MW01164667

THE DOMME

A True Love Story of Me and My Dominatrix Auntie Anna

by Tony Tracia

Dorrance Publishing Co
585 Alpha Drive
Suite 103
Pittsburgh, PA 15238
Visit our website at www.dorrancebookstore.com

ISBN: 978-1-6853-7490-7
eISBN: 978-1-6853-7628-4

INTRODUCTION

This IS a true story of the most popular Dominatrix In All of New England during the 1960s. "The Domme," aka Anthony's Auntie Anna, will Blow you away when this Fetish-filled story takes a turn and Auntie Anna falls for her Charming, well-Endowed and confident Italian teenage nephew Anthony. He gives her a taste of her own Jaw-dropping flaunting and taunting now teasing his gorgeous Aunt in his new bulging Sicily jeans. His Cocky Confident Dominating presence and protective instincts towards her and Cousin Carol has Unlocked his Aunt's heart and Unleashed the hungry Animal Deep within the Fetish-providing Dominatrix a.k.a. HIS Auntie Anna...the Stunning 32-year-old Auntie Anna Looking NO older than 25 still with a killer body Flaunts right back to him in the finest custom-made Italian woman's skirt suits and recent HOT pants/miniskirt look with Perfect curvy legs leading up to her solid heart-shaped ass, in Expensive high-heel Stilettos looking Like NO other woman ever born, the confident Nephew crumbled!

The Domme Just watches, smiling, standing Over her nephew with NO contest to the Dominating Goddess as he dropped to his knees surrendering to his Fantasy woman willing and READY TO SERVE... "From now on the words 'Mistress' Or 'Goddess' shall replace the words Auntie Anna,'" he was told as his Goddess #1 claimed him HER Personal Property!

Cousin Carol, who is Auntie Anna's Beautiful carbon-copy daughter with identical purple eyes as her mom and SOON the same hourglass figure...just six months older than Cousin Anthony, the determined Cousin Carol Will NOT be denied her chance to KEEP her fondling kissing 1st Cousin Anthony INSISTING He be SHARED!... Carol has been developing into a Goddess herself but Can't stop the infatuated Nephew from Straying to the intimidating Mom Goddess overwhelming his desire to serve her, who by the way is also Anthony's Mother's sister....

Carol NEVER surrenders and is determined to WIN Him back knowing her soulmate, she has learned to crawl with as infants Will come crawling back To her Again.

The Insatiable Fetish-Providing Domme Auntie Anna had been grooming her handsome Italian nephew for a few years now after seeing the MAN he had become in EVERY way and decides to "Collar and Own" the confident hung Womanizer as Her Own Fantasy MAN she has chosen to do without, until Now! Can Carol Stop her Mother's Lust and Desire for the flirting Nephew that Worships the ground THEY BOTH walk on? Will Anthony

be forced to choose between the two Goddesses OR simply keep PLEASING BOTH of them, stay silent, and NOT CHANCE LOSING BOTH of them??...

Auntie Anna, Cousin Carol and their groomed Submissive always READY TO SERVE nephew Anthony will have you on the edge of your seat OR UP all night as you read IN DETAIL about their forbidden taboo desires, cravings and kinky Fetishes they explore with each other in the BDISM lifestyle that "The Domme" has introduced the 1st Cousins into as they mature, the Determined knockout daughter Carol is as smart or Smarter than her very successful MommeDomme and becoming just AS Gorgeous, Carol takes Mom's business practices to a whole new level with her Soulmate Cousin Anthony LEGITIMATELY Into the Therapeutic business world while MommeDomme Mentors them to be the best they crave to be. Many Special Clients of The Domme will interact with ALL three Of them in this Fetish thriller love triangle in explicit detail!

With a long Sicilian bloodline on BOTH sides of The Domme AND On the 1st Cousin's Mother's and Father's Sides, Mafioso Uncles come into play with Homicide detectives and Investigators that come and go Looking for answers in this Fetish thriller, leaving the detectives scratching their heads as they always leave embarrassed by Auntie Anna and with NO answers when her daughter's Fiancé is found dead thrown off the Tobin Bridge with all leads pointing to her now "Collared and Owned" Nephew Anthony....

In East Boston a Mafioso war is going on in the 1960s -70s, where 60 men will die in the street, mostly in Boston that Auntie Anna and her nephew know Nothing about, but detectives from E. Boston think otherwise.... The Domme's FAVORITE Uncle Angelo is found hung on a meat hook in SanDiego and messages of retaliation are traced back to Anthony and another Uncle in Chicago, but Still NO answers OR evidence to charge ANYONE.

New Special Clients are "Collared" Favoring mostly Gorgeous Bicurious Women VIPs from Boston's financial district and Major Companies along the North Shore that hear of the Fetish-providing services that Charge the Clients' Business Expense account directly for the expensive Fetish services as "Work-related" Physical Therapy, etc. The Cousin's Personal friends are "Collared and Owned" into their new venture, "SIR" LLC (Sports Injury Rehabilitation). Along the way, the BDISM lifestyle will take them all deep into their "Darkside," never to return to Vanilla Sexual gratification Ever again! HOW will they All handle it?

Lay back and Enjoy MY Story....

CHAPTER

1

Being only six years old and my brother Steven three years old, I CAN STILL remember the day vividly. It's been repeated a million times that you ALWAYS remember a bad day and it's also true that such a day CAN DEVASTATE a Young child. Images OR statements made they DON'T understand will scar their brains forever. Some strongminded kids come out of it, some don't!

I knew it was going to be a bad day when I saw My Mother crying and throwing garbage bags full of my father's clothes out the 3rd-floor window onto his car below on London St. in East Boston, Mass., ONE OF MANY apartments we were constantly moving to and from.

My Aunt Anna (mom's sister) had come over to help her pack my Loser Father's things and was throwing him out for NOT paying bills, NOT having money for food, drinking and hitting

her again, THEN got caught cheating with cheap whores at the local bar, AGAIN!

My mom was too upset so Auntie Anna said SHE would bring me down to say goodbye to My father, that he needed to speak to me privately. As Auntie Anna let My hand go RELUC-TANTLY to his hand she pointed to his face saying to him, "DON'T EVEN TRY to move this fucking car with MY nephew in it!" Then she walked to the front of the car and STOOD THERE until he was done saying, "Anthony, your Dad has to move away but will be around to see you and your baby brother Steven on weekends for Tripe at Morellis on Saturdays. And YOU'RE THE man of the family now!" WTF? WHAT? Am I supposed to start working now at six years old or something? And just lunch? Don't we get a whole visitation Day, Trip on Saturday visitation day, lol, wtf!

I was just confused, scared, AND couldn't believe MY Auntie Anna was sitting right on the hood of a car that I DIDN'T KNOW was going to run her over OR NOT!!

It was at THAT MOMENT I knew I would never leave MY loyal Auntie Anna's side and still was trying to listen to what My drunken father was trying to say TO A SIX-YEAR-OLD!

"YOU'RE THE MAN OF THE FAMILY NOW, CAN YOU FATHOM THAT STATEMENT?"

What REALLY mattered, AND I KNEW IT RIGHT AT THAT MOMENT as well, is I had to make sure My drunken father didn't try to start that car, I was ALREADY protecting

"MY AUNTIE ANNA" as she was protecting me! SO I TOOK HIS KEYS while he babbled some more bullshit AND STARED at her 24-year-old perfect heart-shaped Ass sitting on his Car's hood.

When Auntie Anna heard the door open she rushed to take my hand and started walking me away while My father arrogantly said, "HOW DID YOU KNOW I WASN'T GOING TO JUST RUN YOU OVER, YOU CRAZY BITCH? NOBODY WOULD EVEN MISS YOU!" he arrogantly added.

"BECAUSE YOU NEVER HAD ANY BALLS!" my Quick-witted Aunt shot right back laughing at him, I'll never forget that and walking me away.

"AND WE ALL CERTAINLY WON'T MISS YOU! NOW GO DIE SOMEWHERE, WIFE BEATER, AND OH, by the way!! I ALREADY CALLED YOUR UNCLE JOHNNY DI-FRONZO. I told him you hit your wife again (HIS NIECE) in front of your kids so You should be getting ANOTHER call From Uncle Johnny Boy, ha-ha, ASSHOLE!" my cocky and beautiful Auntie Anna taunting him again. In disgust DROPPING HIS KEYS from MY hands as we walked away, "HE WILL MISS ME," as she pointed to his keys on the ground. "AND FOREVER, I WOULD NEVER LEAVE HER SIDE." Read on....

Auntie Anna's words were the ones that mattered most, that and her words made MORE SENSE as the days, weeks, even as years went by, BUT it was "WHAT SHE DID" I remembered the most by putting HER LIFE in front of mine by standing in

front of a car with a drunk in the driver's seat just thrown out of his house by an Angry, Hungry, and Brokenhearted mother of his two kids. That is what I would WORSHIP, This beautiful Goddess I called Auntie Anna for FOREVER! Also for helping her sister Joanie (MY Mom) who couldn't get away from my father's persistent advances because of a BROKEN legal system, AND PEOPLE WONDERED WHY Domestic wars were fought out in the streets And NOT in court, although it was wrong, it was also self-defense OR protecting a loved one.

"LIFE has its own way of working things out," AUNTIE ANNA would always say. Intelligence AND Beauty, "ALL IN ONE WOMAN," AND She was hardly EVER wrong about anything!

Uncle JohnnyBoy DiFronzo was My father's Uncle on his Mother's side (Millie DiFronzo). My grandmother's notorious gangster brother from Chicago for almost 50 years! And he didn't like woman beaters OR disrespecting women, period....

London St. is forever burned into my brain, but I came out of it STRONGER than anyone could have Ever imagined, EXCEPT for Auntie Anna, SHE ALREADY KNEW I WOULD! Auntie Anna could see the determination I had at a very young age as I grew. She would see just how determined I was to keep This Goddess close to me forever! I melted in her presence, but she was my Auntie Anna.

After the talk in the car I went back upstairs, I looked at my younger three-year-old brother holding my mother's hand, and

my Cousin Carol, Auntie Anna's daughter, also six years old, looked on at me returning with "No, Father," and I could remember saying was...

"Everything's going to be alright," I said.

Cousin Carol came rushing over to take my hand for comfort and support and made both our moms begin to cry at the sight of such a gesture from two six-year-olds.... I had already resumed the role of the Man in the house now at six years old, something my selfish father Never was. Cousin Carol was my rock and stood in front of ANYONE getting close to me.

We were all happy my father was gone from our lives. He was an abusive alcoholic towards my mother and back in those days of the 1950s-60s women were afraid to speak out and were ignored and just took the abuse. I seen it not only in my house but in all my friends' households with single moms as well, and SOME domestic abuses were even worse than mine.

Usually in East Boston kids that came from broken homes found each other and we kind of watched out for one another, we had a common bond and protected one another, and rarely did we hang out much with kids from normal functioning families OR rich kids, which weren't many in the triple-decker rowhouse city of East Boston.

Our family depended on welfare benefits now since there was no income from my alcoholic father, a bad gene that he had inherited from his father, who ALSO gambled and Drank heavily! A two-time loser!!

It was life as usual since he really didn't give much to his own family for food and rent, he would rather drink it away and spend it on whores than take care of his wife and two young kids.

I can still remember walking down London St. to the welfare office in East Boston with my mother to get a monthly supply of free cheese, bread and butter and didn't like it at that young age and thought of ways I could pay for my own cheese and butter, and soon I would.

I was around ten years old when I seen a few kids my age shining shoes for ten cents a shine so I began to build a Shoeshine box of my own. While I was putting the wooden shoeshine box together sweating on a hot summer day, I was imagining making my own money and buying things I wanted. Along comes this punk teenager with his girlfriend and he kicked my shoeshine box and broke it in pieces!! This punk laughed about it, and kept walking and she was laughing too!

I was so angry and all of a sudden it just comes steaming out of me, and I knew at that moment that Nobody was going to stop me from doing what I needed to do to buy my own food and help my family. I picked up a piece of the wood 2x4 he kicked and walked up behind that punk and split his head open, there was blood everywhere and he was out cold.

His girlfriend wasn't laughing anymore, instead she was screaming and followed me into my house and told my mother what I had done, I got yelled at a little by Mom, but so didn't the girlfriend and the punk for kicking my shine box.

I finished my shoeshine box the next day and began shining shoes at Post Time Coffee Shop, a well-known front at the time for Mafia hitmen Joe Barboza, Nicky Femia, and some others that knew my mother and father and already had heard about me splitting the punk's head open and Nicky started to call me "Shoe-Shine," and whenever he saw me he made everybody he was with get a shine from me and paid me $5.00 No. 10 cents. Nicky Femia knew the punk's father and hated him and joked about me whacking the kid's father, Nicky and I would meet up later in life as well.

Auntie Anna had just scared the shit out of my father when she said she called Uncle JohnnyBoy for hitting His wife again, the past Christmas while My NOTORIOUS Great Uncle JohnnyBoy From Chicago (ON MY FATHER'S SIDE) showed up for Christmas Eve to see his sister MY GRANDMA MILLIE (DeFRONZO) TRACCIA, wasn't good for Dad!!

Uncle Johnny "The Nose" DEFRONZO, and my other GANGSTER Great Uncle ON MY MOTHER'S SIDE from San Diego (ANGELO DINUNZIO) Visiting His brother (GRANDPA) LARRY DINUNZIO, My Mom and Anna's Dad, Uncle Johnny and Uncle Angelo hung my father by his ankles OUT THE 3RD-FLOOR WINDOW FOR HITTING His wife, "THEIR NIECE." "NEXT TIME YOU HIT THE GROUND!!!" they told him. My father wasn't allowed back for Christmas dinner with piss on his pants, NOR did he ever want To see them again!

Both great uncles knew each other from their earlier days in Sicily And eventually came to New York's Ellis Island together and "MADE" their names known and were relocated by "THE FAMOUS FIVE FAMILIES," Where they would become MOST NEEDED when the Italian Boys Club that some called the "Mafia" was Reorganized in NYC in the early 30s by Uncle Johnny Boy's "UNCLE CHARLIE."

"When either of your 'Great Uncles' are talking 'YOU NEVER INTERRUPT,' just listen," said Auntie Anna, "and you will learn more that way, Being RESPECTED and to be LOYAL, THEN when people know that they can trust you, they WILL RESPECT YOU!"

Needless to say Christmas came and NO DAD, just Uncles, Aunts, Brother and new sister and YES! A developing Cousin Carol To take my hand like she always did, Auntie Anna LOVED to see Carol work me and take me aside FOR herself and Auntie to say in so many words, "THIS IS WHERE YOU BELONG!"

Around 1965, I would say eleven or twelve years Old, My mom and Auntie Anna stopped associating with My Father's side completely. My mom and Auntie Anna decided we have enough people for nice and quiet Thanksgivings and Christmas.

"We don't need you, and MY boys don't want your bullshit" were the last words to my dad from My mom, with the VERY last words coming from Auntie Anna, of course, as she took the phone from her sister with tears in her eyes, "STAY THE FUCK IN REVERE, away from my sister and MY nephews, that's where

you belong! With Peggy, Die there!" an unmercifully Auntie Anna said so coldly. She just smiled and rubbed my head, slamming the phone for a goodbye, then watched her protective daughter walk me away from what Carol automatically knew what was bothering me.

My proudly developing Cousin Carol put the colored pencils out with some paper snuggling in next to me, just as close as she could possibly get to comfort, protect and complete me.

It was February school vacation and was freezing out today and I was being dropped off at Auntie Anna's so my mom could go away for the weekend and I would better off at Auntie Anna's with Carol since we were both the same age; Carol had just turned a teenager and I would be in six months in June, Carol's birthday was in Jan. and she was six month older and would tease me about it that She was older than me. Carol was even looking older now and I could see it today and couldn't take my eyes off her sweater and curious what I was seeing protruding through her tight white knitted sweater.

I wasn't angry anymore in her presence and immediately she would go get her art supplies out and colored pencils and pastels and we would draw and color for hours as we always for each other if she was over my house or I was at Her house.

Cousin Carol was a mini Auntie Anna with one in 100 million, had purple eyes and jet-black hair with the curves of a Goddess, both men and women would stare at how stunning Auntie always looked and impeccably dressed like a movie star. Although only

thirteen now she would be the carbon copy of Auntie Anna and I could see it immediately.

As we kept drawing and she kept sliding closer like she always did to see my work and I could see hers we would be shoulder to shoulder and leg on leg within fifteen minutes' time, but time was different, way different! We both noticed it and it was reflecting through our art as she commented on why I was drawing her today in the tight white sweater as she smiled with approval. Cousin Carol was not shy around me at all; in fact, she was aggressive because she thought being older made her more dominant over me, so I would oblige her every time because the smiles that came from both Auntie Anna and cousin Carol gave me a feeling unlike I'd never felt at home or anywhere on earth. It was heavenly. Pleasing the both of them and having their approval was what I wanted and it was I eventually Needed.

It was already an hour of drawing and Auntie tried to see what we were drawing as she usually did out of curiosity and to my surprise Carol took it and said, "You can see it yet, we're not finished," as she held it against her new protruding nipples I had been drawing the whole time. "We are starving," she added, changing the subject immediately and running to kitchen holding my hand. We made sandwiches, ate them and then put my drawing in her drawer for safekeeping and got more fresh paper. Auntie Anna was on the phone with a "Client" from the Real estate office so she said and had to show a property for half an hour and

would be right back and we said we were ok, go ahead and we would keep busy.

Carol couldn't wait until Auntie left to show me the "Secret closet" she had discovered inside her closet that led into another room. Behind a loose plywood door was another closet that was boarded up and was loose enough to open and enter into. It had had an old Auntie Anna's client Journal and old items that only a Dominatrix would possess or keep, Carol shut the flashlight and took my hand in the dark and placed it on her new amazing puffy nipples that felt the size and shape of a strawberry and just as firm. "These are what you were drawing, aren't they?"

"Yes, I couldn't take my eyes off you all day," I said, and in the dark she found my mouth to feed them to me and asked if I would like to kiss and suck on them in the dark closet till We heard Auntie coming.

CHAPTER

2

Still in grammar school but also spending a lot of time at my aunt's house on Havre St. at Sharon Ct., a small alleyway that had three small shabby houses in a row that eventually was bought up by eminent domain for the expansion of the Callahan Tunnel. I remember that's where me and my brother Steven would have visitations with my father there and where my father had hung out at Napoli's Bar, along with Joe Piantedsi Sr., who also lived at Sharon Ct. with his nine children and wife Betty. Joe Sr. and my dad and Betty and my mom were longtime friends and won dance contests together.

Joe Jr. and I became good friends and his seven sisters were like my sisters and Joe Jr. and I would go to Fenway Park by train for ten cents, buy a bleacher seat for $1.00 and climb the fence and sit in the box seats behind the Sox dugout and even get a hotdog and a Coke all for $3.00.

Joe Jr. and I had got a job one Saturday down Haymarket Sq. on the pushcarts where Joe Sr. worked on Saturday. I had got a job nearby with another vendor while he worked with his dad but we both got our first jobs together and we were just eleven turning twelve years old. Joe Jr. and his eight other siblings would lose Both parents to cancer and within just a few years of each other. Whenever I would think I was having a bad day I would always think of Joe Jr. He remains my friend still and the strongest guy I know to take care and watch over all his younger sisters and baby brother when he lost both his parents at such a young age. Joe Jr. is a perfect example of the power of "You," when you put your mind to something that "you" and Only you can do because it's about survival, plain and simple!

I would work down Blackstone St. in Haymarket Sq. every Friday and Saturday for the next twenty years and was amazed the kids I met that were also working there on weekends. Silvio Petraglia, whose dad was working there and brought him in. Joey Testa, whose brother owned a stand and right next to me in 100-degree heat or -2 degrees where the fruit would actually freeze and the health inspectors would close us down. We kept warm with portable kerosene heaters or burn wooden fruit boxes in 55-gallon steel oil barrels.

I worked for the same two brothers, Freddy and Sonny, who became family to me from the first year to the last and still think of Freddy as my dad but didn't work on the stand with me and Sonny since he did all the buying and me and Sonny spent all

week picking up and selling the fruit on Friday and Saturday. The pushcarts were only a weekend permit licensing setup and it was enough! We worked on Friday morning at 5 A.M. till 11 P.M., that's an 18-hr. day, and get right back down there and do it again on Saturday! 35-36 hrs. in two days, that was before Faneuil Hall existed or the Rose Kennedy garden.

Cars would pull over on the expressway and walk down and buy fruit and vegetables as early as 6 A.M. on their way to work and Never get ticketed or have to worry about police or being towed ever! Fruit and vegetables were below wholesale prices and the meats were right there too in front of the fruit peddlers, you could go home with a huge box of meats and fruit and vegetables for 10-20 dollars for the week, people loved it and I met everyone from everywhere and connected with good and bad people and I was on my way drinking more and more and the drugs more and more.

Auntie Anna did teach me a very important lesson one day. The lesson to be learned was TRUST NOBODY so Carol and I yelled at Patty for telling OUR secrets to her girlfriend Gina and punished her by excluding Patty from the "Secret Journal" secret Client Fetishes and exploring them with us. Carol and I had NOT told Patty about the Journal OR our recent exploring in Carol's Secret Closet, Auntie Anna would have gone CRAZY if she knew about our reading about her Clients' Fetishes and fantasies then exploring Them with each other.

Carol was Just as horny as I was as a preteen and just as creative from the gifted artists we Both were. We even communicated by

drawing out a fantasy and gave the drawing to one another to act it out the next time we could sneak into the closet without Auntie Anna seeing us. As a teenager Carol And Patty became Even MORE aggressive with me with NO COMPLAINTS from Me, Her eager soulmate cousin, Piccolo Diavolo.

Carol was even exploring with Bi/Patty while their friends and families thought Patty was MY girlfriend, again with NO COM-PLAINTS from Me when they BOTH rewarded me for "OUR three-way SECRET For MANY years to cum," Gina would NEVER know About!

Another lesson from the same lecture was from the point Auntie Anna was making, that was RESPECT and LOYALTY! Both Carol and Patty KNEW I was Loyal to them and Respected BOTH of them as well, I would jump in front of a train for either of them And never let ANYONE at school talk bad or be dis-respectful To either of them, especially Cousin Carol, ALL the horny punks knew better! or would hear from me.

Auntie was so right about Getting MORE out of any woman With Respect and Loyalty, Carol and Patty rewarded Me WITHOUT ever asking!

What Auntie Anna didn't talk much about was WHY, WHY was my Auntie Anna so mad and angry yelling about Me being Just ANOTHER disrespectful man, and She wasn't going to allow that to happen to Me, I was just having a little fun with Carol and Patty getting a hand job in the popcorn box as THEY also thought it was fun, BUT NOT FUNNY to Auntie Anna?

WHO had disrespected Or Abused this Goddess as a Child or Preteen being as gifted and beautiful as Carol at a Developing vulnerable age?? The more conversations we would have, the more I THINK she was Physically abused or even raped by her own father and uncle, I did hear her Yelling at my grandmother In Italian saying she was hit many times, and "where the fuck were you" ("Dove cazzo sei?") a few times during her rages. I would pretend NOT to hear her volatile Italian rants to Grandma while my mom was working, but could always calm her down with a strong hug, or interrupt her In some way when Carol and I were very little drawing nearby while Auntie babysat me weekly. Carol would then ask to GO and get some Gelato at the Cafe Pompee in the N. End, which was her favorite homemade Italian Ice Cream of all.

Auntie Anna would become MY GELATO in a few years from that day making me wait until I was age 16, the controversial legal sexual consenting Age at the time.

As I walked into Auntie's house after the movies Auntie Anna approached me and grabbed my thick head of hair and pulled me over yelling in Italian, ("Vini qui, Piccolo Diavolo") = ("Come here, little Devil"), pointing to the kitchen away from Carol. A very pissed-off Auntie Anna asked, "Were You doing the Popcorn trick with Cousin Carol as well as with Patty?" Patty told her friend Gina and thought this all funny. "And Gina told me Carol was putting her hand in the popcorn box between your legs with your dick sticking through the box?? Is that true, Diavolo?!!" I

firmly said, "No Way, that's my cousin, Auntie! It was ONLY Patty and Me and Gina got mad she couldn't try, Patty told her she couldn't come to the movies with us, Carol doesn't know, Please don't tell her, Auntie? She'll be mad at me!" I begged Auntie. "WTF," Auntie replied, "I'M MAD AT YOU!!"

Patty tells Gina everything, "Are you Stupid? And WTF is the 'Pencil Test'?" Gina said, "YOU put a pencil UNDER Patty's tits to see if the pencil falls down OR stays. That means she has firm titties," Auntie said, trying NOT to laugh and turned away from me.

"CAROL!" Auntie shouted for her to come in now and ask the same question to which Carol had heard from listening in, "NO WAY, Mom, I had My own Popcorn box," looking at Auntie very seriously. Carol replied, "I was just a third wheel on their date to the movies because Patty wanted me there because it was a girly movie." I sat on Patty's side and couldn't even SEE Anthony's popcorn box Or Patty's hand in the box, Carol now raising more doubt as Carol LIED to Auntie Anna Looking directly into her Hypnotic Purple eyes, but Carol's eyes were JUST AS hypnotic and JUST AS gorgeous.

"OK, you're excused!!" Auntie told a smiling Carol as she looked over to me, Leaving the room giving me a hand job sign with her fist while Auntie was turned and pointing in my face and lecturing about "RESPECT," she went on and on. "There is a time and PLACE for everything and a Movie theater IS NOT a place for young teens to be experimenting! I won't allow YOU

to be just ANOTHER pig of a man that disrespects women!! YOU UNDERSTAND ME! Gabeesh!" I had NEVER seen My fantasy woman MY AUNTIE ANNA so angry as she went directly back into an Italian rage. She said again and again that "You will get MORE from any woman with RESPECT and LOYALTY than you will from lies and tricks, you won't even have to Ask her! REMEMBER what I'm saying Today, Diavolo," Auntie concluded and walked away with half a smile KNOWING she would have her days OR nights with me as soon as I was groomed to perfection, sixteen years old and legal to be Collared and Owned to serve And Please My Mistress/Goddess However, Wherever, whenever needed or scheduled, I WOULD DO SO DAILY AT HER OFFICE!

CHAPTER
3

Auntie Anna and Carol were packing and talking about what things to take up to Derry, NH, where Auntie Anna had just bought a small cottage at a great deal from her Real Estate connections right on Beaver Lake! She had asked for me and Carol to help do some of the yard cleaning and needed me to help with insulation in some drafty walls and ceiling and I agreed totally. I would be with her and Carol for the next week anyway and happy now I was with her no matter where I went. They were now becoming my addiction! Auntie Anna had done what No drug counselor could ever do, She took me from my craving of getting high, bad friends and very close to an addiction on Methadone at only fifteen years old to being addicted to serving "Her," A Goddess and My "Domme." This would become a Taboo love triangle with My first Cousin and her age mother, my own mother's sister.

Auntie bought Carol some expensive feminine supplies and wanted her looking as Feminine and neatly groomed as she was and insisted that Cousin Carol keep her Italian complexion clean-shaven and smooth, I could hear her say. I also continued to pack when Carol whispered for me to get the "Journal" to bring up to the Lake to read from. She was really intrigued as was I of some of these "Fetishes" Auntie's clientele had possessed and we soon will explore them for ourselves to the extreme and create some "Fetishes" of our own. We would perform each Fetish/Fantasy for each other and in time groomed to obey the commands of "My Mistress, My Domme," My Auntie Anna! As Carol kept Auntie distracted I snuck past them and into Carol's room, then into her closet leading to the loose plywood wall and opened it just enough to get the secret journal filled with Kinks and Fetishes that would make even the Marquis DeSade blush! We had already skimmed through some Clients' Fetishes for both men and women she served or rather "They served" Dominatrix Auntie Anna on a regular schedule. She was in great demand all over N.E. being as beautiful and talented as she was and highly paid. I packed the valuable kinky journal in my jacket and would have Carol eating out of my hands now that I now had the journal she had been possessed by, lol. We all were excited about seeing this new fixer-upper and taking on the task and making it our own getaway and enjoyed some down time, enjoyed some fresh air away from the city and all the bullshit of everyday life. The best part of it all was that it was only 45 minutes away just over the Massachusetts border.

Auntie had already bought a few small twin beds, had some furniture delivered to fill the five small rooms in this ranch-style cottage steps away from a well-cared-for Lake by the neighbored cottages all owned by the Onessimo family. They were ironically from the North End of Boston, where I worked on the pushcarts at Haymarket. Sonny had told me, "Go see Joe Onessimo and tell him your Aunt is the new owner of the end unit he was trying to buy." Auntie Anna beat him to it, lol.

We just needed to fill the new fridge now and we were hungry and ready to work and then swim and relax a little and just enjoy the times with these two Goddesses that would become my life of eternal devotion born to serve them in "Any" way! Auntie took me to my new assigned room and then showed Carol to her room right beside mine and in between both of them. The bedrooms were all on the right and kitchen and living room and one bathroom and only one shower on the left, but plumbers were coming to add a full bath off Auntie's room to accommodate Auntie Anna, of course.

As I put my clothes away in my new bureau and hid the secret journal, Carol walked past flashing the drawing I had given her the night before of me submitting to her in a very Oral Domination scenario I needed from her desperately. I just wanted her to drown me and gag on her pussycum for whom I had acquired a very special and unique taste for and needed almost daily if possible, like an addiction of no other.

She was smiling and said softly, "Get ready." She was going to the Hardware store!! Carol had just got out of the shower and

Auntie Anna was dressed and asked if I needed anything, so to keep her out longer I told her a few things to get for me for painting and staples for the insulation. This would keep Carol and I together longer on my fantasy I had drawn out in detail that would become my "Fetish" and my addiction.

"Get busy, I'll be back very soon!" Auntie yelled out as she left and Carol ran to make sure the door was locked. We got busy, alright! I started to shower real quick to be as clean as I always would be for her and she loved sexual foreplay in the shower and the ways we would clean and wash each other slowly and sensually with lubricants and moisturizers would be automatic always. When she faced me in the shower and would place her hands on my shoulders, I knew it was time to get on my knees and she would lift a leg to put it up on the bath and grab my thick curly hair to move my head where she wanted me between her legs or something kinky like rimming or tonging her ass with my large tongue. Or taking a Golden Shower she knew I enjoyed from her turned her into a natural wild Dominant watching me submit to her in this way. Moaning and holding her ass while she pumped my mouth as she peed would make her cum as well and I would choke and gag and only ask for more. She would always reply back and say, "I have more." She would cum again and again every time while deeply fingering her G-Spot and I would take every drop from her with pleasure.

As I showered fast this time I was just concentrating on getting onto the bed and my head onto the pillow I had drawn out

for her. Carol was already kneeling beside the pillow tapping on it for me to place my head and she could squat over me like illustrated and I could see her nipples were hard as stones and sucked on both of them as she lowered me down on the pillow and eased her neatly trimmed and soaking-wet pussy to my mouth. I reached up and held her rock-hard nipples between my fingers and she held my rock-hard cock in her left hand and had my head cradled in her right hand and started humping my mouth and my tongue slowly at first with her pussy. As she moved in a circular motion and rocked back and forth she had me eating both her pussy and her ass and using my oversized tongue where she wanted it and when. When she wanted her ass serviced while riding my face, I was actually gasping for air and loved every second watching her face and coming all over my mouth and soaking the new pillow she had placed under my head for my drawn-out fantasy. I was ready to explode with some cum of my own and not having fucked her yet. She lowered her pussy onto my throbbing-hard 9" cock and put it in her pussy and immediately squirted and screamed at the same time. I did Not want to cum inside my cousin Carol's squirting pussy and took it out of her pussy and eased the head into her moist saliva-lubed ass and pumped her asshole full of cum for the first time of many for years to cum.

We had to clean up this cum-soaked bed and both pillows now and Auntie would be coming back any minute now after at least a half-hour of multiple orgasms she had fed to me for my addiction and her first Fuck and Anal experience that we would talk

about for years, even using that special day as foreplay. It still makes me hard to this day.

We were cleaned up and both raking outside when Auntie pulled up and I walked up to take the bags and groceries from the car. We put everything away and Auntie said, "So I see you two kept yourselves busy." We just nodded and replied, "Yes, we were very busy! We're going to love it here!"

I continued to unpack, then Carol whispered as she walked by to "go get the Journal!" and she'd keep Auntie busy. I snuck by as they still talked and looked at feminine products and into the secret closet and put the Clients' secret Journal with all their kinks and fetishes listed inside alongside of their names into my pants and went back to my spare room. I stuck the journal inside my jacket and Carol would beg me to read from it tomorrow. Carol was intrigued and curious with the need to explore these Fantasies and Fetishes and became an obsession with her as was I. Why would both men and women crave these sexual desires and submit to a Dominatrix and be used and serve in such demeaning and submissive ways? I had just drawn out a Fetish I had been curious about ever since I tasted Carol's pussycum from my fingers while fingering her when I was getting my cock sucked from the most gorgeous teen I'd ever seen and was now addicted to.

CHAPTER

4

The ride up to the new fixer-upper was only forty minutes and a world apart from the city and all the bullshit we were growing up in. Auntie needed this not only for herself but for Carol and I and she was grooming the both of us for a different place in time, especially Me! As we unpacked and were putting my stuff in the new bureau Auntie had bought to furnish the place and had delivered a week before, Carol walked past smiling and shaking the illustration to show me and whispered, "Get ready." She was going to the Hardware store to get supplies for painting! Auntie asked out loud, "Do you need anything?" I told her a few things to get so she would take longer and I could keep Carol squirting that hot pussycum even longer and I licked her up clean. As soon as the door closed Carol ran over to lock the door and followed me into the shower, where I wanted her first while on my knees.

I had told her I wanted to wash her in the moisturizer and applied it generously on her pussy and asshole and tongued it into both her hot moist openings and she was opening up enough to fit two fingers in her ass, to my surprise. She had lifted her leg over me and onto my shoulder while I rimmed and ate her ass with my long thick tongue.

I needed to slow it down and get my head on the pillow next to finish the illustration and my Fetish of drowning in her pussy-cum. We took towels and wrapped each other with them in an attempt to dry off but we just kept kissing and touching and couldn't stop long enough. She took both pillows to prop my head up like in the illustration, and while on her knees next to the laid-out pillows I took a minute to suckle on both her unique Large nipples and she lowered her body and cradled my head down on the pillow and squatted over my face and looked down at me to show me how wet she was opening up her pussylips. She was dripping wet and dripped a few drops in my mouth to taste just before riding my waiting long thick tongue circulating and holding onto my thick black hair and holding my hard 9" with the other hand for balance just like in the drawing.

With my head being pumped into two already cum-soaked pillows, Carol was propping my head high enough to take another squirting orgasm into my open waiting mouth. She was grasping on to my thick black hair from behind and I couldn't swallow her combination of pussycum and seemed like hot salty pee down my throat fast enough. She was having a series of mul-

tiple orgasms and I was witnessing her first experience of many more to cum. Carol was a multi-cumsquirter when her G-Spot was reached and stimulated. I had the long cock to reach it and knew how to use my fingers to reach up and pull forward to tickle the "magic trigger" while eating her always wet and manicured pussy. I just lay there submitted and wrapped my arms around her tiny sculptured lower back and ass and took all her cum juice while she moaned like an animal in heat. I had to reach up and actually cover her mouth so the moans and screaming like I'd never heard from her wouldn't be heard from the front door. Carol was demanding to be fucked and lowered herself off my mouth and holding my rock-hard cock she sat right on it and her tight wet pussy swallowed all of me. She instantly screamed and squirting she rode me hard. I was cumming any second and Did Not want to cum inside of her! I forced her off me and held her down sideways and could feel the cum oozing to a boil and with just my head I found her asshole and slowly put my throbbing and now ejaculating head in and pumped a few times into her now loosened-up tasty asshole. Carol was screaming into the cum-soaked pillows and lifting her ass and reaching around onto my legs and humping back to take more cock in her asshole and telling me to "fuck it harder" and "I love it."

This was an unbelievable experience that we still talk about today. It was her first fuck and first Anal experience and was my first multi-orgasmic woman to release a River of pee and cum while I was helplessly being drowned in it and still able to swallow

all my cousin Carol's PussyPeeCum. We still keep the fantasy drawing in the same bureau from fifty years ago, and we still have those sessions every time we go to Derry, NH, to the cottage.

Little was said by MommeDomme to Carol OR vice versa, I would take care of MY END and see Patty on the way to school FOR NOW, and Explore with Carol As usual "IN THE SE-CRET CLOSET." As Carol loved playing in there in the dark, IT TURNED HER ON immediately while we read from the Descriptive Kinky Journal "The Domme" kept Secret.

The Domme and I had OUR OWN PLAN laid out, I WOULD DO WHATEVER IT TOOK! To be one of Auntie's SexSlaves she Dominated While administering their Fetish.

We planned on raking leaves and insulation for drafty walls And ceilings, she noticed And would be busy at Home Depot In nearby Derry. This would give ME and Carol a nice long session for MY fantasy and HERS. Carol was talking about more ANAL SEX next on her list For that beautiful ass of hers and I COULD-N'T WAIT, yum.

Auntie Anna would also have plenty of time Seducing and taunting with HER Diavolo

Il suo Diavolo, AS She demanded the attention RIGHT BACK at her with MY PLEASURE getting My beautiful Auntie Anna visibly excited when her nipples hardened like stones!

I would soon have them FED TO ME once I was COL-LARED And Owned, when I would be sixteen Soon. As we drove I reminded My fantasy Goddess that Both Carol and I would be

old enough for our driver's permits SOON and asked when could we start Driving her car, lol.

"YAAAY," Carol came to life and wasn't mad anymore to start asking MommeDomme to teach her soon, "I'M OLDER, I'll be first, ha-ha," Carol laughed and smiled at me, Taunting JUST LIKE HER GODDESS MOM Did to me, lol.

CHAPTER

5

I could smell the food as Auntie called out to us, "Who hungry? I have pizza for my hardworking kids." Auntie had No idea just how hard we had been working on each other with Cousin Carol creating a Sea of teenage cumjuices. The pillows and bedspread on my new bed were drying out with the fan blowing on them but needed a washing too. We sat and ate some great local Italian pizza and talked about the Lake, then Auntie had mentioned my new job at Haymarket, I told her about and to tell her and Carol about it. I was going to be fifteen this June 21st, always the 1st day of summer and always loved that my birthday fell on that day. I was working to help my mom out and myself, of course, or I'd have to wear bargain basement clothes and horrible shoes Mom would have to buy and then hand them down to my poor brother, lol.

As we sat and talked for hours about the two brothers that hired me, Auntie got a call and took the plates away and Carol was leaning on me and falling fast asleep. I decided to just let her sleep aside me like the angel she was and wait for Auntie to return and let her walk Carol to her room. We were both so exhausted from the multi-orgasm session we just experienced that I fell asleep right with her sitting up in the very comfortable soft leather sofa Auntie had bought. I could feel something and looked up and it was Auntie covering us with a fleece blanket, and my cock was rock hard sticking out of the side of my shorts. Auntie was looking as she covered it and said, smiling, "Don't want Carol to see that big boy just yet, lol, you're becoming a Man very quickly."

Auntie had just approved of my almost full adult-sized manhood of at least 8" at that moment and thick enough for Carol to hold without touching her middle finger to her thumb while she held it tightly and would try. I still wonder if Auntie was sucking or riding me while I sleeping because my cock did seem wet and was very hard. When I woke she was covering my 8" that was coincidentally "out" of my shorts and the covering me up could have been a diversion, she never admitted to it but I always suspected it.

At fifteen to eighteen years a man's penis size is about 80-90% fully grown, and by eighteen to twenty-one years it is fully grown and at eighteen My cock was 10" and my tongue was about 7". I would touch my nose with it and show the girls at school for fun. I'd put the tip of my thick pointy clit licker in my nostrils and they would squirm and blush, lol.

When my cousin Carol's good friend saw this one day in corridor at school she was obsessed with meeting me and asked Patty to introduce her and that she "liked liked me!" and two likes meant she wanted to date me. Seeing my tongue and wanting her pussy licked by me would happen very quickly.

Meanwhile Auntie had still more to say and was done covering Carol and I as she was still sleeping and totally exhausted and all drained out from at least three different multiple orgasms in three different positions. Auntie was explaining how important it is and why a man should Always be a gentleman and treat a woman with the utmost respect even if she is a bad woman. Even a pure slut/whore likes roses for her birthday and as the door opened for her she continued. "You see how comfortable you make my little girl? She knows she's safe next to you and feels your presence, she won't even move because while she sleeps she knows it's you next to her," she added. My eyes opened wide and I could now see the philosopher she was besides being a "Goddess" that she was! I thought she was always smart because my mom and family would always say she was a straight-A student and now I was hearing her speak, she possessed Both beauty and brains, I was hypnotized by her either watching her walk by or listening to her speak to me or Carol.

"Get some sleep and we will do more work tomorrow raking those leaves that are blocking our path to the lake, ok?" And I agreed totally, we had Lakefront property from the back door right into the Lake as did the neighboring cottages with a great

space between them all and all four other cottages were owned by one family, the Onessimos, and ironically one of the brothers, Joe Onessimo, was a pushcart vendor at Haymarket near us that my boss Sonny was very good friends with. Auntie bought the property before they even knew it was sale because of her real estate connections.

Auntie lifted Carol to take her to her room and Carol neglected to move from my side, I smiled and was flattered, then helped her up to go to bed and told her I'd see her in the morning for breakfast. She let go of my arm and walked away and At that moment I felt like a part of my body just walked away. Auntie smiled and said, "You see?" I looked at her smiling back and said, "Yes, I do, I understand."

At breakfast we continued our conversation and Carol remembering talking about me having a job and was so excited for me. I told them a lot of kids from East Boston were going to the North End at Haymarket Square and working for the fruit peddlers on Blackstone St. Joey Piantedosi's Dad told Joey to come down and just around and bring a friend because the summertime is very busy and the peddlers are always looking for help, so Joey asked me to go with him and try to find a job with him. We both got jobs that day and my life would change forever!

I started to tell Auntie and Carol about the two brothers that hired me. Freddy and Sonny Sarno of "Sarno Fruit and Produce Inc." and they were like night and day as far as personalities go but they both loved my loyalty to them, so they loved me and respected

that I always went the extra mile for them and Never missed a day or called out sick. They both were not married and did not have any kids, so they treated me like I was their son in time to come, I even called Freddy "Dad" and they both related my mom and their mom and on my own at only six and my little brother was three! Their Father did exactly the same thing to them at an early age. I told Auntie and the similarities of circumstances in their childhood really hit home with them. They would make sure I had money in my pocket and take food home from the other peddlers and meats from the butcher stores also on Black-stone St. We would swap fruit and vegetables for meats and we were All like Family.

Auntie listened in amazement and said, "I hear they even pick you up at 5 A.M. to take you to work so you don't take the train?" I said, "Of course, they want me in early to set up with them so if they want me at 5 A.M., that's the only way, lol."

I'd been working for them for about six months just on Saturday and then they wanted me a half-day on Thursday to pick up the fruits and vegetables in Chelsea, where Freddy was the Buyer and smarter, and Sonny would take me to pick it up with the truck and store it in the North End and then sell it on Friday and Saturday, the only two days the peddler's permit was valid.

As they listened to me still talk about where I working and all the new people I was meeting, we were making plans to get back home by Friday and work 5 A.M. – 9 P.M. = 16 hrs.! Then on Saturday was the same thing = 32 hrs. in just (two days)!! and a

lot of my friends from East Boston were flocking down Haymarket to work as well, Silvio Petraglia, a lifelong friend, Carmen Ciancio, Ralphie Petrillo, Tony Tango, Jimmy Langley, Joey Piantedosi, Joey Testa, and Fiore Gianetassio, we were All East Boston Kids, and All worked at the ripe age of thirteen years old! The respect and bond we had for each other would last a lifetime.

Auntie was smiling, then pinched my cheek as she walked by and said, "My little 'Big' man is a working man now." I knew exactly what she was referring to and knew my 8" Cock and long thick pointy tongue was in her plans as she continued to groom me into her willing submissive sex slave and serve her totally and unconditionally. Our talks continued on rides to NH and Auntie Anna would sometimes show up to drive me home from work and on Holiday occasions at my house or hers. She would confide in me as I did with her and Carol and would jump in front of a train for either one of them. Carol was dating and I was seeing a lady from the North End that was ten years older than me. Alice was her name and her husband had just left her for another man!! She was a hot brunette on a mission to fuck every young Italian guy working Haymarket and loved to show me things. Alice taught me the G-Spot secret that Carol would squirt multiple Orgasms when I used the method of reaching up and in and pulling forward and moving my index and middle finger in a tickling motion slowly until her pussy becomes very wet, then add a third finger and go faster as she becomes wetter or opens wider and begins to squirt her pussycum when you exit your fingers, I was

learning a lot and having a blast with this intelligent Psychology major just like Auntie was, and they would meet later in the story with my persuasion and introduce them for my own curiosity.

I was warning Carol about her dating this football athlete Mikey Forletty and he was an asshole to girls he dated in the past and was very possessive and either hit them or embarrassed them, grabbing or pushing them around. So when I got a call from Auntie asking about him and that he in fact Did grab her and left a mark on her upper arm muscle, I went wild and hung up the phone and got a ride down the schoolyard when he hung out. I saw the cocky muscular good-looking asshole woman abuser and my mind went blank thinking of how my father would hit my mother. I jumped out from Sonny's car and without saying a word ripped the antenna from the car this scared coward little prick was leaning back on and now running from and I whipped his legs first so he would stop running. I beat him so bad it took three of his friends to pull me off of him and was at least forty or fifty lads lighter than he was but I was in excellent physical shape from lifting 50-lb. boxes of fruit and produce all day long for sixteen hrs. Mickey had to have one of his balls removed in the hospital, and as I walked away I told him and his friends that if anybody ever touches anyone that's family Or even a friend of mine they will die in this schoolyard, period!!

It didn't take long "at all" for this news to spread like wildfire throughout East Boston and the North End because it was Sonny. I called for the ride down to the schoolyard and he just watched

my back from inside the car and just said, "Wow!" When I jumped back in the car to leave, when I was back home in just under an hour Auntie and Carol called and the only thing Auntie said was "We love you so much, I always knew you would become a very special man and come for lunch Friday and We'll drive you to work." My mom asked, "Who was it this time? I hope you don't get arrested for this!" I assured my mom that I'd be bailed out and home in time for work, she wouldn't have to worry about me, just call Freddy or Sonny.

CHAPTER

6

Labor Day came and we were almost finished fixing up our newly purchased summer cottage on Beaver Lake, Derry, NH, Auntie Anna had just purchased in the spring, and the neighboring Onessimo family was stunned. They owned the other four surrounding spaced-out cottages and would have paid triple the price to acquire the property so they would have owned the entire Beaver Lakes properties and soon I would introduce myself and my two Goddesses or Joe Onessimo that Sonny was very good friends with ironically. When people say, "It's a small world," it really is! What are the odds that I worked on the same street as the man who owned the neighboring cottages right next to Auntie Anna's?? When Joe got to see either Auntie or Carol sunbathing on our hundreds of private beaches He'd have a hard-on all day and wouldn't say a word, lol.

It was time, however, to wrap things up and visit on special warm weekends and get more done but for now we'd made a lot of progress and preparing for 1969, which would be very memorable for me and Carol. She would be sixteen years on Jan. 6 and I would be sixteen on June 21st and she was getting her driving permit first to tease me. Auntie would teach us both to drive soon and I would become "legal property" to her at sixteen to sign a sexual consent contract. In Massachusetts it is Legal to have consensual sex but was and is still controversial. In MY case it was more than willingly, it was a privilege and Auntie had worded it perfectly so that even my mother signed it not knowing it was for "my personal sexual consent," but thought it was for Auntie's professional "Life Coaching/Wellness Therapy Counseling" that she was certified in along with "Physical Therapy" degrees and certifications for her massage and marriage counseling. Auntie had certificates and degrees on her walls and was very impressive and intimidating at the same time, and all her clients loved her advice and her BDSM practices and sessions of exploration of Fetish/Fantasy for both men and woman or special couples, as you will read about "Special Clients" from her hidden Journal.

My mother had told her sister Auntie Anna to try and talk some sense into me because I was becoming a real wiseass and had some bad friends now and thought I was doing drugs, so it was a perfect opportunity for Auntie to have my mom sign the complicated contract just for legal business, she told her, and Mom signed without ever reading a word. She told her that I

would have private sessions with her once or twice a week and cared very much about what I had been through when my Dad left home when I was only six. My alcoholic and verbally abusive father told me in the car that was filled with his clothes in garbage bags that I was the man of the family now. I had told this to my Aunt and Carol on a ride one day and she never forgot that devastating day that really Did have a dramatic impact in later years to come. So my Aunt told this to her on that day as well. I still remember my Aunt being involved ever since my mom was with my dad and Auntie was watching me while Mom worked and my dad tried to take me out to play catch. Auntie said to him, "Take your hands off that fuckin' kid I'm babysitting till his mother gets home, and if you ever hit my sister again I'll cut your fucking hands off!" She was a serious and an adamant Italian woman and tough as any you've heard about! They screamed at each other and then she called the cops and he ran out. She laughed and called him "Asshole." I knew she would be very special one day and I felt protected and secure around her like she and Carol are protected with me now.

Carol was all excited as she smiled and teased me from the driver's seat and I was being picked up to go driving with her and Auntie. I was going to get a private lesson later while Carol went out with her friend Patty today. Auntie had plans to talk for a few hours with me and she was dressed so hot that she had my undivided attention and her nipples were at attention as well in her tight Italian knitted Sweater. She knew I was a horny little Italian

wiseass and really played me well and teased me to no end in short hot pants and Sicily jeans in style at the time. I'd never seen such toned perfect legs in my life and they would be serviced by only me soon, along with any other of her instructions for my "on-call" submissive sessions.

On one hot Spring day in 1969 Carol, now Sweet 16, and her friend Patty was older and now seventeen, were at the house alone. Auntie was on a Real Estate call showing a property and Carol called me to come over to read about a woman from the Journal and did not tell Patty about "our secret closet nor the Journal" but instead wanted to experiment and explore on Patty. This really got me hot and hard in an instant and I ran the two city blocks to hear what my kinky female counterpart cousin was up to. Carol had read about a "Special Client," Evelyn McKay, and she was the Executive Director of Bell Telephone on old Atlantic Ave. in Boston and was a massage Client and billing was charged to the company as a perk. Evelyn received other Kinky services as well from Auntie Anna, and Carol was reading her Fetishes to me while Patty was watching TV and waiting to "make out" with me and Carol to see if she was truly a lesbian or liked guys, she was curious about her sexual feelings for Carol but liked me too. Carol said she was a good friend and agreed to explore with her with me present to really tell if she liked cock or pussy or both. Patty was also wondering why I hadn't asked her out yet and if I was interested in dating her, so Not to cause suspicion on our fucking and sucking five times a week we decided to play and explore with her today.

We had smoked a few joints of really strong weed and Carol had said, "Patty wants to play Spin the Bottle but you're my cousin so I don't think it's a good idea, but if we blindfold you would you mind? Just think that it's Patty all the time, ok, lol." So I played along and let Carol blindfold me, I could see everything through the silky cloth she used so I "could" see and she wanted me to see Patty kissing her and eventually eating her out!

Ok, here we go! Patty spun first and The bottle spun 'round and around and landed on Carol, sure enough. So Carol said out loud, "Patty wants to kiss us anyway, Anthony, to see if she likes girls and particularly me, so I agreed and then I want her to kiss you, Ok?" I nodded and said, "Ok, can I kiss her titties too, lol?" Patty said eagerly, "Of course you can, I'm dying to see that tongue again and French kissing is my favorite." So Patty and Carol started to make out and I could see everything. Patty was kissing her passionately and running her fingers along her arms and easing her halter top down to expose her unique large nipples that Patty knew she possessed and wanted to suck them as bad as I always did. Carol's nipples were one of a kind and Patty now was kissing on one and twisting the other one slowly, and Carol took my hand to play with Patty's nipples and so I did and we were all busy now exploring on each other and I was still blindfolded as far as Patty knew.

Patty was very pretty and fully developed for sure with nice solid 36D cups for sure but her nipples were nowhere as large as Cousin Carol's, which I now started to suck on. I took out my

hard 9" throbbing hot cock and put it into Patty's hand. "Omg," she smiled and said, "I knew you had a big tongue but this big dick is a nice surprise!" Cousin Carol said to come and "I told you I saw his big cock when he was taking a shower at the cottage" (but never mentioned she loved to suck my 9" and jerk my cum all over her hot nipples for me to rub into).

Patty wasted no time and went right down on Carol's pussy and moaning with my cock in her hand as well. Patty looked up at Carol with pussycum already on her face from Carol's wetness and said, "I've been waiting to eat you up forever, you're so gorgeous!"

I could tell immediately this wasn't Patty's first pussy and she wanted to date me to get to Carol's full lips and meaty soaked pussy, but Carol didn't seem to mind and kept fingering her pussy as Patty was climbing over her face in a 69 position, since it now was 1969, Carol and I were doing a lot of 69s since her 16th birthday on Jan. 6, 1969.

I was enjoying this so much and my cock was like stone and I decided to see if Patty would like some cock in her ass, and Carol could get a great view of my cock fucking her friend's asshole while she licked some pussy like Evelyn licked her "Mistress" Auntie Anna in the Journal. I had warm oil ready to give them a massage but Spin the Bottle was Carol's idea to get the ball rolling. I lubed Patty's asshole with some oil and she took two fingers as I lubed her hole, then immediately half my 9" right in and gasped, "Oh, yes!" Carol took one of my balls in her mouth that were hanging in her face, then to my surprise

Carol was rimming my ass and tonging my asshole and spanked me hard, "Bad Boy!" She laughed. She was become my demon, And my dream come true all in one, I loved her and her mother, "My two Goddesses," so much, I couldn't think of anything else anymore. Carol was trying to read all of her mother's Clients' Fetishes and Fantasies and wanted me to act out the ones she liked and then the ones I found interesting as well and were starting it off right.

Carol had whispered to me, "When we get in the shower are you ready for 'Eddy Duncan'?" I said, "Omg, yes!!" Eddy was the guy that loved Auntie giving him a "Golden Shower" while on his knees in the shower eating her pussy, then to his surprise he would take her pee while she pulled his hair and demanded he open his mouth. When I read this with Cousin Carol just a few days ago I was rock hard as she jerked my cock reading. I always was intrigued with pussycum squirting and where their piss came out from and how wet their pussy got. I could drink Cousin Carol's pussycum by the mouthful and soon I would swallow all of "my Goddess Auntie Anna" once I was "Collared and Owned" to serve and obey and her Personal Property alone!

Carol was now on the couch with her arms resting on top of the couch facing the wall. She knelt on the sofa and signaled Patty with her finger in her pussy to finish eating her out so they could shower with me. While Patty was on her knees eating this beautiful soaking-wet pussy and taking her cum, I was pounding both her holes from behind Doggy style and I came what seemed like

forever in her ass and all over her back and in her hair, My cum went everywhere! It even reached Carol's back over Patty's head.

Carol said, "Omg, you cum so good, I think it's safe to say Yes! You are definitely bisexual," and Patty said, "Yes, I am, and I've been dying to taste you, lol, and I hope we all can keep this going and have more fun."

Carol looked for my approval and asked me, "It's up to you, Cousin Anthony, what do you say?" I said, "Let's take a shower before Auntie gets home!" We all walked slowly to the shower because we were all fucked out and just came so intensely but the shower woke us up right away and Carol put her arms around my shoulders and kissed me as she now pointed down in front of her for me to kneel before her pussy. Patty went behind her to play with her amazing nipples and watched me eating my cousin, slowly anticipating my prize. I was waiting for her to press my head into her pussy like Auntie did to Eddy Duncan as part of his Fetish. I also wanted my mouth held on her pussy as Carol got ready to give me her hot salty stream of piss, then I wanted her to grab my hair and demand I open my mouth to receive her pee and told to swallow it with her command as I was told to obey.

As I was being facefucked slowly I felt one of her legs lift onto the top of the tub and felt my hair being pulled. "Open your mouth!" she yelled. As I was opening my mouth I could see the heavy Golden stream and feel it first on my face, then she got up closer to my opened waiting mouth so She could fill my mouth with hot pee to swallow just like Eddy did, only more willingly for

my Goddesses! I could hear it filling my mouth and tasted her salty pee. I now felt her hand close my mouth as I was told to swallow it. This would become MY Fetish now thanks to Eddy Duncan and his "Darkside" and the willingness to explore the most taboo kinks you can dream of in the BDism world. It would also become Carol's favorite foreplay when she wanted me to play sex slave.

As Patty was watching she was so horny and asked, "Can I have a turn?" At that instant the shower curtain swung open and Auntie Anna was screaming, "What the fuck is going on here!!! Get dressed and in the kitchen in two fucking minutes!!! And Patty, you are in serious trouble, you fucking slut lesbian whore!!! You're eighteen and my nephew is a minor!!! You're going to prison, bitch!!!" Auntie Anna was steaming mad as we all sat and she stood walking back and forth with the "Clients' Journal" in her hand she just discovered on Carol's bill.... "You little fuck!" Looking directly in Carol's face, "Where did you get this?? You're grounded forever! And YOU!" Looking at Patty, "you will be getting a call in the morning and we will discuss your future for fucking my fifteen-year-old nephew and using my daughter!! And YOU," looking directly into my eyes, "You betrayed my trust!!" That was the worst thing you could say to a man that was devoted to her and Carol totally and loved them both unconditionally and was only having fun. It was a lesson to be learned that I "Disobeyed." But in my defense I was Not collared yet!!

Still in a rage Auntie said, "She's not finished," and pointed right at Patty and demanded she be at the house tonight with

Carol at 8 sharp, when she got back from the office and closed the door behind her. Then Auntie said for me to come tomorrow and "don't see Carol anymore, you are first cousins, for God's sake!" Carol was very upset that we were through and went wild on Auntie and said, "What the fuck are you? You're a high-class Dominatrix? Those people in that Journal Pay you for sex, and you're mad at us??"

I interrupted and said I found the journal to protect Carol as she cried and walked out of the room. Auntie could only say, "Stop protecting her now, she's only manipulating you," and I waited for Carol to calm down before I said anything more.

Later that night Carol and I had to talk and decided to take it slower but still continued our exploration into our deep "Darkside" that Nobody would ever stop, Not even My Goddess Auntie Anna. We kept it well hidden and seen other people. I worked for Freddy and Sonny weekends and was working as a prep cook as well and Carol was doing commercial art classes. We met on planned dates in Peabody at the Plaza Motel for the whole night and left early in the morning separately.

Auntie had made Patty her personal submissive slut by threatening her into agreeing to serve her that night at their meeting. Auntie said she wouldn't tell my mother or the police that Patty coerced a fifteen-year-old into Bizarre taboo sex acts with a minor. Patty was "on call" and collared by Auntie now and both Auntie and I would use her as our personal sex slave. I met with Auntie that next day and she told me what Carol told her about

50

me wanting the Golden Shower with them and I was Not coerced by them and we both want the "Darkside." I wanted Auntie to teach me the BDISM Lifestyle that I was now addicted to and to serve her like the Goddess she had been grooming me for.

Auntie continued talking about sixteen years old and being consensual and legal documents signed and what it meant to be "collared and owned." I would be her "Personal property" and "collared and owned" in the BDism lifestyle. "I am ready, My Goddess, will you Collar me tomorrow? I'll be sixteen tomorrow, June 21st."

"I've been waiting a long time for this," and she took my hand and put it right under her loose silk skirt with crotchless panties. She was as wet or more than Cousin Carol's manicured pussy. Auntie said, "You start serving loyally, tomorrow at 8 A.M. at the office, you will have your 1st session and given a list of rules along with your birthday present. Are you willing to submit and obey my instructions and serve your Goddess and never to stray to another Mistress or Goddess?" she asked in a stern voice. I eagerly answered, "I am willing, this is all I ever wanted."

CHAPTER

7

Along with this alternative kinky lifestyle there are rules and safe words and limits to be respected, or rather "Obeyed." You as a willing sub/slave can agree in writing, a written contract and signed by the Mistress and sex Slave, that you have become "Personal Property" to a named Dominant or say it verbally on video while being used, disciplined or serving your Domme/mistress = Goddess, or Dom "Master" = Alpha Male.

Auntie needed two contracts from me and wanted them signed because of personal reasons as well as our Forbidden Taboo relationship we were about to encounter in this BDSM lifestyle and to please her in every way, every day. She went on to tell me about her health issues from before Carol was born and that her Leukemia was in submission for almost twenty years now and she was ill when she was very young at age fifteen or so. She

continued to put in writing that "I" would personally look after her daughter (Carol DiNunzio) and give her a proper and respectful burial in the event of her death and see to it that Carol and I get what's read off in said Will held by Attorney Evan J. Gellant, her personal attorney. I was totally blown away with this news, I'd heard from my mother that she was sick and almost died when they were kids but I had NO idea it was this deep and serious as the deadly disease of Leukemia.

I jumped up to embrace her with tears in both our eyes and I promised her right there that "We die together!" She smiled and just said, "You're Mine for as long as I'm alive!! And If Carol needs you, you take care of her needs because she told me recently she can't have an orgasm like you gave her anymore, you will please me today and show me how you make her have these multiple orgasms."

That was written and signed by both of us on my 16th birthday, June 21st, 1969, and is on my wall to this day. That was Contract #1, as she wrote out Contract #2, I was so filled with anxiety and eager to be collared I was getting so hard in my jeans waiting for my first session in the Dungeon just through the door behind her desk.

She wrote that the Commonwealth of Mass. stated that age sixteen is of legal age to have a consensual sexual relationship. There was a lot of controversy about the statute and whether male or female or the age difference between the two involved. Our age difference was seventeen years, Auntie was 33 and I was now sixteen with a 9"-thick cock and a long hard pointy tongue that she has seen and wanted to "collar and Own" and kept word-

ing it that it was so perfect and professional. I agreed to it immediately and signed my name, Anthony J. Tracia, next to hers, Anna
Maria DiNunzio. My mother would get to read the first contract
of Me being her Beneficiary in part in case of her demise and sign
her name beside mine, Joanne Tracia, and without realizing My
Mistress/Domme slipped in contract #2 of My being in a consensual sexual relationship that my own mother knew about (but
really Would Never know about!) and Mom signed both Contract #1 And Contract #2, lol. I had both Contracts framed and
keep them on my wall.

My whole family was there at my house to have cake and sing
Happy Birthday after the Contracts were signed and a few more
aunts and cousins and my brother and young sister and we were
all there too for my milestone of Sweet 16. But the only thing on
my mind today was to please "my Goddess," "My Mistress," My
gorgeous Auntie Anna!

Carol was still mad at her and I could see the look and feel
her vibe as I always did and whispered in her ear as I kissed her
neck inconspicuously, "I'll see you soon."

It was still early on my special birthday turning sixteen years old
but I was more like 26, I worked like a mature man and made
my own money, bought my own clothes and was saving for a
nice car after I got my license. My New Goddess was giving me
driving lessons now that Carol got her license ahead of me once
again, lol.

Auntie left ahead of me and I was to follow thirty minutes later and she would pick me up at the Chinese restaurant around back so nobody would see me get in her car to go to the office for my first session. I was going to be collared today and now had a signed BDSM contract to abide by and Obey!

I turned the corner and saw her car parked there and looked behind me to make sure nobody seen me, especially Carol since she was at the house also but she had left right after Auntie did and was going shopping. Auntie opened the door as I approached the car and I closed the door and slumped down and we laughed together about our planned afternoon.

Once at the office she showed me through the door behind her desk and locked it behind us. There were certificates and degrees on the walls for marriage counseling, massage, and Physical Therapy and had Clients in each field, she explained, and was not just some high-class call girl like Carol called her. Auntie was qualified in "counseling" and in "Anatomy," so-called therapeutic healing "massage techniques," and was Very "Fetish/Fantasy Qualified" as well for the right Client at the right price, she explained. She paused at the very expensive and comfortable-looking long leather lounge-like massage table big enough for Any large person or a small couple. On the massage table was a box and it said "Happy Birthday my nephew, Open it!"

I anxiously ripped the paper off and took out an engraved leather collar in jade gemstones that read "Slave Tony" and under it read "Property of My Mistress." She told me to now hand it to

her and get on my knees and look up at her while she put the best present ever around my neck and said the words "With this collar I claim 'Slave Tony' to be my personal property and serve my needs when instructed without question. I demand respect, loyalty and dedication in our exploration into your 'Darkside' and to please his Mistress when called upon, daily or whenever needed to serve his Mistress' sexual appetites, which there are many! You begin your training in our lifestyle called BDISM Now and where you kneel before me is now 'Your Spot.' When I order you to 'your Spot' for your instructions for the session, you kneel with your hands behind your and look up at Your Mistress, and you answer 'Yes, Mistress' or 'No, Mistress' always or 'Goddess' is fine also, No more 'Auntie Anna'!! Do you accept this collar?" "Yes, Mistress!" I eagerly answered. "Yes! I will serve My Mistress and obey."

"Let's begin your first session and get up on the table and lay on your back with your clothes off and hands on your head." I immediately obeyed and seen her take a whip from the wall beside the table and continued to talk and walk around the table grazing my chest and belly and hard 9" cock with it. She told me to listen carefully and that I needed to understand the discipline was necessary so that I never disobey ever again and she didn't like that I was fucking her daughter and she cracked the whip hard across my nipples twice to my surprise! It stung so bad like a hundred bee bites. "Ouch!" was all I could say and she kept talking and teasing with the whip softly and said again, "Your cock is MY

Property now!" Crack! Crack! Two more times across my hard cock as I dropped my hands to protect my dick and she ordered me to put my hands back on my head, and she proceeded to cuff me now to the table's eye hooks all around the table for restraints I would be bound in soon and whipped into shape to be reassured she owned "Slave Tony" now and I was her property and would serve No other!

"Repeat it," crack, crack!! Across my nipples again with the long heavy leather strands as she asked, "I hear you like large purple nipples! Today your nipples will be big and purple when I say you can go," she demanded again. "Repeat it, 'I will serve No other, My Mistress,'" and she put her ear to my mouth to listen. I repeated it twice in her ear, "I will serve No other! I will serve No other!" My Mistress lifted my head, grasping my thick wavy black hair in her free hand, and ordered me to the other end of the table and to lay on my front with my face in the 8"-round breathing hole at the edge of the adjustable headrest on the professional leather massage table. Even the table itself was adjustable as she pressed the control on the floor and the table was lowering to the level she needed me in. My Mistress put the leather whip back and took another piece of S&M equipment off the wall, this time it was a long leather riding crop. I stared out of curiosity and she ordered me to put my face in the hole and just listen to her now hypnotic voice. She grazed my ass with the long skinny wooden crop with a 4" rectangular leather end attached to the stick and holding a round leather handle and tapping my ass with it softly all over

the two cheeks of my ass in between right on my hole, crack! Crack twice on one side and then Crack! Crack! Twice on my asshole that stung more than 200 bee bites that time. When she raised my head once again by my hair out of the hole in table, she was wearing only a crotchless corset and said, "So you like ass, I hear?" She was referring to the cottage when I was fucking Carol in her ass and I had cum in Carol's ass that Auntie had heard at the door. She was peeking through the window and waited until we finished, "Yes! I heard and I watched you both."

My Mistress now was rubbing lube on her hands and opened my ass to lube my hole. I could see a strap-on next to me as she wrapped the strap-on belt around her statuesque figure with a long thin silicone skin-like dildo and proceeded to the other end of the table and pulled my legs apart. I could feel my ass was against the thin smooth silicone vibrating dildo and she was entering my ass slowly and could hear her heavy breathing and moaning, "Nice ass, My slave!" She was slapping the end of the crop harder on my back and ass cheeks with each pumping of the dildo into my hole, now opening and loosening up for My Mistress to use me in ways she enjoyed, I could see she did enjoy "Pegging" her new collared Slave, and just started to enjoy it. I knew I was pleasing her "Anal Fetish" and satisfying her on my first day serving this incredible Goddess, "I am all yours, My Mistress, Only yours and will serve NO other!"

"Ahh, Good Slave! You will always belong to me from now on," as she buried the tool all the way in my ass and slapped my

ass with her bare hands while massaging my prostate gland directly behind a man's balls until my cum was oozing out of my hard 9" while being pegged by the most sought-after Domme in New England, and she would Belong to me as well!

She noticed I had cum oozing out and took the well-lubed 6"-thin Dildo out slowly and turned me over to wipe me up and held my hard cock tightly in the towel and jerked it twice until it was clean, then ordered me to wipe up my lubed and used-up Mistress's Anal Pegging Fetish hole. Now at the other end of the table she pulled me forward and with her foot she tilted the headrest down to angle, my head downward and hanging over the table with her soaking-wet manicured pussy moving over to my mouth. "Show Your Mistress the tongue that now belongs to only me! Open your mouth!" she demanded; when I did it was like heaven having her hold me by my hair and ride my tongue and my chin grinding her asshole all over my nose, chin and lips and was just humping my mouth and tongue hard. "Show me your little trick you do with my daughter so I can drown you too," so she told me, and now she couldn't come for other men. "I will, My Mistress, whatever you demand, I will serve."

From her standing position over my face I entered my two fingers, index and middle fingers, Up and towards me into her now eager-to-squirt moist pussy and getting wetter as I moved higher into her outer wall and moved each finger in a ticking motion faster and faster as she became wetter and wetter, I would slow it down when licking and sucking the clit as I licked and

lubed my fingers in my saliva and added a third finger when she was soaking wet and started to hump harder. Then I would know it was time to receive her prize into my open mouth and try to swallow as much if not All of her mixed pussycum and pee when having a G-Spot orgasm or in most cases a multiple orgasm I live for, yum. After about three or minutes my Mistress was breathing so hard and fast I knew she was ready and fingered her with three fingers rapidly, and her cum was squirting out the sides of my three fingers. I pulled my fingers out and quickly opened wide to take my Mistress's pussycum and swallow her down while she just filled my mouth with her hot tasty juices. "Omg," she said, "you will Never, ever take My collar off, Carol wasn't lying when she said that tongue was made for eating pussy. You will be rewarded when good and punished when bad; however, I think that calls for a reward," and she climbed up in the table to ride my hard 9" and give me yet another mouthful of juice and told me to report tomorrow on "my Spot" to serve and go over some more rules. "Are you pleased, My Mistress?" I asked knowingly.

She just smiled and said, "Oh, yes, My Slave T, oh yes, your first session went beyond my expectations and you will 'Belong to only Me'! Repeat it!" she asked one last time for today, I repeated it twice again, "I belong to only you, only you!"

My face was soaked and My Mistress's pussycum cum was now dripping from my thick head of hair and down my neck as she looked down smiling, "We better shower now and I'll have Slave Patty drive you home. By the way, You will be picked up and

driven to work or home from 'Our' new slave, Patty the slut. I have convinced her to sign papers with Me in turn to be our sex slave and for my consensual bisexual relationship and in turn we won't prosecute her for the next fifteen years. That is when the statute of limitations runs out and she will be cleared of rape of a minor under sixteen and using Carol age sixteen to help her trick you into taboo sex acts," she agreed, "and I want YOU to collar her tomorrow in proxy of me on my behalf and We will share her! Do you understand and accept this gift from your Mistress?" Smiling as she walked me into the walk-in shower and placed a towel down and pointed to it for me to kneel before this Goddess that was about to give me the Golden Shower of my life. I'd been daydreaming of this for about as long as I'd been jerking off and feeling up Cousin Carol.

My Mistress ran her fingers through my hair as I waited anticipating her warm Yellow rain on my face. As she held my chin up and bent over to kiss me deep she said, "Open Wide as you can! And you can look or close your eyes so they don't burn from my hot pee." I "did not" want to close my eyes at all, I needed to see and hear this Goddess's stream of salty pee fill my mouth and swallow her every drop she had for her collared slave. I was stunned and gasping from her heavy stream of piss that shot right down my throat and I coughed only for a second. She was drinking a lot of water earlier and now I knew why! Now I knew why My Mistress had three clients that requested this Fetish, one being Eddy Duncan, the guy I read about with Cousin Carol

when She also drowned me in PussyPeeCum that unforgettable day when Patty was about to pee next but never got the chance.

"Ok, then get dressed and ready to be picked up tomorrow and collar that little Bi/slut that will serve us well for the next fifteen years, lol, I want to watch you tear her holes up, you understand! And don't worry about Carol, I don't care if you want to fuck her as long as I don't know, she will try to manipulate you like always and you should let her, she may cum better that way knowing she Is sneaking around as long as 'You belong to me,' Repeat it Now!" she demanded. "Yes, Mistress, I do belong to you, as long as you keep me collared I will never stray!" "Oh, yes! I love that, Good slave, Bring that slut tomorrow and put her next to your spot at 8 A.M. sharp!"

CHAPTER
8

Today I would not have to take the bus or a train to get to my Mistress to serve and please or to work in The N. End. Instead I would be picked up by a new driver and soon-to-be eighteen-year-old and very hot big-tit sex slave Patty Spazola, a bi/pussylicking nympho that would be collared by me today by Proxy for My Mistress. Patty would be Co-Owned and used as our willing submissive Sex toy from an agreement made between My Mistress and (Patricia Spazola) to waive prosecution from a coerced sexual encounter involving Anna Di Nunzio's fifteen-year-old nephew and trying to seduce her sixteen-year-old daughter. When Patty arrived I would show these papers to her that she had already signed and let her know she would be "shared and used" (collared and Owned) in our S&M lifestyle, also known as BDSM, for at least the next fifteen years, when the statute of

limitations ran out on the very taboo and unacceptable charges of rape of a minor under sixteen years of age.

I saw her pulling up and she was crying and worried about her future. Her fate depended on My Mistress and I and how she served and obeyed in this lifestyle we had chosen and cherished. I would groom her and train her as would My Mistress and she would become ours to keep collared and shared for our kinky Fetishes and Fantasies as well.

"Am In trouble today?" She sniffled and wiped the tears from her cheeks.

"I was told to pick you up and bring you to the office and you would bring me in to collar me and own me."

"What does that all mean, Tony? If you help me I'll do anything you say," and that was what she told me. "I can do whatever, For you or for her and I'm ok with that."

"Ok then, so with that being said just drive to the office and I'll explain the situation to you, and when you pick me up or drop me off from now on I want your blouse undone and no bra on so I can play with those melons that now belong to me and My Mistress, Do you understand now? Just say, 'Yes, Master T,' I will calm 'Our Mistress' down and you just do what I tell you to do. I'll keep you out of sight till she calms down. At least you're Bi and going to lick a Goddess' pussy and not any ugly bitch, lol, just think of it that way for now, play your cards right and we will all have fun you get to be fucked by a nice big cock and eaten and used by a Goddess, any bi/slut would give her

right nipple for that! Am I right? Think about it that way, you have no choice now!"

"I guess you're right and I will do my best, I promise you, and will Carol be using me too?" she asked, smiling. I replied, "I'll see what I can do on the QT, I do have a few things in mind for sure, you may love me for later! Just remember, You belong to both of us after I collar you now, let's go in now and meet her, it's 8 A.M. sharp!! Let's go put your collar on and agree to the terms she will state to you while I put your collar on, and when I say, 'Do you accept this collar?' You say, 'Yes, I do, Master T, I accept this collar, I belong to you and My Mistress now,' and then I'll assign you your spot to kneel before us and swear to honor and obey and never to stray! Then I'll have you suck my cock while already on your knees to break the ice and she will play with your tits for your initiation on accepting your privilege to serve. You're now co-owned by both a big cock and a juicy Goddess of a pussy. This was a lucky day for you."

Everything was running smoothly for My Mistress now and she was super busy with real estate this summer. People were calling like crazy to get appointments to see houses up for sale and the interest rates were very low, she claimed. People were buying houses and summer houses just like she had done last winter. I would be assisting her on some showings because she didn't want to go alone with single guy meetings, she always looked so beautiful. Those asshole rude men always hit on her and she was a professional when it came to business. She had just told me that

when she wanted her pussy serviced, "I'll have my stud/slave T tear it up good and the new bi/slut clean us up."

Carol was up at the cottage staying there now because it was closer to Lawrence, MA, where she was working as a commercial artist and taking classes at the community college to be even better as an artist. I would sneak up there when I could and hadn't decided when to tell her about my new co-Owned bi/slut sex slave her mom had made "Me" collar and own on her behalf. The best part of all was that I'd be "on call" to assist her with the "Special Clients" Journal, the section of the Journal that Carol's pussy became wet as a sponge when she was reading about their graphic taboo Fetishes. Then she made me act them out with her after drawing her scenes out to perform on her. Having this new assignment, however, was a problem for my obligations with Freddy and Sonny, who had been like two fathers to me, and I could not just leave Haymarket selling fruit and being with all my friends on the weekends so I'd compromise with them and work Only on Saturdays and if a "Special Client" was in town it would wait until Saturday night, which was always the case anyway! I had a ride now back and forth so if I needed to leave a few hours early once in a great while it was no problem.

Auntie (My Mistress) wanted to meet with Freddy one Saturday to discuss an envelope Freddy had for her to help buy me my dream car. They both had been taking ten a week from my pay and saving it for my yellow Corvette when I got my license soon. My Vanilla life and my "Darkside" were well organized now

thanks to My Mistress, who was a genius at keeping the two extremely different lifestyles separate with careful thought-out planning. My Mistress was even thinking ahead when she trapped and collared "Our new Co-Owned bi/slut sex slave," who would also appear to be my "Vanilla" girlfriend and take attention away from Me and Auntie or Carol and I. I had made an appointment to get the windows tinted also so my Big-tit driver sex slave would drive topless while I played with them or bring a friend along to play with them from the back seat. I had a lot of plans for her, lol.

Patricia Bergman was a very pretty and petite sandy-blonde, German/Irish descent, and the high cheekbone look, green eyes, her tits were big for her size, which made them look even bigger on her, about a 38D, nice and full and firm being only nineteen in few weeks and now an eager willing participant in her new venture to explore her "Darkside" through Me and My Mistress and to get her mouth on Carol's pussy and unique long strawberry-like nipples once more or on a regular basis, which she would try by pleasing "Me" to get to her. She definitely had the appearance of being my Vanilla Girlfriend and I'd portray her in that way for now while serving "My Goddess" and her daughter with Loyalty and Submit to both of them when I was called on to serve or pleasure either of them. Meanwhile it was time to collar this new bisexual beauty as a member of our extending BDSM family and explore with her and open up her "Darkside" to determine her future with Master T and his two Goddesses. It was time for her Induction now!!

It was the morning after June 21st, 1969, the day I was collared and Owned by a Goddess that only came by once in lifetime. I was delivering a bi/slut slave that would be co-Owned by My Mistress. "I" would be doing her induction by Proxy as I was instructed to do so by My Mistress the day before when I was inducted (Collared and Owned) into our BDSM lifestyle (as my 16th birthday present).

I wanted this morning to go special, I told my new Big-tit Sex/Slave and Driver, So to impress my Goddess that was sitting on her antique Marquis DeSade chair I walked our willing sub/sex slave in the soft-lit Dungeon with her hands behind her back and holding on to her ponytail. My Mistress was pointing down to a pillow next to "My Spot" so I walked her over and tugged her ponytail down to kneel before us to proceed with the induction, then My Mistress and I would begin to "consummate and Initiate" this hot-looking big-tit firm nineteen-year-old to make it "Official"! She had a remarkable resemblance to Rachel Welch with the high cheekbones and big tits, only a lighter complexion. She was infatuated with Cousin Carol's beauty but she was only sixteen and Not gay, Patty was on a mission to eat her pussy and get those huge nipples in her mouth and that was why she was becoming our slave today!! She had violated My Goddess's code of ethics both in her Vanilla life And in our "Darkside" of the BDism world, She simply Got Caught!! And with Me as well in a three-way, I was only fifteen and being used up by both of them.

My Mistress was walking over now to hand me the long Black box with her collar and two chain-linked leashes unattached (one leash belonged to me, the other was for her). All I needed for right now was the collar that was engraved "Cum Slut Whore" in red ruby stones and under it read "Property of Master T and his Goddess" in smaller green jade stones. It was a beautiful 3" soft leather Burgundy collar and you could tell it was expensive too!! Also in the box was a smaller chain with nipple clamps on each end for those big tits and it matched the collar. Patty was now looking at her new collar with matching nipple clamps and she was impressed as I was, She wanted to wear it now with pride, she wasn't shaking anymore and not afraid anymore like when she was walked in, then put on her knees. Patty was as willing as I was yesterday to serve this Goddess of a lifetime.

I took the collar first from the box and stood behind Patty to place the collar to fit comfortably, then locked it in place as I repeated those words that she would take an oath to, "With this collar you will be 'Owned' and become 'our' Property Property that you kneel before, to serve and obey, and serve no other; Do you accept this collar??"

"Yes! Master T and My Mistress, I Do accept! I will serve you faithfully, I promise, and you won't be disappointed with my service." Patty was ready now as I took the nipple clamps from the box and adjusted them to fit so they weren't tight enough to make her bleed nor loose enough to fall of her 38D-cup firm and smooth nineteen-year-old melons with pink nipples that matched

the burgundy-colored collar and clamp handles perfectly. Our "Mistress" now was tying her hands behind her back to get the full effect of her tits as she held them up for me to clamp and straddled her thumbs over her nipples from behind her to harden them for me to clamp more easily.

"Nicely Done, My Stud/Slave T, Master T in training, you will become a great 'Dom/Master' one day. But for now you are my Slave as is my new asslicker and toe-sucking slut, slave, I need her up on the table now to discipline her for trying to steal my Stud/Slave and using my daughter's pussy! And to make this ceremony official, I will accept my punishment, My Mistress, and I'm sorry I disappointed you that day in the shower, I had No idea he was 'your property.' And Carol would be a 'Domme's' daughter, Yes! That's right, He 'Belongs to Me,' Not you!"

And as I sat her on the table My Mistress reached over to take a long thin paddle from the wall and walked over slowly and with her hands still tied behind her back started paddling her clamped tits and nipples. I could hear Patty now whimpering and moaning from the discipline treatment and begin to cry. My Mistress kept scolding her with every crack of the paddle, "Never, Ever try to take 'My Property,' Always Obey and Never Stray, Repeat it, 'I will Obey and Never stray, Mistress!'"

"Yes, My Mistress, I will Obey, I will Never stray, I belong to you and Stud/Slave T, My Master T...."

My Mistress now gave the order for me to hold her head over the adjustable table and lower it so she could watch me first lube

my now very hard 9" with olive oil and deep-throat fuck her while My Mistress put on the large 12" dildo into her strap-on belt and fucked both her other holes from on the table with Patty's legs held up high by me.

Patty was being fucked very forcefully by Our Mistress, who showed Patty on her induction day that she was being disciplined and just who actually did own her and who was in Charge. To my surprise, however, Patty had a "No Gag" reflux and I liked her already!!

I was starting to see that our Mistress was really into her strap-on and Anal play on her submissives, she also liked to inflict pain and Dominate as she was doing right at this moment. She was enjoying our new collared slut/slave being tortured in all three holes and loving pushing her limits to take even more. She was amazed as she looked closer to rub her throat and saw and felt my cock moving in her throat. "Awee! That's beautiful, my Stud/Slave, look at her take all that 9", I'm going to cum any minute, Get over here and finish your Mistress with that big boy from behind me and I want to watch you cum between those tits and finish in her mouth while I hold her mouth open, understand? This slut just came all over my legs while I was fucking her asshole with a 12"! She's a hot one! Just remember, you belong to me!"

"Yes, Mistress, I will not stray no matter how hot she is, You are my Goddess and much hotter to me, I'm loyal to only you and you never have to tell me that."

"I love to hear it, my loyal Stud/Slave T," My Mistress said, moaning as I entered her soaking-wet pussy to do what I was just ordered to do.

I could feel her lowering herself onto Patty to bury her face between her tits and lubing her with her saliva and removed the nipple clamps off her nipples to suck on them while I started to pound My Mistress as she was telling me to fuck her Hard. "Fuck me Harder, fuck that pussy Hard, My Stud!" I placed both my hands on her solid lower back and rode her wet pussy fast and Hard and deep. She screamed like Patty was screaming earlier with the 12" silicone dildo up her ass while My Mistress pumped her hard. I angled my cock to reach her G-Spot and she squirted and reached around to hold my ass and kept my cock in until she was done multi-cumming and then let go slowly and just rested on Patty without moving. As I walked around to finish my instructions My Mistress was squeezing Patty's cheeks and holding her mouth open as Patty played with her Mistress' nipples, "Give it to her, Stud/Slave! I want to see you cum in her mouth, Yes, Yes," said Patty, "I want it all and I want to swallow every drop of My Master T." I almost didn't make it, they were making me so fucking hot. But my cum held back just enough and I exploded all over her face and in Patty's mouth and on My Mistress' hands on Patty's face, and accidentally on purpose I gave a little to My Mistress' tits. Patty licked My cum off our Mistress' hands and sucked her fingers and I licked my cum off My Mistress' tits. "Omg! That was so fucking hot, My Stud, This is why You'll al-

ways belong to only me!! Now that was the best 'collaring ceremony session' since yesterday," My Mistress said, looking and
smiling at me. "You both served very well today, I just came three
times. I look forward to more shared sessions with our new Co-
Owned deepthroater." My Mistress looked down at a drop of my
cum I missed, now dripping down towards her belly. She pointed
to it and told Patty, "That Stud Slave T missed a spot, lol, would
you lick that clean and while you're down there your Mistress has
a few drops from your cum too. You can clean my pussy up good
also while I give you instructions for later, My Stud will take a
shower 'alone'!" she said clearly and firmly.

While My Mistress was being lapped up and licked clean she
was telling Patty to go to see her attorney in Chelsea and to give
her information to be on the books working for her and taking certain massage Clients. "You will need to be certified and I'll enroll
you to take the course so you will be a legal masseuse and we don't
get busted, you understand?" Patty answered, "MmmHmm," from
Our Mistress's squeaky-clean pussy. "You're going to do that for
me, Mistress? That is awesome, thank you so much, Mistress, I
really would love to get my own place and serve you even better,
I will make you feel like today 'every day.' I won't disappoint you
ever again, you'll see."

"You better not," pinching her now visible swollen puffy nipples in between her fingers. "Now we will shower together quickly
and you can do my back for me, then drive 'Anthony' to the North
End and you go to Evans' office and fill out your paperwork, you

will call My Stud/Slave by his name, 'Anthony,' outside in the Vanilla world as our whole family does or Tony as his friends do, and you will call me 'Anna' in public or during business since we will be working together.

"I'm going to assign you to a few 'Special Clients' of mine that have been steadies for years and pay me well for their 'Kinky Fetishes.' I will teach you what they desire and From what I just witnessed here today I'm convinced You can handle it, lol. I thought I was going to have to beat the fucking piss out of your nineteen-year-old solid ass and big tits but you're going to be a huge asset. I'll take you far if you're loyal and dedicated to my offer and work alongside your Co-Owner, My StudSlave T and your Master T in training. He's going to be a Great 'Dom'/ Master one day! You will assist with his assigned Females and couples and serve when he needs you, Gabeesh (in Italian)?"

"Oh, Yes, My Goddess and Mistress! I do Understand completely," as she drew a nice warm bath and wrapped a towel over her Mistress's sculptured torso. "I'm All Yours and 'Your' Stud/Slave T's now and privileged to be both your Slut/Slave forever."

"That's All I wanted to hear. Good Girl!"

Patty watched closely as her "Domme" Goddess's magnificent unblemished body climbed into her warm oiled bath to be handwashed by her new co-owned sex/slave she had craved to be.

CHAPTER

9

My Goddess and now the Co-Owner of this incredibly talented slut Patricia had persuaded our newly collared slut in just one day to promise to be the best slut ever! It just took one session with My Mistress and I to open up her "Darkside." She Never realized she had cravings to be used like a whore over and over that went so deep with desires to please and serve as some submissive masochists tended to crave for. However, Patty still had an infatuation for Carol, she would try and use her own Master T and promise to throat my 10" every day just to get to those one-in-a-billion strawberry-sized nipples and always wet juicy pussy that we had both had the pleasure now to have sucked on.

I told Patty she needed to drive me to Carol and that I needed to talk to her about all that had been going on here, she had even been calling her mom (our Mistress) to ask questions about what

happened to you and me after the bad shower scene when our Mistress caught us all together, "Carol doesn't know yet that you belong to Me and our Mistress now and you're 'collared and Owned,' your soon-to-be-in-a-business venture involving the three of us in regular business and pleasure sessions that our Mistress is incredibly turned on by." My Goddess was having multiple orgasms and now submitting to my 10" cock and pussy and ass eating and training me to become a Dom/Master.

I needed to come up with something fast and I never wanted to lose Carol, she was my rock and my soulmate since we could walk. Carol had someone now keeping her busy, but Not keeping her happy. Carol had called several times.

My Mistress had given me instructions to go see her and calm her down but didn't say Mistress said so! I was given instructions to please and serve her if needed, although she was engaged now to a very wealthy man. The problem was this man who tried to buy my soulmate's love because he wanted this unique beautiful woman by his side, "could not" please her sexually! She had told her mom she could not have an orgasm with this man and that he only had a 4" penis. Then My Mistress yelled, "She didn't even want to say 'cock' or 'dick,' she called it a 4" 'Penis'! And Not a single orgasm in six months and it's 'Your fault'! You have spoiled my little girl for All other men and children someday, Omg! You go and take care of this and don't tell her I talked to you about this! You have the slut drop you off at the Marriott in Derry and send her right back here for work, No fucking three-ways with

Carol, 'Only here!'" as She pointed down, "I'll reserve the room tonight for tomorrow night, have Patty call her in case Shortdick answers the phone and tell her where to meet you when, Spend the day there and I'll come up to get you when she goes to class."

I had Patty call and Carol did answer and passed me the phone (No cell phones in 1969/70), lol. It would have been much easier communicating with her but instead I found other ways to be with her, I was never really away from her long because she wouldn't allow it no matter who she was involved with or I was involved with, we had a bond since we could walk and talk. We just automatically knew each other's thoughts like genetic twins, only we were 1st cousins. Both artists, Both sensual, Both pleasers or Dominants (switch) in BDism terms, I had a plan that would give her the multiple Orgasms she'd been missing and it had to be at the cottage, I would build her a "secret closet" within her closer that led to outside so I could sneak in while her fiancé was out (or at home), the thrill and the darkness and my voice in the dark whispering in her ear up close while I twisted and suckled her nipples, automatically giving her orgasm #1 and then the fun really began. Carol started to flow like a river after her first orgasm and she didn't stop streaming or squirting for hours when I got to her G-Spot, licking her clit hard held my cum back for a while and gave her another one or two orgasms, then when I entered that soaking-wet and meaty manicured pussy with my hard 9" hot cock she became a river of pussycum I wanted to drown in and what I lived for.

My driver and personal nineteen-year-old sandy-blonde slut/slave Patty had arrived with newly tinted windows on my new leased business car, a gorgeous E-Class Mercedes that My Mistress would write off as an expense to Massage Therapy And Rehabilitation Inc. Slut/Slave Patty and I would run this part of My Mistress's Inc. conglomerate. As I got in I noticed she had obeyed my second demand besides the tinted windows, she was topless in a corset holding up those 38Ds for her new Master to play with while she drove as I instructed her to do. But we had big problems today to solve as I fondled her lovely, firm smooth breasts a little to show my appreciation and gave each hard nipple a kiss and told her, "Drive!"

I told her today wasn't a good time to even try and ask to get at Carol but I would make it happen another time. "It will be our secret, though, or Your Mistress will simply cut those hard pink nipples right off, lol."

"I know, Master! And your dick too, lol, I belong to you as well and I will follow your instructions when you think it's time for me to serve you both together again, I won't go against her wishes, Master, but if it's an order from you, My Co-Owner, I'll do you both in a second 'with pleasure'!" she added, smiling, and padded my inner thigh as I sat next to her softly pinching and twisting her now rock-hard nipples.

"I have some tools I just put in the trunk with my suitcase and I'll be spending the Night at the Marriott."

"You have to get your ass right back there to work," Mistress said, "but first go to a Hardware store for hinges for a door I'm

going to make from a piece of plywood at the cottage I have there. Carol will love this and I'll explain what the problem is and just maybe you can give me some ideas too. She's engaged to a guy now that can't please her, she's told her mom and me she can't have an orgasm with him and that he only has a 4" dick and don't eat pussy right at all, but he has like a few Million bucks and building her a house and staying at the cottage for now."

"Well, just like the Beatles' new song says, 'Money can't buy you love,'" Patty said seriously. "She's been a friend of mine for two years now and I know her very well. She won't last with him, she's in love with her art and you! The only two things that she's comfortable with."

"How do you know this, Patty, did she tell you?" I asked.

"I'm a woman first and I just know, I can see just like you see it and you know it too!

It'll come to you and my Master is smart enough to handle this, you don't need my advice, just go with your heart."

Our Mistress/Her mom had told me something similar, she said it was all my fault and that I spoiled her for all other men. She was demanding that I make things right, but don't say she told me to go to her.

"I'll build a 'Secret Closet' first and then have her take him to 'marriage Counseling' and He don't know what we look like and 'We' will give Carol and Lewis an ultimatum into sex sessions to show him how to please or he must leave her for her happiness. He will never leave a Goddess like her and Carol can

have the best of both worlds! What do you think about that idea, My slut, lol??"

"I think you better talk to our Mistress about that one!" she said, laughing.

"Ok; stop here at this Hardware store and I'll be right out and drop me at the cottage, then get to work fast, I don't want Mistress to think we're all in the shower somewhere."

All the supplies were bought and I was dropped off at the cottage first. I then sent Patty back to our worried Mistress for some training in her new massage venture. I found the outside wall leading to the her room between her bedroom closet and the linen closet were back to back just like at her house, where her closet and her mom's closet were also back to back. That was how we were able to find Mistress's journal and some S&M equipment. I began cutting an entry from the outside with my power saw, everyone was out for two hrs. so I had to work fast, and then I'd be able to sneak in and meet Carol when she needed me to service and please her. She had been spoiled sexually by Me and now I must continue to serve and please my kinky soulmate, I needed to for myself as well as for her. I knew how to make her have multiple orgasms that "no other man was able to do for her," she insisted. I myself didn't have an orgasm 1/2 as intense as she enabled me to as well, And she couldn't have an orgasm "At All" if it was not with me!

Now I had to attach hinges I bought to the opening to make a door out of it so I could use it as a door to walk right into her

closet and loosen the back wall of the closet to wait for her in the linen closet to fuck her brains out on the towels and soak them in her pussycum, and mine. She'd been missing my 9" cock and the G-Spot massaging that made her flow like a river that I couldn't drink down fast enough at times.

Many men had done the unimaginable for the woman they loved. This was No different and the least I could, I had only built a "secret closet" recreation of our first sexual experiences together and how she had realized she exploded in sea of pussycum "now missing " in her sex life...although I was dying inside that she was engaged to another man to all of our surprise, I was infatuated that I was the only man that could make her squirt in a sea of her tasty Mango Nectar juice. After her first orgasm she continued to stream from her meaty pussy for at least five-ten minutes, just touching or kissing her "anywhere" on her sculptured Italian body.... Today I'd have to show her just how much I still needed her in my life Without demanding or suggesting she change her engagement plans.

I'd told her where I'd be and when she had time to sneak up to my room at the Marriott that evening, I'd be there for her. I'd work out a preplanned schedule for us to follow after that where and when to meet to please her in the ways she was accustomed to. Reading from the journal and then creating scenarios on paper for me to perform for her WAS her foreplay, the hot Cousin Carol with the huge nipples always protruding through her halter tops and awesome ass as all my friends described her knew exactly

how to manipulate me, and I loved to watch her set me up, that was MY foreplay!

The two double knocks on the door put a smile on my face immediately! I opened the door to see that in only a few months she had become more beautiful as I'd ever seen her before. Maybe it was because I missed her so much or both. She immediately closed the door and kissed me so passionately I could feel that familiar heat and moisture off her lips when "she was ready" to drown me in in a combination of Mango and pee from uncontrollable multiple orgasms. I couldn't wait to drink her down today!!

First we needed to talk as adults and not just kinky, horny adolescent cousins in a closet. This was a serious situation and needed to be addressed. This decision would affect "Both" our future and the approvals of her "Mother," My Mother, "My Aunt/Mistress," My mother's sister and niece, "My younger brother," and the new Short dick in her life, her fiancé. "Oh! Let's not forget our 'Grandma'!! OMG! She will fall on the floor and die there, lol. Do we sneak around or do we tell everyone to just fuck off and mind your own business? What do we do?? That's right, we Sneak around! It makes her squirt more intensely multiple times and we don't want to rock the boat with 'My Mistress,' her volatile 'Domme' Italian Mother (for now)...."

Carol and I started to walk the bathroom, undressing each other and still talking, however, about her involvement with this guy and how she worked for Paramount Pictures, where He (Louis Aronstein) was an executive with the company. He was 28

years old and rich already. She added, "Big money, little dick! I thought I could get some pleasure out of it but I just can't fake it anymore, Anthony! You see what you did to me?" now crying with her naked body against mine. "Yes; I can see. Do You see what you've done to Me? There's not an hour that goes by that I see something, then start to daydream of you!"

"Good!" She took my two hands now and placed them over her swollen hard beet-red huge nipples. "I know these are your favorite possessions and will always be yours no matter what happens." As I was pinching on them and twisting them slowly I could feel her take my 10" cock in both her hands and jerk me the way I was missing. She had a special way of taking my cock in her two hands, gripping me hard and tugging forward slowly and holding it there for a second, then back down, and always straddled with my asshole a bit and circled my inner hole with her fingers. This stimulated bloodflow and I was rock hard in an instant, especially with Carol. I missed washing her flawless unblemished backside, from her neck all the way down to her ankles. She didn't have a pimple or a freckle or a beauty mark on her, just pure silky olive complexion, smooth and tight as it got. She would belong to me soon but there needed to be a careful plan with careful manipulating and who was better than that? Yes! My Mistress/Carol's mo.

The Room at the Marriott My Mistress reserved was a suite, of course, nothing but the best when it came to her daughter, or her Stud/slave she had groomed. This Shower/bath had a sauna

attached to it as well as a built-out seat on the tiled wall right in the shower itself, which you really didn't see in 1970. My Mistress had a similar shower built at her Dungeon already by tile masons to match, even bigger for her (water sports) kinksters. Tonight, however, I would play musical Chairs with the younger Goddess and the love of my life. I would sit on a bed of hot coal to take her continuous streams of warm Mango juice from her meaty pussy to satisfy my addiction, Yes! It was that good! After teasing her nipples for only a minute she sat me right down forcefully when I was teasing with her, then put one leg up on the rim of the bath and grabbed onto the shower head, then the other, and was now "Standing" over me while I sat trapped between her strong, long toned legs. She was positioning my head with her foot and putting her toes in my mouth and told me to suck on them. She was a carbon copy of her Mistress Mother and just as Dominant with me in the beginning of a session, but they both would submit when they needed to squirt their hot pussycum and be taken hard and deep, and with Mistress the fucking was rough as well!

Once my head was where she wanted me, I finally put my arms hands on her tight, smooth, rounded Italian ass in a submissive gesture. She went crazy when I moaned in approval of her Mango Nectar or sucked my fingers while fingering her as I was being facefucked into submission, always with my head being guided to where she wanted it, and my long thick tongue was demanded to be out and used when giving her oral.

I could always tell Or she would let me know for sure when she was ready to multicum or already flowing, Holding on to her strong lower sculptured DaVinci ass and curvy long smooth legs was a challenge sometimes but I didn't want to lose a single drop of her continuous warm stream of pussycum only she could do, and "No man" could ever stimulate her into Multi-Orgasms like I could, Orally or otherwise.

Looking up at her holding onto the showerhead and watching her tits and nipples bouncing overhead and her facial expression when she unloaded a hot squirt that blasted like a broken water balloon was a sight that is still burnt into my brain. I caught only a mouthful of my Young eighteen-year-old Goddesses Mango Nectar, but in my defense, I wasn't ready for six months of pussycum built up in my kinky Female counterpart.

She climbed down slowly so not to slip and sat down in exhaustion while I got up for "My turn." I kneeled down and just wanted to lick up what I didn't catch in my mouth for a minute that was all over her inner thighs, she smiled with approval, satisfaction and gratitude, and while sitting she gave me the Blowjob of my life before we napped.

Carol and I spent the night and we fucked from 7 P.M. when we got up from the nap until 1 A.M. (six hrs.)! In every room, on every table in every chair, in every room in that suite!! My cock was Purple to match her eyes and her nipples were swollen to the size of plums and purple to match her eyes as well, when Carol left she told me she was going to end her engagement when she

went back and moving back to her mom's or to live with me in Haverhill near her work. I told her I thought we should play it a different way and still get the house he was building for her in an out-of-court settlement for cheating and breaking a contract with her, and we would use Patty to it. "He was trying to buy your love and would Never please you in the ways you need. Rich men find beautiful women to have by their side for appearance and he was using you so let's use him now, you may as well leave him and get something for your pain and suffering, lol."

Carol and I finished eating our room service meal and were thinking of a plan to either stay with her rich 28-year-old Jew short 4"-dick fiancé in the movie business or frame him with Slut/Slave Patty and cancel the engagement. Carol was told that (Co-owned and collared Slut/Slave Patty by Master T and our Mistress) was only a driver, which she would also be a slut masseuse for rich kinky Clients that our Mistress didn't need or want anymore. As my pleased, exhausted and multi/orgasmatic Italian eighteen-year-old beauty doodled on the block of Marriott Hotel stationeries I told her about the "Secret closet" I built for her earlier in the day and to meet me in there in two days to spruce up her spirits again. "You have been missing the foreplay," I tried To explain, she interrupted immediately and said, "I've been missing You!!" As she handed me my assignment all drawn out as she demanded, "Make it Happen."

The Illustration she sketched with Initials as usual was My insatiable kinky Goddess Cousin Carol (C) riding L (4" Louie

Aronstein) in her pussy with (A) Anthony 10" taking her from behind in her smooth, rounded well-lubed asshole and being whipped on her smooth solid ass cheeks. Carol's hair was wrapped around Anthony's (A) right hand with my left hand, whipping her beet-red ass, (P) Patty was sitting on Louie's face and feeding him some ass while (P) was pulling lightly on Carol's huge nipples and kissing her passionately.

"This is the only way I'll stay," she explicitly demanded. "If YOU stay with me!!"

"Patty's going to love this," I joked, "but I don't think your Mom will, lol."

Carol explained in a devious tone (just like her mom) that "if we get this on video from your secret closet you built today that I'm dying to fuck you in by the way, then It would be grounds to divorce him or cancel our engagement and Not marry him at all. I'll expect you in two days, Anthony! I'll call."

We kissed goodbye and I answered immediately smiling and said, "I'll crawl to New Hampshire for you!"

CHAPTER
10

As I was waiting for my ride to head back to the N. End to get to work and My Mistress was going to get Freddy's envelope and combine that money with hers they had been saving up for me, Both of them had been making sure I was not taking any drugs and staying away from the bad crowd I was running with but no longer had an interest for. There was No way they were going to allow me to drive a car while on drugs; Not on their watch!! So Auntie Anna along with my two Father figures said, "NO car!!"

In my Vanilla life Auntie Anna was the best "Auntie" you could ask for. She along with Freddy and Sonny (Father figures) did what No drug counselor could ever do. They laid it out plain and simple that even a fool could understand: "It's ALL up to 'You' If 'YOU' want to choose the loser's way of life and not 'US,'

the people who love you, we promise not to interfere and walk past you when we see you in the street. You Can't have both!" That advice came from Sonny. Auntie, however, whipped the fucking piss out of me while she pegged my ass and pulled my hair, slapping my swollen face in a sadistic but disappointed-with-me session when she heard of my drug using. "You lose Me and you lose Carol! It's your call, Anthony! It's All on 'YOU' now!"

To make a long Story short, "I CHOSE THEM" and my life would change forever. Things just fall in place when "YOU" make things happen and make wise decisions, I've always believed that "Life has a way of working itself out!" (Freddy's advice). They always knew what to say and when to say it and more importantly HOW to say it!

Freddy said a few words to Auntie in Italian as he handed her the envelope and the only word I understood was "Gracias," "Thank You" in English. And the only word that I needed to hear from them both, I had a tear in my ear and just whispered to myself, "Gracias to you three," as Sonny looked on.

Auntie Anna (My Goddess/Mistress) could switch to her Vanilla life in an instant and would teach me and Carol how simple it Really was. "That's one reason we call it our Darkside," she explained carefully. "Our alternate kinky sexual lifestyle is Not for everyone and we should respect that, but on the flip side they should never criticize those who enjoy a wonderful sexual experience filed with Fantasies and fetishes they don't explore or just won't!" But tomorrow I would pick up my yellow Corvette and

driving this car turned me into Master T the moment I sat behind the wheel of this Powerful 8-cylinder 454 hp machine that I took total control of. Thanks to Commonwealth Chevy in Brookline for holding it for me with a small deposit till I smartened up, Needless to say I really didn't need my personal Slut/Slave big-tit topless driver Patty anymore but I enjoyed her company and I really DID need her for the plans Carol had, and I needed to carry out that she had assigned to me in her illustration for a couples session. That was what drove her, That was her foreplay! Instructions and Illustrations that I must perform in turn was foreplay for me as well. The Thrill once we complete the "Big Picture" was an orgasm in itself once we had completed all the details and I submitted to her request...once I had submitted to her and she came like a river, I took charge of her now more forceful than before now that she was older and demanding her limits be pushed.

My Mistress decided to have our Slut/Slave Patty drive her up to NH To check on the cottage and Carol to see what she had to say out of curiosity. She would instantly see whether her mood had changed and if she was now satisfied for a few days until she needed to be serviced again like we had planned in the new "secret closet" I built for secret trips to serve her kinks, and mine! As Patty pulled up and Mistress got it the new company, Mercedes, with the tinted windows, she noticed Patty's silk see-through blouse with suspenders on squeezing her 38Ds together looking like 40DD in another outfit Master T made her wear.

"Nice to see you today, My Mistress, and how may I be of service? Does your Master T, My Stud/Slave, make you dress like that?"

"No, not always, sometimes I have to drive topless but I don't mind if you don't. All men are pigs!" She giggled to her new collared pussylicker and deepthroater.

Patty replied, "Yes, Mistress, I know, I have four brothers that all feel me up since I started growing tits."

"Really? And some people wonder Why I 'Enjoy' pegging a man's ass till he screams or whip them until they cry like my bitch, lol. They all think with their little head and not the brains God gave them."

"Very true, My Mistress! I'm so happy to serve such a wise woman and you're so gorgeous. I envy you and thank you so much for the opportunity you have given me."

"You're welcome, my Slut, now let's go get the 'Big Pig'! that has the tongue of a lizard, lol!" They both enjoyed a laugh.

"He has his license and a Corvette now, yet he still prefers you to drive him? I hope you're not planning to steal him again!"

"No, Mistress, Never, that would mean I'd lose you and you're far more my type I'd love to please daily."

"Good answer, my slut, you're very smart and together we are all going to get this new fiancé of Carol's out of her and back to L.A., where the fuck he belongs, with the phonies!"

"I'm in all the way, Mistress, I'll jump in front of a bus for any one of you three, just tell me what to do."

"Just go along with Your Master T as if he's your Vanilla boy-friend. Her fiancé don't know he's her cousin and is told 'You' are her longtime school girlfriend friend and over for double-date nights and dinner parties, soon-to-be Maid of honor wedding plans."

This guy was worth a few million and building her a million-dollar home. My beautiful daughter signed a contract with her company, Paramount, in which he was an executive to have her play Natalie Wood. Carol had a striking resemblance to Natalie Wood, only Carol was even "Prettier" with purple eyes. They would have to change to shit brown and cut her long silky jet-black hair that Natalie wore shorter.

"When we pick him up at the entrance I want him to drive and you in the middle in front with me, ok? Lol."

"Ok, Mistress, just me what you want and I'll do it, you know that."

"I know, my slut, I know. I was so blown away watching you suck his dick and watching his cock's head in your throat moving when I touched it, I almost cum right there."

"Yes, Mistress, I Remember, lol. Do you want to watch me blow him while he drives home, Mistress?"

"That will be fun and my pleasure to suck on My Master's 10" while you feel him in my throat and then I can eat you when I'm done with him, ok?"

"Excellent idea, my creative slut/whore; let's go with that! There he is! Get in the middle and pop the trunk for his suitcase. Good morning, my Pig StudSlave Master T, I see you bought our

slut some new outfits? And one is her birthday suit? You can drive home while we all chat about our little dilemma with my daughter that you have caused!"

Mistress said firmly, "ME? It's not entirely MY fault here in my defense, we can talk over lunch on Rte. 1 when we get to Saugus and for right now I'd like to watch this No-Gag cocksucker blow you while you drive, so drive slow and don't kill us all, lol."

"I want to feel that lump in her throat and her big tits while I spank her with your belt while she deepthroater your amazing cock topless, so take that blouse off and keep the suspenders on, hot-looking slut we have collared here, My Stud, she's dedicated and belongs to us all the way, so use her wisely! Gabeesh!"

"Gabeesh," I said as my cock was swallowed balls deep and my belt was in Mistress' hands, already cracking her tits from the side and fingers in Patty's both holes, working them slowly while watching her throat up close. She followed and felt the head of my cock up and down Patty's neck with her fingers as it moved in her throat with very little gagging or coughing until I just held my cock deep in her throat and came right down her throat without spilling a drop on the new heated leather seats in our company Mercedes.

"That was so fucking hot, Mistress, and that was my first blowjob while driving."

As Patty milked the last drops into her mouth, then rested her head on her Master's lap, The newly collared slut/slave was now being fisted by her Mistress and flogging her big tits and nipples

with the belt back and forth on each visible swollen nipple. Now her Mistress was twisting all four fingers in her pussy and whipping her tits right in the front seat while I was trying to drive and then asked, "Could you please get her on the floor or somewhere else before I crash, lol."

Patty was ordered to kneel on the floor while Our Mistress lifted her skirt and had Patty slip off her wet panties and put them on my lap as they giggled.

"Keep your eyes on the road," my Mistress said, but I couldn't resist glimpses of Patty being facefucked and having her hair pulled.

My Mistress had both her feet on The dashboard and holding Patty's head buried in her neatly trimmed soaking-wet pussy, and all I could hear was Our Mistress cumming so good, "Take it! Take it all! Don't get any pussycum on the new seats!" I repeated to Patty, only this time it was for My Mistress's cumjuice and not mine. Patty had just sucked the cum out of both of us and showed us how good of a collared slave cumslut she Really was. We were going to have her serve us both daily, Patty smiled and said, "I'll do that every day if you want me to, that was so fucking hot and I loved both your cum, My Master T's or My Mistress's, either one or both together, just give me the order to serve...."

Mistress just smiled at me and said, "Find somewhere to get some food so we can eat and talk about the cottage and that short-dick fiancé, please? And how are your courses going?" looking at both of us now.

Patty answered first proudly, "I'm almost done, just two more classes and I get my Massage certificate in Massage Therapy and Physical Rehabilitation will be two months more, Mistress," she quickly answered.

"Awesome, my Slut, then that's when you can start taking some of these kinksters off my hands and you can assist with a few others as does our Stud/Master T in training. Evelyn has made her appointment for this month, Stud T, and she wants you there again."

"I'll be there for sure, you two made me so fucking hard that day I could have cum two more times, omg, Mistress, I want to see you and her go at it again, and please give the order to do Whatever I want again, Will you? Please, Mistress?"

"Yes, with Evelyn and I only, for Now! I give you the order Now and for always. Do whatever you want during our sessions together, starting Saturday afternoon...."

"You are Master T in training soon to become a caring but Dominating Master. And I will be your Mentor to train you properly in BDSM, to please by Domination, and to discipline into submission and have them worship you for it, Wow!" said Patty.

"Just like I have become for both of you, You are a pleasure to serve, My Mistress. I'll be here to help Master T any way I can, please let me help, Mistress?"

"Yes! My slut, I will tell you soon what to do and how to help, Your loyalty is with both of us And will always be. I've seen that in you from the beginning."

Our new co-Owned cumslut deepthroater Patty had become very dedicated and loyal to her Mistress now and would do "Anything" to please and to serve now. Patty was really showing her appreciation for the scholarships she was earning in both her Vanilla life and in BDism and together My Mistress and I had opened the door deep into her "Darkside" and nothing would take her away from us now, Not now and not ever!

Patty and Her Master T would rock our Mistresses BDism world with pleasure through pain beyond her expectations and would soon multi/cum just like her eighteen-year-old daughter did for Her kinky male counterpart soulmate and addiction, Cousin Anthony.

Patty took her new venture of Massage Therapy and Physical Rehabilitation to the top and even added sports figures from the Boston Red Sox and Boston Bruins' injured players and nursed and nurtured them into recovery in "Special Clients" sessions!

Master T was being tested on Saturday for his "Master's" degree and would take on His Mistress, and her tantalizing and extremely sensual 45-year-old (Masochist) Executive Director of Bell Telecom in Boston could pass for 35 years old at the most, Evelyn M'Kay, a light-skinned Scandinavian Beauty from the "Special Clients" section of the secret journal. Evelyn has awesome solid 40D-cup natural tits that needed to be whipped, nibbled, bitten, slapped, and still called out for more. My Mistress was consumed by Evelyn's beauty, sensuality and passionate pussylicking that was equivalent to hers, also being stunned by

her limits of pain that My Mistress (sadistic) could deliver was causing her to submit to Master T, who would take control of these very erotic and sensual S&M sessions into "Both" their Darksides and push their limits to No end!

Patty was the "on-call driver" and would deliver Evelyn today, it was Saturday and her day-off day for her Massage or Physical Therapy, it was how the Bell Telegraph company would receive the bill from the Physical Therapy Rehabilitation Center. Master T had taken the liberty to have Evelyn picked up from "our stunning big-tit Co-Owned cumslut," Master T was feeling out Evelyn's thoughts about Patty and if Patty had caught her interest or not.

"Well, this is a pleasant surprise. Nice car! And even nicer driver, omg, I love your outfit too! You're a stunning young thing, are you new?"

"Yes, I'm in training and getting my Massage Therapy license, My Mistress and Stud/Slave T picked out the outfits for me to drive in."

"Did Mistress tell you we started off with Massage sessions and now we have taken it further than I've dreamed? She is extremely brilliant besides being beautiful, as you probably see that by now, it only took me one day!" Evelyn said in a sexy voice.

"Me too, lol," Patty anxiously said back. Patty had that "gift to gab" and could have you eating out of her hand in five minutes as did she now have Evelyn.

Evelyn had already known Master T in training would be joining the session today and quickly said to Patty, "Since I did

request Master T in training to join us again today in Our Mistress's steamy sessions, maybe I'll have him come out here later to get you too, would you like that? Will you be waiting here to drive me back?"

"Oh, Yes! And Yes again! You won't be disappointed, I promise."

Patty jumped out to open her door and very professionally offered her hand to help her out of the Sparkling-Black Mercedes with tinted windows to drive the very "Special Clients" with a very special seductive driver also with brains that matched her beauty.

"I'll be right here, and May I say you look stunning today yourself!"

"Thank you, sweetie!" Evelyn shot right back. "You wait right here till Master T comes for you to join the three of us today, let's make it a very special Saturday today...."

It was early on Saturday morning and I was flying up to NH In my new yellow Corvette to Be with My Younger Goddess in the new "Secret closet" I'd just built for her up at the cottage. I could get in from the outside, then close the camouflaged entrance and be in a closet space used for linens and towels inside the six-room ranch cottage right on Beaver Lake, Derry, NH, right behind the loose plywood wall. I squeezed into the adjacent closet in Carol's room, My kinky eighteen-year-old stunning beauty would keep her closet locked from now on so that no unwanted fiancés walked in on us fucking and sucking like he didn't even read about! I didn't have much time, however, because "Special Client" Evelyn, she had her scheduled session today with My

Mistress and wanted me there to "assist" as I did once at my Mistress' request.

It was early and Carol's four-inch short-dick fiancé was going to out in the morning anyway and Carol was dying to try out the new hidden closet right in the house where her fiancé and soon-to-be husband would be living, the thrill of him being right there in the house and her pussy being pounded by My cock that was 2½ times the size of his really got her panties wet. I figured I would please her at least once and still have plenty of my young cum left for the session later on the same day, which happened often when I was only eighteen years old, lol! I really wanted her approval and to see the look on her face from what I had built for my gorgeous kinky soulmate. When I arrived I had a plan to park outside the fence on the city property, only a minute's walk to the covered entrance. Our plan was to have her waiting for me "already in" the pitch-black dark closet in just a robe and very easy to disrobe her or just have her wrap my face under the robe while I lick every inch of her sculptured Italian flawless masterpiece of a body.

Just as We planned, I was in the closet and she was giggling with excitement and had the flashlight on for just a second or two to greet me. She kissed me so hard and grabbed my cock immediately and just dropped to her knees to give me the most slurpy and violent deep blowjob, so excited like I'd never seen her do so far. I tried to fuck her but she just wanted to keep blowing me, she said to do her asshole instead. She told me she had her period

and to cum all over her tits, then to eat some of my own cum from her amazing nipples that drove her wild, she would use the robe to wipe clean after. I loved that she had become my Anal slut, with the right amount of lube she loved to be fucked slowly in her amazing solid ass while being spanked or whipped.

Mission accomplished! Carol and I made plans before I left while licking some of my cum own off her large puffy nipple. We would have a double date next week with "My Vanilla Girlfriend" And Co-Owned Big-tit cumSlut Patty and kinky Cousin Carol, My younger Goddess and her fiancé' to "get acquainted" and see if Carol wanted to keep him and use him for his money or dump him and come up with a plan to frame him for cheating with Patty. Mistress was in with this plan, "All the way in"!!

I had time to rest and planned to shower with the ladies today and be tested for my Master's degree (Master T to be) with My BDism mentor and Goddess I'd dreamed of serving since I was old enough to jerk off to her sexy pictures I kept in my drawer. Carol was becoming the Carbon Copy of her before my eyes and now I had "Both of them" to drink up and lick clean whenever I wanted. Today I would conduct the session and "DO WHATEVER YOU WANT!" were My Mistress's words in our first session with "Special Client" Evelyn and My Mistress and had shown signs of submissive behavior while squirting and having Multiple orgasms with my pleasing methods she had become addicted to and now needed from "Master T." My Mistress had groomed young Anthony into "Her Master T" and now was reaping the rewards' intensity into

her "Darkside" with her favorite kinksters of all time, (Masochistic) Evelyn M'Kay, who had submitted to My Mistress's demands five years ago and couldn't cum without her presence or her touch!

CHAPTER

11

On my ride home and while I napped I had been thinking All Morning about My Mistress And Evelyn. I knew I was being tested today for me to really push both their limits. My Mistress was now loving the G-Spot and Clitoral stimulations and positions and how I fucked her rough, but also with the respect and passion that made her multi/cum that Alice from the N. End had taught me. My inflicting of Hard spankings with various wooden paddles and leather whips, along with my long thick tongue to match my big cock, drove Evelyn wild. The 40D Scandinavian and young-looking 45-year-old knockout, wealthy, and very beautiful CEO wanted the same treatment from Master T Even "harder." Evelyn was more (masochistic) than her slowly submitting "Bi/Sexual favorite pussylicking and ass-eating passionate lover and Dominatrix," "Our Mistress Anna," My Mistress as well as hers.

I did come up with something nice, sweet and simple that also sent the message I wanted them to agree to and accept me as Master T today. I wrote out a testimonial and would conduct a "Ceremony" like My Mistress did for her "Collared and Owned" subSlutSlaves, Only today I, Master T, would collar them Both!!

As I pulled up in my Corvette I noticed Patty and the Mercedes outside the Office and Secret Dungeon behind the office walls at the Washington Ave. location in Chelsea, MA.

Patty saw me and opened the window and smiled and prepared me by saying, "You're in for the afternoon of your lifetime, Master!"

I replied right back, "Aren't I always lately, lol. Did Evelyn like being picked up? Did she talk nice to you?"

"Ohh, yea! Evelyn is going to ask you to come out and bring ME in on her three-way session, So that means it's three on one, lol. So I think Yes, She liked me a lot and the outfits you picked out, Master, she especially loved, lol. I'll be right here when you're ready, Master!"

Waiting for my arrival was My Mistress and Evelyn having a drink and brushing each other's hair back into ponytails and giggling like fifteen-year-old schoolgirls who loved each other's company, they had become best of friends. I could tell immediately this was much more than "Special Client" and Domme sessions. They become lovers and Evelyn was married with kids and a very powerful woman at Bell Telecom in Boston. She ran All New England branches. For the past five years My Mistress and Hers

had given the pleasing she lacked from her very Vanilla husband who didn't and wouldn't take her rough or beat her ass, pull her hair, slap her face, or just spank the Fucking cum out of her while pounding both her holes from behind and calling her a filthy fuck whore! Which she NEEDED Desperately as a (masochist) and Slut she craved to be. Evelyn was in awe of her beauty the first day she arrived for her first massage. My Mistress hadn't realized just yet just how much she would enjoy the touch of another woman that matched her beauty and kinky lifestyle.

Evelyn and Auntie Anna just clicked right away while Evelyn was talking about her husband and how she would just wish sometimes he would give her a strong massage like My Mistress could, she also jokingly said, "But I really wish he would just fuck my brains out and spank my hard ass, lol," as they both enjoyed a laugh. Auntie Anna said, "I know how you feel, men are so fucking clueless as to what we really need so they buy us jewelry and flowers, we need to tell them or we will never get a good spanking," both laughing out loud now. "My husband is not that way at all, he's a minister and I'd hate to find a nice young playmate to fuck but I'm afraid I need to real soon," Evelyn replied back seriously. Auntie Anna said right back, "I'll see what I can do for you, I have friends that would love you! You're beautiful!" Evelyn lifted her head in envy and could only say, "Not nearly as beautiful as you, omg! I wish I looked like you!"

With the immediate attention and the magnetic attraction by Both these gorgeous women, their faces were buried in each

other's pussies in a matter of that one-hr. warm oil massage session that sent them both into a river of pussycum. Evelyn and Auntie Anna's sessions would escalate into more kinkier sessions as they explored each other's needs and desires on that massage table each week and billed to Bell Telecom in Boston, where she was the Executive Director and very wealthy with a very kinky side.

Today was just around five years they had experienced and explored on each other, they giggled, fondled and kissed. It was their foreplay for today and Evelyn now mentioning how much she appreciated her and without her she'd be home listening to prepared sermons by her boring Vanilla sex minister husband but couldn't leave just yet because of three kids. "I LOVE your new two Additions, Anna!" Evelyn pointed at Stud/Slave and soon-to-be Master T, "and the hot big-tits young driver, Can she join us??" Evelyn asked curiously.

"Sure, but ask Master T if it's ok also, He will be in charge after I set us all up to begin the session and it's your day anyway! Lol." My Mistress giggled, then told Me, "Go get our slut and bring her in here and change into something nice, YOU help her pick something off the wall she'll look hot in," Mistress added.

Patty seen me open the door to get her to serve at today's session and immediately smiled with excitement. Patty hurried to lock the car and run to me, knowing her pussy and mouth would be used by two Goddesses' PussyPeeCum And nipples to die for, not to mention a 10" cock she was now becoming addicted to

had respect and admiration for his Gorgeous Auntie Anna and her cloned artist daughter. She groomed him well and stressed early on that No woman liked to be treated like a whore or a slut "UNLESS SHE wants him to! Remember that!" she would say, "There's a BIG difference!"

Today Master T's Mistress and Goddess Auntie Anna WANTED him to treat her like the whore she craved to be that day, she said those words to him, looking at the bulge in his pants, "Even a pure slut likes roses sent to her for her birthday," she added, she would also fantasize about his unique long thick tongue while young Anthony would tease Carol by sticking the point of his wet hard tongue UP his nostrils and pretend to eat his snot. He'd gross her out, not realizing he was getting his kinky Auntie wet in her pussy and causing her nipples to tingle, although she knew she had to wait till he turned sixteen to be legal, she would wait patiently to collect her reward, His future Mistress admired his cocky demeanor and quick-witted mind, it was nothing she couldn't tame As he melted when she walked by him in a short skirt and bent over into the cabinet, catching his wandering eyes at only fourteen years old.

Master T now helping his newly "collared And Owned" Goddess up from her knees, he put his hand up her skirt, there were No wet panties to be found. Evelyn had removed them already while applying the moisturizer to Her sculptured long legs, pussy and ass, all Master T would get was a handful of pussycum that needed some cleaning up and so he did what any good Master

would do, HE CLEANED HER up and drank her down as he sat her on the edge of her desk, it was only proper that his newly collared Mistress and now whore would take a mouthful of cock while getting her face pumped up for a minute before leading the way to the others waiting for their turn to be passed around the room. Evelyn and Patty would be violated in all their holes by Master T's 10" hard cock and Vibrating massage toys from Mistress's toybox for hours, No time limits for "Special Client" sessions, especially Evelyn M'Kay, she was one of us now!

I took a leather whip from the wall as Evelyn and Mistress sat on the Massage table and turned towards the wheel of torture a few feet behind to watch me whip Patty's big tits, and dripping-wet pussy, they were hugging and Fondling each other's pussies and pinching and twisting each other's nipples while they kissed and played watching the live sex show I was performing for them both. Patty was loving this, she did exactly what I had told her to do, I was pretending to be scolding her and whipping her across her nipples and large breasts hard and loud enough to excite any Sadistic or Masochist slut or Dom. She began to cry and was tied up and was trying to break free but couldn't, I would whip her pussy and she would scream and cry louder. making Evelyn moan in envy wanting some of that abuse. My Mistress with Sadistic qualities also envious of giving the beating or whipping wanted to take the whip and inflict some pain as well, the more I whipped and beat Patty into tears the more Evelyn was cumming right on the table to My Mistress's mouth and flicking of the tongue buried

in Evelyn's pussy as they watched. I now wanted to tie Evelyn on the wheel since she was begging so badly for a whipping. She desperately wanted and needed to be humiliated and beaten as some Masochist sluts did crave.

I paused to approach Patty to respect her limits and she whispered that she was fine and wanted more, Patty was actually getting off on watching Evelyn coming to Mistress's double-ended dildo as she was fucking her from behind with one end and the other end in her Mistress's pussy and both were humping watching Master T discipline Patty's pussy now, while moving the wheel to another position. Patty was Upside down now and Master T was whipping her pussy that was at eye level now.

"Omg," said Evelyn desperately, "Mistress, please, can I please get some of that from your Stud/Slave T? Patty's Master T, please? Or maybe you can whip me like that tied to the wheel?"

"Ok, you may have both if you let Master T in training co-own you like Patty is to Master T and I, that would make you and Patty BDSM sisters! Will you accept his collar?" said Mistress curiously.

"Oh, yes, Mistress! I do want that so bad to be co-Owned and beat like her like he's doing, I need my tits whipped just like that. Patty has tits and nipples just like me when I was her age and still desire to be slapped, bitted, whipped and violated, they are twitching right now and oozing out to be beat or bitten or nibbled, can you arrange this For me and I'll be your slave every day along with Master T and Patty too? I knew this session would be special today."

"Yes, my slut Evelyn, I will take cumslut Patty down and have Master T collar you now to tie you up to be beaten and gagged till you squirt in front of us all, ok?" said the smiling Mistress, looking at her Master T.

Master T nodded with approval and waited for Evelyn to be delivered with a coownership collar for Painslut big-tits Evelyn, Master T untied smiling Patty as she whispered, "Thank you, Master T, I'll keep our Mistress busy now while you beat my BDSM sister into submission and watch her cum in a river of PussyPeeCum enough to lick up for all three of us."

My Mistress now holding Evelyn's arms behind her back and holding a new collar from the wall told Evelyn to kneel and repeat after Master T, "I Do accept your collar, I will obey and Never stray, I am begging to Master T, bound me, beat me, violate me. I am now co-owned and property of Master T." Mistress now walked Evelyn over to the wheel with cum visibly streaming down Evelyn's legs with anticipation to be whipped into ecstasy as a Masochist would cum in buckets while being tortured, it was what they enjoyed and what they desired to stimulate themselves into multi/orgasms and Mistress had found her weakness now. We would have fun with Evelyn and send Patty for her after work quite often after she'd Been collared and co-Owned and BDism sisters with Patty, whom she now admired and insisted on her presence as with all of us for wheel of torture sessions, which she was addicted to now thanks to Patty and Master T.

Evelyn, very ambitious, awaited the first lashing from the long leather strands across her firm large breasts and visibly pulsating red nipples. Her Mistress Anna was just slapping and biting them on the massage table while watching Patty being whipped by Master T and was begging Master T as he teased and toyed with her wet pussy with four fingers deep in her open-wide pussy streaming with hot wet cum, "Fuck me, please, and beat me, Master T, I'm cumming and I can't stop," Evelyn said, whimpering and almost in tears. WHACK!! WHACK!! Twice very hard across each nipple and a sigh of relief from Evelyn, "Ahh! Omg, again, please! I need this, Master T, nobody has ever slapped or beaten me the way I've needed except for our Mistress and now this, I loved watching this and know I needed this with the whipping all tied up, Do more and harder, I'm begging you, Master T."

Master T now took another whip from the wall and called Mistress up to the wheel of torture and demanding she whip co-Owned painslut from the right side and Master T from the left side with two whips simultaneously, beating her on each tit/nipple as Patty turned the wheel, as Evelyn was being turned and beaten all over her body she began to scream in ecstasy and squirting and pissing all over herself and all three of us. Master T gave his whip to Patty for some fun while he stopped the wheel with her head at the bottom and her pussy at the top, being fist fucked by Mistress, and her ass was used up with the double-ended dildo by Patty, Evelyn's head was at the bottom and Master T pulled Evelyn by her hair and opened her mouth to throat fuck her while

slapping her beet-red face into orgasm after orgasm, Master T took his cock from her mouth and slapped it over her finger-printed face, she fucking loved it and thanked everybody more than twice.

It was now time for Mistress to be initiated and used by All now and take Her Master T deep in all three holes while the others watched and got instructions from their "True Dominant and Master T," they were loyal, dedicated and now obedient to "or else"!!! Master T's Mistress and Goddess was now tied to the wheel backwards while he blindfolded Evelyn and Patty so they didn't see What Master T was about to do to their Dominant Mistress. He didn't want them to Ever disrespect his Goddess and still Mistress while he pounded her pussy into multiple orgasms. From behind Master T sodomized her asshole wide open with his thick hard 10", while pulling her hair and calling her his whore that she craved to be, and wide enough for four fingers to scoop out some cum to show her while he licked his fingers for her to show his appreciation for her, she cried in a happy puddle of both their hot, salty and sticky cumjuice for cumslut Patty to happily lap up. The admired Goddess again laid there in total submission just as she had from the last pussy pounding from a true Master and couldn't move a muscle from satisfaction and gratification, Master T now had his Goddess eating from his hand now, It was indeed a very special afternoon for "Everyone" now, family in their new "four-way playday," as Evelyn liked to call it when she scheduled her next "family session...."

CHAPTER
12

Mistress called Patty and Master T in to congratulate them on a job well done. The Mercedes and the Corvette pulled up together and parked in the rear of the Real Estate office where Mistress was on the phone with Evelyn, reminiscing about the previous afternoon that lasted until the evening, as Master T leaned against the desk his Goddess/Mistress pointed to her expensive alligator high-heels to be taken off and foot massaged while she giggled. Co-owned Patty began to massage her Mistress' neck lightly, waiting for her mentor to instruct her also. The Goddess looking all happy and pleased this lovely morning reached behind for Patty's hand, massaging her neck, and brought it down and into her halter top to have her tits played with, while still talking and giggling like a schoolgirl with overexcited Co-Owned painslut Evelyn. Master T took the moisturizer and

started to apply the silky cream to her long beautiful toned legs like Evelyn did yesterday while he looked on. Mistress was now leaning back and being pampered by her two favorite dedicated and collared pleasers in a matter of minutes, she was ready to cum all over again. Starting to get hard now and couldn't get over how smooth this moisturizer was making her legs feel, Master T put it All over her and signaled for her to hang up the phone and to bend over the desk, and Patty to do the same. Both of them hurried to obey in anticipation knowing what was to cum next!

As The Dom and Now "Alpha Male" Master T placed both of his sluts side by side, they kissed and began to submit onto the desk and held flat down, one hand on each of their curvy lower backs and ordered to "stay" and "Open," only two words were spoken before their Lord and Master would enter both of their streaming cum-soaked pussies and asses one at a time, back and forth he went slapping, spanking and pushing them back down if they moved. Patty had came first and screamed as she began to suck mistress's nipples from the side, Grabbing Mistress by the hair now with two hands and fucking her hard and fast from behind she screamed and only could say! "Yes, Master! Omg, Yes: you're a fucking animal! Please Fuck ME like an Animal! Don't ever stop! I'm cumming like a fucking teenager and can't stop." Mistress looked at Patty and smiled, "That Man is ours!! Don't let Anybody near him and that's an order from your Mistress, lol, no wonder why Carol can't cum for that 4" cock you two are going to convince to leave my Carol."

"Now I was coming up with a plan here before I got pleasingly interrupted, and he made me come once again," Mistress said jokingly.

"Noooo," Master T shot right back, "you are so fucking beautiful, I still get hard just smelling your hair or looking at you, I'm addicted to you and so is Patty over here, oh, Yes!" Patty agreed, and after yesterday, I'm obsessed and possessed, lol.

"So, I just got off the phone earlier this morning with an agent that tells me a four-family brick house in East Boston is in Foreclosure and it's selling for only 15K and I want to buy it and rent all the units, I want Patty in one of the units and get her away from her fucking asshole brothers that rape her, Understand! I don't want Anyone touching her except for you or I," Mistress said firmly! "We will fix the building up a little here and there and get the income from it."

"Thank you, My Mistress!" Patty said, wiping a tear from her cheek.

"Don't worry, Mistress, I don't think they will be touching her ever again, Her older brother heard I'm her boyfriend and that I'm dangerous, lol. This Vanilla thing we are about to play out with Carol and get this guy out of here should be interesting, Carol should be back here close to us where she belongs," Master assured his still beloved Mistress he couldn't resist pleasing.

"I'll need the both of you to keep the building in decent shape in your spare time, If you have any now that we are doing great and Patty will be getting her massage and Physical Therapy license and

Master T, YOU should also study for the Real Estate part of it, buildings are selling fast and we can all make a fortune together."

"So Patty, you call Carol and make a dinner date," Mistress told Patty. "Tell Carol you really want her fiancé to meet your new boyfriend, OK? Now I really need to soak in the Hot tub for a while, lol."

"OK, My Mistress, I'll make the call and let you know when the date is. Now please, let me bathe you, My Goddess, for letting me in your life, it doesn't matter how I got to serve you, it only matters I'm here now to please both of you, one by one, or together!!"

Patty took her Mistress's hand to help her up to bathe the Goddess as Master T sat in exhaustion from fucking the pussy-cum from his two appreciative kinky beauties. But before Patty could take another step she noticed her Master's cock had a combination of his cum and her Mistress's pussycum and took his entire manhood down her throat for Mistress to see and to clean him off before he left to do errands. "Omg!" Mistress replied, "you have to show me how you do that to Master T, lol," they all laughed.

"Let me draw your bath now, Mistress, and wash your back before I go," Patty insisted.

"Ok," Mistress agreed, "but I just need to soak a while and relax, Master T fucked me so good I think I came ten times yesterday and twice just now. Omg! He's an amazing fuck."

"Yes, Master T is the best fuck I've ever had, that's for sure," Patty said right back. "He is loving that you made him your

Master T as well. He's even more dominating and confident than ever and still caring about hurting you at the same time, that's amazing control he has also not to cum so fast and can last for hours," Patty added.

As Mistress entered the bath and Patty washed her flawless toned shoulders and backside she said, "It's very important that you make your man feel he is in charge, Even if you know you hold the control button, lol, understand?" Mistress replied.

"Oh, I see! Lol, you're a genius, Mistress," Patty giggled, "and I can't begin to thank you enough again, Mistress. Get in the bath with me So I can wash your back too!"

Mistress ordered, "You wash my back and I'll wash yours, Ok? That's a famous saying for a reason, I know how loyal and appreciative you are and Master T is also, so I will go all out for people that are dedicated and loyal to me, the BDism lifestyle is one thing, but everyday Vanilla life is a much longer day and we have watch each other's back, as we wash each other's Back behind closed doors, Gabeesh?" Mistress explained as she washed Patty's back, reaching around to her large firm breasts as well with Patty now melting in her strong toned caressing arms. Mistress kissed her relaxed neck as Patty's head leaned back onto Mistress's shoulders, Patty's clit was being massaged so firmly and methodically with the fondling of her big firm tits from a professional masseuse were overwhelming. Patty uncontrollably squirted her pussycum into the bathwater for the end of her mentor/Mistress's sermon.

"Let's dry off now, my beautiful little cumslut, we need to plan your Vanilla date night with a not-so-Vanilla boyfriend, lol."

Patty kissed her so passionately, and jumped up to escort her Goddess out of the warm oiled bath and cover her with her robe.

"Carol is calling for you, Anthony," Mom told Anthony. "I asked her if everything was OK and she just said to come up for the Art showing, He'll understand!"

"Ok, I'll call her."

"Thanks, Mom, I haven't seen you in days since you bought that sports car."

"I hope you're eating OK," Mom said.

"Oh, yea! I'm eating out a lot lately!" Master T said, smiling.

His mom didn't have a clue to as WHAT he'd been eating, or WHOM he had been eating almost daily and sometimes more than once in a day!! He'd been drowning in her sister's pussycum or PussyPeeCum mixtures, his favorite, or Evelyn's Or Patty's Or Carol's (Multiple orgasms) that streamed for minutes at a time while he choked down mouthfuls that she could produce in his mouth in a given moment.

Master T had not had Carol's "Mango Nectar" pussycum in a while and he needed it bad!!! Carol's Mango-tasting pussycum addiction was making him shake like a junkie and he "Needed" her NOW!! Patty was supposed to call her like Mistress said but I needed to calm her down first, she was calling me and that meant she was ready and horny and couldn't wait, but what if the little-dick fiancé answered, what would jealousy do to him? This

was his Soulmate!! His kinky female counterpart!! The clone of the Goddess he now owned! OR did Master T want to own them both?? Let's play it out!!

Patty came to Master T's house to pick him up and discuss what Patty just arranged on the phone with Carol so Anthony was off the hook, for now! Master T now told Patty to call her, Now! He demanded to talk to Carol, and so he did! He told her that when he called at 3:00 exactly it would be him and for a only "Her" to answer, he otherwise would call her work or for her to call him at exactly 5 P.M. and only He would answer at Mom's house (Master T was wishing cell phones were invented by now, lol).

Patty would have a new apartment soon and the calls would be easier if Patty answered and handed the phone over to Master T, Or would they?? Let's play that out too!

Mistress called Patty to pick up their Stud, she wanted them Both to get over to Evan's office in Chelsea, MA, Mistress/Auntie Anna's Family and Business lawyer, Mistress had purchased the four-unit brick building on Sumner St. at Maverick Sq. in East Boston. The Foreclosure went down in the morning and she made the final bid of $21,500. Which was still a steal even for 1973, the building was worth two million in today's 2020 Real Estate Market. Its (Waterfront) views alone were worth a million in itself overlooking the Boston Harbor and in direct view of the Custom house and N. End waterfront. The building needed some minor repointing and the inside needed cosmetic work, the electrical and Plumbing ALL needed to be replaced for about

another $5,000. In those days the top unit (penthouse) Unit would be split up into three units (Yes, it was long enough to do) and each unit would be small, But! The entire top floor would be Mistress's office/Patty's living and office space, and Master T's office and living space...and Mistress had put them to work and teaching them Both (Work Ethic) and that Nobody just handed you something (for nothing) work, work, and more work, she stressed to all three students now in her apprenticeship, Master T, Patty, and Maybe Her Carol, she was hoping.

The two insatiable young kinksters that could please any sex maniac arrived and were so happy with news, Patty was skipping like a six-year-old to the door holding Master's hand. "This is unbelievable, I love you, Mistress!" Patty yelled out to her mentor. "We will make that place look fantastic while we work and promote (Massage Therapy and Sports Injury Rehabilitation Center)." "Sir" = Sports Injury Rehabilitation, along with Patty would bring in clients from the Boston Bruins and Boston Red Sox contracts, Master T would make sure "Nobody" stood in their way. He protected them like A Lion watching over his cubs, and His Mistress and Goddess knew he would, more importantly, He could! "Sir" or "Master" are the two formal ways to greet your Dom/Dominant in the BDism world and anyone in the alternate lifestyle Knows this, the rest would just fall into place for the three kinksters, now exploring every aspect of the lifestyle on each other and anyone of interest that could afford their "expensive services"! Corporate, Enterprises, Trusts, Sports Celebrities, All

Client services would be billed to their Insurance company or be write-offs anyway, so price was no issue, Cash (tipping) was always OK too, lol.

Mistress sat and held a large drawing of her ideas of the top Penthouse Unit with a roof garden that Patty would be watering, lol. Mistress joked as she glanced over to Master T, Patty laughed and pointed at herself, then to Mistress, and the finger went back and forth as in a Question; Mistress Nodded, and whispered, "Oh, yea!" And continued with her presentation, Mistress continued talking about leasing the bottom units (a total of six smaller condo-sized units), OR to be used as a rehab facility site once they had enough clients, either way the building's income would pay for itself in just five years, she said, and would be paid off, Mistress added.

I don't know to this day if Auntie Anna was more beautiful than intelligent, OR more intelligent than she was beautiful, it was as fascinating to me to listen to her talk or to watch her walk by me with her hourglass figure and long perfect toned legs. I would inhale to smell her Shalimar perfume she wore that made my cock hard instantly. I was Always in awe of her, I still have images of My Goddess as kid burnt into my brain, absolutely one of a kind, until she reproduced her clone daughter, Carol.

"Patty, you go home and get some clothes, bring them to your new place, then we are going shopping for some new clothes for you and I today to celebrate, then we go and sign papers for the company. Master T, I want you to go to Evan's

and sign your paperwork and give him this envelope for me, we will meet up for dinner at Rita's in Chelsea for our Reservation."

The Goddess had a kinky scheme and wanted Patty to hear it without Master T knowing, So Mistress finally got close enough to whisper in her ear at the new Building in East Boston, checking out the Penthouse plans and where Patty and Master T would reside, the office and Desk would be facing the waterfront for Mistress, of course, Mistress whispered to Patty, "I want you to wear a dress or skirt to Rita's restaurant with NO panties, Rita's has long tablecloths and I'm going to have Master T eat our Pussies at dinner for his dessert, lol, but don't say anything, Ok? I'm going to drop my fork, then ask him to go under the table and pick it up and then tell him to eat both our pussies under the table and nobody will see anything, so don't make any orgasm noises. We will top off the night's celebration with some pee for him back at my office in the jacuzzi, I know it was him that was asking for you and Carol to pee on him when I walked in on you," Mistress admitted.

Patty replied, "Oh, Mistress! That's fine, No worries, you have done more than enough for me and so has Master T."

"I know, Patty, I just want to have some fun with Master T to celebrate. He loves Pussycum and has a strong pee Fetish so we will oblige our Master T tonight and give it to him good, OK?" Mistress stressed.

"Lol, Absolutely, Mistress, Let's drown him in what he loves so much, I'm totally down for that tonight," Patty giggled.

Mistress made sure Master T sat in the middle at dinner as they talked about the new building, with just a few bites left Mistress dropped her fork on the floor and pointed to the floor and asked Master T, "Would you get under the table, please, and search for my fork, Master?" Mistress said, smiling, when Master T lowered himself to the floor Mistress lifted her skirt and said, "While you're down there! Give Me and Patty a lick with that Lizard tongue, I made sure Rita's had the long tablecloths tonight so Nobody can see you," Mistress whispered to him as she lifted Patty's skirt up and to her hips and fondled her clit while Master T lapped up Pussy #1.

"Are you ready, Master T, for a shower now? Your face is all sticky and your shirt is soaking wet, lol," Mistress giggled to Patty.

"Oh, Yes! I'm ready, are both of you going to make it rain?"

"Oh, yea!" Patty shouted. "My Mistress gave me orders, lol, she knows about YOU were asking for the Golden Shower when Our Mistress walked in on me ready to pee on you after Carol gave you a mouthful. We just want to please you tonight for being a great Master and the Pussylicking was nice tonight too."

As they all undressed at the walk-In shower for four with seats built onto the tiled walls, Patty walked him in and sat him down on the floor between two of the seats, and then Patty sat on his right side and held his head up with his mouth open. Mistress stood in her heels towering over him and squatted over his opened mouth held by Patty. "Are you ready, Stud-Master? Say Yes, Mistress!!"

"Yes, Mistress! Please give it to me, My Goddess and Mistress," Master T said, begging for her piss.

Mistress squirted a stream right into the open mouth of Master T, so heavy and so long, he was choking as she was ordering him to "Swallow, Swallow that piss!" As Mistress closed his mouth full of pee and now ordered Patty, "You now! Do it! Do it! Give him what he needs," As Mistress held his arms back with one hand, she pulled his hair and ordered him, "Open! Open wide and take her piss!"

Patty squatted directly over his mouth and shot her hot piss right into his open mouth and they enjoyed hearing the mouth fill up with piss so close up, it was going directly down his throat and gagging. Master T was actually Drowning in both their piss and was loving it. Mistress was playing with her pussy watching this and started squirting pussycum for the second time tonight, while Patty was still pissing, Mistress was now cum squirting on the other side of her on his face. He had both Piss and Pussycum in one mouthful as Patty closed his mouth shut and told him to swallow.

"Wow!" Patty said, "that was so fucking hot, My Mistress, We owe him a good blowjob."

"He gets plenty already from you, lol, but we will blow him together like he did us together tonight, lol, now shower for real and go home, I'm tired, see you two tomorrow and go over your plans to go see Carol."

Patty asked Carol if they could up this Thursday night for a dinner date at the house or just go out to a restaurant, then go

back to the house to stay in the spare room with Master T, Patty was also trying to feel Carol out as to why she was still with this guy if he didn't please her. Carol replied to her question by saying that she was in a sighted contract with him, she accepted his proposal, which Carol now realized was a big mistake. "I'm trying to cum with this inexperienced 4" small-cock man, but just can't," Carol explained. "I need my kinky cousin, lol, he's the only one that knows what I need."

Patty said to Carol, "How far do you want to go with this? Do you want to marry him and then get out of it and try for an annulment if I can get him to cheat on you?"

Carol replied, "That May be a good idea! He's worth millions, I'm told, and he's building us a million-dollar home to compensate for his little dick, lol," Carol giggled.

"Yea, but be careful, He May have powerful friends with that kind of money! We are coming up as Girlfriend and boyfriend, are YOU OK with that? We will play it out and fool him but We don't want to hurt your feelings."

"I'm a woman and I know You love him! I know he loves you and I'm OK with that! We are in a BDISM relationship as Master and slut/slave and our Mistress is your Mom and you know that, I just don't want to Ever lose your friendship over this or I have to tell your mom I'm out!! OK?" Patty explained.

"Oh, No, Patty, I do understand All of that and this will be fun to play out. We can have our fun playing with pussy, then with My Anthony, Your Master T, and finish our golden shower

scenario that he loves, let's get my Fiancé' Louie involved in a four-way swap and this can be an ongoing thing. If love does get in the way and spoil the fun, then I'll choose love!" Carol replied.

Patty shot right back, "That's when people get hurt, when it goes too far, Carol, but I'll do this for you and Anthony, My Master T, and for me to get at you, lol, we're going to go over the plan and how we met and all that stuff and then I'll try and seduce your fiancé in the kitchen alone, I'll flash my tits at him and see what his reaction is and then I'll know if we can play him or not, you OK with that?" Patty asked.

"Absolutely," Carol said, "I'll be blowing my man in the closet While you're in the kitchen, see if he'll feel you up and we can get the ball rolling from there and do the swap. I can't wait," Carol giggled. "Master T has a sketch I gave him, I want to do with the four of us, ask him to show it to you," Carol asked of Patty.

Patty told Carol, "Your mom is buying a four-unit building in East Boston and setting me up in a unit, why don't you just come home and take a unit too, I think Master T will take a unit or take a room in my unit so we can work on the building and live here at the same time, being his driver and driving 'special clients' like Evelyn. She was so fucking hot, Carol!! You should have seen her taking a beating and cumming and peeing all over the place. I'll keep you in the loop when I meet with them and watch Master T and Mistress use them up just how they like it, we will talk and play Thursday night. This is going to be one great fucking ride, Carol, get ready!" Patty told her.

"I'm ready as I always am, take care of him for me until Thursday, Patty," Carol said.

"I promise I will, Carol! I will deliver Our Master Thursday night and finish his fantasy in the shower, when we go in before bedtime, You pop in while we are in there waiting for you, drink a lot of water, he loves that, lol," Patty replied, smiling!

"Ha-ha, I love the way you think, Patty," Carol replied, laughing.

After a very memorable evening with his two submissives, Master T had been the submissive the night before in a Big way! His Mistress and Goddess showed him what Domination actually meant! Just one of the "Ds" He was learning to Master, He was manipulated into eating "two" pussies during dinner, then receiving his favorite Fetish, a forced (Golden Shower) by not one but TWO women at the same time, pissing all over his head, face and in his mouth while being scolded, slapped by his Goddess with his mouth held open and closed to swallow the warm yellow salty rain, Mistress Anna was the most highly recommended (Golden Shower Dominatrix) in All of New England at the time, let me remind you, and Master T clearly knew why now!

Patty was being groomed now, very loyal and dedicated, she'd already been collared by both Master T and her Mentor/Mistress, She was in awe last night after her schooling on how to properly give a "Golden Shower" to her "Special Clients" in the Journal she was about to study, Mistress had six men and women who desperately craved this Pee fetish or squirting Pussycum, Pee fetishes and fantasies (Water Sports)

are more common in BDism kinkster world than one may think, Just ask a Dominatrix, lol.

Mistress started off just as Patty was starting, a beautiful young lady very clean, very intelligent and manipulating with men (and women), Patty had a talent that not too many women had also, she could deepthroat a large cock balls deep and Mistress loved watching her work on Master T's 10". Mistress massaged her throat and watched the thick cock's head move when she blew him in front of her and kinkster Evelyn, Mistress knew Patty was an asset to her new venture "Sir" and would take her deep into the "Darkside" and how to be very successful on the Vanilla side as well. "Patty is here to stay, and will never stray."

It was Thursday and Patty arrived at the office for her plan and any other instructions that her mentor may have for her outside of Master T knowing, just like the Rita plan, lol.

Women are smarter, so you better be a smart man if you play with any of these three main lady characters, Mistress Anna being #1, Patty or Carol, Mistress's carbon copy.

Master T arrived a few minutes later and was definitely excited about this Vanilla double-date night, Patty was loving this even more, although she was playing Master T's "Girlfriend" AND was going to be in the presence with the opportunity to lick up this younger beautiful Goddess to the older yet wiser One, how's that for manipulation!

The plan was going down to arrive, look around and have a drink, go out to eat and come back for a nightcap because the

only two old enough to drink at a bar were Louie, 28, and Patty, now just 21, Carol and Master T both now twenty respectably, and went to bed or (hopefully played out a swap), which WAS the ultimate Goal to accomplish. Master T and Patty would take a room (his room) that he decorated and help remodel this whole cottage, when Patty had the opportunity she was to flash her tits or sexually Provoke Louie Aronstein, a young 28-year-old wealthy good-looking movie scout, only Problem with him was that he had a small 4" dick and Couldn't stand eating pussy, lol. "Poor Carol," as Mistress described him to Patty, "Get that short dick out of here and back to L.A., where movie people belong," she ordered Patty.

"I'll work on him, Mistress, please don't worry so much," Patty said consolingly.

Also part of the plan was to arrive early before Louie got there, as they would in the future also so Master T could give Carol what she'd been missing and give his cumslut deepthroater Patty a taste of her and Carol enjoyed pussy just as much now, like mother like daughter, they say, lol.

Patty and Master were still talking about the great evening with their Mistress and especially the end of the night, when they Both got Schooled on "Golden Shower" performance by the best and a Master T was smiling ear to ear, "Oh, yea!" remembering, "I was drowning in your piss and her pussycum at the very end was a nice touch I wasn't expecting, omg, so fucking hot, Both of you. Thank You, My slut!" Master T implied.

"You're welcome, Anytime, Master T, I belong to you now, in My Vanilla life as well, I can do what our Mistress did at the end for you too when she masturbated and squirted on you while I peed in your mouth if you want," Patty suggested.

"Really? Can you do it this weekend? If we get the chance with Carol?" Master T asked curiously!

"Yes, Sir, My Master T, YOU CAN COUNT ON IT," Patty said in confidence!

Just as they all had planned, Patty and Master T arrived in the Mercedes and Patty was dressed in her driving attire for Master T to enjoy on long rides, in today's event, however, Patty wanted to be ready for anything. It was a warm day and she was also driving so she wore a loose skirt with No Panties, and a revealing halter top to really show Carol these solid 21-year-old 38DD cup breasts on a beautiful Petite Hourglass Frame.

Carol rushed out to great them and kissed Master T very passionately on the lips and grinded her pussy against his hip while grabbing his ass, Patty looked on curiously and then she got the same greeting, with her appreciation and approval, of course.

Carol took Anthony, her artist and kinky male counterpart cousin by the hand and told Patty to follow down the trail by the rear of the cottage that Master T hadn't seen yet on their property, there was a broken-down shack right on the stream that shot off Beaver Lake, It was a gorgeous setting and very secluded and Carol wanted to fix it up, she told her cousin and My Mom, "Don't even know it's ours yet, our neighbor's

property ends on the other end of the stream and this side is ours," Carol pointed.

"Let's go inside," Carol said, smiling and holding both their hands. Carol led them past a small prepared table for three, to the rear Barn door with a large blanket with a picnic basket "outside" surrounded by brush a few yards from nature's well-placed stream.

"Omg, I've been waiting for you for days to bring you here, and to show you this and finish what we started in the shower, lol," Carol said, giggling.

"I don't know," Patty shot back, "Mistress almost beat me to death once, lol, the order would HAVE TO come My Co-Owner and then I would have to OBEY his command, The Male Dom overrides a 'FemmeDomme.'"

Carol explained, "That's Right! I am the Alpha Male in the room, or by the Lake, and I demand that you take that top off and let Carol suck those Melons while I start taking her top off for those nipples we've missed so badly, Ok, Master T, I'm your property as well and this is our secret, today, and always when it's us three, I don't want Mistress angry with us ever again, Gabeesh, lol," they all giggled!

Master T now gave the order for both of them to get on their knees and kiss facing each other and rub tits together while he sucked all four nipples, suffocating in ecstasy. Master T's cock was so hard he couldn't take it anymore and went behind Carol. He opened her legs wide from the rear, to the inviting soaked pulsating starved pussy to take his 10" deep for a pounding on the

blanket she never had forgotten. Patty was now feeding her nipples like a baby while Carol sucked her DDs from the front with her head being guided under Patty's control and totally under submission to the Domme's apprentice, Master T positioned her to stimulate her G-Spot for the orgasms she lived for and was missing in her life, only his technique, Dominant approach with the caring touch along with Master's long 10" cock could reach her G, causing explosive ongoing Multiple Orgasms that lasted for minutes at time, producing streams of pussycum and pee together, leaving her totally drained and sexually satisfied, but for only at least a day or two, then she desperately needed the Master all over again. Carol simply couldn't cum for anybody else, unless it was pussylicking and that took a long time that Patty had the patience for and could satisfy any insatiable Male or Female, she WAS that good, Master knew from the last time she had an urge for her ass to be fucked also and now opened her ass and tongued her to lube her hole and slid it halfway in as she screamed and Patty held her down, "Take it All!" Master T and Patty were yelling in her ears. Patty put her tits in her mouth to silence her and Master T buried all 10" in her asshole and pounded her with Patty holding her tightly now.

Taking it out slowly, Master T put it back in her now gushing pussy to finish her off in a series of hard pounding all the way in and out again right aside of her G-Spot and Carol just squirted everywhere for at least two whole minutes while Master T and Patty buried their faces in her pussy to reap the hot MangoNectar

pussycum rewards of this young beauty that could multi/cum like a breached River, but Only for Master T!!

Master T was holding back for his now Vanilla Girlfriend, His BDism Property and loyal pleaser to finish and then "get his fantasy" that Patty promised she would do for him. Master T laid Patty down with her legs up and knees at her neck and entered her soaked pussy so deep she moaned like bear, this WAS another way to get to the G and he got her good in this position that she liked with her Master because he tit Fucked her to sometimes finish that way, OR in her ass which was convenient in the missionary position. Master T instructed Carol to sit on her face and feed her that used-up still-streaming pussy and give her that cum, "Don't waste any of that Mango," he joked.

Patty was Now in heaven being pounded by HER Master T again and again five-six times a week and now needed him as much (maybe more) than the other two insatiable women, now submissive and under his complete control, in a second's notice she screamed, "I'm coming, Master!!! I'm coming like I've never cum before, Master T!" Patty too let out a bucket of PussPeeCum mix that Master rushed down to lap up along with Carol, Patty was all flushed and red and said, "Master T, that was amazing!"

Patty jumped up and pushed him down to beat Carol to the dead to devour his massive 10" throbbing cock deep in her throat and took his cumm right in her throat while nodding and not letting it out of her throat until he was drained of every drop of cum while Carol sucked on balls, Patty let his still hard out of her

mouth and French Kissed Carol to give her some of her Master's cum and Carol was very appreciative and kissed her softly and whispered in her ear, "Patty, let's finish his shower in the Lake."

After the two young kinky beauty queens now eating out of Master T's hands to see who had the Master's #1 rating, Carol and Patty each took a hand and walked him into the lake, Carol didn't know what Mistress had just taught Patty about the Masturbating cum squirting that was an added Bonus for the piss-hungry Fetish Master, He now had acquired a taste for both and loved to drink up either one, gladly! They stood kissing and naked and rubbing tits with their legs apart while Master T sat in the water directly under them, caressing their asses and kissing their legs in anticipation of a stream from the two that would turn into one river of hot piss. Patty grabbed him by the hair, then squeezed his mouth open for her piss, and then here came Carol's also!! You could hear the mouth fill up and Master T, helpless, started to gulp down the hot salty yellow rain. Then to Carol's surprise, Patty rubbed and fingered herself so rapidly and let go to administer a pussycum squirt right into his waiting mouth that he was expecting, just like Promised her Master T.

"Wow!" Carol said in awe and disbelief, "that was so fucking hot!! Let me try now."

So not to be outdone Carol did the same, "Yummy!!!"

CHAPTER

13

Carol thanked her now Secret Serving cousin for the "Secret Closet" he had built for them to meet in, whenever she needed to be fucked by a real cock, she would call the day before to be there to please her "that late evening OR first thing in the morning," right in her own bedroom closet behind the loose plywood just like at home when the kinksters experimented on each other and Carol's first multi/orgasm that only Cousin Anthony now (Master T) could do for her. But Carol knew Patty would be coming and She just HAD to show them the old shack at the end of the trail on their property right on a secluded rocky stream. Carol had sketched out on paper the way her and Patty would finish young Anthony's pee fetish that was interrupted in the shower on that embarrassing afternoon by Auntie Anna, And she gave him what he needed as he gave her exactly what she needed!

"Thank you so much, Anthony, for my closet! I LOVE IT! Soon I promise, but today we needed more space!" she giggled, and the three young kinksters all laughed loudly in agreement.

"Let's go in now and put your stuff away, we can wait for Louie to go out, and you two can meet, talk to him and tell me what you think," Carol added. "Both your opinions really matter to me and if I see he don't like you or he's jealous of my Friends I leave the deal, OR if YOU two see something I don't I also walk, OK? I already know what your Mistress thinks, LOL," Carol added, smiling as they all agreed in laughter once again.

Everyone was dressed and waiting over a glass of wine, showing Patty around the new cottage they broke their backs working on to enjoy times like these by the Lake and get away from the "City bullshit," as Mistress called it.

Louie Aronstein had met Carol and immediately seen what a star she could be on the big screen, Carol had natural beauty just like her cautious and protective mom, Auntie Anna had seen a million guys like this and was offered a million dollars once to marry a wealthy executive that frequented her first "massage job" at the "The Parisian Men's Club" in Peabody, MA. The Exclusive Men's massage Parlor had cars' license plates from all over New England the day it was busted. Auntie Anna had slipped out the back and simply walked away untouched that day in the Early 70s, she recalled.

"There are guys that just want a beautiful woman by their side all the time and they will pay for that! I refuse to be a fucking tro-

phy wife!" Mistress stressed. "And I don't want my daughter to be one Neither!! You two try and talk to her," Mistress demanded.

Patty jumped in and said, "I talk to her woman to woman, I promise, Mistress. We all wanna her to come home and be part of this venture we will take to the top. Master T has the power over her, though, and if He can't persuade her NOBODY can. I'll call you after dinner at 8:00 like I do every night, Mistress, and report in," Patty said secretly in Mistress's ear.

"Thank You, my Favorite slut, I know you will, and I know you're smarter than them too, lol, We will take this to the top, you know that, right??" Mistress said, confirming.

"We can't miss!" Patty said in confidence of the three business partners, and hopefully all four of them.

Louie arrived and was greeted by Carol, then introduced Patty and her (BOYFRIEND) Anthony to her Fiancé Louie Aronstein, a coworker at Paramount Pictures, where Carol was in the art dept. and Louie was a scout and movie casting consultant. He got ready for dinner while the three continued to speak softly about Evelyn's last session with Patty and Master T that Carol was missing out on, Patty told her of Evelyn being whipped across her tits and being turned on the "wheel of torture" and squirting and peeing going 'round and 'round and pussycum flying everywhere while she was crying in ecstasy and loving it, calling out for "harder" and "more, more!"

"Lol, it was so fucking hot, Carol, I wish You were there with us."

"REALLY! Oh, Fuck! That's one Hot Slut, OMG! Leave it to Mom, lol, What a Journal She has, I'm enjoying just reading the Fetishes and exploring with My kinky big man here, I'm looking forward to even more!" Carol added in confidence.

Carol made reservations at a nice Italian restaurant on a hill overlooking a stream in Derry, NH, and they all ate, Patty and Louie had IDs to order the wine that we all shared, Patty made a statement that she got really Horny when she drank wine lol and Carol giggled, setting the mood, and said, "Yes! I remember, ha-ha."

"What did she do?" asked the Kidding Master T to Carol.

"She flashes her big boobs to people that are staring at them, lol."

"They are fucking huge for her petite frame," Carol added. "You must have a party with them, Anthony, don't you," Carol now fishing for answers.

"Yes! Yes, I do, in fact, She's very hot in that department, I must say."

As Patty quickly changed the subject, Patty now asked about Louie's professional life and education during dinner, she admired his position and flattered the 28-year-old and told him how handsome he was and how lucky Carol was to run into such an influential successful young man, Patty was a natural with feeding a man's ego and Mistress seen that quality Patty possessed instantly! Carol and Anthony talked a bit like they were strangers and playing the fantasy game they played so well together. This was actually making Carol hot, she wanted that swap she drew out for

Master T to happen soon, if not tonight!!! Patty had two more glasses of wine and pretended to be drunker than she actually was. Master T didn't know exactly what she was up to, but she had something brewing he knew but didn't know What was to come from this unpredictable, intellectual knockout. On the ride home he would see what she had in mind.

They had taken the Company's Leased Mercedes and Master T took the keys and the wheel to drive home.

"Can I rest my head on Your lap, Anthony, for a minute?" as she giggled and slumped down with her head facing her Master T and her hand now unzipping his pants, with Carol and Louie Not being able to see, Patty took out Master's hard 10" and started blowing him right there, and said, "I told you I get horny when I drink wine," she giggled and then made slurping sounds on Master's Masterpiece for the others to hear, but could not see.

He looked behind and signaled down with his finger pointing to Patty's head bobbing up and down and for them to watch and touch her exposed ass and smooth-shaven moisturized legs.

Carol peeked first, then she said, "Wow! You weren't lying, your Boyfriend does have a big cock! That's huge!" Carol repeated for Louie to hear, Carol then motioned for him to lean over and told Louie feel her tits Anthony had taken out of her low-cut dress she wore to dinner. Patty certainly had the ball rolling and they weren't even home yet, Carol was caressing her ass and hips and sliding her finger in her asshole easily while Louie had his eyes

glued to Anthony's cock and Patty throating his manhood and now moaning in appreciation.

"OK, baby!" Master T lifted Patty's head, "let's finish this inside, please? We're here!"

On the way in, the two couples talked about Patty Not lying about "Drinking wine makes her horny," they all enjoyed a curious laugh, they all were very curious about What was next. Especially Carol, Carol wanted there to be an ongoing swapping 4way to have her two favorites that made her squirt and be available on Saturday nights into Sunday morning after Anthony was done in the N. End working and went up to the cottage with Patty to please her and be used like the slut she needed to be for her Anthony, Patty's Master T!

Patty whispered to Carol as they walked in that she had to make a call and to send Louie in while she was on the phone to get some glasses of wine, and start working on Anthony, hopefully she would handle Louie, she would ask Louie if he liked the deepthoating. Patty made her 8:00 P.M. call as promised to her Mistress and Mentor to give her the news that they were going to swap tonight and that Louie's eyes were glued to Master T's cock and not really on my pussy and was squeezing my tits, in not a very experienced way either, lol.

Mistress shot back and said, "HE must be a cuckold then OR Bi/Curious then, OK, change of plans then, see if you can get him interested in Master's cock and have him suck it while Master's face is blocked, I don't think Master is Bi at all but he

will let another guy blow him, though. He's a pussycum eater all the way, but this guy watched you suck and watched Carol finger you? Omg, sounds like he is a cuckold to me and I've seen this type before, He will watch Carol get fucked by a big cock and jerk off while being humiliated by his woman teasing him with a bigger cock in all three holes, DO It, My loyal slut! I know you can, and if he is a cuckold and Bi we will use HIS money to build our new Physical Therapy Facility. I have a nice present for you when you come home," Mistress said before hanging up.

"Goodnight, My Mistress, I'll take care it," Patty replied.

Louie walked in and started to pour the four glasses of wine as Patty walked over and watched him pour grazing her tits against his free arm, Louie said, "YOU have an amazing deep-throating talent there, Patty, Anthony has a nice big cock too for you to challenge your skill, Is He Bi/also like you and Carol? I didn't know until tonight that Carol really did like girls until I seen her caressing your beautiful tits and legs!! Omg, you do have a beautiful body just like Carol does," Louie added.

Patty took out her DDs, then grabbed Louie's hand to feel her light-skinned, smooth and firm breasts with pulsating red nipples waiting for tonight's abuse by Master T and Carol. But first, Patty's curiosity had her wondering if this young and handsome fiancé was in fact Bi, or a Cuckold like Mistress suggested.

So Patty asked the simple question, "Why did you ask if My boyfriend was Bi? Are you Bi? It's OK if you are Bi/gay, you know, Carol is, so she can't say a fucking thing about it. Have you ever

sucked a guy's cock?" Patty asked firmly, "truthfully now, tonight is the night you can Get it all out, and I'll help," Patty added.

Louie discreetly said, "I haven't sucked one yet, but as I watched you blowing Anthony and looking at his long thick cock in your mouth I got an amazing hard-on and I wanted to suck it too, so I guess, maybe, I could be Bi, I did experiment and gave a guy in college a hand job, because I chickened out on blowing him, but he did blow me," Louie said in confidence.

Patty, now all excited and getting so wet, she took off her panties and was rubbing her pussy and unzipping Louie's pants to suck his tiny 4" hard-on right at the counter as she sat down to take all his 4" with ease,. Patty sucked on Louie in the kitchen and had a plan she told Louie about, While Carol fed him some pussy squatting on top of Anthony while he was lying flat on his back, He couldn't see who was blowing him. Patty would then take Anthony's cock from HER mouth and give it to Louie to try.

Not at all surprised, Louie said, "I'll do it, Patty! I'm dying to try it now and on a nice big dick too, Thank You, Patty," Louie added.

"Don't thank me yet, we still have to get Carol in on it, lol, but Carol will love our plan," Patty giggled.

Patty and Louie entered the living room from the kitchen, each holding two glasses of wine each to find Nobody there, so they searched the next room to find Anthony and his cousin Carol fucking like sex-starved animals in heat.

CousinAnthony/Master T had Carol by her hair Doggy style and was ramming her from behind hard while she was screaming into the pillow So Patty and Louie wouldn't hear them in the kitchen, too late now.

"Here we are, you two!!! You started without US, lol," Patty joked, then started to undress Louie and get right back on his dick down her throat while Louie played with Carol's huge pulsating purple nipples. The whole time Louie was witnessing Master T pounding his Fiancé in the ass and in her juicy pussy back and forth admiring the "Alpha Male" Silverback, in the room, IN ENVY!

Patty now jumped in to get at HER Vanilla BOYFRIEND Anthony, Carol's Cousin and MASTER, Patty was caressing Carol's lovely nipples and suckling on the throbbing raw red flesh being slapped, pinched and used up by her Master as well.

Patty began to whisper in Carol's ear to sit on Anthony's face Backwards, and that Louie had agreed to suck cock for his first time, "But don't tell your Cousin, just turn around and watch it while I Blow your Cousin, THEN just block Anthony so he don't know When I hand his cock to your Fiancé Cuckold/Louie to suck his cock, OK?" Patty was whispering and kissing Carol's ears.

"ABSOLUTELY! I LOVE IT," Carol said with pleasure. "You're plan is unbelievable, Patty! This is going to be one great summer," Carol said, kissing and whispering into Patty's ears.

As Carol did exactly what Patty suggested, Carol hopped up onto her kinky cousin Anthony's face, she fed him his favorite

meal, JuicyRipeMango, and was riding his mouth and demanded his tongue stay out of his mouth and into her holes as she rode the long hard wet lizard tongue, blocking his view as Patty and Louie were passing his 10" cock.

Patty was blowing Her Master T, making Louie take turns sucking his cock and forcing his head down until he just submitted and started to take the hard cock himself with pleasure while Patty started to blow Louie's little dick "as Louie's reward."

Carol was amazed while watching her Bi/Fiancé sucking Her favorite man in the whole world and now realized, SHE NOW HAD THE BEST OF BOTH WORLDS, and SO did Patty now.

Carol's Cousin Anthony, And Patty's Master/Anthony did NOW realize it was NOT Patty blowing him, and it was Louie, but didn't respond Knowing Patty and Carol had something up their sleeve and just let the cuckold have some cock to suck on for them to watch.

Master T knew Carol, Patty and his Goddess/Mistress had planned this and he would just say silent and let them play him for his money, Which the three devious kinky Domme Goddesses would do, IN A BIG WAY!

Carol, Patty and Mistress's plan to somehow make Cuckold Louie Aronstein walk away from the engagement to Carol because of their Bi/sexual behavior and BDism lifestyle had "backfired" on them.

INSTEAD, Fiancé Louie had now exposed himself as a bi/cuckold that loved to watch His Fiancé Carol AND Cousin/

Master T, OR any big-cock Stud for that matter, taking his Wife/Girlfriend while he masturbated and was humiliated by his Wife or Girlfriend while fucking and/or sucking a bigger cock in front of him.

In some instances the Cuckold is ordered to lap up the Cum/Mess from the loaded pussy or asshole, and suck the guy's cock clean if she Orders him to do a Cream Pie, in Bdism terms.

Carol's craving for multiple cocks at the same time along with her love for eating pussy wasn't going to chase Fiancé/Cuck Louie away at all, in fact Louie was now IN the lifestyle now to be used and wanted MORE after Patty had opened up his Darkside.

Would Master T collar Louie now? Would Patty collar Louie, or would Louie search elsewhere and bring strangers home and put Carol in danger? Let's see what The Domme Anna had to say about this strange turn of events.

Carol was still facefucking her Favorite Man and being fingered deep in her streaming pussy on her G, the Master of producing multiple Orgasms for His young Goddess was ready with his mouth open. He needed to drink down some MangoJuice from Carol he had become addicted to and with a loud scream, Carol grabbed onto Cousin Anthony's hair and pumped his mouth full of her Pussycum while Louie watched a river of Pee/Cum squirt directly into his mouth as he choked momentarily, but got it all down.

"WOW!" Patty said in disbelief. "Now THAT is how you suppose to Squirt, lol."

"OK," Carol said to Master T, "I want your cum now, Anthony," as Carol started to blow her cousin she signaled her Cuckold Fiancé Louie to fuck her while watching her blowing another guy and taking his cum in her mouth.

Carol's Master T/cousin let out a grunt and filled Carol's mouth in reciprocation, Patty ran over to cumswap with Carol by kissing her, Patty then spit some cum in Louie's open mouth she held open to make him taste her Master's cum as well humiliating him.

"Good job, Louie, We're proud of you to 'come out' now and we will all have a good time together, and maybe YOU can come in on our venture as an investor and we can introduce you to lots of people you will love in our lifestyle. Carol can give you an idea IF you're interested in this being ongoing with Me and MY Boyfriend/Anthony. We will have to Collar you! We'll explain in the morning," Domme Patty said in exhaustion.

"Come to bed, Anthony," Patty said, smiling, waving goodnight to all, taking her VANILLA Boyfriend Cousin Anthony's hand as Carol rolled her eyes.

Carol, still a little confused at just WTF went down, watching HER MAN, Her soulmate, and Her addiction walk off to bed to sleep on Patty's 38DDs most men and women dream of, But in their lifestyle there is NO room for jealousy, or is there? Carol had also just witnessed her fiancé get played into sucking her OTHER Man's cock by the Same manipulative young insatiable Patty with unmatched Oral skills, the same woman who'd also

been groomed to be a ruthless Dominatrix by the most popular Domme in All New England! Carol's own Mom! And GOD-DESS Auntie Anna, read on.

Patty had called Her Mistress/Domme Anna first thing in the morning and gave her report as Nephew Master T listened on. The Domme gave Patty new instructions to her apprentice Domme in training.

The Domme /Auntie Anna then ordered her nephew/Master to "do whatever necessary to keep both Carol and Louie close to home, Get them involved in SIR any way you can, maybe even 'Collar' Carol!! Carol would love that, especially now that she sees YOU and PATTY are getting too close for her comfort! Carol is very Possessive of YOU even around ME, Carol wants you ALL to herself, SO REEL HER IN, my nephew and Master T, just as you've reeled Me and Patty In, lol. You know what to do, Patty will have your back, she's All business," The Domme concluded.

At breakfast Carol made sure SHE made the breakfast HER Anthony loved, Homemade waffles with whipped cream and Real Maple Syrup with corned beef hash. Carol already had everything ready, knowing the Love of her life and Diabolical Patty were coming for the weekend so she wasn't going to go out.

Carol wanted to play house, just like Patty was doing with him, as Carol was flipping the waffles Anthony yelled out as he was walking over, "I SMELL WAFFLES." Carol's eyes lit up and she yelled back to her Soulmate, lover, Cousin and Master, "HOMEMADE with Maple syrup and whipped cream, MMMMmmm," Carol taunted.

"Yummy, just like you!" Cousin Anthony whispered in her ear and kissed her neck passionately with nobody downstairs yet and they both knew it.

But Patty was right behind him as usual, watching his every move to be careful.

"OK, Louie, it's homemade Waffle time!" Master T yelled out.

Patty now started the conversation, "Louie, are you familiar with the BDism lifestyle? You're much older than everyone here, so you MUST have heard of the alternate lifestyle, right?

Kinky sex, Vanilla and Non-Vanilla sex? Whips, spankings, Bondage and all that stuff?" Carol curiously asked to take her Cuckold even DEEPER into their plan to Use him up real good.

To everyone's surprise Louie said, "NO, Not really! I just always thought of sex as either Gay or straight and I knew I liked women, But I'd have to say I was curious about men too but not to the extent of yesterday's experience, when I really enjoyed sucking on a cock. Thanks, Bi the way, Patty, for getting my nerve up to do it and especially you, Anthony, Patty's boyfriend, for having such a great cock to really enjoy it for my first time. Will you two consider an ongoing thing with Carol and I?" Louie said, looking for a Yes.

Carol JUMPED UP in anger and said, "Hold on there, Mister! I'll have the say in that! These are MY friends, NOT yours!!" Carol Snapped and pointed in his face.

Patty walked over to Calm Carol down and Said, "If you really want this engagement you better talk it out OR end it

now! Marriage is hard enough without other things that may get in the way, We should Propose something, Master T," Patty said to Louie's surprise.

Louie asked, "Why did you just call him Master T instead of Anthony?"

Patty replied, "He is my Master T when we swap or play out fantasies in our BDism lifestyle and that's how we keep it separated from our Vanilla life, I am Collared and Owned."

Louie asked curiously, "How can we learn? If Carol agrees, of course," looking to her.

Master T now replied, "We will teach you both if you're serious, if not we will leave now!"

Carol jumped up, AGAIN, "No, No, wait a second here, how will YOU, ANTHONY, do this 'Collaring' thing YOU are suggesting, SIR?"

Master T said firmly, "I put a collar around your neck as you repeat an oath to me, you promise to obey and never stray, You promise to submit, serve and to be the slut you crave to be, you will now be 'Collared and Owned,' you call me Master or Sir and you're rewarded when good, or spanked, whipped and punished when bad or disobey a command, very simple."

Carol now curiously said, "ANTHONY, Will YOU do this for ME? TODAY, and Patty collars Louie? Is that how it goes, Man/woman, AND woman/man?"

Patty now said, "Sure, it can go either way, but that sounds right in this situation, I would go along with that. My Master says

it's OK, A Master/Dom has the last say in BDism, An Alpha Male is most Dominant and sets the guidelines and teaches sub/sluts in training."

Louie jumped in, "I would like to serve under Master T AND Patty as well, could I do both?"

Master T replied, "Yes, by proxy as I've done before, Carol would belong to only me! Are you two OK with all of the rules, I will use our two collars in the car and give them to you two and it will be official if you agree."

Carol immediately approving, "YES, YES! GO, Get the Collars now, Master, please? I agree to everything you said and I'm getting so fucking hot for this now, COLLAR ME NOW!"

"I'm sure MY Master/Anthony will collar you, Carol, AND I'll take your Cuckold Fiancé to another level also so he can explore a lot more of his sexuality with Us AND our venture at 'SIR.'"

Louie continued to ask questions, "What is 'Sir' your venture, I heard you say something about Investing Also?"

"Yes, we can talk about that at lunch later, Louie, and save some whipped cream, Carol," her cousin/soulmate said.

Carol quickly replied, "I already did, SIR, Do you and Patty have many clients yet?"

Master T confirmed, "Yes, we do, we have a 'Secret Journal,' SOME are very 'Special'!"

Carol, all wet now, said, "I'd love to hear more, wouldn't you, Patty? And Louie?"

"Let's Not get ahead of ourselves now, I'll be right back with your collars!" Master said.

"I can't wait, Master T, I'm first, OK?" Carol said, squirming in her chair.

Carol's cousin Anthony/Master T came back in holding Carol's new red ruby collar he had been holding onto, AND handed Patty Louie's collar, which was Master T's old one, to make it an official Collaring on the Cuckold Louie.

"I have Carol's collar right here that IS a new one and didn't realize it was a new collar, it was an extra Collar from Evelyn's order at MY jewelers, I think," Master T said inadvertently.

Although Carol was so excited to get it around her neck she interrupted to look closer, "OMG, I LOVE IT! I want it on me Now, Please, Master, Collar me NOW? What Oath do I need to repeat to you, Master?"

Master T handed the other collar to Patty for Louie's neck. Patty then pointed to the floor for Louie to kneel before her, right next to his fiancé, Carol.

Cousin Anthony, AND Master stood directly over Carol, holding her chin up, and said, "Repeat after Me: 'I promise to serve only you, Or beat me until I'm black and blue, I agree to be "collared and Owned," To be the property of Master T, And To be the submissive slut/Slave I crave to be,' Do You accept My collar, Slave Carol?" Master T recited to the eager Carol.

"Yes! Yes! I accept your collar and need to be the Slut/Slave I crave to be, ONLY for My Master T, now Please, Master T, put it

around my neck, It's So beautiful! Thank you, Master/Sir," Carol cried out, then hugged, and kissed her Lover/cousin with passion.

Master T placed the very Expensive red ruby on Black leather Collar/Necklace around his young Goddess's neck, pinching her excited hard nipples protruding through her thin blouse along the way.

"You are now the property of Master T in our alternative BDSM lifestyle and will explore your Darkside together on our journey," explained Master T.

"I'm All yours, FOREVER, Anthony, MY Master T," Carol replied.

Master T now said, "We have to Consummate your Initiation with a kinky sexual command you will obey now, So bend over that kitchen table while we wait for Domme Patty to finish collaring Your Cuck Louie."

"Yes, Master T, DO what you want to me. I will obey, and I do whatever you say," Carol was rhyming her words to her Soulmate.

Carol bent over the kitchen table and rested her elbows on the long Granite countertop and waited for her Fiancé to be placed next to her for his Initiation and penetrated by Patty.

Master T had officially given the command to Patty to Collar and Own Louie by Proxy as He had done before by Proxy Co-Owning Patty, while Goddess/AuntieAnna was present. Master T had also taken in the double-ended dildo next to the collar in the box from the car, now handing it to Patty after her ceremonial for Initiation to Louie to be her "Bitch."

Patty now placed the collar around Louie's neck while Carol held his head up, pulling his hair, wasted No time bending the eager submissive Cuckold over the table right next to Carol to be "Pegged," WATCHING Carol being Pounded in her ass by Her Master/Lover/and Cousin, Domme Patty, and Carol couldn't wait to watch Cuckold Louie "cleaning Up" everyone's Mess, taking more of Master T's cock cum from Carol's ass, "Creampie style."

Carol's Master grinded his now Collared young Goddess up close from behind and put both his hands around her to find her raw swollen nipples to toy with while Louie watched the Master work on her, continuously POUNDING her gorgeous round Italian Ass.

Carol just closed her eyes and moaned while she was crying as her soaked pussy was entered by the rock-hard 10" cock, from her ass, Master T shoved her down onto the table and held her lower back and ordered her to "STAY." Exciting her cuckold Fiancé needing to cum,

Carol's turned-On Cousin and Master pounded her harder and harder and Carol just cried louder and louder, causing Louie to masturbate. Cuck/Slave Louie was ordered down onto the table and held down by His new Domme/Mistress Patty, then lubed his asshole.

Patty entered his asshole with her strap-on dildo attached to fuck the cuck in his ass while his Fiancé was being violated and fucked by a much bigger cock he Envied. "These are the rules!"

Master T implied, "and whatever the girls tell you, Louie, You must Obey, or be beat and pegged until you learn your place."

Carol was holding back a river of Pussycum from all this fore-play that there was a huge puddle on the floor when Master took out his cock from Carol's dripping pussy to cum in Carol's ass for Louie to Clean Up.

Patty was given the signal by Master T to have the Cuck/Louie get on his knees to lick out Carol's ass of Master's cum load oozing out of her asshole (Cream pie) as it was called. Master and Patty watched in amazement as Collared Louie Cuckold sucked the oozing cock cum from her winking asshole and off Their Master's cock being held in Patty's hand, feeding the 10" cum-covered cock to her new Eager Sub/Slave that Fiancé Carol couldn't even look at anymore and ONLY wanted her Cousin/Master back FOREVER.

Mistress got a call that night and she was in heaven and Praised Both of her S&M Master/Domme of BDism.

"We need to have that Cuckold Louie sign a contract this week," Mistress Anna was saying. "Let's do this right and remodel the building with the Sports Injury Rehab, facility 'Sir' on the ground floor facing the waterfront, and our Suite's on the top floor."

"Get that little-dick Cuckold to Evan's office soon before he runs away from Patty, lol," the Domme and Goddess Anna joked.

CHAPTER

14

Carol jumped at the opportunity when she heard about TERMS and conditions in the BDism world about being Collared and Owned by a Master during their kinky-filled four-way swap weekend with HER Cousin Anthony, and male counterpart ever since they could walk. Being Owned also meant SHE would become "The Property" of the Master or Mistress collaring her, which in this instance would be HER Anthony/now Master T. Carol would use this BDism Terminology to her advantage to get out of the Vanilla relationship with her fiancé Louie Aronstein. Carol was Displeased, Disgusted and sexually unsatisfied and could NOT have an orgasm with this Cuckold man's 4" dick, Louie could not please her, not even Orally!

Now Carol found out he was Bi! A cuckold! And now He wanted cock instead, AND have her watch him eat Creampies from her pussy or ass!

Carol needed the advice of a Wise Goddess, So she called no other than the wisest woman she knew, Yes, Carol's Mom, The Domme, Goddess AuntieAnna.

"Mom?" Carol pleaded. "I should have listened to you, I'm sorry once again, I didn't take this seriously and it got way out of my control. I'm sure Patty or Cousin/Master T has told you by now but I need to tell you too, I'm your daughter, Not Patty! I know you confide in her a lot, she IS very good for business and knows how to work it, thanks to you, I'm sure, lol," Carol joked to show she was Not angry with Mom.

"Ha-ha!" said MommeDomme. "I got her some new outfits and she is stunning with the right clothes, just a blush of makeup, YOU, My clone, don't need Any makeup At All," Carol's Mom added.

"When I was younger I was offered a part in movie as well, AND a bigshot executive offered me a million dollars to be his wife! Can you imagine? ME, a fucking trophy wife?"

Mistress added again, "Listen, MY little girl I love More than life itself, It's NOT about the money, It's about Happiness, just simple things you need that make YOU happy, Not the things you want that make Other people happy they CAN buy for you!! What makes YOU happy, Carol? Then you make plans to pout and get it, Work for it! Educate yourself HOW to get it, And then once YOU have it, You are Happier than you thought you would ever be, because YOU earned it, and went out to get it, NOBODY just handed you some money and told you, here buy

it, be happy now, LIFE JUST DON'T WORK THAT WAY, BABY!!" the Domme, MommeDomme, said.

"I love you, Mom! YOU always know what to Say, I understand now! This was an interesting weekend to say the least and I'm more determined now than ever to help you, and be closer to you and My Anthony and NOW My Master T, and Patty I think will be a great asset as you already have groomed her to be, lol... As you probably have heard I convinced Our Master/Anthony to 'Collar and own me.' I finally realize now MY COUSIN ANTHONY MAKES ME HAPPY, In Your world, his world, and now our world, NO more Vanilla for this girl, ONLY WHEN IT'S BUSINESS," Carol added adamantly. "I'm going to stress to Louie that we need to invest in 'SIR' Patty, Anthony and I already have an idea and we will run it by YOU first for approval, if that's OK with you?" Carol suggested.

"Now THAT'S my girl, lol! That's OK for sure!" Momme-Domme confirmed. "Let me know when you're coming and I'll call our lawyer Evan, You met him, He will write up something for Louie, You and I to sign. Don't break up with him totally just yet, I'll explain when I see you for dinner tonight, I'll make sure your Master T is here! lol! I want You to cook for him, He's YOUR man now, You earned it!"

Carol cooked her Master his favorite Sicilian dish called "Scungilli Diavolo" that night, it's sea conch, an eel, a seafood dish with a dash of Tabasco and "Mango juice" to wash it down, a joke between the two cousins.

MommeDomme/MistressAnna made sure that She had BOTH their attention and started to talk about the elephant, OR maybe two elephants in the room, One which was that the two kinksters were "1st cousins" and should be Very, Very discreet about their Passion and Desire for each other around family OR business matters, AND should be very careful OR give second thoughts about having children since there was a greater chance of birth deformities with incest babies, Both their mothers were also sisters. The Second Elephant in the room was that "Master T" had collared Both Mother and Daughter, and they MUST be OK with Master T serving them both, AND being served BY both.

They DID AGREE that they BOTH could serve him as HE would reciprocate and please them now that they were all dependent on each other sexually and the lifestyle had NO room for jealousy, IT WAS PURELY SEXUAL and part of the commitment of being Collared and owned.

Master T now had the "Green light" for Mother and Daughter FOR LIFE!

Patty wasted NO time whatsoever under her Mentor and Mistress's direction on organizing and remodeling the Penthouse into three units/sections. One unit would be Patty's, then next to her on the right would be her Master's, and on her left would be her Mistress and Mentor in the corner office. The petite sandy-blonde Patty with natural DDs on her curvy frame now had the clothes, shoes and Jewelry to make any man drop their jaws with desire, and most women too. The only problem Patty had was that she

was in the company of two Goddesses with even more natural beauty Sharing the same Master. Patty, however, had "unmatched Oral skills" the two Goddesses Wished they had! Patty already got her stuff in the new Building, and getting more stuff at her old place. Her abusive older brother of the three that were raping her tried to hold her back for one last blowjob, BIG Mistake!

The abusive Older brother was undoubtedly missing her unmatched oral skills and Patty got on the phone to her Master, and within minutes Anthony/Master T arrived in his Corvette and honked the horn standing outside, looking up to the third-floor apartment.

When the older brother opened the window to answer Master T yelling out his name, "Hey, Asshole, YOU have 30 seconds to send My Girlfriend Patty downstairs, or you're going OUT THAT FUCKING WINDOW when I come up for her!!" the angry Master Demanded.

The Asshole was already quite aware of Carol's cousin Anthony's temper and tough reputation. It only took seconds for Patty to come running downstairs and hug her Master T in tears as he drove her to her NEW HOME into Her new Venture, with the three New people that depended and care for her and now "Owned" her in Their Darkside, AND on the Vanilla side for EVERYONE to see.

Mistress Anna was in a Meeting with Her Master and Carol and continued going over the legal and financial matters, there were Documents Mistress insisted on being signed by all four of

the others while Patty was waiting outside, when Carol and Patty's (Vanilla Boyfriend) walked out Patty felt a little slighted, but understood.

Patty's Mistress GoddessAnna Gave the other two kinksters a few last words before leaving (hurry up back to work!), the Domme concluded, THEN Patty was called in to get today's instructions from her Mistress Anna and wasted NO time to put Patty's mind at ease about her NOT being at that meeting and why Only them two and NOT Patty.

Mistress explained, "IT'S CAROL'S MESS, not yours, you have your own problems. I heard from your Master T, You're with ME now! MY family is now your family! Fuck them, and I don't mean in a good way," DommeAnna said angrily. "I hate rapists and disrespectful men, they're not MEN at all, they take up the air we breathe and should all die, Motherfuckers!" she continued her anger for Patty's mistreatment yesterday!! "With that said, would you like to do more shopping today, lol," Domme Anna hugged her crying apprentice Patty, then sat her down in her luxurious office chair.

To Patty's surprise her Mistress took off Patty's shoes on her knees, then reached for the bottle of moisturizer and applied the expensive oily lotion to her young silky and milky-white toned curvy calves, feet and smooth legs by the professional Masseuse and Domme, Mistress Anna ordered Patty to just lean back and relax and put her legs up on her desk for the next half-hour or so. "I'm just so in the mood to eat your pussy all morning, Patty. The

other two won't be back for a while, I gave them four hours' worth of work," Patty's Mistress Anna giggled.

Mistress/Goddess Anna was really starting to enjoy pussy now and realized that with Masochist kinkster Evelyn in particular and began telling that to her NEW Pet Patty as she professionally massaged this gorgeous young and perfect petite body.

Patty was getting noticed more and more by her Mistress as she was now also Dressing the part, Mistress/DommeAnna was picking out the "Perfect Attire" for Patty to look even better and hotter for DommeAnna, Special Clients and for the Sports world Celebrities at "Sir," their new venture together.

"I have to admit to you now, THIS is the other reason I had you wait for the other two to leave," Patty's Mistress applied more warm oil onto her hands and told Patty to take her top completely off. Her soaking-wet Mistress reached up as she was now on her knees in front of Patty, with Patty's legs up on her desk.

Mistress/Goddess buried her face in Patty's cum-streaming Pussy and Massaged her firm 38DDs from her kneeling position. Patty went into a squirting orgasm that had the approval of her Domme and Mistress Anna as she just kept her mouth on Patty's gushing fruit-flavored pussy until the Domme Anna had taken every drip/drop of Patty holding and humping DommeAnna's face as if Patty was Anna's Domme.

Patty, now all drained out and playing with her Mistress's cum-soaked hair, said, "Your turn now! I'm going to lick your pussy so good now in the shower while I wash my pussycum

off your hair, lol. Then we better go before they cum back," Patty joked.

"OK, My Slut! I seen a great outfit I got for you yesterday I want you wearing next week. We have a few appointments lined up, Between You, Carol and I, WE will have these sports figures EATING out of our hands and land these Team contracts. There will be NO looking back from now on, Patty. We have the Finance, the Location, Experience, and the Class. Let's get the Clients," Domme Anna ordered.

Patty dropped to her knees in the shower to lick her Mentor Goddess into two consecutive orgasms that she choked on, but kept on licking till the Goddess was finished and pleased. The satisfied Mistress lifted her up in appreciation and kissed Patty very passionately to put an end to a perfect morning. "Let's get dressed and go shopping!" the Domme Anna concluded.

At the family Attorney's office of Evan J, Gellant in Chelsea, MA, Cousins Carol and Anthony went over the documents and signed them respectably. Louie, Mistress and Patty needed to sign and there would be legal obligations specified by Mistress Anna and she was a genius in these matters. Louie had better be more educated than good-looking or rich to play with the Goddess/Domme of good looks, and pretty well off herself, On her way to becoming rich!

Everything fell in place fast and the contractors were done in a few weeks. The place looked awesome as everyone knew it

would, with Mistress and Patty designing it along with Professionals they sought out together and played hard together as well along the way.

Patty was eating out BOTH Mother and Daughter, but could only have Carol's pussy if ordered by Master T, lol. Which was often, after all Patty and Anthony were in a Vanilla life also that portrayed them as Boyfriend and Girlfriend for business and family discretions.

Patty could SUCK a golf ball from a garden hose, OR LICK the paint off a Cadillac, Cousin Anthony would joke to Carol and watch Carol roll her eyes at him.

Master T never refused a blowjob from Patty's aggressiveness when Nobody was around, Master T always kept Patty close by as his Vanilla life demanded it, OR his Mom Joan came by.

Eddy Dugan, CEO and head of Advertising at DUGAN & SON ADVERTISING, INC., was a "Special Client" kinkster in The Domme/Auntie Anna's old Journal and Eddy Dugan's son Eddy Jr. was in tight with the Boston Red Sox Organization. Eddy Jr. had scheduled an interview with the three Goddesses for a Proposal and Contract with "SIR."

Eddy Dugan continued into My Mistress's New Journal, which meant they went WAY back to her Parisian Sauna massage days, when The Domme started out. Eddy had known The Domme and a few other Privileged clients for many years now and Eddy had a Fetish that even stirred MY Interests into the Water sports Fetish, OR the more popular term, GOLDEN SHOWERS.

Carol and I had read of this GS Fetish in the secret closet and I got such an amazing hard-on fantasizing about Carol pissing on me at that moment. I'll never forget while she was jerking me off, making me suck her new developing nipples and finger her wet pussy.

We soon did act it out as we did with ALL the Fetishes from the old journal of The Domme and WERE now still a Favorite Fetish of mine, with MY three Goddesses I now had Collared and own.

Eddy was chatting on the massage table with The Domme Anna, she was explaining about her New venture as she took some fresh warmed oil and applied it to his asshole slowly. Using just one finger, then two, and then three, and deep to find his Prostate gland, he was now spotting drops of cum oozing from his 50-year-old cock that Mistress would also massage with the other hand.

Today Eddy was getting a scheduled Prostate Massage BEFORE his Golden Shower session, THEN pegged for HIS happy ending, as everyone called it. She didn't even have to Blow him for $300.00 sessions EVERY WEEK, billed to his advertising Co. Eddy was Bi/Curious but old-fashioned and wouldn't come out of the closet, only by the glory hole with Mistress's "Stand In" and On-Call She-Male Varney.

Varney got His cock sucked by Eddy from a hole in the wall (Glory hole) while getting his ass fucked by Mistress's 9" strapon, getting paddled and whipped hard at the same time while Eddy masturbated to please himself. Varney was a Professional

SheMale Dancer from Saugus' Green Apple Night Club for female Impersonators. The most wanted Golden Shower Domme Anna met Varney at the club while working up on the popular Rte. 1, soon putting Varney to work.

Eddy mentioned his son and His son's connections in the Boston sports world, Especially Red Sox AND Bruins players he knew very well. He played pro ball but gave it up to be an advertising exec with Dad.

Eddy Jr. reached out and made an appointment for the three Goddesses with the President and GM of the Boston Red Sox, and the rest was History. "SIR" Sports Injury Rehabilitation would DO ALL the Physical Therapy for the Organization and bill their insurance. Tipping would be EXTRA and there would be LOT$ of tipping!!

At the meeting on Yawkey Way, Fenway Park, Boston, MA, the three impeccably dressed and manicured Goddesses walked into the office and in two minutes EVERY MAN was on the phone and one minute later the conference room was full of the ballplayers trying to sneak a peek. No Man in the room had EVER seen a woman so Gorgeous as Auntie Anna looked that day, never mind (three) Jaw-dropping women in the same room.

Tony Conig And Carl Maz, the two big names in baseball in the 60s, wanted to be FIRST on the list for "SIR." "I DON'T CARE WHAT IT COSTS!!" the two Celebrities had told the GM after the meeting and the Contract was signed that very day!

Back at the Building, Master T finished up with labor contractors for the roof garden, over the Penthouse for plumbing and lighting, there was even a toilet and a waterfall installed to relax on the open-air roof to enjoy the Boston skyline view.

"The celebrities will LOVE it!" The Mistress stressed. Everything was ready, except for Carol; she wanted to be back in Boston with her Cousin Anthony, now her Master.

Master T's collaring was personal to her, It's like a marriage in the BDism world, and Carol wanted NO part of Louie now, Only her Master.

MommeDomme and Patty had to convince Carol to KEEP LOUIE around for now. "Anthony isn't going anywhere, You don't have to live with Louie, just keep him as your Cuckold and that's all," Patty and HER Anthony explained. "He IS a financial partner!"

"OK, but I want to stay in the Penthouse too," Carol adamantly demanded, "with MY Master. I'm NOT getting stuck up in N.H. while you all are here in Condo suites!"

Carol's arrogance and disrespect was getting Her Mom pissed off, The wiser Goddess started to yell and school her cloned spoiled daughter by telling her Carol put herself in this position.

The MommeDomme further explained that her Fiancé already had a fucking million-dollar home being built as they spoke. "Just stay in your Mansion a while, Then you get him to leave it to you, BE SMART and just play this out until we get 'SIR' off the ground. Your Cousin/Master and Patty will come there some nights to play or whenever possible AND you'll come

here Sat/Sun and work and stay at the Penthouse on weekends, OK?" Mom reasoned. "Stop fucking complaining, YOU did this to yourself, taking his offers, NOT US, but we're going to get you out of this, Just listen to me on this one," The Domme sternly told Carol.

Carol's Master T looked on grinning, and said to HIS young speechless beauty, "Carol, It's going to be fine! Do what she's telling you and I'll be up to see you with or without Patty. You'll be closer to your Artwork in N.H. and your Job that way, THEN all weekends here with us, OK? Deal?" Master T convincingly told his female kinky counterpart with a wet kiss, and a pat on her ass.

"I guess for now, Master, but weekends HERE with you and Mom," Carol said and pushing away, "Just for now," Spoiled Carol ended.

The Domme/Mistress added, "It's Not going to be ALL fun and games either, you know. YOU will work at SIR like the three of us and we will all meet and greet 'Our new Clients.' These spoiled young Athletes may actually have an Injury, lol. Work with Patty on the Physical Therapy techniques and exercises," Mistress seriously stressed.

"Ok, and maybe Patty can show me how to deepthroat while we're at it, lol," Carol joked.

Mistress Anna called in Master T to have Patty pick up Carol after work this week. "I'd like to start introducing you three to My 'Old Secret Clients,' as I call them in the old Journal My

daughter loves to read about to you, lol. I Don't want Louie to hear, let him get here by himself and you take him to the sauna when he gets here also and let me know, I want YOU especially to meet Eddy Dugan that you envy. He's Bi but won't 'come out.' I want to do something special for him since 'Eddy Showers' Got Us The fucking Red Sox account, THAT was BIG for 'Sir' and YOU and I so YOU and I will bring him 'Out of the closet' and be OK with his sexuality and not hide anymore!" Mistress Anna stressed to Master T.

"I agree totally and I have an idea how," Replied Master T, "I'll have Carol and Patty whipping and pegging Louie's ass, just walk Eddy in the Massage room that YOU THOUGHT was empty, then tell him this show is free for you and so aren't your massages for life, courtesy of 'The Domme,' Queen Golden of the Golden Shower, as he knows you, lol, THEN Patty and Carol will make Louie Blow him. I'll stand in front of Eddy and see if he goes for my 10" right in front of his mouth, just like he does Only for the Gloryhole," Master T added.

"THAT is a beautiful plan, My Nephew, I'm all soaking wet now! SEE WHAT YOU DO TO US, lol," The Domme said in a raspy voice. She then took her wet panties off and showed him, His Domme Anna now unzipping his pants and taking out his 10" hard-on from watching her squirm when he talked out his plan to the kinkiest Goddess of all time.

Wasting No more time, Master T knew now She liked to be taken hard and rough. His Goddess had undeniably submitted

and surrendered to his Dominance now. Goddess Auntie Anna was forcefully laid flat down on her desk and held down as Her Master T pounded both her holes while spanking her with consecutive backhanders on each cheek of her still-firm 38-year-old heart-shaped ass.

Pulling his Goddess up by her hair while fucking her hard doggie style, the Master turned his now Submissive Aunt Anna around with her ass on the edge of the desk, and finished her off with a G-Spot Orgasm her Daughter Carol loved as well.

Her Nephew/Master was ready to eat her explosive orgasm now, squirting everywhere as The Domme/Goddess screamed and pulled her nephew's head in close and squeezed with her powerhouse legs and released ANOTHER hot stream of PussyPee-Cum he was ready for. He lived and loved to drink her down while she also Loved squeezing his head until she was completely drained. Master T would not move his mouth until she let go off his thick curly black hair and made sure he had every last drop of his Childhood dream and Goddess Auntie Anna.

Patty was on the way to get Carol while Master T rested up and prepared for the Grand Opening coming up. A party was being planned at the Building On the rooftop Garden for the four Kinkster Partners, And Oh! Louie too. Carol was always anxious but this weekend was more special because she was getting to stay with her Anthony/Master at his Penthouse, Next door to Patty's, lol. And The Domme's corner office suite overlooking the Boston skyline.

Carol could stay in there, but no way! Carol had to be with Cousin Anthony, period! And so it went down, Patty drove the Mercedes in a very special linen top with Suspenders.

As Carol got in Patty said, "Do You like my outfit, Master T bought it for me."

"Ha-ha, Wow! You are the hottest driver I've ever seen, lol," Carol giggled while reaching for the sandy blonde's tits and played with them on the 30-min. ride from Derry, NH, to Boston, and Patty told Carol of the plan to lure Louie into the Sauna and cuckold him into some play for "Eddy Showers" Dugan.

"I was also thinking later maybe You and I do Master T??" Patty asked.

"Yes! He would love that," Carol replied, "we are neighbors now pinching her nipple, lol."

It was Friday evening and Louie was supposed to meet the Ladies at the Sumner St. building, Carol and Patty were waiting for Master T to bring "Eddy Showers" to the new Whirlpool bath for "Therapeutic stimulating" as a result of a work injury and be billed to Eddy's Insurance co. for $500.00.... The Therapy Room had a few more expensive Physical Therapy Items "Louie" had paid for with his investment. A custom-built Hot rocks Sauna Bath was right next to the whirlpool bath and then a Massive standup walk-in shower with tiled seating built into the shower walls was last before you dried off and went into one of four private locked Massage rooms. Each room had

soothing music as you lay down on a luxurious padded full-sized electronic adjustable massage table, to the right was a small table of lubricants, moisturizers and fruit-flavored oils, a microwave for warming the oils and fresh hot wet towels ready to wash the oils off of you.

Behind door #3 Is a brand-new "Dungeon" designed by none other than "The Domme."

Short or long, leather or wooden Whips, paddles, and riding crops lined the wall on one side and collars/leashes, Hoods, corsets, ropes, blindfolds and cuffs lined another wall. A New "remote control wheel of torture" was added and a padded leather sex swing with restraints, right next to that.

Mistress was very proud to show her Masterpiece design to the girls first and then leave because Louie was about to arrive with Master T. Mistress Anna was waiting for Eddy Showers Dugan to pull up for his surprise Live sex show in appreciation for the Red Sox account.

Carol took a few toys off the wall for the show and Patty nodded in approval, the girls were ready with crotchless S&M attire under their Gucci dress suits and quickly undressed to wait for their submissive men to play with the double-dong 18" dildo. They had Never seen one before till today.

"Omg! Mom thinks of everything, lol, Let's try this, Patty," Carol said, lubing them both up before giving Patty her 9" and then Carol's already soaking-wet pussy swallowed the other 9". Their pussies took both sides of the 18" double-dong respectively

until their throbbing meaty clits and flat tight bellies touched and the Dildo couldn't be seen anymore.

Master T drove Louie to the facility, The girls greeted them both at the door and Carol asked what was in Louie's bag he was holding. He said it was a surprise he'd been trying to tell her and thought today was the right time.

In Louie's bag was woman's makeup and women's clothing and he wanted them to dress him up in for today's session. Louie asked Carol and Patty curiously.

"OMG, Really? You're a Crossdresser?" Patty asked, but Carol was all excited to see her Master T, hugged him and said, "Did YOU know about this!?" Carol asked.

Master T, in Shock, now said, "FUCK NO! lol. "I'm as surprised as you, But let's get him Dressed up and in the Sauna, Eddy will be walking in and really going to see a great show."

Louie had shaven his legs and Patty put his pantyhose on him as Carol put on his Lipstick and called him Her little 4" cuckold and just humiliation that a "cuckold" LOVED hearing, verbal abuse and sexual abuse combined, and today Louie would get it ALL by three ruthless FemDommes.

"All dressed up and nowhere to go." Carol put a collar on Louie and led him by a leash to the top bench, where Master T was sitting and watching, waiting as Carol led Louie up on all fours, instructing Louie to get up there, and she said, "Suck on My Master's 10"," Carol Demanded.

Master T was watching and waiting for the Crossdresser Louie Lipstick, drooling like a dog in heat with saliva actually dripping from his lips, and Patty starting to whip him with a long leather whip. Patty had put in half the 9" double-dong dildo in Patty's pussy, and the other 9" of the double-dong was about to go into Louie's ass.

Eddy Showers got a short tour and a quick massage by The Domme, who told him now to take a Sauna first before he sat down in the shower and was peed on forcefully by the "Domme of the Golden Showers," which WAS Eddy's Fetish.

When Eddy walked in to this surprise of Patty pegging the Crossdressing Cuckold Louie, while being whipped by Domme Patty, Eddy got an immediate hard-on and Master T yelled, "Surprise!" standing up for Eddy to see his massive cock in front of his face.

Patty sat him down and said, "WATCH THIS," as Patty DEEPTHROATED his 10" in front of Eddy and Louie, THEN Carol now led her Cuck Louie Lipstick over to Eddy Showers to see if Louie wanted to try some sucking dick.

Eddy was so overwhelmed at Patty's deepthroating skills and eager to try it and finally "come out," he asked, "HOW do you do that, Patty?"

Patty now said to Eddy, "Care to Give it a try?"

Eddy wasted No time putting Master's cock in his mouth and sucked like a ten-dollar hooker while Louie's mouth was still full and his face smudged in Lipstick. Patty continued to beat Louie

again and fucked his ass more with the double dong. The Cross-dressing Louie and Eddy Showers BOTH took a nice load and exchanged phone numbers on the way out.

On the way out of the Sauna, that is, Eddy Showers still needed his fill of the Fetish he had become addicted to. He daydreamed of his monthly sessions with the Goddess and Domme of the Golden Shower. Master T had also acquired the salty addiction of this Fetish secretly hidden by Millions of kinksters around the world.

There are "Pee Clubs," "Pee Dating" and Masters/Doms, Dominatrix/Mistress, High-Priced Gorgeous tasty College-aged girls providing this "GS" service as well. Discretion And Excellent Personal Hygiene is a Must; therefore, the receiving party usually will stay with only one Special Golden Shower "Giver" to assure personal health safety. "The Domme" Mistress/Goddess Anna was ALL of that, and more.

Patty was instructed to deliver Eddy into the walk-in shower when the kinky Trio were done with him and succeeded in getting him to "come out" AND give Eddy a Very special treatment today for the Boston Ball Club's contract. So Domme Patty sat him down on the built-in tiled seat, looked up and Eddy said, "It looks like rain!! Lol." They both enjoyed a laugh as Patty held Eddy's head steady for his fill of the blonde bombshell's long hot stream.

Patty ran back for Carol and her Master, abusing the Cross-dressing Fiancé Louie, who Now also had "come out" in a big way and wanted more and more dick now. Carol told her Cousin

in disbelief, Carol couldn't get the Sex Swing out her mind and begged Master T to put her up in it and fuck her while suspended in the air, and he swung back and forth while her wrists and ankles were tied up by her shoulders, exposing Carol's Meaty pussy and welcoming asshole on the edge of the seat for some (DP) Double Penetration, also reaching her G-Spot very Easily.

Being the aggressor that Carol always was towards her Cousin and Master/Anthony, she just took his hand and led him back there and stubbornly told her Master T, "I'm soaking wet for this, now pick me up and put me in that swing and Pump me, Fuck Both my holes, I'll pound back into you, I Can't wait, Master," Carol begged. "Patty! Make sure My Cuckold is watching this!! Your lipstick is smudged all over your face, " Carol yelled to her. "Cuck Louie Lipstick," that they all called him now.

Master T lifted his stubborn younger Goddess/Cousin Carol into the Sex Swing seat, then lifted her legs, ankles, and wrists high UP into the left restraints by her shoulders, and then the right side, exposing both her dripping holes down at the edge of the swing's seat.

Cousin Anthony/Master was just as excited as Carol now for the latest new sex toy on the market and penetrated her streaming Pussy slowly at first. Carol felt his 10" deeper than any time before she said, Master humped and pumped, pushing the kinky nymph Carol backwards, and she came back down violently into her Master humping his 10" over and over and finally let out her loud explosive scream when she squirted....

As Master took out his cum-covered cock to enter her oozing, winking asshole, reaching her G-Spot in yet another way, Carol was able to multi-Cum while her asshole was being fucked and that IS a hard thing to achieve, but her Master knew how to please her. Only her Master T,

Carol's cousin and Master, was actually now standing in a puddle of her unbelievable amount of Pussycum and her Master's cum was oozing out of her ass.

Patty dragged Louie Lipstick over by his leash to clean out her creampied ass with lipstick smeared all over his face while the three kinksters were enjoying this as Louie cleaned up their mess.

Carol was still panting and catching her breath from multiple orgasms she was having again, now that she got her Anthony/Master back, and asked Cousin Anthony if She and Patty could be on the "Receiving end of HIS Golden Shower." "We talked about it and want to see what all the Hype is about with Pee Play. So many kinksters Love it, I see, So We want to try it too, then Patty and I will give you yours that you love from us, Ok?"

The Master smiled and agreed, "Mistress should be done in there with Eddy, Then I'll sit you both down together and pee on those two awesome racks and lick them right after, but I'll give both of you a taste in your mouth too, I promise. Then you better be extra special for Your Master T," said excited Master T of this request.

"You can count on it, Master!!" replied an eager Patty, taking Carol's hand.

Patty checked the walk-in shower to make sure The Domme of the Golden Showers was done giving Eddy Dugan his fill of her tasty Yellow Rain. To Patty's surprise she was still at it with him and ordered Patty to watch her finale. The Goddess in High heels was squatting over Eddy's head, squeezing his face to open his mouth. Eddy was already lying in a puddle of his Domme's tasty piss, now giving Eddy more after drinking four large iced coffees.

Patty was watching and listening to her mentor DommeAnna order Eddy to

"Open your mouth." The Domme squirted a heavy thick stream of hot piss, filling Eddy's mouth, tilting his head forward towards her by his piss-soaked hair.

"Swallow that Piss!! You fucking Dog," slapping his face twice and asking Patty, "Do you see? Can you see and hear what the Piss lovers like? You do exactly what I do for this Piss head, and the others, and they will keep coming back for more, You believe your Mistress!!" said the Domme in a stern voice, making sure Eddy still had his mouth still opened.

The Domme aimed a last heavy spurt of her tasty PeeCum she had just masturbated into the Piss addict's drooling mouth while Patty was ordered to watch and learn for future "Golden Shower" clients Patty would soon have coming back for more.

"Wow," the Dominant Patty, now very impressed, said, "I will ENJOY giving the Showers immensely, my Mistress, you won't be disappointed whatsoever." Patty giggled.

Patty went back to the sauna, where the KinkyCousins were waiting and Carol drinking More Water for their Golden Shower session with Master T once Mistress let Eddy up from her GS session, then Patty and Carol would get to experience this taboo GS Fetish and give Master T what he enjoyed as well.

The coast was clear and Master T sat down Patty and Carol facing each other on a longer bench seat in the walk-In shower. Their Master/cousin ordered the two kinky FemDomme explorers to kiss and rub their firm titties against each other and share the new double-dong dildo, taking half each.

He caressed both of their heads and took aim while they kissed and released a hard Hot stream of built-up piss onto their two awesome sets of nipples and then up onto their faces as they were French kissing. They each let out a sigh of ooohs and awes to show their enjoyment for the taste of his hot salty piss, and to satisfy their craving for this Fetish that they LOVED doing to please their Master in this way.

To show his approval and appreciation, Master T began licking his own piss off them as he French kissed Both of his new Piss sluts back and forth.

Patty now took the Dominating position like her Mistress Anna and following her instructions, laying Master T on the tiled floor Eddy had laid in. Patty was showing and telling Carol what The Goddess, MommeDomme, had just done to Eddy and told Carol to "Watch this."

Domme Patty put on high heels to squat over their Master's face and squeezed his mouth open, ordering him to "Drink my Piss, OR Swallow that juice," then Carol would take a turn, then hold back, Patty would pee some more, then Carol, then both of them, one behind his head and one standing over his head while standing on his wrists, holding him down in place.

Master T was drowning in their hot piss AND their Mango-Cum as they Both Rubbed One Off on him from being SO horny doing this GS together, pleasing their Master one after the other.

CHAPTER

15

The four insatiable kinksters got to play a while today before business. Mistress was at her desk and waited for the kissing-kousins to sit as she curiously looked them all over. She Knew something went down, but she Had NO idea what her cloned gorgeous daughter was doing on her knees just a half-hour ago to please her Anthony/Master T.

The Boss "Domme" Auntie Anna started off by saying, "Good afternoon, you all look happy this morning, at least I am," glancing at her apprentice for a second, smiling as Patty nodded. President and CEO Anna DeNunzio, founder of "SIR" Sports Injury Rehabilitation, A Physical Massage Therapy Center, had structured her Corporation with the officers needed to start a Corporate Organization and ALL of the Kinkster/Partners had an equal share of "SIR" because They had All worked hard to

promote the New Legitimate venture. SIR would also Serve as a front for a much more lucrative enterprise for these four young Dominant sex-driven talented Fetish providers for their Mistress's long-time Clientele of Submissives, ranging from simple Prostate massages to Fisting their ass, Or a simple spanking and scolding to Whipping and Paddling you on the Wheel of torture until they pissed and came all over themselves, spinning around the remote-controlled wheel while tied up and stretched out.

"So today I'll reveal some names, and Fetishes they request and which one of you I think is best suited for each Client as you take them over while training with me in their sessions.

"The Sports teams, however! Boston Red Sox and Bruins clients will be treated as Non/Sexual! Until you know them personally, you consult with ME first. NEVER let your guard down and trust NOBODY who mentions money for sex. IT's a setup and you'll be busted on a recording. Simply say, 'NO, SIR, We DON'T do that sort of thing here. We will make enough money legitimately, and WE DON'T even need to go down that road.'

"Just for well-known established 'Special Clients' OR referrals by the established Clients we serve already like Evelyn or Eddy Showers that you all have met already, I'll give you each a list of a few more names coming in soon for their monthly, Bi/weekly or weekly sessions. I'm SO happy to have help now with talent beyond my dreams from My Master T and yours now too.

"Domme Patty! What else can I say about her Oral talents for Male OR Female? Carol, you're my daughter. Do whatever

you want when you're here to work on weekends, just Don't let me know, OK? My nephew Anthony/Master T is in charge of you. You consult with him and he has things for you to do.

"Patty, YOU consult with me, I own YOU all day at SIR except with Vanilla meetings and family times, then Master T is your Boyfriend like before so the kinky Cousins don't cause problems within our family or her engagement," the Domme said, glancing at Carol's stubborn smirking face. "Master T, my nephew Anthony, spoiled her rotten, now HE will take care of her, ha-ha," she added.

Master was working hard on the "Grand Opening" party where family, friends and low-key Special clients would get invited to The Roof Lounge Party. Then the Clients that needed discretion like the Ballplayers and married clients Or the Professions, CEOs and Execs that DIDN'T want to be seen out at Events, they would come to another party more exciting and Private, soon.

"So read your paperwork and sign them, then look at the names and Fetishes with the billing or cash next to each name. I'll go over them in a few minutes, each of you bring your own stuff to our lawyer Evan's office and I want you ALL to get to know him better. It's not just Me on this one," the Boss Domme Anna continued. "How's your 'New house' coming along, Carol?"

MommeDomme, Patty, And Master enjoyed a big smile as Carol just stared, smirking at the quick-witted MommeDomme.

"Like I said before to ALL of you, Money ISN'T everything so don't get greedy and be careful with new clients we don't know. Just Massage Therapy, not even a hand job!" said the wise Domme.

A lot of Invitations were sent out already, mostly family and friends, Anthony's bosses from the Market, North End friends, East Boston friends and some of My old friends. In two weeks the roof party would be a nice touch from all the hard work we'd done so far.

"So with that said, I want you ALL to meet an old associate and 'friend of mine' now to become a 'friend of Ours,' THE MOST beautiful She-Male, Female impersonating dancer YOU will ever see, OR I have ever seen and have had the pleasure to work with, When she's available, that is, lol. I met Her/Him at the Green Apple nightclub on Rte. 1 in Saugus, having a drink after work during my Parisian Sauna days.

"She goes by only 'Varney,' Sunny Varinella is her name but you didn't hear that from me, 5'9", Blonde, long beautiful legs, and the best 38DD implants ever. They look like Our Patty's big natural beauties, she's got a fully functional 10" like Our Master's. Blue eyes and sooo fucking pretty, you would NEVER know she packed a 10" dick, and the perfect heart-shaped ass ever, like mine and Carol's. I Even used her a few times myself, lol," Domme Anna joked.

"There are two couples and an (alleged) E. Boston retired Mafia enforcer I went to school with named Nicky," the Domme told her crew. "I named him Nicky Nipples in the old Journal,

just smile while you whip him hard across the Nipples. The two couples want Me and Varney only but I want them to meet all of you now because Varney is just too hard to get anymore, SHE'S that good!" The Domme giggled.

"The two couples are Lenny Bolanese and Allie from NBC, then there's Millionaire Paul Travilla and his wife Lisa, who loves Dominance and three-ways with Bi/women. So I want Patty on them for sure, OR if Carol wants to try, you two work it out. They're going to love Both of you! By the way, Patty, My EVE-LYN asked about you for next weekend AGAIN! My slut!" Mistress added.

Patty nodded and smiled in agreement. "Oh, yes, My Mistress! I'll pick her up in My new outfit she likes, YOU just tell me when," Patty said happily.

"So YOU'RE going to be busy and Master T will have to join us in Evelyn's session or maybe Carol because My little Angel never seen what the Masochist Evelyn turns into when she's being pushed to her limits by Forced Domination inflicting pain."

Each session Evelyn had asked for harder limits, along with more passion.

"Omg, Evelyn come like a fire hose last session. Carol, you have to join me on this one!" Patty remembered as they all laughed.

"The two couples are here next week. I want to try Master T on each of the women with one lady in a strap-on. Allie called me and asked to be DP'd without Lenny knowing she requested this for herself, just have the Dildo in her ass laying on one of the girls

189

on her back while Master T pounds her pussy from on top while she sucks her husband Lenny off. I'm sure he'll watch and enjoy his wife screaming and squirting all over him. Allie will love it, it'll spice things up a bit for them. Allie loves to be aggressive like you, Carol, with your cousin/Master, SO YOU TWO do that one, OK?" MommeDomme smiled to the 1st Cousins.

"For sure, Mistress, Sounds like fun," Master said.

"MORE Than happy to do it," Carol added, not really knowing or sure what to call her DOMME MOM just yet.

"Mistress," Master T suggested, "I got a call from Alice in the North End that I mentioned to you about before, she had my two work buddies over and wanted Another guy too. Alice likes at least three BIG cocks at once standing in a circle while she sucks them off, making noises, and I told her YOU would love to watch that someday. I want you to meet her soon AND I can get those two guys, Joey C and Carmen, to do DPs or use them in certain sessions, IF YOU give the OK," Master T suggested.

"FOR SURE, Master, YOU make the decision if you know them personally, as long as they're safe and clean," Mistress agreed, smiling.

"Fuck Yea!" Carol added, looking at her cousin Master T and Patty laughing out loud.

"Can we pick them up next week with you, Master?" Patty added, smiling, stroking his arm.

"OK, Let's focus here!" the Domme said. "Have you ALL been to see Evan at our lawyer's office? Did YOU, Carol, give

your signed paperwork that I also signed for him and your Lenny Lipstick to sign?" MomDomme asked firmly.

"Yes, I did, all set, now let's see how it goes, and the house is just about done too."

Carol was still explaining about her Movie contract that Louie said she may have to go to California to shoot more scenes, "and I may have to show my nipples and breasts, I'm NOT going to California to do Porn, I'm here for My Family business now."

"NO! You won't! Don't worry about that, I wrote something nice Evan told me to write and we ALL signed it, So Fuck Him! You stay here with us And YOU get the house too. These movie guys that LOVE using and exploiting women can burn in fucking hell. They want trophy wives for appearances' sake, then put on their wives' lipstick and panties," the angry DommeMomme joked to her cloned daughter. "We will tear him a brand-new asshole here in Boston. He came to the wrong city!" the Goddess/Domme angrily stated. "Let's go over today's agenda now!"

Mistress looked to Master T first and asked if He invited Alice and his two Work friends from the North End to the Grand Opening for SIR. Then she suggested having them for a few upcoming sessions.

Master T quickly responded, "Yes, Mistress, I invited all three and my bosses Freddy and Sonny as well. They all know each other from the N. End. Mistress Alice is a counselor with a Physical Therapist and Radiology degree working at the Linderman

Center in Boston, Alice is just like us, a real kinkster Mistress that loves to explore and her ex/husband couldn't handle.

She even wants ME to drive up to the Tobin Bridge toll booths, where her Ex/husband will be collecting tolls while she is blowing me with his favorite N.Y. Yankees Hat on." Master laughed.

"Alice will hand him the 15 cents for the toll, then after HE says thank you, she will look up and say 'thank you' while drooling saliva from her mouth and tipping the Yankees Cap, laughing."

"WOW!" The Domme/Mistress laughed, and everyone enjoyed a great laugh.

"Alice's Ex/husband left her scared after learning He left her for another MAN. She has been having revenge sex with all of us younger Italian guys from Haymarket Produce Market,

'Every Weekend'! On her days off Alice has fucked or sucked at least nine out of the twelve young dicks from East Boston and the N. End. The other three have steady girlfriends, lol, but they're tempted. She's very kinky with a great body, being in her 30s. Alice wants and needs two-three at a time or more and she's asking ME if she can get us all together," Master concluded.

"I'd say she's a little pissed off," the Domme/Mistress shot back, and Patty laughed so hard she was crying and fell off the chair. We ALL laughed so hard for at least ten whole minutes.

As I was talking, Carol was drawing her Fantasy for me to make happen like she always did. I knew she was drawing Me and my two friends 'Gang-bangin' Carol in a DP style. Sure enough It was, with a quote saying "Make it happen...!"

"I'm yours, Master T, Your slut I crave to be." As Cousin Carol handed me the folded sketch she added, "THAT story made ME soaking wet, Can WE take a ride over the Tobin Bridge tonight, Pleeeez? I'll wear your Red Sox cap," Carol giggled to her lover and Master, cousin Anthony.

"Next on our list is the scheduled sessions for the next four days, then three days off. We will do a four-day week with four people and have plenty of time for ourselves. There was a request from the Red Sox star player for Patty, Eddy Showers' son called and said He wants to meet you, lol! He asked about you and if you were involved with anyone, I told him I'll ask you if you're interested. Reel him In, Sweetie," Mistress suggested. "He's loaded, BIG money contract this guy just signed with the Sox, AND he's only 21!" The Mentor Domme smiled to her apprentice Patty.

"Just Don't forget Who you belong to! You Promised to Obey and Never stray!" Master T quoted her BDism oath.

"I NEVER WILL STRAY, MY MASTER, This here is My life now! What you three have done for me I'll NEVER forget," Patty responded, looking her Master T in the eye, then glancing over to Her Mistress.

"WE know, Patty! He's only teasing you!" Mistress added, lol. "We don't mind if you Fuck the guy, though, that's all he wants anyway, Just another BIG fish with Money. Reel him In, honey; You have MY permission," the Domme added.

"So, Lenny and Allie will be first this week, pick them up in Charlestown, Patty, and then you all get to meet the prettiest

She-Male you ever saw, with a big dick and the best expensive L.A. boob job ever. He/she will be for our millionaire Clients, Paul and Lisa Travello."

"Master, you make plans for a few days out to get your two friends for Allie and Lenny, then dinner with Me AND your friends," as the Domme/AuntieAnna told her Dominate Master/ Nephew in his ear on the way out. "Do whatever you want to me...," his Auntie teased.

"OH, I CAN'T WAIT, My Mistress!" Nephew/Master T concluded.

The four-day weekly agenda was already full. Even an eight-day agenda would fill up fast for these HOT and talented kinkster "Fetish Providers."

Patty was on her way to pick up Lenny and Allie, this couple lived in a new Condo in Charlestown, the very next town over, bordered with the N. End, and Lenny worked in Walking distance to Channel 7 TV station in Boston, AND Channel 2 in NYC as well.

Lenny was 25, 5'10", maybe 180 and toned, in great shape. His wife Allie was 22, great solid smaller tits, great legs with a hard rounded ass. He made six figures and was IN-LOVE with his Swedish Blonde that wanted to explore with other couples and had a Fantasy she wanted to turn into a steady Fetish and share it with him, but he hadn't come around to sharing her YET!

So that was why Allie's arrangement with their Domme Anna was a private call. Lenny had an expense account with NBC and

Varney, the very Passable She/Male, Don't come cheap. Mistress figured that if Lenny saw a woman with a big dick HE may consider Varney just another Lady with a dildo strap-on or fisting Allie's pussy, Needing to be filled as usual in their three-ways, but Allie wanted two or three guys in her fantasy and Not another woman with a strap-on or toys. Allie wanted the real DP deal, Double Penetration in BOTH her holes OR even two cocks in either her pussy or asshole. Allie wanted to be stretched out in Both holes and pounded HARD, she insisted while her husband watched her, not really a cuckold situation but more a slut/whore voyeur-type session showing Lenny what she wanted to do sexually while exploring her "Darkside," as we say in the BDism lifestyle. AND Allie had some Fantasies for her husband as well.

Mistress assured Allie, "One way or another, YOU will get what you need today and Master T May also participate because he has already established a friendship with Lenny, talking sports, and both love Corvettes, and When Lenny sees Varney HE may want HER too, cock and all!" Mistress told Allie confidently.

Allie responded, "YES! I'D LOVE THAT, MISTRESS!!! See if Master T can talk to him, OK?"

"Done!" the Domme Quickly responded to Allie.

Mistress called for Master T to intervene and get Patty to have Varney AND Master in the Mercedes when Allie was picked up and Master knowing Lenny would introduce Varney as his date for the swap party session.

Allie LOVED MISTRESS' IDEA at this point where they were all happy and talking and Lenny was saying how Pretty Master's date was, and he Couldn't wait to Start in the new Dungeon with the new S&M equipment.

Lenny had NO IDEA He was about to witness two ten-inchers in his lovely insatiable Swedish bombshell wife, at the same time pounding her while she blew Lenny's smaller thick 7" dick.

As They all entered the hall leading to the Sauna and Jacuzzi where Master wanted to start this off slowly and get Lenny's further approval of the voluptuous and gorgeous She/male Varney, Lenny played with Varney's revealing tits and ass in her expensive tight Gucci skirt and vest suit. Master T, Varney and Allie enjoyed a nice private giggle, lol. Needless to say Varney was flattered as always but was enjoying THIS session immediately because He/She was completely comfortable around Master T, and even if Lenny didn't approve Varney could just walk away, WITH the money too, BUT that was NOT going to happen at all, NOT by a long shot!

Lenny not only approved of Master T exploring with his Precious voyeur Blonde nymph wife Allie, even when it came time to stand up and out of the jacuzzi, VARNEY had taken off HIS bikini bottom revealing A long hard 10" just like Master T did, and they were both holding their cocks in their hands and walking towards Allie while she was laughing.

All Lenny could say was "WOW! YOU PLAYED ME REAL GOOD! LOL," and he just laughed about it and said, "HEY, WHY NOT! I LOVE YOU, BABY," he said to wife Allie.

The party was started, and We walked Allie over to the massage table for a four-hand warmed oil massage while Lenny was told to have Allie Suck his cock while Master And Varney fucked her ass and Pussy from the other end of Allie, which was her "DP" fantasy today arranged by The Domme/Anna, "A Double Penetration."

Lenny would have to hold up her long legs in certain positions to lay down on her back with Varney's cock in her ass while Master T pounded her streaming pussy. Lenny was getting tempted and sucking on Varney's perfect 38DD implants, Varney even grazed him a few times with his 10" to see if he would start to blow him in the position HE/SHE was in while fucking the Swede Allie's hard heart-shaped ass while Master T drilled her into a puddle, squirting all over everything and everyone.

Varney did notice Lenny had grabbed his cock when Nobody was looking, however, and now sensed he could get the two voyeurs to share his 10" she/male dick by having Allie lay on Lenny's cock in her ass and Varney standing, feeding the Swede's full pink sensual lips. Varney's cock would be RIGHT THERE at Lenny's eye level, all Varney would have to do was FEED IT to Lenny as well, and that was just what Varney did!!!

Lenny took a look around and NOBODY was looking, NOT Master, NOT his precious blonde wife, SO LENNY WENT FOR THE HARD 10" And Varney's balls too, Varney told to Master T and Mistress later.

Lenny was sucking on Varney right after his cock had been taken from Allie's Ass, but Lenny didn't seem to care, he was that

turned on by this whole session with his wife Allie's moaning and squirting, having Multiple Orgasms over and over until EVERY-ONE came on Allie for Lenny to watch Allie rubbing cum onto her milky-white Swedish skin, looking towards Lenny for his approval.

Husband Lenny DID APPROVE, alright, Totally! Then booked future sessions for the first of EVERY MONTH, requesting two or three men for the kinky Voyeur couple, courtesy of their NBC expense account.

MomDomme continued lecturing her distracted daughte6r, TRYING her hardest to keep Carol to stay with her Art profession and come home weekends to work at SIR, which she would hold a major interest in every way eventually. Cousin Carol would, of course, stay with her Soulmate/Master to keep her relationship with her Alpha Male counterpart in HIS Condo.

All that was on the beautiful young Goddess Carol's mind today was her Master coming back home to fuck her hard against the wall and listen to the China cabinet plates rattle while she squirted all over his hard 10" dick, but Not only that, today Carol was expecting to be gangbanged by Cousin Anthony and his two friends he mentioned to the Domme already.

Carol had already drawn it out on paper for her Cousin/ Master and we all know now HE HAD spoiled The Nymph to no end. Master T had the go-ahead for a few wealthy "Special Clients" with some recent special requests for DP exploration and gangbang Domination for the Rich Developer Paul Travello and wife Lisa.

Master T was on his way to pick up his two friends today, along with Alice in the N. End, and introduce the trio to his Goddess/Domme Auntie Anna.Au

His buddies would each get 50 bucks for the use of their 10", and fucked and sucked ALL day long with beautiful young kinky beautiful woman. The Client would be charged $500 for Discreet special requests. The two friends Joey C and Carmen just had to get blown by a guy once in a while (just close your eyes).

"Look at Patty or Carol, that should be there too," Master T told them, "a mouth is a mouth!"

They all laughed.

Alice was already addicted to Anthony/Master T and his two buddies' big cocks that she had been chasing on weekends while they worked at Haymarket, getting the much younger sex-hungry hung guys over to her condo.

Alice sucked them all off until she drained their young balls and loved to swallow it all. Alice would get a LOT of Revenge Sex after her Ex-Husband left her for another man with these 21-year-old horny exploring boys, Ouch!

TODAY Master T was taking the Tobin Bridge So Alice could fulfill her request to Anthony months ago. Alice's Ex worked as a toll collector on the Tobin Bridge in a small booth, when you pulled up to pay your toll and handed over 15 cents, the collector said, "Thank you," and you said, "You're welcome." SO today Alice would be sucking Master T's big cock for her EX to see,

ALICE planned to hand over the 15 cents WHILE SUCKING COCK in her Ex's favorite NY YANKEES HAT she stole from his stuff, THEN TRY to say "thank you" with her mouth full of cock!!

Master T was in his Corvette with the T-Tops off, so it was looking just like a convertible today, it was very OPEN, Alice's Ex-Husband could see his Yankees hat perfectly bobbing up and down on a huge dick. Master/Anthony's friends were behind him in Joey's car just in case of a chase, Joey would interfere and cut them off.

They COULDN'T WAIT for this to play out, Joey and Carmen had been laughing and waiting ALL MORNING for CRAZY Alice to perform this revenge sex fantasy on kinky friend Master T.

As Anthony said, "Good Morning, buddy," the Ex saw he was getting a blowjob while taking the toll from Alice's left hand and said, "YES! YOU are Definitely having a great morning," the ex/husband laughed, then noticed his N.Y. cap! AND her wedding ring. "HEY! WAIT! YOU Motherfucker! I'LL KILL YOU! MY FUCKIN' WIFE??? MY FUCKING YANKEE HAT!!" the Ex/hubby screamed and ran out from the toll booth.

Master T sped away in the 454 Corvette while ALICE was waving His Yankees hat and we both were giving him the finger as he ran out of the booth and into the lane to yell at us. Joey pulled right up to his back and HONKED the horn, scaring the piss out of him as he slapped the hood of Joey's car, then went back into his booth, TRUE STORY!!

We ALL enjoyed this story for years to come! Alice LOVED ME for doing that revenge sex fantasy for her, but I was just happy to ease her pain and help put it behind her!

Alice, Mistress/Anna, Cousin Carol, Patty, Joey And Carmen ALL told this story at parties and it was STILL just as funny today as it was that Special day in the summer of 1973.

Patty had just picked up millionaire Paul Travello and his wife Grace in her sexy, skimpy driving attire, and his wife was in awe of the young beautiful driver Patty and stroked her shoulder, looking over from the back seat of the Mercedes, and asked if her tits were real.

"FEEL THEM," Patty permitted to Grace, and so she did!

"WOW! You are beautiful, young lady," said the 45-year-old spoiled kinky trophy wife.

"Thank You," Patty said politely, "Master T will be delivering your two guys in a few moments and I'm sure you both will be very pleased today. IF there's ANYTHING else you may need before I drive you there just LET ME KNOW," Patty Curiously asked.

"OH!" said Grace quickly. "I think I may ask Mistress Anna if YOU can join us. Is THAT something YOU DO, or you just drive?" the wife now CURIOUSLY asked an excited Patty.

Patty in turn replied, "I can do whatever you want me to do. Just put your request in with Master T to OK it and what YOU will request from Me. YOU are very pretty, Grace, and I'd LOVE to join you and Paul today," Patty added, and Paul nodded in agreement to wife Grace."

"Soooo, We're gonna need a bigger bed, lol," Grace excitingly suggested and rubbed her hubby's cock in anticipation of adding a beautiful blonde woman to their session today.

As Master T pulled up with Alice, Joey pulled up parking behind the yellow Corvette and met Paul and Grace inside for the three-on-one OR possibly four-on-two session when Patty got her OK and the PRICE was adjusted.

Patty had a personal persuasion to match her talent, skills and her looks. Price made NO difference to the WEALTHY kinksters exploring their Darkside, also spicing up their 20-yr. sexually happy marriage. Grace wanted what she wanted AND Paul GOT it done for her like Anthony spoiled his Cousin Carol.

"A happy wife IS a happy life," Paul told Master T on the way to the Sauna first to start things off, relaxing in the tub waiting for Patty and the boys to put on skimpy bathing suits to have drinks and enjoy in some intelligent conversation with the educated married couple of 20 years and NEEDED to know you were worthy of their submission in this BDism Darkside kinky play.

Mistress/Domme Anna came highly recommended and now she had New partners that NEEDED to be felt out by most to be reassured of the Discretion that was VERY IMPORTANT to the prominent Celebrities that could RUIN careers and their livelihoods.... Today, Grace wanted ALL three of Her holes filled at once forcefully and dominated with her husband being one of them watching and participating.

Grace now wanted to add Patty's neatly trimmed pussy to suck on, play with her DDs, and had NO idea just how Dominant Patty was, and would LOVE Domme Patty's Domination for sure. Joey and Carmen would be the two other cocks taking her pussy and asshole hard, passing her around like a ten whore and calling her filthy dirty names, which she LOVED to be called, whore, slut, cocksucker, filthy Pig, cumSlut, And Sex-Slave. Patty got the "information" on WHAT Grace wanted to do today and LOVED what she heard from the Domme: "OH, yes! I WILL give her dominance, Mistress Anna taking her orders for the session, lol."

After a few drinks and a few laughs, Patty started to pinch Grace's long nipples and commented on how hard they'd become in the water and wanted to take her over to the table with the guys now, also playing with her as her husband Paul kissed her in comfort, relaxing her.

Grace was melting and jerking both hard cocks at the table while Patty had three fingers in her pussy now, twisting her 4th finger in Grace's soaking-wet, cock-starving Pussy.

Paul stopped kissing for a moment when Patty took Grace by the hair and forced Grace to blow the 11" cock on Joey and let out a choking cough, taking at least half the huge cock eagerly and forcefully at the same time.

"Take them slowly," her husband suggested, smiling.

"OMG, I LOVE IT," Grace told Patty face to face, now kissing Patty.

"Make me do More, Patty! I want ALL three in Me, Please Do it, DP me, you guys! I NEED THIS SO BAD!"

Grace moaned as Patty took a small whip and put Grace on all fours and told her to crawl to cock #1, Carmen, and then ordered her to SIT on it and ride him while Patty whipped her ass hard and had Joey put his huge 11" in her asshole to "DP" Grace while she blew her husband. Patty was pinching and slapping her stone-hard nipples and whispered in her ears with a firm Domme voice, "What a filthy fucking Slut You are!" Slapping her face lightly, looking to Push her limits, She then called her more names Patty knew Grace liked to hear and whispered again, "You are A Cocksucking, asslicking, Pig," and slapped her harder and told her to "eat Carmen's ass NOW, you fucking whore!"

Grace started moaning while screaming into multi/orgasms one after the other as Paul was smiling ear to ear, listening to his wife's appreciation and gratitude for Domme Patty now building a name for herself.

Patty made Grace eat and tongue everyone's ass for the next 20 minutes while being fucked repeatedly and alternately by the two hard young big cocks in both holes while Patty HELD her down! Slut wife Grace was squirting like she was sixteen years old again and couldn't have thanked Patty enough on the way out, crying like a baby in complete satisfaction, and booked Domme Patty for BI/WEEKLY private sessions, and DP sessions with and without her husband with his approval, of course.

Master T and his two work buddies were relaxing with a few cold ones, still laughing their balls off since Alice's Tobin Bridge fantasy. Anthony/Master T to the BDism world helped his friends understand a little what was exactly going on. As their work buddy, friend now since Eastie boys were working alongside of N. End Fruit peddlers, Fathers, sons, Uncles, cousins, WE ALL had a certain bond also, WE had each other's back, AND one thing for sure, WE ALL waited for Alice to show up to give a few of us a well-deserved blowjob Or a ride on our young hard Italian cocks. ALICE LOVED ITALIANS!! She liked to suck on BIG dicks while using her toys on her pussy at the condo, she knew the three biggest cocks out of nine of us Alice would always look for first, ME 10", Joey 11" and Carmen 10" respectively. Alice was very kinky too, along with being very intelligent. She hung degrees over her desk just like My Goddess Auntie Anna. She was a Physical Therapist and a Psychology major Just like Mistress Auntie Anna too.

I JUST HAD TO introduce them and today was the day since I was going to the N. End for the guys. Alice always listened to me tell her ALL ladies I was involved with were ALL Bi/sexual. They all liked Pussy but NOT as much as good young hard cocks in them.

Alice was NOT surprised from the "psychological stand-point," she explained. "Women ALWAYS look at other women MORE than Men look at other men sexually," Alice told me. "I may try A nice pussy someday, who knows?" Alice giggled.

"I KNEW IT," I said to myself. I just HAD to let MY MIS-TRESS/Anna talk to Alice for ten minutes OR Patty in five minutes, lol, and Alice would be on her knees eating both of the Persuasive Femme Dommes TOGETHER.

Alice and Carol were on the roof, where I left them planting flowers and decorating for our Grand Opening coming up. I told Alice to take a ride to My Mistress Anna's and Carol to "The fantasy drawing of the three Guys" that she had placed in my pocket last week.

On the way Carol laughed and said, "Alice, I was so happy what YOU two did on the Tobin Bridge, AND Did you say three guys, Master? I thought there were two," Carol remembered.

Then I corrected Carol and said, "Joey, Carmen AND MASTER T IS THREE."

TODAY I planned on Carol's gangbang she drew out on paper, and My Mistress Anna to OPEN UP Alice into her "Darkside," to put Alice's guilty feelings behind her for what her husband did to her psychologically.

The three of us walked up to the Penthouse, where Mistress Anna was expecting me to introduce Alice. Alice was promised and expecting a massage today, and also to see the New MRI Scanner/Physical Therapy Establishment to get Alice ON BOARD as a Technician. ALICE WAS WELL QUALIFIED for Our new SIR Venture, AND at the same time while Alice got a four-handed massage by Patty and her mentor Mistress Anna,

ALICE would be squirting in no time at all on the table with these two savages for a good-looking woman with a great body that Alice DID have! THEN we could Collar Alice and get her onboard with ALL of us Kinksters, where Alice belonged!

My two hung friends, Joey and Carmen, were in MY SUITE waiting for me to deliver Cousin Carol to fulfill her Fantasy of Multiple cocks she craved lately, THEN to visit MY cock-hungry Mistress AuntieAnna for a last three-on-one with The Domme to finish a long day testing their Stamina at the same time, A Mother/Daughter three-on-one, but in separate rooms.

I told Carol to shower and wait for us in a nice S&M corset and heels in the room as I took the guys to the rooftop lounge to show it off to them and to wait for me to get back in a few minutes.

I was running back and forth like a crazy man, organizing TWO Fantastic Fantasies at the same time, and just decided to leave the three girls to work out the Massage scenario with Alice first, then EITHER ONE of them would tell me EVERYTHING later.

I needed to get Carol's "Fantasy Drawing" done first as I always did to Please Carol, My Younger Goddess and kinky female cousin counterpart. I yelled up to the guys to come down to my Condo and meet My excited Carol.

I walked my half-naked Cousin Carol out to the couch where they were sitting and told them to stand up, then sat her down in my office swivel chair. I lowered the chair ALL the way down for her to swivel back and forth from one big cock to another with her hands tied behind her back while I whipped her Unique

visibly throbbing nipples lightly. The studs were STUNNED by
seeing such amazing large purple nipples that matched her stunning purple eyes. The guys were so hard and horny from the sight
of her, they immediately went into fuck mode as Carol bent over
the swivel chair, NEEDING to be fucked.

So I walked my dripping-wet Cousin over to the table, sat her
up to eat up her MangoJuice while she continued to suck two big
hard cocks uncontrollably while streaming her pussycum for her
Master to enjoy.

The Mangopussycum of My young Nympho Goddess Carol I
was addicted to just kept flowing when I'd given her the Fantasies
she demanded from me EVERY TIME! Carol WAS The biggest
Multi/Cummer I'd ever seen! Carol had her collar on like I told
her to and I connected her leash onto the collar and passed her
around the room, Fucking her three holes to WHOEVER took
the leash from WHEREVER she was taken from in the room. We
ALL ended up in the bed with three dicks in ALL her holes while
Crying in tears holding on to her Master T, just calling out for
more and Moaning like the Nymphomaniac Carol was.

Carol was squirting pussycum all over everyone and everything, I told the guys to cum on her tits to finish her off and that
ONLY ME, MASTER T, could cum in My cousin Carol's mouth
while she happily opened her mouth wide for ONLY COUSIN/
ANTHONY, MASTER T.

Master T now told Joey and Carmen to go see how Alice was
doing with the two Natural-born Dommes Mistress Anna and

MY Vanilla Girlfriend Patty. I left Alice talking to My Mistress and Patty while getting the free Full treatment for prominent and Classy women, the 4handed massage OR electric Vibrating massage with warmed flavored oil moisturizer, a manicure, pedicure, sauna, steam, jacuzzi, and "Happy ending," IF requested.

Alice was tall for a woman, 5'7", 130, toned-out and long curvy legs, normal-size 34C with Cherry nipples and a smooth, firm, Great Ass, however, to make up for everything she may be lacking on beauty, but NOT ugly by any means. Alice could suck cock ALL DAY long and that was ALL that mattered to most guys anyway, AND SHE LOVED TO SWALLOW, every drop, lol. "The bigger the cock, the better!" Alice said.

Joey checked in on Alice like I told him to do and I/Master T also wanted to see this for myself so I decided to find Joey, who was taking too long. The three ladies were softly kissing on each other everywhere and were partially dressed in S&M gear Mistress Anna was trying on with Alice. She was exploring with her Darkside having Alice watch Patty lick Domme Anna into an orgasm that turned Alice on immediately and wanted some pussylicking as well. So Alice ASKED Patty if she could lick HER pussy too.

Mistress Anna caressed, nibbled, twisted and sucked on Alice's firm, standing Cherry nipples, in a milking technique that drove Alice wild as Alice played with the Domme's long black hair while she nursed from Alice.

DommePatty was bringing Alice to the ultimate orgasm with the electric massager, along with her full hot lips, suckling on

Alice's very Meaty labia and erect clit. Patty also rimmed her lubed-up ass, tonging it deep, in and out.

Alice had submitted totally to NO surprise to me as they Both held Alice in position by the Two Dommes to have Alice TASTE HER FIRST PUSSY.

Domme Patty held Alice's arms out by the wrist and was kissing her belly up to her nipples and back down again slowly. Their Dominating Mistress Anna was on the other end facing Patty and smiling as she squatted and humped over Alice's mouth and visible tongue flicking the Beautiful Goddess. Alice was gasping on dripping pussycum into Alice's squeezed open mouth. The Domme's free hand was caressing Alice's hard standup Cherry nipples between her skilled fingers, making Alice Explode in Patty's face while Alice's face was smothered and covered in the Mistress Anna's cream. Alice was making her demonic growling sounds again just like she did when sucking multiple cocks when she drained her young studs on Saturdays and Sundays.

"Alice, you're a natural, are YOU SURE you NEVER licked a pussy before, lol?" said the Domme, quivering her last drops into Alice's mouth and smiling.

"NO, NEVER, Mistress Anna, and I do want to try Patty now too, OK? I love the warm cum, so please feel free to give it all to me, and you too, Patty," Alice begged. "I LOVE the guys when they cum in my mouth, THIS should be even more fun since WE ladies can squirt a LOT more." Alice giggled. TRYING to say it

with Domme Anna still riding her mouth at the same time only now even harder as the Domme started squirting hard!

As The Domme/Mistress Anna stopped humping, she grabbed onto Alice's hair with both hands. I could see the juice squirting into Alice's mouth.

I could hear the brief choking as Alice was taking ALL Domme Anna's hard squirting stream down her throat, swallowing the hot MangoJuice just like Alice did for her Multiple men on Saturdays and Sundays.

Patty immediately hopped on Alice's mouth when MY Mistress/Domme Anna signaled Patty with her finger to Alice's mouth to "get on top! And give Alice More Pussy/Mango she said she loved."

I NOW made Myself visible and told Mistress Anna, who had just released a gallon of cream and HotMango down Alice's throat, "The guys will see YOU, now follow me." Master ordered his Mistress Auntie Anna, now HIS Property.

"Yes, my Master T, I've been waiting to serve you, Sir!"

As the Goddess submitted, I took her hand and walked her to the eager Big-cock studs along with Myself to USE My Goddess/Aunt Anna alternately Gang-Bang style and to Fuck her HARD like she was asking for.

My Domme/Mistress Aunt once again whispered in my ear, "DO WHATEVER YOU WANT TO ME! SIR, Only for you! I will submit to ONLY you that I have groomed and trust in ways I NEED from only you, That Only YOU know how to do to me.

I promise to OBEY AND NEVER STRAY," she would always say, "THAT is our oath! THAT IS OUR OATH to each other!" Mistress added, "I will give YOU whatever YOU NEED when you're DONE using me, I will start to include Alice along with Patty and Myself in YOUR Golden Shower sessions IF you would like three women for your Fetish, Master!" my Domme and also MY Submissive added to my surprise.

I told the guys to wait In Mistress/Anna's office and We would Fuck the Life out of her in there while Carol wasn't around to get herself in the middle. The DommeMomme didn't want sex play with her daughter, AT LEAST NOT YET! Carol didn't seem to care WHO it was when it came to sex, although the old-school Momme did.

As I took My Domme/Auntie Anna's hand and sat her down between my buddies, I knelt down and kissed her deeply and pushed her back on the extra-large sofa and lifted her skirt, NO panties to reveal her beautiful legs and groomed pussy for the guys to see in AWE!

"She is so beautiful, Anthony. YOU are the luckiest guy ever and I want to be Collared BY THIS ONE for sure, I will do anything. I'D even suck your dick to get to her pussy," Joey added (unintentionally), OR was it?

"YOU KNOW, there is meaning to what you just said, young man!" the quick-witted Domme told Joey, "just ask, that's what WE do here, WE explore people's 'Darkside' and IF you have one 'I' PERSONALLY will bring it out of you, AND YES, I

WANT TO COLLAR YOU AND YOU WILL BELONG TO ME and Master T next week, OK?"

The Domme/Goddess Anna nodded as she ran her sweating hands on their naked thighs and slid off the couch to her knees to suck the three Huge young hard cocks while her Master was using his wide black leather belt on her heart-shaped ass while she gagged but enjoyed ALL three guys, one at a time.

I told Joey to sit and put My Mistress facing him and then leaned her forward to put Carmen's cock in My Goddess' Asshole, then told Joey to bury his 11" in her streaming cum-soaked pussy, A BEAUTIFUL DOUBLE PENETRATION to see, while her Master was Pumping her throat behind the couch as all three holes were being violated like The Domme asked her Master for.

My Mistress Auntie Anna was being fucked DP style so hard by my friends' two big cocks that were fascinated by her beauty, that she started squirting enough HotCum to fill a river and soaked the coach and all three of us. My Submitted/Domme Aunt was throating my 10" so deep and hard, I thought Patty had been giving her lessons.

I was starting to cum and wanted to shoot it on her tits, but the Cock-Hungry Auntie Anna held My cock in her mouth and wouldn't stop until she took it all in her mouth to show it to me just for fun, then swallowed it while the guys also watched her show us the cum, then kept fucking the Goddess even harder into another puddle of Auntie's hot creamy MangoCum I was addicted to for life.

All in all it was a very productive day, to say the least in our world of BDism, and added a few more players and Professional services from Alice and two more "Collared and Owned" young studs for My Goddess's collection to service her needs and the needs of her clientele! The Domme would also start to EX-PLORE Joey's Darkside that caught her ear and her EYES.

Needless to say, Joey And Carmen were drenched in pussy-cum that was squirting everywhere Just like I Told them she did, AND her daughter Carol could do as much if not more.

When THEY started to have an orgasm, it turned into a "series" of multiple orgasms they couldn't control and that was when I just buried my face In EITHER pussy and tried to drink as much MangoJuice down as I could.

Carol's Cum was fucking Delicious!! And I was addicted to Her sweet Hot MangoCum, Or her Pee!! Carol always drank Iced Coffee with four sugars and could be the reason why, Just sayin'....

The guys were begging already to come back next week, for Free! They Didn't want the Money, they said, "Just pick us up any time, Anthony, we LOVE this place and You're the luckiest guy EVER. Wow, You take care of all this? We want to help you, my friend! You know Me and Carmen Won't say a word to ANYONE about the Fetish-providing part, We're N. End guys Just like YOU for life and would 'NEVER RAT' On anyone, 'Especially a guy like You'!!! I like my life, LOL," Joey Respectfully added to his work buddy.

"OK, Joey! But there are BDism rules, and You both will have to be 'Collared and Owned' by My Mistress Aunt Anna or Domme Patty. I will belong to Carol, Will YOU BOTH accept the conditions??" the Master asked Joey and Carmen.

"Yes, Yes, Yes! Fuck Yes!!" Joey yelled and hugged his buddy Anthony/Master T.

"There's one more thing before I go get Alice after her Massage and take her back to the N. End. We're going to do a three-on-one with The Domme, MY Aunt Anna, I OWN HER NOW!! I'll explain all of it to you both when we have a final Sit-Down, Gabeesh?" the Master said.

"Anything you say, Anthony," the two sex-hungry hung studs anxiously replied at the same time to an intimidating and worried Master T.

CHAPTER

16

It was looking like Mistress Anna had a lot on her agenda for the upcoming week ahead. Dealing with Carol and Louie's drama engagement, replied to invitations coming in all at once, she wanted to be sure the roof garden was to HER approval for hosting "The Grand Opening" of Her start-up "SIR" AND now wanted to OK the request by Joey to be 'Collared and Owned.'

Joey had Eagerly agreed to be her Submissive Stud, pussy and asslicking/slave as nephew/Master T also WAS to his longtime Mistress and Goddess Auntie Anna.

The Domme/Mistress Anna wanted to call Joey in discreetly to talk about the blurted-out statement he made about sucking a cock to get to HER Gorgeous Mistress' meaty pussy the day they gangbanged the Insatiable Bi/sexual peaking FemmeDomme. She

friends cumming back and become involved in SIR, and in all the ladies' Vanilla lives as well.

Master's Mistress Aunt always preached to Master T about BALANCE in the BDism lifestyle. "Domination is great, but once in while it is also 'Great or Greater' to be Submissive to someone you can trust totally to Dominate YOU, IF they want to switch and just let them take control to DO WHATEVER THEY WANT TO YOU, with respect!"

The Domme/Goddess Aunt Anna had totally groomed Her well-hung and tongue-taunting teen nephew to be just that and more. He was loyal and faithful to his family and HER family as well, especially when it came to soulmate Cousin Carol. THEN the Goddess Aunt didn't mind taking the back seat as long as Her nephew Anthony/Master was there for HER TOO!

Master T/Anthony's Love for BOTH Mother/Daughter was unconditional! Their NEED for his services and approval was Unmistakable. They fed off of each other's presence but Carol was always overreacting, thinking she could NEVER lose Her loyal Cousin Anthony to Patty, and Patty forever told Carol, "He belongs to YOU!" Patty was more sensible and wanted to keep the peace, so taking on Joey as her Vanilla Boyfriend was a smart move for Patty.

Joey and Carmen arrived with only a day's rest from their young balls being drained by three big cock-craving nymphs and Master T needed to Deliver Joey to the Domme for more "Stand-Up"

pounding against the wall and deep penetration she couldn't forget. Then she would Collar Joey as HER PERSONAL PROPERTY for future use.

Patty would get to use 11" Joey to use as her deepthroat Vanilla BF and for Carol's schooling "Deepthroat 101," but Carol's Master/Cousin Anthony would be Patty's to practice on this evening.

Joey yelled out, "THIS IS SO FUCKING HOT, I CAN DIE NOW!" Joey joked as they all laughed out loud, then Patty slowly showed Carol how to take 10, even 11 Inches of hard cock down her throat without gagging, a/k/a "NO REFLUX."

Carol then tried the same thing as Patty explained on her Cousin/Master holding her tongue OUT of the way and holding her nose NOT to gag, and it seemed to work with some more practice.

Master T then held her head over the bed while standing and the angle was even better while Carol was taking Master's 10" ALL THE WAY DOWN HER THROAT. Carol was so relieved she could now do this for her Soulmate Cousin Anthony, she hugged and kissed Patty all night while the two couples swapped until they were drowned in each other's juices, Especially from these two beautiful young unique women, Carol and Patty, that could fill a bucket with their multiple-orgasm gift, Carol in particular, MuchoMango!

Meanwhile The Domme was impressed and stroking Joey's biceps and asked if he worked out at an All-Male gym Or was it for both male/female? To No surprise of the interest Mistress Anna had of Joey's sexuality, He answered, "It's Mostly Men that lift weights, not many women."

The Domme's eyes opened wide as her next question to Joey was "Do YOU Shower there before you leave with other men to see your long thick dick, and do YOU look at them?"

As the curious Goddess/Anna now dug deeper, holding his hard cock tight with BOTH her skilled hands, stroking his massive tool slowly while Joey weakly answered, "Yes, I do! Sometimes I DO look at them, I do see them, All look at mine in envy. I KNOW where you're going with this, Mistress Anna, and I guess I could say I AM kind of Bi/curious but I could NEVER let MY friends know this," Joey admitted.

"I know YOU do understand these things, and can WE please keep this to ourselves, and I want desperately to be collared and learn to please a beautiful Goddess like yourself, I DO KNOW THAT I LOVE WOMEN way more than men! Meeting You, Domme Anna, is a dream come true and I'll gladly be collared and Owned and learn This BDism lifestyle of Yours and Anthony's. I'll do anything you want," Joey added.

"Even if it means sucking a dick to get to this??" as the quick-witted Goddess Anna placed Joey's hand on her dripping-wet pussy and kissed him deeply, jumping up onto Joey Again for him to carry the perfect curvy, long-legged Domme/Goddess to be Fucked HARD and DEEP against the same wall for the second time in as many days.

Joey replied while gasping for air while the Domme's legs were squeezing his 32-inch trim waist to hold on to the well-built Bi/curious 25-year-old Stud Joey.

"WE'LL SEE when the time comes the things I Will do for you." The moaning Goddess was squirting yet again in her new Favorite position of hers and told Joey to put her down on her knees for him to cum on her tits and lick HIS own cum off her full 36DDs, Just like Her collared nephew Anthony and Master does for her! AND to see if Joey would obey and maybe like CockCum, even if it was his own.

AS NO surprise to the Domme's curiosity, Joey ATE ALL the cum up being fed to Joey by the Goddess after jerking off on the Domme's perfect breasts. She even MADE Joey lick and suck all her fingers clean.

Carmen and Joey were hooked, needless to say, and Patty, Carol and Cousin Master T all enjoyed swapping the night's stories and laughing as they prepared for the next day in dealing with Louie Lipstick, Carol's soon-to-be EX/FIANCÉ now that things took a turn for the talent scout who had been outsmarted by the MommeDomme.

"He certainly did mess with the wrong woman's daughter! AND the wrong Master's Cousin Carol. Everyone to the roof garden!" Mistress stood and said. "It's a beautiful night and I feel fucking great today, How about all of you??" Mistress giggled as she fixed her blouse, smiling.

Up on the roof overlooking the Boston skyline, she approved of ALL their preparation and in a few days it would be packed with family and friends to see her successful foundation officially incorporated as "SIR" Sports Injury Rehabilitation, through Physical Massage Therapy treatments.

Today Mistress assured her New Boytoy Joey that Being Bi/Sexual was the Best of Both worlds and that She enjoyed Both Men AND women sexually. "Your Secret is safe with Me and We'll explore much more of your secret Darkside with or without your friend Master T when I put this Collar on you, making you officially MY personal Slave, but I May share you with others for MY amusement, and explore your Bi/curiosity. Repeat after Mistress Anna: 'I will Obey and Never stray, Or be whipped and pegged every day.' You are now MY slave and serve only Me, Do you accept this Collar from Me? To be the best Pussy/Slave you crave to be, You are now MY Sub/Slave/Joey C," the Domme Anna recited and got her answer very quickly from the eager Pussy Slave.

Without hesitating Joey answered, "Oh, Yes! My Mistress, I accept this Collar and I would NEVER stray, always obey and learn your new way. It will be an honor to serve you and Call you MY Mistress/Goddess Domme Anna, TO BE Whipped OR Pegged ANY day."

"Now it's time for your induction into our BDism lifestyle, Discipline 101. Have you ever been pegged before, my slave?" Mistress Anna asked, smiling at her new hung man-slave Joey.

"No, What is pegging?" Joey curiously asked his New Domme and Goddess of the Golden Shower AND Pegging a man's ass just for fun today, but MOSTLY for a LOT of money.

Slave Joey would soon learn to please this borderline Sadistic Dominatrix in HER particular Erotic Fetish's through force and humiliation to amuse and PLEASE herself, OR be replaced!

The Domme's nephew Anthony/Master T had warned Joey already NOT to fall in Love or be too needy or HIS MISTRESS would eat him up for breakfast and spit out his bones before taking her beauty nap.

"Just wait until she calls for you," Master T stressed to his work buddy and friend Joey. "Then fuck her brains out HARD and rough, but always with respect if there is such a thing, lol, Don't EVER humiliate Our Mistress, THAT'S FOR ME ONLY!" the Master joked.

Carol was all over Master T, showing off her new "Deep-throating" skill, and called Patty twice a day to thank her and wanted to repay her with an oral session for Patty to show her appreciation and to get a taste of some pussy since she'd been throating her cousin Master T for two days straight now, enhancing her skills.

Patty told Carol to KEEP DOING it until it just slid right down without ever thinking about it, like when Patty's brothers used HER mouth before their parents got home from work, Every day!

Patty would Only Suck her Master's cock when HE wanted her to on rides while playing with her perfect DDs squeezed together in suspenders in driving outfits HE alone picked out for her to wear. Patty DID have amazing Oral skills NO man could just forget about OR overlook, So Patty would STILL be serving on her Master's command or Mistress Anna's cravings for the stacked pussy-loving blonde. Patty would NEVER refuse sucking

the cum down from her Master while his 10" was buried deep in her throat, like a vacuum! He was having a harder time than he thought staying away from Patty's oral skills, even though Carol had replaced his addiction.

Patty's brothers had been warned for a second time now to KEEP AWAY From Patty as Master T shouted and pointed at the older brother coming out of a restaurant in Boston's N. End,

"LAST WARNING!" The angry Master T pointed to him, walking away with Patty and Carol after dinner in a nearby restaurant, Café Pompei. Another favorite Italian Restaurant of Carol's besides Rita's in Chelsea, MA, bordering E. Boston.

Carol's Fiancé Louie was adding to Master's distraction and focus on his agenda and needed to calm down and take a fast ride in his Corvette up to the cottage, where he knew Carol was getting her stuff. He always would forget everything once He and Carol would fuck in the dark Secret Closet, reading from the Domme's journal. He hadn't used the NEW SECRET CLOSET yet he had just built for Carol. They went straight to the stream to finish off the Golden Shower Fetish that day, he wanted to show Cousin Carol how much he loved her.

Master called to make sure Carol would be in there waiting and she was THRILLED that Cousin Anthony, now her Master T as well, was driving up to fuck her in their secret way.

Carol was always waiting in the secret closet with her halter top ready to be peeled off for her new developing oversized thick purple nipples to be sucked on, pinched, twisted and cummed on

in their younger Curious exploring days when Carol would squirt when her cousin touched and kissed her like NOBODY else could. Carol was trembling and creaming out from her pussy. Her asshole, which now was being used a lot to her liking, was throbbing, just waiting to be taken hard and deep by her Master's hard 10, once again.

Insatiable Carol was just hoping Louie wouldn't interfere and that trouble would start if he showed up unexpectedly, and unwelcomed.

When her soulmate Anthony/Master T arrived and opened the secret door, Carol was just waiting to be Violated in both holes, bent right over, and took every inch from her Dominant 1st Cousin and love of her life in "hungry animal fashion" while being whipped with Master's strap across her perfect unblemished heart-shaped ass, inherited from her Momme.

Frustrated Cousin Anthony and Master to all her needs was unwinding hard, Fucking his Young Goddess/Cousin Carol into a puddle of her Mango. She couldn't have been happier to satisfy her addiction that she just COULDN'T live without anymore, AND vice versa.

"Louie is history," Carol began to tell her cousin right after taking his drained dick out of her mouth, stroking the last few drops, looking up at her Master for life in the new secret closet he built for her.

"GET YOUR STUFF, and let's go for now, we'll talk on the way back," Master said, kissing her deep and licking a few stray

drops of his own cum from her chin. "I'LL take you home now!
And WE will figure this whole thing out like we always do,"
Carol's confident and Protecting Cousin Anthony said, ALWAYS
putting her mind at ease.

"Let's get the party started!" Mistress Anna was saying as the Corvette pulled up, pointing at her main man and business partner
of four, including Patty.

The caterers, the planners, the flowers, everyone was arriving
at once and it was early afternoon. Carol was gleaming like a
lightbulb and Momme/Domme Anna was happy to see THE IN-
SEPARABLE cousins so happy together without hiding anymore,
Outside of business or Family, of course. Patty wasn't worried
and would take on Joey anyway to keep best friend Carol happy,
her Master T would Always be there for Patty in a New York minute, and Patty KNEW it.

Mistress' Family, Anthony's Mom, brother Steven, Aunt and
Cousin came first, Then his two bosses, brothers Sonny And
Freddy, twelve young East Boston and N. End coworkers, including Carmen and Joey, now addicted kinksters, and Alice tagged
along with them. There were others like Nicky Flemia, who was
Anthony's older friend and Mistress Anna's old school days friend,
aka Secret Client, known as Nicky Nipples in the old Journal.
Nicky knew Freddy and Sonny and came to the opening party
with them. Nicky Flemia was a well-connected, well-known Mafia
enforcer, along with the infamous Joe Barboza turned informer,

who was later assassinated from East Boston during the Winter Hill Irish Mafia wars in the 60s. Nicky met Anthony when he was an eleven-year-old shoeshine boy. Whenever Nicky Flemia seen the younger hungry, angry Anthony around E. Boston, he would call him "Shoeshine" to get a smile from the troubled kid, and when Anthony got older, Nicky would call him "Mustache" when the kid got old enough to grow a nice thick black "flavor saver," as Auntie Anna called it.

Nicky Flemia, Joe Barboza, And Chico Amico were three of the baddest Mafia enforcers in New England until they all turned on each other. They walked the streets in E. Boston and Everyone crossed the street when they saw the trio walking and talking.

Nicky was bad but he was loyal to friends, NOT into bad business OR the street wars that were going on between the Italians and the Irish rivals of Southie, and that was why My Auntie Anna/The Domme STILL associated with him. She called him Nicky Nipples because it was said Nicky cut off his sister's nipples because his sister brought home a black man back in the 60s and that wasn't allowed so much back then.

The Grand Opening for SIR was in motion, friends and family and some special guests were already here, Master T and Patty sat together in the Vanilla life as GF and BF. Carol and Joey chatted right next to them as BF and GF and life was good. The caterer was here and stayed to serve food and drinks. The DJ would play some music and it was an open bar, just like a wedding, Only nobody here was getting married anytime soon!

Police Captain Tom Evans from Chelsea walked in to ask some questions to Master T about his whereabouts today and asked to see his hands as Carol AND Patty stood to defend him as Anthony's MOM Joan took their hands and walked them away.

"WHAT IS THIS?!" the startled Domme Anna asked the detective.

"This will only take a second to see his hands, and I KNOW you will ALL say he's been here ALL DAY, but this needs to done now ASAP so we can rule him IN or OUT. I'M not stupid," Detective Evans said, "I'll explain over here with YOU, Anna," and Anthony and his Mom as The Police Captain from Chelsea who was in East Boston District with permission from the East Boston Police, accompanied by Head Detective Bobby Faucette to question the murder of Carol's Fiancé Louie Aronstein, who was just thrown off the Tobin Bridge in Chelsea just a few hours ago. Louie's body was found with "Blood-Red Lipstick" smeared all over his face.

"I need to see if Anthony has lipstick on his hands AND if his hands are bruised," the two detectives were now looking over the Domme's Nephew and prized possession for evidence.

"Patty's older brother was also badly beaten this morning with a pipe and he is in Intensive care and NOT supposed to make it through tonight," Detective Faucette added.

"I find it VERY IRONIC that YOU, SIR, are sitting with HER, the badly beaten brother's sister, who I'm told is YOUR girlfriend AND the fiancé of a dead man who is your cousin?? CAN

YOU ALL PLEASE EXPLAIN THIS FUCKING COINCI-
DENCE!" the Angry and confused Police captain yelled out!

"My hands are clean, Sir, except for some breadcrumbs," Anthony grinned as Detective Bobby Faucette talked with Anthony's
mom, who was an old-school friend of hers, and Anthony's father's
school friend as well.

"HE'S BEEN HERE ALL DAY GETTING THIS PLACE
READY WITH ME! And My sister Anna! It's her Grand Opening, FOR GOD'S SAKE!" Joan yelled.

"I Know, Joan, But a murder has just been committed today
and all he has do is answer a few questions and show us his hands
for bruises or blood or lipstick found on the dead body, THAT'S
ALL! and we will leave, if there's anything more he will get sub-
poenaed at a later time."

"Chelsea Police can't charge him if he's clean! I'll make sure
of that, Joanie," the brawny East Boston most fearful detective
promised Anthony's Mom and Angry Auntie Anna and the trembling Carol and Patty consoling each other, looking at their
Master, crying that they may lose him!

After taking pictures of Anthony's hands inside the house and
a few questions, the Police Detectives left in complete confusion.
They were Certain they had their guy but a whole party full of
people was a pretty "solid alibi," I would say, Along with NO lipstick OR bruises nor blood on his hands.

"OMG! Louie is dead? The Tobin Bridge? Where did I hear
that word 'Tobin' before?" Carol asked.

"I told you a story about the Tobin Bridge and My Ex/Husband's Yankees hat!" Alice jumped in to change the subject and enjoy a laugh. "ARE YOU OK?" Alice hugged Carol and asked her, "What are you drinking? Let's all have a drink and ENJOY this day," Alice insisted, smiling, caressing Carol's flawless lower back.

"YES, Everything is fine, I'M SURE this is something LOUIE and his L.A. Porno asshole friends have gotten themselves into," the MommeDomme arrogantly jumped in to say.

Patty stared into her glass, smiling, and then turned to glance at her Master for a second before following Carol and Alice.

"Why are YOU smiling?" Anthony asked Patty.

"It felt nice when He said I was your Girlfriend," Patty Replied, walking away, smiling.

Joey then put his hand on His friend Anthony and said, "IF they had ANYTHING at all, they would have taken you away, Fuck them! You're clean, Anthony, and you answered everything they threw at you, shame on them! Let's Party, my friend! This is your grand opening!" Joey said, comforting his work buddy and mentor.

Before Chief of Detectives Bobby Faucette left, He noticed Nicky Flemia was at the party and nodded, smiling, and asked Anthony, "What in the world is HE doing here? And who are those Two characters he's with?"

"Nicky is a friend of MINE, and a friend of OURS," the Domme snapped at Bobby, "and those two men are my nephew Anthony's bosses from Haymarket Sq. in the N. End! They're in

the Fruit and Produce business, STOP overthinking this right now, Bobby. You know Nicky in only a bad way! I know the real Nicky!" the Domme was pointing at Detective Faucette.

Detective Faucette laughed in Anna's face, "There's ONLY ONE Nicky!!" he laughed.

"Yes, Our longtime schoolyard friend Nicky!" the Witty, angry Domme Replied. "Joan and I have known him since grammar school and he needs Physical Therapy for his back and 'I' am His Physical Therapist," the Domme added.

"HE needs Therapy, alright!! Don't call us when he cuts YOUR nipples off!" the pissed-off Detective warned her, referring to Nicky's sister's incident.

"Is that all, Detectives? Can we get back out there now for our guests, Please?" the Domme pleaded sarcastically.

"I guess so, And now they've given a Well-known mobster enforcer, an alibi Today also!" the E. Boston detective told the Chelsea police Captain. "Good luck solving this one," as they headed out the door baffled!

Detectives Bobby and Captain Evans could only watch Nicky wave goodbye to them, smiling, then saluted with his drink to a smiling Anthony, aka "Mustache" to Nicky.

Nobody really spoke of that day again and many questions went without being answered, Or questioned at all, and the party went on.

The Grand Opening went on and everyone was told it was a big Coincidence and that Louie "Lipstick" Aronstein was involved

with bad characters from L.A., and Carol should be more careful of the men she chose to live with, OR promised to marry.

There are women that will defend their families, and then there's ITALIAN women, THEY will rip you a new asshole if you embarrass their family, and this Goddess Italian "Femme-Domme," Auntie Anna, had done exactly that For her Groomed nephew that was now Master to ALL her needs.

His loyal Goddess had even stepped in front of his own mother, her sister Joan, pleading for her son to protect her Now Dominant nephew/Master. She even went as far to defend her longtime Schoolyard friend Nicky Flemia to the most feared Chief detective, Bobby Faucette of East Boston Police Dept., while Nicky watched, smiling, KNOWING Bobby was in for a Free Discipline Session 101…. Watching Italian women Get in someone's face using their hands to talk as well as demeaning you is somewhat Hypnotizing, and ITALIAN MEN know better than to stay and take the Losing lecture, SO WE JUST WALK AWAY!…period.

Bobby rolled his eyes in the air in embarrassment at least five times before losing HIS case to the Domme Anna and signaled to Chief of Police Tommy Evans of Chelsea to GO now.

Once they left Nicky walked over to his longtime friend and "Physical Therapist" to say, "IF I knew for sure YOU wouldn't be in harm's way for the things I do, I'd give my right arm to MARRY you!" Then Nicky kissed Anna on the cheek.

Domme Anna snapped back, smiling, and said, "Then how would you spank me?"

BOTH laughed and enjoyed her witty joke as he left the party happy as the 5th-grader she once knew.

With EVERYONE totally confused, things were forgotten in a few hours as speeches were made about the new foundation SIR and by its Founders, assistants, associates and partners alike. Alice and Patty were introduced to family and friends that hadn't met Patty yet.

"Patty IS FAMILY," the DOMME and BDism sister/kinkster Carol Insisted to the Grand opening crowd. "Alice and Patty are licensed, Certified and experienced with degrees in Physical Therapy Rehabilitation, and Radiology scanning. We are looking to service our Boston Sports World players to overcome their injuries through Physical Therapy In our new up-to-date facility, financed by our own 'Carol DiNunzio Financial & Realty' Trust Co."

Carol was about to inherit two million in an Insurance Business protection policy just for starters with her Fiancé OUT of the picture. So with the addendum clause, that made her 50% interest a 100% controlling interest In "SIR" Sports Injury Rehabilitation... Yes, Sir! Carol was well on her way to the top."

CHAPTER
17

The Grand Opening for "SIR" Had come and gone. It was confusing to a few Detectives that left the party embarrassed but mostly to Anthony's Mom Joan, who had NOT seen this "Bond" between her oldest son and youngest sister Anna.

MAYBE curious mom Joan could see the bond between her oldest artist Niece Carol and her oldest artist son Anthony of the same age, who had stood in front of the investigating detectives immediately to protect him. Carol would have stood in front of a train if she had to.

The Soulmate 1st Cousins Carol and Anthony were only six months apart and learned to draw and color together, they crawled together as infants and soon learned how to Crawl "FOR EACH OTHER" in their most Sexual Taboo/Fantasies. But their Bizarre Sexual Appetites were unknown to Mom Joan, who had

babysat Niece Carol OR sometimes her sister Anna watched Nephew Anthony over her house with daughter Carol to draw their fantasies out on paper.

Joan and Anna were only ten months apart and DID NOT have much in common at all while the two 1st cousins Anthony and Carol DID have Everything in common. They had a Mental Telepathy connection through their art to explore each other's Cravings in the most Sexual taboo ways, much deeper than simple incest.

Auntie Anna was first to see it as the psychological wizard she was, and tried to figure it out to stop the 1st cousins' sexual relationship but failed miserably. Then later on a Broken-hearted Alice with a Psychology degree would try as well, and still the cousins could NOT be torn apart.

Carol herself tried to break away and got engaged to do the right thing but couldn't have an orgasm without Her telepathic/ Cousin Anthony, NOR could Carol bear the thought of HER Cousin Anthony being sexually involved with her best friend, Bi/sexual kinkster Patty, with Unmatched Oral Skills, OR with any other woman with him sexually. So Carol NEEDED to get her Soulmate, Master/Cousin Anthony, BACK where he belonged, TO HER!

Patty was always very happy and willing to take second place, AND still be #1 for Carol's meaty pussy and huge purple nipples with a solid heart-shaped ass inherited from her DommeMomme. Patty STILL got to play Cousin Anthony's Vanilla girlfriend in business AND for Family gatherings with a close eye from Carol. Patty

was always holding Anthony's hand in Vanilla life, grinning ear to ear from the HONOR to be introduced as Anthony's girlfriend.

Today everyone was getting ready for the 2nd Party for "Special Clients'" OLD AND NEW journals, only with a NEW title on the cover called "SIR." Celebrities from the Boston Sports Organizations would be coming, Executives of major N.E. Utility companies, and Financial Institutions, Wealthy couples, OR Single entrepreneur VIPs with Sexual Fetishes and Fantasies to "Spice-Up" their sex lives, all provided by "The Domme" Anna all by herself for years, now had the talented help she so desperately needed.

Nephew/Master T would take the leash from his Goddess Aunt Anna, and lifelong fantasy. She had now surrendered and submitted totally to his Dominance and Abilities to please the insatiable Goddess and Fetish provider, along with her masochistic gorgeous Redheaded Bi/lover Evelyn.

The surrendering Domme told Her groomed Master T that it was the "Balance" she so desperately needed to give herself what SHE had been inflicting for so many years. The "Switch" Dominatrix Aunt now on occasion LOVED to be Dominated and Used ONLY by who she trusted and knew could and would satisfy her much-needed cravings to be the Sub/Slut/Slave she craved to be. ONLY for her hung Nephew/Master she had groomed for the past five years. The most Popular Domme Anna and Queen of the Golden Showers needed to feel what so many were coming back to her for, and her Loyal Nephew Anthony/ Master T would show her why!

While locked in Evelyn's arms today, The Domme Aunt Anna would get the "Balance" she had begged her Master for, A Golden Shower on both of them while French kissing, tasting the Hot Salty Piss of her Master right on their lips while kissing, and on Evelyn's huge tits to lick off.

"Will your boytoy Joey be joining you girls today for the party, My slut?" Master asked of his Submitted Mistress Aunt, respectfully. "Do you wish to watch him suck cock soon like you've said? I have plans for Patty, Joey, Carol and I to use Evelyn on the wheel of torture later, I could come up with something if you like," Master of the Domme added.

"DO WHATEVER YOU WANT TO ME! Only you can satisfy thee," His Goddess Aunt replied. "Give me the Balance I seek, and I will give you whatever you want from me," the Domme's hot wet lips whispered into the Master Alpha male's ear slowly, lowering herself to her knees, grinding her wet body against her Dominant nephew lover, taking his hard cock deep as he pulled her hair, pumped and slapped her face violently just like SHE did with her Slaves, and HAD done to him!

Grand Opening Party #2 Would be more Discreet but still took place on the impressive Roof Garden overlooking the Boston Harbor and Skyline from the East Boston side of the Harbor. The Maverick St. Section 8 projects were ½-mile down the road and the poor and unfortunate paid poverty rates while the other side of the Boston Harbor Looking at the broken-down brick buildings and dirty water paid tens of Thousands for their New Construction Condos.

The Smart real estate Domme Anna had purchased her four-story brick building in need of repairs for short money and now was worth a fortune with a Million-dollar view to top it all off.

There were three suites for Domme Anna herself, the main office On the Right corner, Master's unit on the other corner, and Patty in the middle (Both easy access to Patty). Patty's unit was a gift from Her Mistress, and Master T would see to it this was where THEIR Co-Owned Oral Slave Patty stayed, BUT would Carol approve?

"This is where you belong, Fuck them!" referring to Patty's abusive brothers that raped her on a daily basis. The Domme told Patty, The roof garden was ALSO Patty's other daily duty to see the plants were watered daily and keep it clean for clients to come up and relax and enjoy the view, having a drink or two while Patty unzipped the clients' pants and dropped to her knees to deep-throat the scheduled generou$ Special VIP client, Man or Woman, OR wealthy Bi/couple while they play with her natural 38DDs and gorgeous petite 22-year-old body.

This rooftop garden was as close to HEAVEN as Patty would ever get, Patty would take a bullet for EITHER Mistress Anna or her Master T, who protected her and Carol like a Lion protected their cubs.

Today Patty would pick up Alice, Joey and Carmen from the N. End so they didn't have to drive and lose their Parking spots in the dense parking of the Tiny North End streets of Boston designed for the horse and buggy and NOT for today's pickup trucks and long expensive cars.

Patty wore her skimpiest top to catch her Joey's eye and maybe a feel from Alice also. "How do you like THIS Driving outfit That Anthony wants me wearing, Alice? lol," Patty asked to get her attention and DID get a nice nipple twisting and caressing by the Bi/Curious cock cum lover Alice.

Patty was NOW learning that Alice also DID love to eat pussycum as well, Especially from the three wet gorgeous co-workers on hand daily that loved to use her up, and vice versa. Joey leaned in to give both nipples a good-morning kiss and a pinch as well as Patty rubbed his impressive 11" cock that she was loving as her new toy also from the front seat.

Joey was A gift from her Master T AND Domme Auntie Anna, but Patty did have to share Slave/Joey with Carol in Vanilla life for appearance's sake while cousin Anthony was Patty's Vanilla Guy (WHICH PATTY PREFERRED Anyway).

"WE are going to have a blast today!" Patty told them. "Red Sox players are coming into SIR today and VIPs from Boston Business we recruited recently. So let's treat them right, Alice, and they will run back to us, OK?" Patty said.

"I can't wait!" Alice eagerly replied, Holding both of Patty's firm 38s in her skilled hands, leaning over from the back seat, feeding them to Joey. Alice got so excited she unzipped Joey to start blowing him right there, although Joey had cock on HIS mind Today as well.

Joey wanted to suck dick today too and had told His NEW Mistress Anna that had Collared and Owned the Confused and Bi/curious work buddy Joey.

Master T had a plan that would tempt his friend Joey even further when He planned to DP his Mistress Anna and lover Evelyn. The plan was When Master slid His hard 10" IN The Goddess Anna beside Joey's and Joey felt another cock on his, Joey might go crazy for it, but it was all in a session for the Master thinking of the two men as only pleasing his now submissive Slut/Mistress Aunt, craving to be the whore SHE now Needed to be, and the Master paid NO attention to the other dick involved.

Master's Goddess and Mistress LOVED to watch her submissive masochistic lover Evelyn being used and slapped while in her arms, feeling the trembling emotion from Evelyn's body being whipped from the dominant ruthless Master T, giving Evelyn EXACTLY what she Needed to cum.

The Domme/Mistress Lover Anna came just from holding Evelyn, comforting Her and restraining her at the same time while experiencing One orgasm after the other from Evelyn's Pleasure through pain.

Nephew/Master would alternate whipping The Domme/Goddess Auntie Anna also while she kissed and caressed Evelyn, squirting uncontrollably. The Hot submissive pussy-pleasing Mistress desperately NEEDED Evelyn in her life now. The Weakened Submissive Domme Had surrendered her dominance to share the pain with her lesbian lover Evelyn as "Balance." The Domme/Aunt's Nephew LOVED what he was experiencing and GAVE THEM BOTH a hard whipping and double-penetrated DP'd BOTH their assholes and creaming Pussies one at a time

with Joey as the second cock in the SAME HOLE for Joey to feel the hard meat and to see what Joey did about it.

"Balance," as the Domme described it, "IS the transfer of power to another to whom you can totally trust to submit to, who YOU Have confided in to PLEASE YOU without instructions in case you are ball gagged and CAN'T instruct them literally, after all YOU are being tied up at times, whipped with a Collar around your neck, SO YOU better know what you're doing and WHO you let Dominate you."

The Domme's Nephew and His Goddess Aunt had Mastered EACH OTHER'S pleasures, cravings and desires and needed NO instructions as to what made Each other Cum all day long.

Today Master T would have His Goddess watch what she enjoyed most of all. She loved probing the ASSHOLE of a man, humiliating him through Pegging, Prostate Massaging, OR Butt plugs while paddling them or whipping them into a moaning Plea once their limits were being reached, OR breached!

The Domme Aunt's Nephew/Master T knew this firsthand but allowed his Fantasy Goddess Auntie Anna to go "PAST his limit" just to please HER Fetish.

The Domme Aunt whispered, calling him nasty names, pleasing his Fantasy Goddess Aunt into multi/Orgasms HE then licked up for HIS pleasure, then got to Cum in her verbally abusive mouth.

So today Master T had a FEW guys for his Goddess and Mistress to watch sucking cock while their Asses were opened wide in front of her and Evelyn while they watched and used each other.

Evelyn had learned "Balance" from her Mistress/Domme Anna as an Executive Director of the telephone Co. in Boston. Evelyn was IN CHARGE all day long, then looked forward to transfer power over to Her Dominatrix Bi/lover, telling her what to do! But more than that, the Domme had taken her even deeper into her Evelyn's Darkside to find the Hidden Masochist Evelyn craved to be, who enjoyed being whipped, beaten, nipple tortured, slapped and Fucked hard and rough.

While Evelyn's vanilla husband Couldn't provide her ANY Kinky satisfaction, Evelyn was now Collared and Owned, Pleased and satisfied BY three Sadists by her side, one Domme/Mistress Anna, two A very Dominant Patty, AND three, Nephew/Master T.

Master T called on Domme Patty today to slide two massage tables together that Husband Cuck/Lenny and mean Domme-Wife Allie would be performing on right beside the other table, where masochist Evelyn and her Domme Bi/lover Anna would be watching and Sharing/Humping on an 18" DoubleDongDildo locked together while their two Pussies rotate on each other, taking their 9" share of the 18" toy until it was BURIED and their two big clits met.

Lenny and Allie were Putting on a live sex show for the Goddess Anna and Evelyn that would have them squirting continuously all afternoon. The Dominating Goddess Aunt had become her Master Nephew Anthony's surrendered submissive whore the Domme/Aunt always craved to be for Only her Nephew/Master T.

Master T had already told Joey that if he wanted to keep the Domme's Interest, then Today was the day to do it!

"Mistress/Auntie Anna told me you said YOU wanted to suck a dick to get to her pussy? Now you better keep your promise OR she will replace you! Today, Joey, I will introduce you to Lenny, who WE just got to come out of the closet last week. This week YOU will come out too! YOU are Mistress Anna's property now and let's KEEP it that way so we can all work and play together, there's a lot of money to be made for you, Joey. You can do that if you want and I won't say a word, but it WILL come out from Domme Patty eventually, So YOU will be getting a nice massage by Lenny and Allie and then WHEN they start to massage your ass and open you up from lubing you with warm oil, YOU reach for Lenny's cock for the Domme Anna, YOUR MISTRESS, to see You, SHE will go crazy for you after that, OK?" implied Master T.

"Yes, DEFINITELY! I want this today, I'll do it!" replied BI/Curious Joey.

"Allie and Lenny is in on the plan for today, Joey, so that Allie gets HER paid fantasy being DP'd by two guys today, WHEN you start on Lenny WE will ALL move over to the Domme's table and DP Evelyn, Then Fuck Allie DP style by you and Me, that's the plan. You'll suck Lenny's dick and Fuck his wife Allie at the same time! Lol, Gabeesh?" the Master Joked to an erect and very excited Joey listening to Master T. "Oh! By the way, After that you have to take a Strap-on toy in

your ass from Domme Patty, requested by YOUR Mistress Anna for her and Evelyn's amusement. It's up to you now if you want to stay and be their Slave/Joey," Master T said seriously to his work buddy Joey C.

Carol, Joey, and Alice would participate in another scenario today while MommeDomme was busy in the other room and WAS NOT allowed to play with Momme or vice versa, much too tacky for the Goddess. "Mother/Daughter pussy licking is for ten-dollar hookers and hillbillies," Mistress Anna would always say.

ALTHOUGH the millionaire Paul Travello had offered The Gorgeous Domme/Anna, Mother and Clone Daughter Carol $50,000 to PERFORM a Mother/Daughter pussy-licking session in front of him and his kinky trophy wife Grace while they watched and Fucked, Daughter and Goddess Carol replied back to Paul and Grace, "Make it $100k," and she would consult with her Domme/Momme to DO it.

That offer was after Carol cashed in on a 2M life insurance policy from a dead Fiancé, Louie Lipstick. It was all about the excitement with Carol anyway and she didn't need the money, but THIS request just made Insatiable kinky Carol all soaking wet! Momme just DIDN'T WANT that kind of money, Butt would her kinky daughter PERSUADE the older Goddess??

Master T was going ALL OUT for his Mistress Aunt today to please her in the EXACT ways she had groomed him to do, SHE KNEW her Master's needs as well and happily obliged her

245

Master when he required her services in return, when Soulmate Carol was working, of course.

Domme Patty placed and tied Joey's legs apart, leaving his hands free to grab Lenny's cock when the lights went down and Joey's ass was being Lubed-Up by ruthless Patty fingering Joey's hole, which WAS the signal to start sucking Lenny's dick for his first time.

Joey was all excited with his visible 11" hard-on standing UP at attention, exciting the wet Goddess Anna already and her slut/slave Evelyn as well. Allie started on Joey's legs and Lenny started on the other end at Joey's shoulders as they walked around the massage table twice, massaging and oiling the young muscular 25-year-old Bi/curious Stud/Slave Joey.

As Allie poured the warm oil onto her hands and opened Joey's solid bubble ass to apply the oil, Allie AND Domme Patty took turns sliding their two larger fingers right into Joey's asshole slowly and easily opening him right up. Master T turned the lights down as the signal for Joey to go for Lenny's thick dick.

Joey reached for Lenny's cock right at his eye level now, along with Lenny's large hanging ballsack, and just sucked and licked with ambition and excitement to finally get it over with. Domme Patty held her Slave/Joey still to take Allie's third and fourth fingers into his hot wet oiled-up ass, moaning with enjoyment, making his Goddess Anna explode into a multi/orgasm while sucking on Evelyn's DDs, gasping at the sight of Slave/Joey's cock-filled mouth AND Joey's asshole being fisted by Lenny's

dominant wife Allie, All while being whipped by the Dominating Patty calling Joey "My Cocksucking Man/Slave."

Master T whispered in his Domme/Aunt's ear now that HE was going to FUCK HER ROUGH and her lesbian lover Evelyn in the ass and OPEN HER UP just like Cruel Allie was doing to Joey. "DO WHAT I TELL YOU, My slut Mistress Auntie Anna, YOU belong to ME now!" the Master/Nephew whispered yet again in her hot tingling ears as she kept streaming and dripping PussyCumMango onto Evelyn's mouth below, sucking her Lesbian Mistress Anna's neatly trimmed Pussy and choking on her thick hot creaming MangoJuice.

"YES, MASTER, YES, SIR, DO WHATEVER YOU WANT TO ME," the weakened and helpless Nephew's Goddess turned Sub/Slut/Whore Auntie Anna repeated again and again, watching this LIVE Planned-Out Fantasy Sex Show right before the Domme Anna and Bi/Lover Masochist Evelyn's eyes just six feet away on two massage tables pulled together.

Allie hadn't been this happy in a long time to have her fantasies and the hidden desires of her AND her husband Lenny finally come out in the open. They were so grateful to the most sought-after Fetish-Providing Domme/Anna on the North Shore of Massachusetts AND known all over New England, a/k/a/ "The Domme."

Allie and Lenny thanked Master T for his loyalty to please his Goddess Aunt and to help others liberate themselves sexually through Fantasies. "IF only people would be more honest with

themselves, they would ENJOY their sex lives much much more," the Domme would stress.

Lenny had a small request for his part in liberating Joey today. He asked of Master T, "Could we show the Domme my wife Allie getting DP'd now while I throat fuck My Allie's head hanging over the massage table for The Domme to get a real nice view?"

"ABSOLUTELY!" replied Master T. "Have your wife Allie lay down on Joey's 11" cock in her ass and I'll slide my 10" in the same hole Right next to Joey's Cock, Then BOTH her holes after that until she squirts. Then I want you to put Allie's head over the side of the table and I'll have My Mistress Aunt rub Allie's Lumpy Throat while your cock is down there moving back and forth in her throat. Mistress Auntie Anna LOVES DOING THAT when Patty deepthroats ME," Master T replied to Lenny.

The "DP" (Double Penetration) Fantasy request was a BIG hit and now ALL four kinksters would be DP'd and would be present, Starting with Allie, who had been getting her pussy gangbanged recently from Master T and His well-endowed N. End friends.

Then the Masochistic Evelyn's Asshole was violently DP'd By Joey and Lenny while Patty whipped and cropped her into a puddle of her own pussycum, SCREAMING at times while being Face-Slapped HARD by ruthless Domme Patty.

Master T LOVED Licking Evelyn clean, Sharing her MangoJuice with his Mistress/Goddess Aunt Anna, French kissing her and PussyCum swapping Evelyn's continuous long hot Squirting

multiple/orgasms while being beaten, Screaming into one orgasm after another.

Allie fed Evelyn her Pussy, pulling her hair until Evelyn choked on her explosive squirts of built-up MangoJuice, exciting all watching cruel Allie Burst like a broken water hose on the Masochist's face, humping her mouth.

Patty was Very Dominating and The Domme was very impressed and encouraging her favorite Domme Patty along the way, shouting to her "More" OR "Harder," giving The Domme's Masochist Evelyn what she Needed!!

EVERYONE WAS SOAKED IN MANGO JUICE and Master T still had to get to Carol, Alice and other Special clients' Requests on this busy day's Agenda.

Mistress/Goddess AuntieAnna was last to be DP'd In her ass and in her pussy by Joey and Lenny, Nephew/Anthony was the one to hang his Sub/Domme Aunt's head and waiting opened mouth over the massage table to FACE-FUCK his dream fantasy down her throat and empty a huge load for her to gag on while Evelyn rubbed and squeezed the LUMP moving up and down in Auntie Anna's neck.

My Goddess knew enough to give ME her Creaming MangoCum that I was so addicted to just when she was ready to squirt a longer HOT steady stream of her Cum. So she squatted into position over his face, She took her Nephew by the hair like she always did and filled my mouth, TWICE!! while everyone looked on giggling as I choked on the Gushing Goddess, showing HER dominance in Our Power exchange.

The 2nd Grand Opening party for Special Clients was turning into a full-blown orgy for the staff and well-established regular Clients in particular. The Domme and Evelyn were drained completely and needed a nap. Master T needed food for more energy along with Vanilla girlfriend/Collared and Co-Owned Domme Patty.

Carol was busy greeting Clients at the door and just chatting with the Sports players on the Injury Reserve list needing Physical Therapy appointments already! Their star ballplayer Tony Coniglione was there looking for Patty and had an eye/head injury, mind you! The blonde Goddess had already caught his good eye and he was now staring at the young Goddess Carol as well.

Carol's nipples were a bit nippy tonight and protruding through her thin light Blouse for everyone to see how amazing they really were, although Goddess Carol loved to flaunt them. Alice was even drooling over Carol's stunning outfit, and Joey knew NOT to even try to touch her Crazy Cousin Anthony's property without Permission, So Joey would have to wait until later!

Carol told the amazed baseball star that Patty was with guests to avoid his advances, and said, "I will tell Patty you're here, Tony C," then offered him some hot food delivered from the Spinelli's Italian catering Co. in Day Sq., E. Boston, with the best Italian Pastry from Mike's Pastry from the N. End, and Homemade wine from friends in E. Boston.

Master T also took the liberty to send Patty to pick up a few of his favorite pizzas from Santarpio's Pizza very close by, Garlic/Sau-

sage combo, and told Patty he'd be ready again tonight for his petite Vanilla knockout G/F with a soft squeeze to her solid ass.

"I want You and Carol to finish MY night off in the shower,"
Master T then told Patty,

"I want YOU to train Alice how to give a GS."

"THAT will be MY PLEASURE, MASTER! I'll work on it
immediately, I'm All wet now, SIR, you know exactly how to get
me all wet every time, Master, lol," Patty giggled.

"Carol is one Lucky woman," Patty added, grazing by her
Master's visible semi-hard-on with the back of her skilled hand
as she walked away smiling.

Joey and Alice were enjoying the guests and greeting people with
Carol as the others were cleaning each other up in a DP session
for all the ladies involved. Two double-sized, state-of-the-art adjustable massage tables were pulled aside of one another so the
Domme Anna and Evelyn could have a perfect view of her newly
collared sex/slave boytoy Joey sucking Lenny's dick while his asshole got opened up by wife Allie fisting Joey's hole while watching
her husband Lenny get blown by another man, which Allie had
Paid for today.

Patty was whipping Joey and Lenny, walking around the tables
and enticing them in Patty's Domme debut. The Domme Anna
herself was locked into Evelyn with a 18" double-dong buried in
both their pussies as they humped the long thick toy, French kissing Evelyn while Patty whipped the Masochistic Evelyn as well,

but her Mistress Anna consoled Evelyn's quivering body after every Painful SNAP of the whip By the ruthless Dominating Patty showing NO mercy.

Carol would get her chance later with Alice and Joey and a few chosen guests who needed discretion that PAID well for it, Eddy Showers was back again and "out of the closet" this time and looking for Lenny to blow again, and to have his hole filled today.

Alice would be trained to give Golden Showers and she WOULD BE A natural for it! Women that were hurt or used by men saw this Pee Fetish as one of demeaning and humiliating men that had hurt them. But some men just LOVED the taboo Fetish of the warm shower of yellow rain over their body as well as being Dominated, Scolded, OR humiliated, PLEASING the woman's desire of demeaning the Submissive guy/lady while taking control of him/her. NOT resisting her Dominance and giving up control to her was well worth it in the end. Your lady will WANT YOU to Dominate HER sooner than you think, for the Balance and Power exchange in the BDism lifestyle.

Alice had been finding herself lately with her new circle of friends and Co/workers she once considered "Her Prey" from the Haymarket fruit produce days. The young Pushcart Boys, seventeen- eighteen-year-olds that could cum all day and still fuck her ALL NIGHT. Alice LOVED to blow, All day long if she could. And now she had these same young hung men as her Kinky Co/workers to have ANYTIME she wanted. Alice was now also

exploring with exceptionally beautiful bi-Sexual WOMEN she had found to be even more exciting Orally, reaping MORE and sweeter Mango to swallow down.

Master T had a thick long tongue that was made to eat Pussy, OR tongue fuck a nice heart-shaped ass such as Cousin Carol's Ass OR her Momme's. The Cocky wiseass Italian teen was groomed to do this very young at fifteen-sixteen years old, being disciplined after school serving the Domme Aunt under her desk at her Real Estate office in Chelsea, MA, one town away from their Suites in E. Boston. The Goddess Aunt was teaching her nephew TWO lessons at the same time, HOW to Master a woman ORALLY, and how NOT to make her Daughter/Cousin Carol SUCK his cock in her own house in a secret closet.

Alice appreciated being Eaten-Out as well while blowing multiple men standing in a circle one by one. Alice remembered well and reminded Anthony/Master T today about her hunting down the teenage pushcart boys to get her fantasy revenge sex. She LOVED me for Doing her Tobin Bridge PAYBACK fantasy, "Framing" the Cummed-On Yankees hat She wore that day and kept it hanging in her office.

Now Alice Belonged to all of us at SIR willingly and faithfully, she had become one of us on the Darkside and Alice would never go back to Vanilla Sex ever again. Vanilla was NEVER her personality anyway, after all the Tobin Bridge REVENGE Blowjob for her Ex to witness WAS HER IDEA! and a very kinky fantasy.

Patty would bring out the real kinky beast in Alice today when she trained Alice in Golden Shower Pee/Play for Special Clients requesting the well-paid-for taboo Fetish.

Domme Patty was trained in a Golden Shower session by "The Domme" slapping and pulling Eddy's hair as she squeezed his mouth open, yelling at him to drink her piss, filling his mouth with a hot salty stream of her sweet Nectar from the Goddess/Domme Anna herself. I would expect NO LESS from the apprentice and Carol tonight as they trained Alice to do the same for future Pee-Loving Clients in Our new walk-in shower with Built-In seating on the walls.

The Domme/Goddess Auntie Anna would be loving the new live shows I had planned for her. "If it's good enough for the guys, then it's good enough for the ladies," the Domme said.

I enjoyed eating pussy and their assed with my oversized lizard tongue. Patty had recently told me that only I had made her cum orally and no one else. Patty begged about pleasing her more in that way when driving me for SIR business meetings, and NOBODY would ever know Patty pleaded until she got her way, like Patty usually did get her way with the Master.

While Master T told Patty to train Alice in the Golden Shower play, Patty reminded her Master she was always daydreaming of his long thick tongue licking her ever since she seen him touch his nose with his tongue in the school corridor, immediately wetting her panties, and had to change at school. "Then you ATE-OUT

Me and Carol the very next day after school, So WE sucked your dick together to THANK YOU," Patty giggled.

Master chuckled, "You're Welcome."

"Now we have each other anytime we want," Patty said.

Master T, now feeling Patty's tight packed red cashmere sweater, assured her, "I'll have to pay more attention to that soon. YOU deserve a lot more attention and I'LL make it happen with or without Carol, OK?" the Master whispered into her hot ear.

"I belong to you, Master, YOU alone make that decision And I'LL be there," Patty cleverly added.

"DONE!" Master nodded in agreement.

Master T told Patty to be sure about the training of Alice in the walk-in Shower Today and what to do with Eddy "Showers" when he got there at 3 P.M. and then Master wanted his turn when Eddy left, He added to Patty.

"Carol has a meeting today and I'm making arrangements for her to meet with 'Business Women Only,' an Elite Women's-Only club Evelyn told Domme Anna about. They actually hire Male escorts and private studs to go on trips with them for BIG money, I'm told. So When I am done with all that, I want MY shower with the three of you. Be sure to have Carol and Alice hold me down for some of your awesome warm sweet Nectar, I remember you tasting so good," Master whispered softly, kissing Patty's goosebumps on her arms and neck. "I want to concentrate MORE on getting ALL THE GUYS involved in pleasing ALL OUR GIRLS, most of all, and second to get in with this

'Private Women's Club' WE HAVE BIG DICKS right here!"
Master T added.

"ABSOLUTELY!" Patty agreed. "And I deserve this pussy
licked MORE, don't I? Lol," Patty giggled.

Master T then insisted, "Get over here and sit here for a good
licking and be silent."

"YES, SIR!" Patty hurried over to the edge of the desk and lifted
her skirt while Master T ripped off her wet panties, drooling for his
petite deepthroating collared slut Patty's sweet MangoJuice.

THEY were both worked up and HOT for each other as her
owner Anthony/Master T kneeled on a pillow and began to slurp
up the Blonde knockout Domme Patty in training. Patty was
NOT shy at all anymore around her Master T and LOVED
being in his presence, in fact, It made her SECURE and HE
made her belong. Her Master was her world now, But Master T
was Carol's AND The Domme's property, let's NOT forget!

But right now, He belonged to Patty, who was humping his
mouth violently and holding his hair tight, controlling his mouth
and long, thick hard tongue Into position. Patty was feeling Her
Master's fingers reaching Up and In, massaging her G-Spot into
a steady pulsating squirt right into his open mouth, filling his
mouth FULL of her hot MangoD'Nectar.

Patty held his head back to watch him gag a bit before Closing
his mouth shut, "Swallow It all, Master!! I LOVE what you do
to me!" Patty cried, silently kissing stray drops of her cream off
his chin.

Master T assured his collared property Patty after swallowing a full mouthful of Her hot sweet Mango that she had desperately needed to release. "YOU BELONG TO ME." Master T lifted her ass up a bit, then pushed her down slowly to clean out stray drops around her asshole and licked her hole ever so slowly, tonging her ass deep and slowly down to Patty's inner thighs to complete what she was missing for a long while. Needless to say, PATTY GAVE HER MASTER A SECOND MOUTHFUL of Hot Mango, only this time gagging her Master/Pussycum lover, but only momentarily while drinking Patty's Gushing Cum ALL DOWN.

"We have to get out of here, lol," Master T laughed. "I could eat YOU all day long, though, I'll see you AND Alice back here at 6 and take care of Eddy really good like The Domme trained you, you can now train Alice in your way too! I'm looking forward to it."

"I'll do it, Master, THANK YOU. You mean the world to me, and I mean that!" Patty added discreetly, then left to find Alice for training.

"I'm looking forward to it and will bring Carol to join you two 'Blindfolded.' Maybe YOU will have MORE cum with your pee, lol," Master added before washing his cum-soaked face and hair in the shower.

"I'll try, Master, and THANK YOU, You mean the world to me and I mean that!" Patty added discreetly and left to find Alice for training her in the Golden Shower Pee/Fetish.

Patty was smiling ear to ear that Her Master Went all out to please her today. She had a hold on him and WOULDN'T let

go, despite what Carol said, Master T OR the Domme herself had the final say! If He said on your knees, OR for him to kneel for some Juice from the Skilled deepthroater to drink from her Fruit Garden, then THAT was His final decision and Carol must be silent OR join in if told to do so! UNLESS He was Collared by Carol. What Carol didn't know, however, wouldn't cause a problem, so Patty would just stay silent and avoid a confrontation.

The Master surely didn't want to rock the boat! especially since Patty would reciprocate with a deepthroating blowjob real soon when she dressed for him in her revealing driving suits.

Patty KNEW exactly what her Master was addicted to and SHE had the drug he called "Mango" AND the skills to take his 10" cock balls deep until he came right down her throat.

Patty had taught the skill to Carol now but Carol still had to get better at the No-Gag Reflux, which just came natural to a true deepthroater, but you couldn't take anything away from Carol for learning the skill for her Kinky male counterpart Cousin Anthony Carol couldn't live without.

Patty knew this and did try to keep her distance most of the time. Because If Patty wanted to drink from Carol's Ripe and juicy Mango Tree, She better keep a good distance. Carol could cum longer and harder than all three of her BDism sisters combined and far more than any guy. Patty LOVED eating Carol's meaty Pussy, taking all Carol's Squirting Orgasms being squeezed between Carol's powerful legs. Patty loved eating-out Pussy as much OR MORE than sucking cock.

CHAPTER
18

Now that all the questions had been answered and everyone was cleared in The Louie Lipstick murder Investigation, the Insurance company had NOTHING more to say and only to honor the two-million-Dollar policy to business partner and fiancé Carol DiNunzio, as stated in the Insurance protection Policy, in case one of the two were to die or be disabled to carry out their part of the investment into "SIR." Any funds would automatically go into the trust fund set up by Carol, Louie, Momme-Domme/ Anna, and Cousin Anthony! with Carol being the main interest in the policy and could be used by the officers of said corporation "SIR," period....

The new million-dollar house just finished would belong to Carol because that was a gift for agreeing to marry him, it was where he asked her to live once it was completed and they would

stay at Carol's cottage until the house was completed and then married. NOW The new house could be sold for another million and into Carol's PERSONAL bank account.

The investigation had concluded that Carol's fiancé Louie Aronstein was involved in the adult movie industry associated with organized Crime out of L.A. and Las Vegas, Louie's death was an unfortunate accident with NO suspects or any evidence to go on. Chief Detective Bobby Faucette from the Homicide/ Drug Unit wrote on the final report and submitted it to the Insurance Company to close the case and honor the 2M to the surviving insured of the Investment Protection Policy, which was Carol DiNunzio, Louie's business partner as well as his fiancé. Now with Louie's 25% shares of SIR, Carol would own 50% of SIR Inc.

Carol was excited by the news from Evan, the family lawyer, on the phone, telling her the good news on her Settling the Insurance Protection policy For two million. "Come pick up your check and sign for your money and deposit the check right away," Evan said. "Good luck on your business and new addition to the four Controlling Officers of DiNunzio Enterprises Inc.:

Carol DiNunzio, COO; Anna DiNunzio, President, CEO; Anthony J. Tracia, CFO, Senior VP; and Patricia Spazolla, Chief Marketing Director and CEO consultant.

Carol called the girls in right away for an emergency meeting AND SHOPPING SPREE! Patty was told to pick up Alice and then drove to the overwhelmed Carol, who was crying and hugging her Co/working Nymphos Ready for a Newbury St. spend-

ing spree. They would visit Gucci (Carol's favorite), Versace (Mom's fave), and her Mom's Italian tailor/seamstress.

MommeDomme had told her clone daughter Carol to enjoy the day and she would get fitted for something in a day or so, when she returned from the Cliff House in Maine with Evelyn, Joey, Lenny and Allie, just having "Couples' fun."

Master T had told her to buy a case of "Shalimar," his favorite perfume on a woman, And for all the girls at SIR to put it on at work.

Carol shot back, "I DIDN'T KNOW THAT! I'll get a case for Myself then, lol, Hmmm, My Mom wears Shalimar, I think!" she added curiously.

The girls spent the WHOLE DAY shopping, then drinks and dinner in Boston's N. End, where Alice then showed Carol where she would lure the three young hung men up to her Condo on Salem St. in the North End. Carol's Cousin Anthony, Joey, and Carmen, mostly (they all had 10" or more), but there were five-six others also.

While having a few drinks, Allie giggled to Carol, "I'd suck their cocks all day on Friday nights and Saturday during work on their breaks. They are all horny little Italian teenagers that stay Hard all day and night long, lol," Alice admitted to Carol, now getting all wet, listening to Alice's large Cock-Sucking Fetish. "OH, and Your cousin Anthony/Master T is unbelievable with his oral skills as well, NOT many men can eat pussy and rim an ass like he can. His tongue is just not a normal size!" Alice added! The ladies all laughed in Agreement.

"I'm an Anal slut because of that tongue," Carol giggled in to say. "He tongues my ass so good that it opens so wide just itching to be pounded."

Patty curiously and jokingly asked, "Can YOU let us borrow him, Carol? Lol."

"Ha-ha, Patty, YES, YOU CAN, and sooner than you think," she whispered. "I want the three of us on him real soon and see if he can handle it," Carol joked. Carol laughed, saying, "Momme went crazy laughing when I told her about our 'Guessing game,'" as they all laughed so hard remembering him trying to guess who was peeing on him alternately while blindfolded at the lake.

Continuously for a half-hour, the three kinkster sisters were drowning their Master in his favorite fetish by his three favorite women, keeping them happy as always!

Today was a planned-out weekend by the Goddess specifically to show her Bi/lover Evelyn's husband JUST WHAT his wife needed and he better give it to her OR LOSE HER. Collared Slave/Joey was there to accommodate his Goddess Anna and follow the instructions already given to him.

Also involved in today's session were Lenny and Allie, recently sexually liberated in THEIR marriage for Allie's BDism cravings AND Lenny's Bi/curiosity. THIS WAS what The Domme did best, and enjoyed doing it! Domme Anna now KNEW Evelyn NEEDED to be whipped, spanked, and enjoyed pleasure through pain, especially on her large breasts and thick nipples

being nibbled, bitten and clamped (Nipple torture), OR her ass Slapped, Paddled and Spanked, VERY HARD.

Evelyn's husband was a Minister and BDism might NOT have been his thing, But Evelyn's Mistress Anna HAD TO try for Everyone involved, including HERSELF, whom she had developed feelings for and vice versa. The Domme wanted Evelyn to leave the Vanilla life that she DIDN'T BELONG in. Evelyn's Mistress Anna HAD shown her why already for the past five years now WHY Evelyn kept coming back to her for more intense Masochistic sessions, courtesy of the Boston Telephone Co.'s expense account.

Her Domme Anna now consoled Evelyn as Master T AND Domme Patty in training now did the whipping, paddling, hair pulling and face slapping in a very Dominating session to test her Never-ending limits.

Mistress Anna French kissed Evelyn, feeling the passion from every strike of the whip as Evelyn moaned and groaned into one orgasm after the other, making Goddess Anna cum just from holding Evelyn close, feeling her trembling and throbbing bruised nipples pressed against hers. Yet Evelyn taunted and exposed her marked nipples to be abused even more.

She pleaded to be whipped, slapped, and bitten again and again, creating a puddle of her hot Pussycum her Husband WOULD NEVER be able to understand or duplicate. So Evelyn's Mistress and Domme Anna would convince her to leave her husband and NOT worry about her grown kids that KEPT Evelyn at home all those wasted years.

Collared slave Joey and His new Owner/Mistress Anna arrived for dinner as well as Allie and Lenny (now very happy), along with Evelyn and Vanilla Husband Richard the Minister. They all had a nice dinner and more wine than they should have, but it set the mood for Allie, who was more the outgoing type and got right to the point, as well as Domme Anna would with her new collared slave Joey, who was already instructed for today.

Allie started off by saying she was So Happy to have met new people who had sexually liberated HER marriage and new love for life, "and NOT so 'Vanilla' anymore with SO much more to explore," Allie added.

"What is Vanilla?" Richard curiosity asked, and Evelyn responded by saying, "YOU KNOW, when you do the same thing sexually, In the SAME position for twenty years for three minutes (if that)," Evelyn said to her boring Vanilla husband.

"Yeah! and with six inches, IF THAT," the witty Mistress Anna said, and Evelyn giggled! "We are here this weekend to convince Evelyn to make you change, Richard, OR make you leave!" the Domme strongly and adamantly told Evelyn's shocked husband to his face up close and very personal. "You DON'T deserve this woman and She don't deserve to be neglected for twenty years, NOT to mention that she is only 45 and in her sexual prime. Did you even know a woman had a sexual prime, Richard?" the Domme continued.

"We all agreed on this meeting and to take the rest of the night after dinner to OUR SUITE for a Full Wife-swapping session, So

ARE YOU IN, or out?" Evelyn bluntly asked an uninterested husband Richard in a demanding voice, Knowing that the Vanilla Minister would say "NO."

Evelyn turned and then said, "HAVE A NICE LIFE, I already called MY lawyer and WE are done here, and so is our marriage," Evelyn concluded, looking over to her supportive Mistress/ Domme Anna, who had become Evelyn's liberating lesbian lover for life!

After a moment of silence the Domme got up, taking Evelyn's hand, and lifted her lover up and hugged her tight, French kissing Evelyn to take the party upstairs like they planned.

Allie would take control of Lenny and Joey now in a mano-e-mano LIVE sex show to forget about everything that just transpired in the restaurant a moment ago, and the women would control their men to show Evelyn what she'd been missing for twenty years.

The Domme/Mistress wasted NO more time on Richard, the boring Vanilla Husband for twenty years that a neglected Evelyn had to live with. Evelyn was ready for Memorial Day weekend, however, and knew her Goddess of the last five years would be giving her what she deserved.

The Domme had planned the whole weekend out for Evelyn and Herself with an adjoining suite for Lenny and Allie, her Special Clients from Channel 7 in Boston that had been granted their Fantasy a week before.

Allie would also take Control of Lenny while Mistress Anna restrained Evelyn while "Locked In" to the 18" DoubleDong

with Evelyn being pushed to her limits. Evelyn STILL Didn't have a Safe word For when you have had ENOUGH beating OR pain, and WANT to stop.

Allie would get ANOTHER Gangbanging DP from two cocks today As she received for her fantasy last week, along with getting Lenny to suck dick for his second time, SO she would Do exactly what the Domme requested from her today. Allie was a young 28-year-old Swedish knockout kinkster and Lenny was a Good-looking Bi/Italian and would fit right In with the "collared and Owned" slave Joey regularly after today with the Goddess In Full Bi/Swap sessions.

The Domme Mistress Anna had put ALL HER PEOPLE in Place and paired off ALL the young horny insatiable Kinksters that could fuck and suck ALL DAY and cum back ALL NIGHT for more! Including her own daughter Carol with her hung Lover/Nephew Anthony, Patty for Joey. The Mistress wanted Patty to collar Joey also for future Vanilla day appointments. The Blonde knockout Patty WOULD break him down Real soon but Mistress Anna The Domme had Boytoy Slave Joey For now (AND Evelyn!).

Carmen would Soon be paired off to Alice, Allie and Lenny would be called upon for weekend Wife swapping and Bi/swaps, then there was Paul Travello and his Kinky BigCock Craving trophy wife Grace to swap with, AND get paid for it through business expense accounts.

Nephew/Master T would still service his Goddess Aunt upon request when she needed to be the Submissive Whore she craved

to be for Only Her groomed nephew, who had now Mastered The Goddess/Domme Aunt's needs, Period....

Carol would have to share his talented Oral Services and Enduring Fuck sessions that had them BOTH Multi/Cumming, leaving a puddle of their Mango EVERY TIME, that is if he didn't drink down their MangoJuice first!

Both Mother and Daughter knew how to feed him His fetishes and keep him Coming back FOREVER more!! Master T COULD NOT break away from EITHER of these Goddesses! Nor did he want to!

His Ultimate Dream OR taboo Momme/Daughter Fantasy would be to drink from BOTH their "FruityD'Mango Fountains," Nephew/Cousin Anthony and Master to all their needs would gladly go down for either of them and DROWN in their juices while his head was squeezed between either of their long Powerhouse legs.

Neither Mother NOR Daughter let their nephew/cousin Master T get up until they had given him every drop of Mango-CumJuice that he begged for, driving them wild into Squirting Orgasms, hearing his vibrating TURN-ON TALK between their legs while eating them out.

Another bottle of Chatenuef DuPape Wine was opened and shared as would be ALL the Bi/swapping sluts in the room tonight. Mistress warmed some fruit-flavored oils and applied some to Evelyn's ass and pussy as well as herself for the 18" DoubleDong, 9" buried

in BOTH their pussies until their clits were grinding together in a circular motion they enjoyed doing and just kept streaming together all over themselves.

The Domme/Mistress Anna Held Evelyn's arms behind her back and signaled Allie to come over and tie Evelyn's throbbing DDs together for a whipping, slapping, along with some sucking and Biting by the Mistress OR Allie enjoying some "Nipple Torture" for the Masochist Evelyn.

Joey was called over by his Mistress/Anna to stand and turn around for some lube and put her finger in slowly with the warm oil while sucking on his 11" cock to get him going and was hard as a rock at this point to perform ANY instructions by the Goddess.

Allie was instructed to lube Lenny and follow the Sadist/Mistress' lead in what she was doing to get the TWO GUYS to start playing and blowing each other for the Mistress' Amusement and excite Evelyn her Bi/lover to enjoy Evelyn's Oral skills as well. "Evelyn can kiss like nobody I've ever kissed before," the Domme/Goddess claimed! "Very passionately with a talented tongue she uses Extremely well," she joked, telling Allie and getting Everyone comfortable.

Allie lubed her husband Lenny's ass, bending him over and whipping his legs apart further to insert two fingers deeper with more oil. Allie walked over to Joey and did the same.

"OPEN wider," Domme/Anna told Joey. "I want Both of you to have fun exploring some Anal today," Mistress demanded. "Allie will instruct Lenny and I will instruct Joey! ARE

YOU OK with this, my collared man slave?" his Mistress asked Joey directly.

"YES! I am really ready for this, My Mistress. I'll do whatever you say and never stray, I'm here to stay!" Joey, the proud submissive possession, recited to his New owner and gorgeous Sadistic Mistress Anna, having his ass abused today for her amusement and exploring HIS submissive Darkside At the hands of Allie's Domme Debut, using her husband in this session.

Allie sat the two Visibly hard Cocks in excellent view for the panting Mistress and moaning Evelyn to watch as they started blowing each other sideways in a steamy 69 position while their asses were being fingered slowly by Allie and Mistress Anna, now OPENING Joey's hole More now with three fingers halfway in his asshole. The Domme applied MORE oil to get Joey ready for Lenny's Average-sized 7" hard cock in Joey's ass.

Lenny, however, was about to take Joey's big 11-incher. "This is only my second time for Anal and Only with Eddy Showers' 6 inches but NEVER 11," Lenny said to Allie.

"QUIET!" Whipping Lenny's ass harder, "Just bend over and relax, Joey will give you just half!" wife Allie demanded.

The mean Mistress Anna was now so excited watching Allie "CRACK" the whip so hard on her husband's hard dick, she was streaming and visibly dripping PussyCum onto Evelyn as Joey now asked his Cumming Owner/Mistress Anna, "YOU WATCHING?" as Joey held Lenny's lower back Down up close for his Goddess to GUIDE His cock to Lenny's hole just before Joey

Eased the whole 11-inch big Cock "RIGHT IN," feeling the warm oil and some Vaseline!!

Allie was shocked and leaned in to see her husband's ass Violated and sucked on Joey's balls, then whipped Joey hard on the ass. "GIVE HIM MORE, Fuck him hard!" Ruthless Domme Allie was learning to "SNAP" the whip now hard ON BOTH of their asses in her guy-on-guy fantasy.

THEN with the loud scolding and the wife Allie's whipping, LENNY leaned back and began HUMPING at The hard 11" while applying the oil On himself And moaning for his wife and the Mistress to hear, LOUDER and LOUDER, Lenny moaned wanting more and more until ALL the Bi/Slut kinksters were Squirting uncontrollably at the sight of Lenny taking Joey's 11" ALL THE WAY IN while being whipped HARD by Lenny's Domme wife Allie, and Slave/Joey being slapped and spanked by both HIS mean Mistress/Domme Anna and lover Masochist Evelyn wishing it were her.

Carol treated HER girls today to a ten-thousand-dollar Gucci and Versace shopping spree while her cousin/Master rested, Carol's Momme The Domme treated Joey and Evelyn To the five-star Hotel and restaurant "The Cliff House" in Ogunquit, Maine, by the York Beaches and Kennebunkport, where President Bush's Family own property.

The Mercedes S-Class seemed to be a little crowded for Carol's Expensive taste (just like Mom) so she had Patty stop on

Commonwealth Ave. when Carol spotted a New BENTLEY Rolls Royce at a British Dealership, Also selling Jaguars and Aston Martins.

Carol began to say, "You can always tell how successful a business is When you see what kind of car is parked Out in front of their Office! So Patty, YOU will soon be parking a BENTLEY Rolls Royce outside of 'SIR,' OUR Business, with the license Plate that says 'SIR' on it. Have our Insurance co. GET THAT PLATE for us tomorrow! And Drive that Baby home tomorrow morning In one of YOUR new knockout Mini-dress vest suits. We'll pick up Joey and collar the stud to top off YOUR day. I think he's ready To be Co/owned when he sees you tomorrow like he's NEVER seen a woman before, lol," Carol joked, as they ALL laughed out loud. "Master T And Joey are like Brothers From other mothers and WE certainly are Sisters from the same Domme, lol," Carol Also giggled.

Patty now added, "Alice, YOU Belong with us now too. You are hooked and Our Mistress is going to give Carmen to you, I hear! YOU Collar Carmen, We will train both of you together so we can ALL work Hard and play Harder."

Carol Couldn't wait to wake up Master T and have him smell her pussy dabbed in the Expensive Shalimar Perfume.

With his cock halfway down her throat, The Master WOKE-UP in a 69 position to smell the expensive Shalimar perfume and licked Carol into a nice Juicy squirt just by tonging the young

beauty's heart-shaped ass. Carol could even cum for her Cousin/ Master during Anal play now. Her ass had become super sensitive and she Loved to be fucked in her ass now, Even DP'd In her ass recently. Patty had been slowly fisting Carol's ass with her skilled Massage Therapist Hands in Carol's Personal Spa/Massage sessions.

Carol told Cousin Master T about her spending spree AND the Bentley, now a symbol of their Success that was going to be parked outside below their three Penthouse Suites. Carol then asked him if Joey had any interest in being collared Again and Co-Owned by Patty, with Permission, of course, by his Owner/ Mistress Anna.

"OF COURSE HE'S INTERESTED! I THINK HE'S MORE AFRAID OF HER!! LOL, He thinks she's gorgeous," Master/Cousin Anthony added.

"REALLY?" said Carol. "Just wait until tomorrow, when HE sees her pull up in the new Bentley! Can YOU have him here at two for lunch with us, please? I really want them together as a couple like US, and Carmen with Alice," Carol suggested.

"OK, done!" said Master T. "I'll have Joey here for Patty, then lunch," kissing Carol's cheek, whispering to assure her, "HE will do anything for Cousin Carol."

Joey and Lenny had completely satisfied Both their Dominant women in DP fashion one at a time. The Domme couldn't take the excitement anymore and was Dripping wet all over herself and Evelyn from watching Both men bury their hard cocks into each other's

lubed-up Man Pussies. The two Sub/Slaves were moaning and making noises to please and excite their FemDomme owners, Each slapping their humping asses and whipping their balls as one man fucked the other deep, taking ALL of each other's hard cocks in a live ManoE'Mano performance six feet away from the Goddess and her lesbian lover like they BOTH had never seen before.

THE DOMME Demanded the worn-out boys come to "Shower Time" after the Mano-e'mano show to get them both in the shower for a final performance. So Allie guided BOTH submissive Bi/Stud Sluts, still whipping them into the running shower with the Domme waiting to "RUB ONE OFF" on her Sub/Slave Joey's face, kneeling before His Ruthless Goddess Anna to drink any HotMangoJuice OR her SaltyPee.

FemDomme Allie in her Debut was controlling husband Lenny, "RUBBING ONE OFF" in His mouth as well, sitting a few feet away from each other, getting squirted on by the two most Dominating women you would ever find.

BOTH men were now instructed to Clean their cocks off and to DP each of their Dommes right there in the shower, One cock in the pussy in Front and One cock in their ass, One Turned-On FemDomme at a time. They were like three Dogs in heat from watching the incredible Live performance.

EVELYN begged to be gangbanged by ALL of them while Allie and Mistress Anna slapped and bit Evelyn's Visibly red, raw, marked-up nipples On her solid DDs while Taking TWO cocks. Both ManPussies were stretched wide open, But would have to

wait until next week, when their ONGOING ManoE'Mano sessions would be approved by All SIR officers.

The two exhausted studs were forced to cum AGAIN on Evelyn's whip-marked milky-white DDs And on her face while kneeling and Screaming for "MORE" of a beating as her DommeAnna AND Allie slapped her cummed-on Face and pulled her hair in a Sadistic gangbang.

The two Dominating and Sadistic FemDommes Anna and Allie were as pleased with their Men's performance as you could get, So Mistress/Goddess AuntieAnna to Slave/Lover, Nephew Anthony, thanked him ten times for Setting Up the Live Show for HER two-Man Fantasy, while preparing him for the Next day's busy Fetish-Providing agenda.

It was Now TIME TO COLLAR AND CO/OWN 11" Joey, So that Patty had a stud/slave to call her Own and Carol wouldn't have to worry so much about Patty luring Cousin Anthony/her Master OR him straying away to Patty's GOD-GIVEN ORAL SKILLS not many Women had.

Patty had taught Carol to Deepthroat on Cousin Anthony/MasterTony, However, and it would take a while before ALL the Gagging stopped completely with more practice that Carol continued to do on her Cousin whenever she could.

Master T had picked up Joey and was waiting on the rooftop lounge having a drink and waiting for the Bentley to arrive with the blonde knockout Domme Patty driving the NEW BENTLEY and DRESSED TO KILL.

As Master T looked down he ordered, "Joey, Hurry Downstairs, YOU NEED TO SEE THIS."

As the two young Man/Slaves opened the door downstairs to go out front and greet the girls, Patty was getting out of the Bentley in her new Versace Mini-Skirt Hot Pants suit with a vest simulating a Corset that DROPPED THE JAWS of Both Joey AND Master T as Carol looked on.

"She looks better than the fucking Bentley!" Joey shouted to his work buddy Anthony.

Patty liked what she heard and walked over to a hard-on Joey and whispered in his ear, "GOOD ENOUGH TO COLLAR YOU TODAY?" Patty whispered.

"DO IT RIGHT NOW! RIGHT HERE!" Joey said and jokingly dropped to One knee, simulating a marriage. "Patty, you owned me the minute I laid eyes on you weeks ago," Joey said while everyone laughed and nodded, included Patty, Anthony, Cousin Carol, Alice and Carmen, even the Domme was stunned for ALL to see this Magnificent Couple Bond for the first time.

"NOBODY EVEN CARED ABOUT THE NEW BENTLEY!" Patty was getting a Man/Slave today, but would have to SHARE Slave/Joey, who was already collared by Domme/Anna. "OK, then I Love hearing that, MY Slave/Joey, I have your NEW collar In the NEW Rolls just waiting to put around your neck. We'll have lunch and then WE celebrate," Patty added.

"OMG, yes! I'M living a dream," Joey watched in amazement as Patty strutted away with Carol In approval, smiling and tapping

SIR's pearl-white New Bentley Rolls Royce in Her Skin-tight Versace thigh-high leather Boots, and knockout Mini-Skirt Suit, courtesy of Louie Lipstick's 2M Insurance Protection Policy.

Lunch was at Rita's in Chelsea today to celebrate. Slave/Joey wanted to drive his new Mistress/Patty this time to show his appreciation for her, Carol and her Cousin/Master were in the luxurious back seat of the Bentley designed specifically for VIPs AND for comfort, equipped with a mini-refrigerator and mini-bar. You could stretch your legs as far as you wanted to, So your secretary could ride your cock or suck your dick on her knees on the plush rug floor, Just like Insatiable Cousin Carol was about to do right now with the tinted glass UP so neither Joey Nor Patty could see Carol Deepthroating and practicing her Oral skills on her Cousin's hard 10, laying back on the oversized soft leather couch/seat to BREAK IN THE BENTLEY, before Patty did.

Joey and Patty were happier than anyone had thought, they both had tough lives and grew up in abusive households. They both appreciated everything that came their way, but Most of all they had Honor and Loyalty that you were NOT born with, but you learned quickly in the City. THE DOMME/MistressAnna STRESSED that All the time to ALL her BDism enthusiasts. They took Nothing for granted and reciprocated when they could, they could go ALL OUT for friends and family OR in this case CHOOSE their new Family.

"THIS is Family!" Patty said, smiling towards Joey.

"YES! It is," Joey stared into her gleaming green eyes, looking at her new sandy-blonde hairdo, and was Very proud to be in her presence. Joey was About to be "Collared And owned" by a woman from his dreams in this real-life fantasy he had now entered on HIS Darkside.

Master T Could see Joey was indeed living his dream when it came to catching the eye of a beauty like Mistress Anna OR Patty and her unmatched oral skills.

Joey couldn't see straight and it was time for his friend and work buddy Anthony/MasterTony to talk to Joey and BE SURE Joey knew ALL the "BDISM RULES" and not be hurt or disillusioned going into this lifestyle that's NOT for everyone.

The Bentley pulled up to Rita's Secluded parking lot in the rear of the Restaurant as directed by Patty where to park to perform her ceremony on her hypnotized sub/stud soon-to-be Slave/Joey.

Carol put fresh Lipstick on after deepthroating her cousin's load deep down her throat and the Master zipped up, telling the girls he NEEDED a minute to take a piss and talk to Joey before Patty Collared him for life!

"What's up?" Joey asked his concerned buddy Anthony.

"My Pal Joey," the Master started to say, "THIS is NOT a game or a fantasy dream. This IS all REAL, my good friend, and YOU better be ready to SERVE and Protect Patty with your life, AND I MEAN THAT! That goes for THE DOMME herself, Who is also Your Mistress Anna that Co-Owns you. Carol and I will always have your back, you're with us now but I need you to

understand, Joey, I Don't allow anything or Anyone to hurt MY Ladies OR my close friends and Family, and You ARE a close friend! DO YOU UNDERSTAND, MY BUDDY?" Master T/Anthony coldly stressed those words, staring into Joey's eyes.

Joey answered immediately to calm the Master's concern, "OF COURSE, ANTHONY! I can see what I'm doing and I DO understand your concern. I see what you do for them and I WILL ALWAYS have your back too. Nobody is going to get hurt, I promise you," Joey ended.

Patty and Carol heard every word with the windows down a crack to listen. The girls now exited the car and popped the trunk to get Joey's NEW COLLAR purchased yesterday on their shopping spree by Domme Patty. Carol had bought one for Her Cousin/Master T as well while at the leather specialty store, IF and WHEN the time came.

Patty pointed down to a clean spot for Joey to kneel before her $500.00 Gucci stilettos And smooth toned legs, NO Panties on for what was coming after the collar was secured around Slave Joey's neck. Patty now asked her Slave-to-be, "Slave Joey, repeat after me... 'I'll wear this collar you have chosen just for me, Slave/Joey C, To be loyal, obedient and honor Goddess Patty that stands before me! To serve, please and be Used by Mistress/ Domme Patty, To be the loyal slave that I crave to be.' DO YOU ACCEPT MY COLLAR, SLAVE JOEY C?" Patty concluded her Pledge.

Slave/Joey repeated his vow that his NEW Co-Owned Goddess/Mistress Patty had just demanded, "ABSOLUTELY," JOEY

added, "I'll be the best slave to serve your every need, I WILL BE the slave you need me to be, YOU ARE A GODDESS SENT JUST FOR ME."

Patty smiled down on him as he looked up at her neatly trimmed heart-shaped blonde bush while Patty Collared her drooling stud/slave with his new 3"-wide soft leather collar with rubies, emeralds and diamond chips around Slave Joey's thick neck that spelled out "Patty's Man Slave."

The Cousins Carol and Anthony were witnesses to this "Eager Collaring" of Slave Joey to serve Patty's insatiable needs DAILY.

Once inside Rita's Italian restaurant Slave Joey would be "INITIATED" while under the table with the long tablecloths to cover his body and feet as he would be instructed to "EAT OUT" All four ladies present while on his knees ONE AT A TIME To see his stamina, endurance and put his Oral skills to the Ultimate test.

The Domme Patty would take control now to Collared and Co-Owned Slave Joey, along with the Goddess herself, Domme/ Anna. MommeDomme and Daughter Carol had always LOVED Rita's food AS WELL AS THE TABLECLOTHS for their amusement of the Oral play in public. But TODAY, however, was Patty's day and she would get the First pussylicking until she was pleased by HER Slave Joey, Then Domme/Anna 2nd, Then Carol 3rd, Then Alice 4th, ALL four Fetish-Providing insatiable Beauties must be pleased by the end of dinner for Slave Joey's Initiation under Domme Patty.

Master T/Anthony COULD NOT help him in ANY way. He could only Pass him a wet napkin to wipe his mouth after each

serving, OR a glass of water to wash down a heavy Multi/
Cummer like Carol, OR to cheer Joey on.

Master T leaned down under the table, Smiling to say, "YOU
CAN DO IT, JOEY, Just think of four nice Cannolis from the
St. Anthony's feast, take your time with them and ENJOY all 4"
one at a time." Master's ladies enjoyed the clever advice and had
a great laugh as Joey kept on eating now on #2 with two more to
go after the Goddess.

Patty leaned over to whisper in her Master's Ear, who was on
the far left. Carol was in the middle next to her mom and couldn't
hear Patty say, "I HEARD WHAT YOU SAID TO JOEY
ABOUT 'HE BETTER PROTECT ME'! and Carol Wonders
why I love you so much?? THANK YOU, MY MASTER! NO-
BODY COMES CLOSE TO YOU, SIR!" Patty concluded.

As Patty leaned forward a bit to get her cloth napkin to wipe
some pussyCum dripping down her smooth naked legs that Joey
had missed, she passed the cum-soaked napkin onto Master T's
lap. The Master inconspicuously WIPED his mouth with Patty's
CUM on the napkin she passed to him, where Patty said He had
a spot of spaghetti sauce on his lip without Carol ever suspecting
Her Cousin Anthony was TASTING Patty's MangoJuice off the
cum-soaked napkin onto his lips right in the middle of dinner.

Master T and Patty laughed as he used Patty's FruityD-
'Mango Wet-Nap to dab his lips for the next 45 minutes. That
was when Slave Joey would finish Dabbing his mouth after Alice
#4 finally squirted heavily into Joey's mouth for a very Tasty, and

Testy Induction Day Ordered By Joey's new strict and diabolical Mistress/Goddess, "Domme Patty."

Joey now belonged to Patty. He had been inducted and passed her expectations of him eating out the four delicious kinkster women on his knees under the table at Rita's restaurant, hidden by the long tablecloths. Master T, his work buddy, Anthony, could ONLY coach Joey and NOT help him please the fabulous four also employed at SIR along with Joey, Carmen and Master T.

Master T had done three of the four Insatiable women before TWICE in the same day on a Tease bet by his Mistress and Goddess/Domme AuntieAnnaA. The Nephew and Master to ALL his Goddess/Aunt Anna's needs took on the bet with pleasure.

Born with the tongue to eat pussy ALL DAY LONG if He wanted to and make them Squirt, Master T happily slurped ALL the Mango of ALL three Ladies right down and now must teach Joey his technique ordered by Domme Anna AND now by Patty.

Domme Anna had bet her Nephew/Master while at the Cottage on Labor Day weekend that HE COULDN'T Orally please ALL three women in the morning, THEN do it again that same night. His taunting Goddess Aunt bet him That IF SHE LOST the bet, SHE would please HIM Orally two times in the same day.

Nephew Anthony/Master T won the bet and received two BLOWJOBS from the Honorable Domme Auntie Anna the very next day, Once waking him up, Then AGAIN putting him to sleep.

The MommeDomme Insisted Carol and Patty be "Eaten-Out" separately during the tease bet, then the Domme last that

day, NOT wanting to be involved in sexual sessions with her daughter. Master T gave advice to his work Pal Joey while Eating-Out the four women into one juicy orgasm after the other to just think of the Cream-Filled Cannolis from Mike's Pastry in the North End and to savor each succulent slurp. "Eat it SLOWLY and just Relax, enjoy it. Eat it from the inside out like the cannoli. Take ALL the cream that oozes out first, then move up to the top and flick that clit real good and hard, reach inside with a finger or two real slow and tickle the G-Spot a bit, then take more cream, now just wait for your Gushing/Squirting Prize, DON'T move until SHE moves your face away. Let the cannoli melt in your mouth, Then you get yourself ANOTHER Cannoli until you have finished ALL four," the Master advised Joey as his lips and tongue were getting tired blistered and sore, as Joey started on number four.

Poor Joey was SOAKING WET but didn't seem to care one bit as he was almost done with his Initiation and first Demand from Domme Patty, who now Co/Owned Slave Joey, OK'd by Domme Anna Slave/Joey's first Owner and Domme of ALL Dommes in HER Dungeon.

Master T could see Alice WAS the last girl to be orally pleased By the newly Collared Slave Joey when Alice leaned back in her chair, closing her eyes, and opened her mouth, trying so hard NOT to scream as Alice filled Joey's mouth with her Sweet MangoJuice.

Carol smiled at her Cousin and fixed her wide leather belt, lifting her torso to give her Master a glimpse of her hard Pro-

truding huge nipples, showing right through her thin blouse. Cousin Anthony, her Master, could only smile and nod in approval of his younger Goddess sitting next to his First Fantasy Goddess, Her Mom!

When Alice tightly held on to the arms of the chair, closed her eyes tight While throwing her head WE ALL KNEW! "Mission accomplished"! It WAS the last Orgasm exploded from four Nymphomaniacs in a little over an hour!

"VERY GOOD!" replied Alice, gleaming with approval. "I'M GOING TO LOVE IT HERE!" she concluded.

"Adda Boy, Joey!!" replied Master T, talking down under the table so his soaking-wet buddy could hear while Patty took his hand, helping him up, and led him to the Men's room and said to her new Shared Slave and Property, "WASH UP, SLAVE. You're NOT getting in MY Bentley all soaking wet like that," the ruthless Domme Patty told the exhausted PussyCum-licking Slave/Joey.

CHAPTER

18A

The Boss MommeDomme wasted No time to go over tomorrow's agenda. Now all very pleased in their Private reserved Circular Booth with floor-length tablecloths facing the fireplace, "YOU BELONG TO ME NOW!" Patty sternly told her Newly collared Slave Joey for everyone to hear.

Alice put her hand up to go first AFTER the last Squirting Orgasm OF four, and mentioned her three responsibilities to SIR, MRI scanning, and follow-up Physical Therapist. Alice was top of her class, a Psychology Major with a Doctorate Degree in Biochemistry and now a Radiologist. BUT what her ex-Husband did to her head left Alice with some Psychological problems of own that THESE WOMEN WOULD CURE! Period....

Alice met Anthony/Master T, along with at least six other curious Italian horny teenage studs, in the N. End Fruit Market that

loved getting their cocks wet from Alice's revenge sex, Ages ranging from sixteen to twenty. Alice lured them over to drink beer
and get blown or fucked their brains out three-four at a time until
she just wanted the BIG ONES, ten Inches or more, and that was
how Anthony, Joey and Carmen were chosen.

NOW Alice eventually ended up At Rita's as one of the Fabulous Four Getting SERVICED herself, which would be a PERK
now In her NEW POSITION employed at "SIR" after Alice's
FAVORITE Anthony introduced Alice to HIS Aunt Anna.

Alice's favorite Italian hung teen was Anthony, whom She called
Tony OR just plain "T," who always licked Alice's pussyCum Clean
while she sucked off three-four of his buddies at a time in GangBang
style, making her GROWL like an animal that the teens loved hearing, making Us cum faster and harder, sometimes Twice!

"The Boston Red Sox have two MRI appointments for scanning, then to be read and advised on," said a happy Alice. "Our
new MRI Scanner will pay itself off in NO time with the Sports
contracts that use 'SIR' as their MRI service provider. THEN we
get to treat them too in More ways than one with follow-up Physical Therapy, their Insurance Co. approves eight-ten sessions at
a time, Mistress Anna," Alice added confidently.

"NICE! I love it," Mistress Anna added with Carol And Patty
nodding, grinning.

"WE ARE SO HAPPY to have found you, Alice, YOU FIT
RIGHT IN HERE WITH US," Carol said Directly! Taking
control of the conversation now.

"Alice! We would LOVE to continue our concentration On the MRI Lucrative scanning procedures from the Sports Contracts AND Hospital referrals I've been hearing about. Let's reach out to ALL the major Hospitals and let them know WE AT 'SIR' HAVE THE MRI Expertise, Scanning/reading/and treating through Physical Therapy, A BRAND-NEW FACILITY, with Brand-new LICENCED, QUALIFIED, and CERTIFIED THERAPISTS," Carol directly told an ambitious Alice.

Mistress and Domme Mom hugged her brilliant, cloned daughter next To her and just said, "WOW, I couldn't have said it ANY better," with Patty surprised, looking on, nodding in approval. "Let's GO WITH THAT! Alice, BATTER UP!" the Domme Anna concluded.

"LET'S ALL HAVE COFFEE IN THE MORNING, 7 A.M., and go over the appointments, Agenda and what to keep or let wait," Carol ended.

While renovating the new "SIR" facility, Carol was contemplating what equipment would be needed for sports-related injuries. Carol was advised by a Red Sox player that had his eyes GLUED to her long, perfectly toned legs and tight silk/linen blouse with her huge nipples staring right back at him.

He mumbled in his own saliva to say, "MRI scanning was THE most important thing to have to see the extent of the injury immediately and Treat it right away," as the player wiped his chin and licked his lips.

Carol was flattered as always and thanked the player, smiling the day the three knockouts went on a Promotional tour of the City. Carol then got the financial support from her Ex/Fiancé Louie Lipstick for 100k for a deposit and got the MRI Machine ordered and in place in a month for the Grand Opening,.

The Injured Player went directly to "SIR" for scanning and read right there to give the information results to the organization's team Dr. Then billed to the organization's Insurance Co. with eight-twelve treatments of Physical Therapy sessions To Follow!! The very expensive Medical piece of technology was well worth Carol's Investment into her Mom's new legitimate Venture of Massage Therapy.

By 2020 Standards, MRI Scanners pricing went between one million - three million dollars. In 1975 Carol spent 800K for the best one. As the saying goes, "It takes Money to Make Money," Carol told her MommeDomme Anna, and now had the Money! Momme had a lot of money hidden as well and her protector/ nephew Master T would make sure NOBODY tried to take ANY money from them, Even with the "Wiseguys" trying to shake them down would meet their match with Uncle Angelo. Between the Domme's street smarts, connections, skills, beauty and College Degrees, there was A LOT of money to be made for the knockout Fetish-providing "Therapists."

The business SIR was now on a roll, the injured players came in for an MRI. Alice read it and sent a diagnosis to the players' doctor for Physical Therapy treatment. The player would get

better from the time off, AND the physical therapy treatments would eventually help as well. SIR would get a patient for thousands of dollars from the Insurance co. and just maybe a NEW SPECIAL CLIENT would be back for "Private" and more Personal Sessions!

It was 7 A.M., time for coffee and fresh jelly donuts rolled in sugar while still warm. The jelly donuts were made by two old Italian ladies at 3 A.M.- 9 A.M. DAILY and sold from the basement of the triple-decked brick building on Chelsea St. in East Boston by Maverick Sq. near SIR, and the donuts were for the briefing on the day's agenda.

Carol and Patty were first to meet the Boss MommeDomme, since they were ALL living on the Penthouse floor Along with Anthony/Master T, who always gave the Ladies a private talk before walking in after HIS own choice of breakfast.

He told them DONUTS were going to make them fat, So Cousin Carol would then lift up her blouse and slap her hard flat belly and reveal a partially huge nipple to say, "Does this look like fat to you?" Carol teased, while her Momme and Patty enjoyed the witty humor, taking bites of their warm delicious Homemade jelly donuts, now rubbing THEIR solid Flat bellies as well, laughing and taunting their Master and Protector, just shaking his head, smiling, admiring their flawless bodies.

"Alice will be here at 7:15 with Carmen! He will be running Alice's errands and MRI disks into Boston, and whatever else

YOU all need Carmen to do as well. I Won't be needing him all day so I'll let Alice have a nice Man perk around for working so hard. I already gave the OK to put Carmen ON THE PAYROLL for Alice's assistant and deliveries. Alice has already sucked his dick fifty times or more anyway with MR. Donuts over there while working selling fruit, lol. NOW CARMEN CAN GIVE ALICE BLOWJOBS!" the Domme joked in conclusion. "There's Hospital Parking and Valet parking so Patty DON'T need to drive The Bentley EVERY-WHERE all the time, SHE'S NEEDED HERE MORE!" the boss Domme added. "Two Red Sox players are coming in today, 10 A.M. and 2 P.M., for our First MRI scannings and said, 'I'M SO EX-CITED.'" Domme Auntie Anna was now rubbing her belly and asked her nephew and love of her life, Master T, for another donut.

The other two flat-belly beauties, Carol and Patty, teased and smiled, then did the same to copy their Domme, Momme and Mentor.

"Carmen will drive to Landsdown St. in Boston, then hand the package of information to a staff member waiting and drive back here, UNLESS there is hospital business in Boston, In which case THE MAJOR HOSPITALS are right in that area all by LONGWOOD AVE., and BROOKLINE AVE. IT'S PER-FECT!" the Domme concluded.

"Our MRI Machine will be our MONEY Machine once we pay it off," Carol added as they all giggled with approval.

Carol now opened HER NEW JOURNAL with scheduling and planning out meetings for three major hospitals in Boston.

Carol and Patty had appointments for NEW BUSINESS concerning SIR's New facility. Carol's NEW Journal was VERY SIMILAR in size, color and shape to HER Mommes's old journal that the younger fifteen-year-old Breast-Developing, curious Kissing Cousin Carol read from with her ALSO sexually Curious 1st Cousin Anthony in the dark closet, feeling each other up.

The young horny teen Cousins would READ from her MOM/AUNTIE ANNA'S Old Client's Sex/Fetish journal and immediately fondle each other into orgasms in the "Secret Closet," where the Old BDism Clientele Journal was lost and hidden behind a loose Wooden panel in Momme's closet adjoining Carol's walk-in closet.

Cousin Anthony/Master T got up closer for a GOOD look at Carol's NEW journal that she just started writing into and remarked, "WHERE DID YOU BUY THAT?" Master T shouted out, smiling to HIS Cousin Carol.

Carol was now taking charge of the early Agenda meetings and being JUST AS DOMINANT as her Domme/Momme, Carol was Showing EVERYONE that SHE had the major controlling interest AND the intelligence, Marketing skills, along with flawless beauty just Like Mom to take this NEW VENTURE "SIR" right to the top!

The Master Couldn't believe the drive Carol now had and was SO TURNED ON by her dominance. He was sweating and getting hard but WOULD WAIT until later to REWARD HIS YOUNG GODDESS and cousin lover.

"WHY? DO YOU WANT ONE!?" Carol shouted back across the round table to answer Cousin Anthony's question about the new Burgundy and black trimmed Hard-Covered Journal she just purchased lately for SIR Business ONLY.

"ABSOLUTELY!! I want one TODAY, PLEASE, I had one just like it," Master joked.

Mistress/Goddess Auntie Anna was also now smiling and Replied, "YEA, ME TOO! but my nosey daughter and nephew stole it and got it all wet."

"Back to business, please!" Carol interrupted, smiling, turning the page of HER New Business Journal, referring to the day's agenda and a LIST of Hospitals Carol and Patty would INFILTRATE and capture the eyes of jaw-dropping Executives, MALE AND FEMALE ALIKE!

Carol had planned out four days for eight hospital contracts, "Two hospitals a day for four days," she sternly pointed out, saying, "WE SHOULD GET HALF is what I'm shooting for," Carol confidently said.

An even MORE confident blonde Knockout Patty nodding in agreement said, "WE WILL GET THEM ALL! My sweet sister," as they ALL clapped, laughing out loud. Cousin/Master T listening closely WANTED his kinky cousin more than ever now, and to read to him Tonight from the OLD JOURNAL while he drank from HER Mango Tree.

Carol had shown up today for WORK in a Commanding way! She ROCKED the Whole room And EVERYONE in it, including Boss/MommeDomme, who was supposed to be going over the Day's Agenda, BUT CAROL'S AGENDA was Much, Much More, like the whole week and then some!

Carol was planning to SHAKE UP more business in THE MEDICAL WORLD, Hospitals, Major Medical Clinics, OR ANY Facility that could REFER a patient to an "MRI" scanning facility, which Carol had purchased for "SIR" on the advice of Baseball players, and Physical therapists that KNEW how LUCRATIVE they were and a Major piece of Equipment To have in their new business venture BUT WERE VERY EXPENSIVE to purchase.

MRI Scanners in 2020 cost around $3M, equal to the $800k In 1974 that Carol spent on this NEW Medical technology scanner that could detect anything from injured Blood vessels to a torn muscle from the outside, just like an X-Ray machine did for bones.

ALICE KNEW the potential revenue the MRI Scanner would bring in, and PUSHED CAROL, "BUY IT and I'll operate it for you at SIR," Alice pleaded to Carol.

Alice knew how to operate an MRI or CAT scanner and also how to read the complex technology and what to follow up on to waste NO time in TREATING The injury for even more Insurance money from the unfortunate INTERNAL injury.

"Your Mom will be able to retire for good IN A YEAR! and YOU will have more money in YOUR bank account than you know what to do with," Alice promised Carol.

SO, CAROL BOUGHT THE 800-thousand-dollar MRI SCANNER with little convincing that it would pay for itself ten times over sooner than Carol and Cousin Anthony thought it would.

Carol was now in her Italian three-piece Skirt suit with the most perfect cleavage on any woman holding HER brand-New Journal that caught Cousin and lover Anthony's eyes that dropped his jaw today as usual,

In a commanding and intellectual voice, Carol owned the opening of the meeting today. She mentioned all the Potential this new Facility Momme had purchased as a Real Estate foreclosure and turned it into Physical Therapy Treatment Center/ Sports Injury Rehabilitation, a/k/a "SIR."

Carol Now mentioned Alice, who was introduced by Cousin Anthony/Master T To her Momme, was a blessing and that ALICE'S experience and Doctorate Degree Intelligence In this MRI field WE were all entering would take US off the ground floor right to the moon," Carol was Praising Alice, in conclusion getting Alice all wet!

Finally, PATTY! MY KNOCKOUT SISTER, had the confidence AND the smarts to promote, market, and sell you sand in the desert. Like she said earlier, When WE went out to Sell OUR MRI services next week, Patty would be sure WE got ALL eight Medical Accounts, not just one or two, LOL.

Patty ALSO pushed Me to "GET THE MACHINE" like Alice was saying she knew SIR would be big as Patty smiled and was now nodding.

"ALSO, What else can WE all say about Master T, our Rock that keeps us level headed, focused, and gives ME the confidence to stand here today, NOBODY dares to Mess with ANY of us," as Carol's Cousin and Master thanked his Goddess Carol with a wave now with his other hand in his pocket, holding his hard-on from this Vision of Beauty that belonged to ONLY HIM. "DON'T FORGET TO BUY ME A JOURNAL just like yours! Lol," he joked to Cousin Carol.

"That was a brilliant briefing!" MommeDomme Said. "Congratulations, my VP Carol, well done! You Had EVERYONE glued and focused ON YOU and that's how you do it. Get their attention and YOU own them," MommeDomme added. "And You Owned them ALL today."

Carol would now OWN Cousin Master T as if she didn't already, but this time she had a "Collar" for him to wear FOR HER as well as Co/Owner Momme. Carol bought a Collar when Patty bought Joey's, then went to Rita's for his Induction and Initiation, where Slave/Joey was ordered to Eat-Out all four women, kneeling in a puddle of MangoJuice while ON ALL FOURS.

Carol asked Patty to bring Joey and for Alice to bring Carmen to Celebrate over dinner. Master T wanted to cook for everyone tonight and said, "Mom, will you bring Evelyn?"

Carol looked to her Momme, "NO, But thanks for asking. YOU HAVE FUN TONIGHT, My VP, I have a lot of paperwork and forms for the Insurance companies you're making Me do, lol, but I LOVE what you're doing. IT's your turn, Carol.

Have half the fun I've had and I'll be happy for you," Momme-Domme added.

Master T walked up to his confident Goddess Cousin to congratulate her on the prepared speech and opening presentation she had been working So hard on with her Master in their penthouse suite all week. He told her How Incredible SHE Really WAS, "Beauty and Brains," He whispered In her ear, and to DRAW something out on paper for him to do to her tonight as the kinky couple loved to do together.

With a huge smile Carol now insisted to Cousin Master T he wear the Collar SHE bought for him, although SHE was collared by Master T as well.

"YES, of course I will Switch for you ANY TIME You want. I will even take a BDISM oath for you, My Goddess Carol. Just put the Collar on me and give me the drawing like we always did when we weren't So busy, Bring MY Collar tonight and I'll do the Oath for you!"

"REALLY? I'd love that!" Carol added, jumping up and down. "You're Mine, although I think everyone knows that by now," she giggled.

"YES! It's out there for everyone to see, anyway! Fuck all the Vanilla people That Don't understand as far as I'm concerned, You are the air I breathe!" Anthony/Master T continued To tell his lover/cousin, melting her heart where she stood and sending her juices flowing. Carol was ready to take everything off right there but wanted Him in the New Collar first, an Expensive soft

leather Collar with Diamond, Jade and Ruby stones spelling out HER name across the 3"-wide black leather Collar, "PROPERTY Of GODDESS CAROL."

Carol had to wait until tonight and Collar Cousin, Lover Anthony/Master, of all her needs in front of Patty, although She would Share Him With Patty ONLY when Carol wanted to and Carol had everyone KNOW who OWNED her 1st Cousin Anthony... Period.

Domme Patty had already accepted the fact Anthony/Master T would Never leave Carol, So Patty was happy with the sharing and the swapping, having her pussy and ass eaten out hours at a time by his oversized talented tongue with the ability to make Patty squirt like Nobody else could.

Patty just Waited and LOVED when Carol asked her to join in on three-way sessions Patty Domme's Master T really good in Golden Shower sessions trained by Mistress Anna herself just the way He liked it. Carol enjoyed watching Him being held down while giving her Cousin the Master his favorite GS Fetish, the hot salty Yellow Rain.

Carol and Patty Always worked the kissing kinky Cousin over nicely together and the two beauties now had added Alice to special sessions, treating the Master to three ladies when they could.

"In Business and in BDISM, there are rules that one MUST follow," said the Goddess Auntie Anna/MommeDomme to her stubborn cloned Goddess daughter Carol. "In order to Collar and Own someone who IS ALREADY OWNED, They MUST ask

the ORIGINAL Owner to 'Co-Own Property/Slaves,' Like Master T and I Co-Own Patty, then I will SHARE with PERMISSION," added Momme. "Master T has informed ME, His Mistress and Original Owner, that HE wishes to be Shared And collared with MY daughter CAROL. ARE YOU, MY DAUGHTER, CAROL??" the curious Owner and MommeDomme asked her frowning daughter Carol.

"YES! I am!" Carol replied. "Master T said I would have to ask for your permission AFTER he asks you first, then I was going to ask your permission to Co-Own and Collar him tonight and WE could do the INDUCTION AND INITIATION together IF YOU LIKE, GODDESS," Carol curiously asked.

"HMMMMM, Now THAT sounds interesting. I also think Your Anthony and OUR MASTER T will enjoy hearing that! SO YES, YOU have My permission to Co-Own OUR Loyal Master. WHAT'S MINE IS YOURS ALWAYS And MAYBE WE could do A Mother/Daughter thing on OUR Co-owned SLAVE/MASTER T and get PAUL'S $50,000. Without US playing with each other," MommeDomme added to her interested daughter.

Carol told Paul $100,000!! That Carol would DO IT ALL For The Mother/Daughter live pussylicking show with sex toys, strap-ons AND using Paul's kinky wife Grace as well. MOMMEDOMME Still said "NO" To Mom-on-Daughter play, NOT FOR ANY AMOUNT. BUT it now seemed different with the Nephew/Cousin Anthony involved as the center of attention.

"ONLY IF Master T would USE BOTH GODDESSES TO-GETHER, and Give Master T a Golden Shower WITH the wife Grace pissed on too!! PAUL AND HIS WIFE WOULD LOVE THAT OFFER!!" the Domme suggested to her daughter.

"I'll ask Grace right now!" curious Carol anxiously added to her Very Interested MommeDomme, who LOVED giving her groomed nephew and Sub/Stud a good Golden Shower along with a mouthful of her hot MangoJuice in very Dominating sessions.

Later that evening, Carol was waiting on Patty and Joey to arrive while Master T was Chatting with The Older wiser Goddess about His Induction ceremony to his FemDomme kinky counterpart Cousin Carol, who now NEEDED to Co-Own him.

The 1st cousins and artists were Literally crawling TO each other since they were six months old at each other's auntie's house, and STILL DID TODAY only for different reasons.

Carol had Cousin Anthony's Collar all ready to put around his neck and have him recite A prepared oath to her while kneeling before her on BOTH knees.

Tonight, Carol would have HER collared Cousin Sub/Slave Anthony To Initiate and Induct to make it official, THEN his Domme Auntie Anna would make him pay and sit for a Dominating Golden Shower session.

Domme Anna, Millionaire Paul's wife Grace AND her daughter Carol would be the three ladies Master T would be Eating-Out and ALL of them would "RUB ONE OFF" on him!

This was AFTER THE MASTER FUCKED MOM/ DOMME and NEW CO-OWNER DAUGHTER CAROL TOGETHER for his Induction AND TOOK Paul's $100,000 for the Mother/Daughter live sex show act!

Master T, Patty and Joey were READY for Carol's prepared Oath that Master T Must repeat and promise to obey. Carol pointed to the floor for Her New Sub/Slave Cousin and Master, now kneeling repeated, "I Kneel before you today to be your Collared, Co-Owned Property and slave. I always will Obey and do Whatever you say. I will never stray and I'm here to stay! I will Do what you wish to please and pleasure you, I will be Loyal to you, Or beat me Until I'm black and blue," Cousin/Slave Anthony repeated as he kissed her High-Heeled Stilettos.

"DO YOU ACCEPT THIS COLLAR, MY SLAVE?" Carol asked sternly.

"YES, MY GODDESS CAROL, I WILL accept My beautiful collar before me. I promise to serve you in every way and to be the slave I crave to be."

The Co-Owned surrendered and submitted Master Proudly pledged to his Goddess Carol, then looked up begging to be Inducted and Used (BY HIS TWO GODDESSES) in this Ceremonial, which would ALSO serve as a $100K LIVE MOTHER/ DAUGHTER SEX SHOW.

MommeDomme was on the phone and reached Paul Travello and kinky trophy wife Grace. Grace LOVED The two God-

desses' Proposal, then said, "THEY will be there by 7 and will bring the checkbook."

"MONEY IS NO PROBLEM," added Grace. "This kind of thing DON'T come by often, ONLY ONCE IN A LIFETIME YOU GET TO SEE TWO BEAUTIFUL WOMEN LIKE YOU AND YOUR CLONED DAUGHTER IN A LIVE PRIVATE SEX SHOW. My husband Paul and I will be so excited to watch you both, along with ME drowning your Nephew/Master in a Golden Shower session, while eating the three of us out while I Blow my husband. We are dying to see these Screaming Multi-Orgasms that you both claim HE CAN MAKE YOU DO! WE WILL PAY 100K FOR THAT ANY DAY," the Kinkster wife Grace concluded, running her fingers across her hard nipples as she spoke of her very expensive fantasy provided by The Domme Anna.

Carol was holding her Slave/Master Cousin Anthony's New designer collar and smiling, moving ever closer to his mouth as he grabbed Onto her hips to lick her bare wet pussy while she lifted her skirt briefly, buckling the Collar in place that read: "Property of Goddess Carol," spelled out in multi/colored hand-cut Gemstones! (Red Rubies, White diamonds and Green Jade gemstones (Italian Colors)), clearly outdoing her mom's collar to their Master/Lover and now their slave as well!

Master T was then congratulated by Carol and Joey and The Domme was now on the phone, telling Carol that Grace and Paul

were on their way to witness the collaring and participate in the induction for the $100,000 LIVE SHOW, as proposed.

"Really?" Carol giggled.

"WOW!" Master T shouted out! "This is the best collaring ever, lol, and the induction I'll make sure is worthy of My new Owner," as the Co-Owned Cousin pinched Carol's huge hard visible nipple in her see-through top she wore for the Collaring ceremonial.

MommeDomme was there to greet the wealthy high-class Kinksters that had been steadies for a while now. Grace LOVED to be used by Varney, the 10" she/male, and the Domme Anna's huge strap-ons in Bondage sessions while her husband jerked off on her, beating her with his belt.

Grace licked the cum off his belt as he would scold her what a whore she was and Grace sometimes would cum from that alone!!

Recently the three studs had been violently fucking Grace in all three holes while her husband Paul was Loving the New Addition of the two Young studs, Joey and Carmen, and they were coming back Every week! IF Grace wanted it Kinky, they came to the right place!!

Ever since Paul had first seen Carol and she was Legal (eighteen years old), He started his offer of 20k for the two Bi/beauty queens. The Domme just laughed at him, BUT when Carol heard $50,000, She KNEW The kinky millionaire would go $100,000, and so he did!

When someone has fifty Million in Bank accounts all over the world, WTF is 100k to him? His accountants would probably

find a way to deduct it somehow from one of their ten different investments they had, Just like The Domme offered billing For Physical Therapy and its Insurance deductible For business expense accounts for stress, when it was really a massage by Domme Anna OR Domme Patty, "FISTING" Grace's Pussy, TIED to a massage table until she squirted while her husband Paul jerked off on her watching Grace scream, "It's only money!"

Millionaire businessman Paul Travello sat for a minute and Made sure BOTH Gorgeous Mother Anna AND Carbon-Copy Daughter Carol Would be putting on a Live sex show with their 10" Prized possession Master T would be in a kinky three-way that would also involve Paul's wife eating them out, while Fucked doggy style in their gorgeous asses by their Nephew/Cousin and slave.

Paul wrote the check and handed it over to Carol's waiting open hand to look over the check.

"It looks good!" Carol said.

But then Cousin/Anthony/pointed to Paul and said, "If THIS Check bounces, I'll be bouncing YOU off the brick walks up and down this street! Gabeesh?"

"No Problem! I keep my word, just like YOU and Your Mistresses Do," Paul confidently said to a suspicious Master T. "Now please, Can we all just have some fun? And Congratulations, 'T,' on being Collared by such a beautiful woman. Yes, Carol and her Mom told me everything, YOU are the luckiest man alive to have Them Both!!! Omg! Fuck my wife's ass hard as you can and make

her squeal loud like the pig she is," Paul concluded with a hand-shake to Master T, now smiling.

Master T told Patty to "Bring OUR Mistress to the door and have Joey STAY CLOSE by with YOU, Patty, but first hand Me a blindfold so I can put it on the MommeDomme when I walk her out for all to watch MOMME ANNA and DAUGHTER CAROL NAKED TOGETHER."

They would Get BOTH their Pussies and Assholes Pounded hard by THEIR groomed and Trained-to-please Master while blindfolded and tied side by side. Mother and Daughter WOULD BE whipped, Cropped, slapped and flogged by their Master's belt strap. BOTH Mother/Daughter Beauties would be eaten-out by slut trophy wife Grace AND the Master While Paul jerked off on his wife's face while Grace lapped up BOTH Mother and Daughter's PussyCum for a cool $100,000. Carol would be a mouthful and then some!

MommeDomme walked up to Master T as usual when SHE was about to be used by her Nephew/Master T, and would whisper in his ear, "DO WHATEVER YOU WANT TO ME," closing her eyes, NOT to see her daughter putting her hands be-hind herself to be tied and Blindfolded, THEN Kissed her Lover/Nephew deeply.

Domme Auntie Anna then added, "FUCK ME HARD, MASTER! Fuck Me like an Animal, I want to scream while you pound both of YOUR Sluts doggy style all tied up and blindfolded," making her nephew's big 10" cock harder and harder. "I'M SO fuck-

ing HOT for this live show now! I KNOW CAROL WANTED THIS 100K SESSION. So Give them their money's worth, SIR," the Domme Aunt concluded to her Nephew.

Master/Nephew cuffed his Goddess, then Blindfolded The wet Domme of his dreams and Stood her in front of Paul on DISPLAY, leaning her against the massage table With her legs spread apart, revealing His Aunt Anna's flawless trimmed manicured puffy wet pussy. She was manicured so neatly into the shape of a heart, you could see her Full and Meaty Labia.

NEXT was Carol to be displayed with her unique oversized nipples looking more like purple plums now and Visibly pulsating and hard as stone. The millionaire kinkster Paul was jerking his cock, looking at these two gorgeous women ready to be fucked back and forth in each of their three holes while their Master/Slave T was now whipping them softly alternately across BOTH their hard nipples.

Mother/Daughter's heart-shaped solid asses had been lubed up with warm flavored oils for a good Deep tongue fucking, Opening their holes wide before fucking BOTH the beauties' assholes Into orgasms. Master T HAD made BOTH HIS submissive Collared Beauty ANAL SLUTS MULTI/CUM in this way many times before, Especially Carol, who NOW had really learned to relax during ANAL and now loved her ASS fucked by her Cousin/MASTER T.

Carol would often whisper in his ear at home, "WILL YOU PLEASE FUCK MY ASS, 'SIR'?" while relaxing on the sofa In

their suite, driving her Cousin/Lover Anthony WILD for her every time. Carol had taken a page from her Momme's book of foreplay.

Circling Both Mother/Daughter tied to each other and Blindfolded by the Master T , He whipped a little harder each time as he passed their hard, perfectly rounded Italian asses. They BOTH could really handle a hard whipping or the wooden paddle he had used on both of them many times before, sometimes at their own request.

He started to whip harder now on Carol's unique nipples that were marked and pulsating as she gasped to the hard strikes on her enormous plum-sized nipples on a DD cup. This nipple torture started Carol's pussy streaming as only her Master knew how she liked to be treated (like HIS slut). Their Master was visibly hard as a rock and lowered Momme to her knees and teased her with 10" of Hot Meat while blindfolded, first caressing his Mistress Aunt's full sensual lips with his warm hard cock, eagerly opening her mouth wide to take All of her nephew. But then he took it away, slapping her face with his hard 10".

MommeDomme then begged, "PLEASE, Master, Give it back to me! Please, Sir, FaceFuck ME, for Everyone to see, THE WHORE and Slut I crave to be, Only for YOU, Master T," the Domme Auntie Anna recited her plea.

"Not yet, MY SLUT !" slapping the Goddess' hard nipples, then she turned to Daughter Carol's long black thick Ponytail, lowering Cousin Carol to her knees Right next to her Momme shoulder to shoulder so they were now touching and feeling each

other's hot naked flesh, visibly exciting them BOTH While Moving In closer slowly and sensually.

The Bi/Sexual MommeDomme WAS NOT concerned anymore that it was her Daughter Carol and JUST ANOTHER PUSSY ready to be lapped up to enjoy now while Carol HAD ALWAYS taken that attitude in this situation and was even More openminded than her Momme.

Master T squeezed Carol's face and mouth and just ordered, "OPEN WIDE," then slapped Carol with his hard dick on her face, stuffing both his balls into her mouth, and told the heated Cousin Carol, "You Suck my balls!" and then turned to her Momme.

Master/Nephew Anthony now pulled his Goddess Aunt by her hair, Facefucking the beauty with his hard 10" for the millionaire Paul to watch up close as Paul and wife Grace went wild six feet away, jerking off his cock in Grace's mouth, watching this Awesome LIVE Oral Performance with MOTHER and DAUGHTER sharing their Nephew/Cousin's hard 10" cock, sucking on his two huge balls while he pulled their hair and Slapped them as they moaned, drooled and kissed.

"YOU! SLUT GRACE, Get over here and lick My ass, RIGHT NOW!" Master T demanded.

Grace went down on both knees and opened the Master's cheeks to lick his flavor-lubed asshole to her approval and started to finger the Mother/Daughter while BOTH continued to suck on their Master. Their gorgeous faces touched as one was sucking balls and the other taking 10" of thick hard meat.

Master now told his collared Mother/Daughter to switch now for Carol to SHOW OFF her deepthroating skills to Paul and his wife Grace to see as Cousin Anthony fucked Carol down her throat, holding it IN HER THROAT for the Millionaire Paul to see, giving him his money's worth.

"WOW! THAT IS AWESOME, SIR," Paul said in admiration.

"I'm coming, Master! I'm coming right now!" the Domme Aunt begged. "PLEASE fuck me now, SIR, Fuck me hard like the Animal you are!" the Domme Aunt teased and pleaded her groomed Nephew, tearing her pussy up for the past five years now.

SO the MASTER bent Both beautiful Mother and Daughter over the table, opening the Goddess of his dreams NOW who was just a Surrendered Submissive Slut, dripping her pussycum down her legs, onto to the floor.

Now the groomed Nephew was holding his Slut Goddess Aunt down with one hand on her 24inch lower back and the other hand pulling her hair back, Sliding his hard 10 in, pounding her HARD right away, enjoying HIS Goddess Aunt Anna begging and crying tears for "MORE! "HARDER! FUCK ME LIKE AN ANIMAL," Her Nephew's favorite foreplay line!

Carol was being held down now and Fucked deep by her Cousin/Master and STILL pulling his Goddess Aunt's hair with the other as SHE was still squirting everywhere and screaming out for the Millionaire's pleasure and 100K PAID session to really give him his money's worth. Carol was now reaching over to ca-

ress Momme's ass and fingering her wet streaming pussy to taste, making Momme Explode!

"I'M COMING AGAIN! OMG!" the Goddess in a crying explosive orgasm and now moaning like the nymphomaniac that SHE WAS.

"FUCK MY MOMME GOOD, MASTER!" Carol told HER COLLARED COUSIN/MASTER that drove Slut Grace and Paul into ANOTHER ORGASM. "FUCK ME IN MY ASS and MAKE ME EAT MY MOMME'S PUSSY without her knowing, Please? I want her pussy bad!" Carol whispered to her Slave/Cousin Anthony and Master, NOT caring Domme Auntie Anna was her Momme AT ALL!

"Joey! Patty! Get over here!" Master T yelled out, then ordered Patty to hold Grace and lube Grace's ass and for Joey to fuck her ass hard with his big 11", Then to help DP in the Mother/Daughter show.

Patty was now feeding Grace her pussy, rubbing one off on Grace's face while husband Paul also cummed on Grace's wet face.

Back and forth and ready to explode, the hard hung Nephew pounded his Domme Aunt AND her Daughter bent over the massage table side by side, now caressing each other's ass and kissing and stroking each other's hair while being pounded deep and held down defenseless by their Dominating Master.

Master's Domme Aunt and 1st Cousin Carol continued to multi/cum and console each other until their exploding Master turned the Mother/Daughter around to hang their heads OVER the

side of the massage table to FUCK BOTH THEIR THROATS, EJACULATING A HUGE LOAD OF CUM FOR BOTH MOTHER AND DAUGHTER TO SHARE WHILE CUM SWAPPING AS THEY FRENCH KISSED EACH OTHER PASSIONATELY.

The Stunned millionaire Paul was on his second load while his wife Grace was sucking off her excited Husband watching the Master FINISH off his Goddess, then Daughter Carol into a puddle of ALL three of their hot Mango on the two leather massage tables pulled together. To Finish things up, EVERYONE watched Domme Patty put Grace on her knees, humping her mouth up against the massage table, slapping her like an animal, then squirted on Grace's face.

Joey had his 11" buried IN GRACE'S ASS for Paul to see just six feet away, then stood up to jerk off on Grace's face while Patty was ready was now rubbing ANOTHER one off ON GRACE'S FACE, Soaking her with three loads of different cum, and Grace was ready for a shower.

IT WAS NOW MASTER T'S TURN TO BE USED and WAS TO BE an initiation day to remember when MOMMEDOMME AND NEW CO-OWNER DAUGHTER CAROL, DOMME PATTY, And PAID PARTICIPANT GRACE would Initiate Master T Into Being Collared by his Soulmate and aggressive Cousin Carol.

Master T would be blindfolded THIS TIME BY HIS Mistress/Goddess Auntie Anna.

DOMME PATTY and DOMME ANNA Loved to Dominate in these Golden Shower sessions, Carol enjoyed watching him squirm and gagging on the Salty yellow rain And liked to control the Dominating pee play when it came to her Cousin/lover, Master and now Slave.

Carol called to go FIRST. "HE belongs to ME now so I will hold him and Pee first, then you two can pee next!" Carol said to her MommeDomme AND Patty.

"HE BELONGS TO US, You mean! My Dirty Darling Daughter," the Domme reminded Carol.

"YES, MOMME, of course! BUT It's MY Collaring TODAY, haha," Carol reminded Mom. "WE JUST SHARED HIM NICELY, DIDN'T WE? Lol, and made $100K," Carol giggled.

"YES, WE DID! And Yum, It wasn't as bad as I thought, Good job, my Delicious Daughter."

With that out of the way, Carol held her new Slave/Cousin's arms behind him and ordered him to "lay down," standing over him, then gave him a long hot stream of her hot piss directly into her Collared Cousin/Slave's opened mouth.

The Domme Anna held Patty's big tits from behind in line while Patty took Slave/Master's wet hair from Carol, pushing his head Back and squeezing his face.

"OPEN," Patty demanded like always, Filling his mouth full of her hot pee, listening closely to the sound of his mouth being filled up.

Patty then said, "I LOVE THE SOUND OF THAT! Now swallow!" she demanded, closing the Slave's mouth shut and holding it shut until he swallowed ALL of Patty's hot salty Pee.

The ruthless Domme Patty turned and kissed Her MistressAnna, saying, "YOU'RE NEXT."

"Very Dominant! Good job, DommePatty," replied THE DOMME of the Golden Shower! "LAY DOWN, SLAVE!!" demanded The DOMME. "I want to squat And pee like we done for your first time. Do you remember, Nephew?" whispered his Domme/AuntieAnna into his wet ear.

"OH, YES, Mistress! I Remember well," said Slave T on the shower floor.

Carol watched HER Collared Love/Slave LAYING DOWN and taking her MOMMEDOMME'S piss while squatting and squeezing his face, pissing LONG and HARD Right into his mouth From six inches away, choking and gasping for air. The Domme Aunt held her Nephew/Slave down with her knees on his arms and her strong long legs kept his head in place, he was HELPLESS!

"DRINK, DRINK MY PISS! And breathe slowly Like I taught you!" the Domme Aunt had schooled her PussyPeeCum-Drinking teenage Nephew/lover again and again each week in their earlier years at her office after his High School Classes.

"YES, MISTRESS, I do remember," catching his breath, ready to DRINK more as she squatted, still holding him steady as Carol held her Momme's hair back to witness this Dominance

of the Pee/Play MommeDomme had Mastered a long time ago, and ALL the ladies Present would learn "HOW TO GIVE A DOMINATING GOLDEN SHOWER" today.

Grace was NEXT and her First time peeing on a guy and was nervous around the other Pro kinksters, but gave Master a good amount of hot pee before Patty took Grace by her hair to RE-CEIVE Master T's Piss on Grace's Face, and ALL the Ladies were told to "RUB ONE OFF" on Grace's face and in her mouth while husband Paul, who was still jerking off, came up to piss on Grace with Master T and Joey was asked to piss on her too.

Grace was cummed on during the Mother/Daughter session three times, then pissed on by three guys, then Pissed on again By the three women Before being Cum squirted Again by the three women. GRACE WAS DROWNING taking on three women AND three men's Hot Cum and Salty Pee!!

"SO, I hope the millionaires got their $100,000.00 Worth Today," Carol said to her Slave/Master T, kissing him passionately and thanking him for "A COLLARING INDUCTION THEY WOULD NEVER FORGET"!

CHAPTER

19

Carol was now Dominating in every way possible with confidence and admiration from MommeDomme. Also impressed by her dominance now was her Collared Cousin Anthony/Master, who had surrendered to his soulmate and would move mountains that tried to get in her way just to please her stubborn ways.

Patty stood by with Joey doing their own thing, waiting to be called upon by EITHER of the kinky Cousins for a full Couple swap, OR private sessions with the Petite Domme Bombshell with a set of natural 38DDs that stood at attention in her tailored skirt suits. Patty could accommodate EITHER one of the cousins and happy to do so, Patty was also STILL doing Mom's baths and waxing her legs and eating Domme Anna's Pussy out, OR TREATING the Domme To Patty's Sweet young MangoJuice when she was called to serve.

y

z

done

ok

final

.

.

Today Patty picked up Joey and got into a heavy conversation about BOTH their abusive households and how Joey was also used by his sister AND her drug dealer. She knew of HIS 11" cock and that her heroin dealer was gay, Joey's sister Debbie had Joey get his dick sucked by the bi/Dealer. Joey was also asked to fuck the guy's ass for bags of heroin when his sister was shaking and sick for the "horrible heroin."

"But PLEASE, Joey," pleaded to Patty, "don't say anything about this to our Co-workers, especially your Cousin Anthony. I know about YOUR brothers abusing you because Anthony told me he was going over there one day for you and get you out of there and to live with Mistress Anna and Carol and to keep AN EYE ON YOU and a closer eye on your older brother HE DID NOT LIKE at all," Joey added.

"Really? Anthony really said THAT to you?" Patty, smiling, curiously asked Joey.

"Oh, Yeah! I know He really cares about You, and all three of you girls more than ANYTHING! YOU EVEN HEARD HIM TELL ME NOT TO HURT YOU," Joey concluded.

"YES! I heard him say that to you and I told him so, I was Sooo turned on yesterday for his Initiation and especially in the shower with him. I'm getting so fucking wet right now, I want to pull over with you, OK? I need you to fuck my pussy really hard, Joey, I wanted MORE last night but the night ended too quickly!!" Patty added.

"I understand, it DID end fast, but you could have asked Me to stay with you and I would have Pleased you even More! ALL

NIGHT if you needed me to. You're My Mistress, Patty, now, Don't be afraid to ask OR just 'MAKE ME.' Besides, YOU DO OWN ME NOW!" Joey said, smiling. "Do you want me to call you Mistress or Goddess Patty?"

"YEAH, That's right! I DO OWN YOU," Patty agreed. "And right now you're gonna EAT this dripping pussy before pounding the Juice out of me with YOUR HUGE COCK I NOW OWN, And YES, You may call me Mistress OR Goddess."

Patty pulled the Bentley over and got her blanket from the trunk to lay outside on the grassy spot she adored by a line of trees on a hidden path right by a pond she discovered nearby.

Patty and Master T OR Carol visited here in their Private, discreet rendezvous with each one on Sneaky special occasions, only sometimes to Deepthroat Master T until he came down her throat, OR Having Carol in a 69 on the blanket until they were covered in each other's PussycumMango, then wash Each other off in the pond behind the Arbovite trees.

"I'm very pleased, Mistress Patty, that we had this talk and I'd LOVE to hear MORE of what pleases you and FOR YOU TO MAKE ME DO WHAT YOU DESIRE. Whatever Your shared Master T does just show me and I'll do it, I'm all yours," Joey told his new Goddess Patty.

"Is THIS how it works?" asked Joey while fucking Mistress Patty VERY hard from behind, pulling on her Silky Sandy Blonde hair into three consecutive orgasms in a row while his deep dirtytalking voice was driving his Domme Patty wild for More of Joey's big dick.

Patty knelt down and held her tits together For Joey to cum between them just like Her Master T did, Patty told Joey, "MASTER T WILL LICK HIS CUM OFF MY TITS right after he cums on them! Then HE kisses me to CUM-SWAP, telling ME to swallow it all, TOTALLY FUCKING HOT!" Patty continued, "I can cum again right then when He does that To me while pulling my hair and feeding ME his cum from HIS mouth. OMG, I DO WANT to teach you everything now that you're Collared to serve all MY needs and NOT TO repeat this as you promised!" Patty demanded.

"NOT A WORD, Mistress Patty! I NEED to do this to keep you Pleased AND for YOU to NEED ME like you need Master T. I will work on MY ORAL skills, and I promise to DO IT MORE and bring YOU to more multi/Orgasms using HIS techniques. YOU WON'T BE DISAPPOINTED," Joey concluded.

After Patty cleaned every last drop off Joey's cock, she French KISSED him, Patty then took Joey's cum from between her tits with two fingers and ordered Joey, "EAT YOUR CUM, SHOW ME you mean what you say!!" Patty said as she fed Slave/Joey his own cum.

Joey took her hand and licked it clean, THEN took both her tits in his two hands and sucked them clean of every drop from HIS huge cumload. Slave Joey lapped up and swallowed every drop before being dismissed.

"Did I pass your test, Mistress Patty?" Joey seriously asked of an open-eyed Domme Patty.

"YES, INDEED! My Slave/Stud Joey, You get an A+. You will be learning more this week, I'll pick you up whenever we aren't working, OR get together with Carol and Master T will be even better for you to watch him Eat pussy, AND I WANT YOU TO TAKE MY PEE In front of BOTH of them tonight," said Mistress Patty.

"Absolutely, I WANT TO, MISTRESS, To SHOW EVERYONE MY Loyalty to YOU," Joey anxiously and quickly answered His DOMME Patty.

"Awesome! I'm so happy we met and got this out of the way today, now WE can look forward to a great Vanilla AND Kinkster relationship with our Best friends and kissing Cousins Carol and Anthony. This will be so fucking HOT teaching you everything YOU NEED TO KNOW ABOUT PLEASING ME, OR Carol, just watch carefully, listen to Me and learn Our needs and The Domme Anna's BDism rules."

Carol was now preparing for the Medical tour Of Hospitals, medical clinics and facilities in Boston's Brookline Back Bay Fenway locations to get MORE business for the MRI scanning with follow-up Physical Therapy Rehabilitation treatments for an even more Lucrative Venture MommeDomme had started up with Daughter Carol and was now expanding SIR services already.

With the help of Domme Patty and a very experienced Alice in the MRI/CAT scanning field along with her Doctorate in Biology/Physical Therapy, SIR would hit the ground running, Patty

told Joey and They all would be together DAY AND NIGHT, as Patty put it. "Maybe WORKING more than Playing but we will find time to play, I'm sure, lol," she joked. "But it's going to be a great ride with YOU as Slave/Joey, Collared And Owned by MY SIDE. You served me very well just now," Patty said, rubbing her raw swollen pussy for a moment after a pounding from her Slave Joey.

Domme Patty had a meeting with Carol and Anthony to go over tomorrow's agenda and rushed back in time, fixing her smudged lipstick as Joey went around to open her door.

Patty and Joey arrived in the Bentley just in time, But before the meeting Joey told his Goddess Patty, "I'll come every morning to service you, MY Mistress. You won't have to pick me up, I'LL GET HERE on my own to please and serve you, Is that OK?" Joey stared into Patty's eyes, asking for her approval.

"YES! I'd LOVE that, I'm looking forward to it, but I'll call if I have to pick up somebody, just let yourself in and prepare my Bath with the Oils I like!" Patty told Slave/Joey.

"YES, MISTRESS! You're going to love My Bathing You before pleasuring you EVERY morning!" Joey told his pleased Goddess Patty, now gleaming from just cumming TWICE!

Patty was so overjoyed and pleased, you could See her nipples swelled right through her blouse. The Sandy-blonde bombshell's panties were getting moist too from being told she was Going to be bathed, THEN Eaten-Out every Morning by HER SLAVE JOEY, DELIVERED to her door Collared and Owned, and very eager to please the blonde Goddess/Domme Patty.

Carol KNEW the flushed face on Patty meant SHE was just fucked to satisfaction and smiled as Joey greeted his best friend and work buddy Anthony and now Mentor. Joey NEEDED to know some of Master T's Oral techniques that pleased Patty AND ALL the other Ladies at SIR. Joey's tongue might NOT be as big Or as thick but the technique had a lot to do with making them squirt that Slave Joey would learn.

Curious Cousin Carol asked Patty, "Are You OK?"

"YES, Why do you ask?" Patty smiled.

"Ohhh, no reason, You look a little FLUSHED, that's all, lol," Carol giggled.

"Well, there's a good reason for that, IT'S HOT OUT TODAY, Ha-ha," Patty joked.

They both enjoyed a laugh before getting ready for today's meeting, then went out and got some NEW CLIENTELE for "SIR."

The Domme/Anna entered the room to see Patty and say hello now. "YOU look a little Flushed today, Patty, Are you ok?" asked the smiling Goddess.

Patty replied, "Ha-ha, It's a little HOT out today, Mistress Anna."

"YOU ARE THE HOT ONE! A blind man can see that, have fun today, you two, and just take it slow, YOU TWO CAN'T MISS! Have the Valets take the Bentley to save time, Alice and I will stay with clients coming today so don't worry," the mentor Goddess Anna advised them.

A Red Sox player had an Injury so the team Dr. was bringing him in. "I want to be here with Alice when that happens, SO IT'S

YOU TWO, the two most beautiful AND SMART women I know, that will take SIR to the moon and back, So there! THAT'S your pep talk, and I LOVE YOU both, Lol, GOOD LUCK. See you later for dinner when you get back," the Domme concluded.

The two young Goddesses put on Last-minute touches of lipstick and jewelry and were complimenting each other's beauty and were OUT THE DOOR and on their way to Boston's Medical Centers and Major Hospitals, ALL Located within a ten-mile radius!

The Mass General Hospital would be FIRST on the list, because of the Location. It was more in the Old West End of Boston, whereas ALL the others were in Boston's BackBay and Brookline/Fenway Park area of Boston by Longwood Ave. The Massachusetts General Hospital WAS the biggest-Name Hospital IN THE ENTIRE WORLD, and was within five miles of SIR in East Boston, Massachusetts, right through the Callahan Tunnel, which goes UNDER the Boston Harbor.

The two beautiful AND intelligent women WANTED THIS ACCOUNT badly. They BOTH looked their very best and It was morning WHEN most people WERE AT their very best intellectually, and had an appointment with Executive Director Phil LaBella, a 36-year-old Italian single guy the two Persuasive beauties Carol and Patty had already Profiled.

"Phil WON'T be alone long," Alice stressed to the girls after profiling him, "AND Making a decision for their Radiology Department account on MRI/CAT scanning will involve many associates at the MGH, the most reputable Hospital In their entire

world. So DON'T get disappointed, just DO YOUR BEST and talk about the MRI and CAT scanning services with follow-ups. WE ALREADY HAVE the Boston Red Sox AND the Bruins' account to keep very busy, any more business and "YOU'RE GONNA NEED A BIGGER BOAT," Alice joked.

While the girls were out and busy getting some NEW business, The Domme Anna and her talented nephew Master T were doing a little OLD business and he was told By the Goddess to come and see her in the office. So Nephew/Anthony told Joey to go down to see Carmen and Alice and he'd be there shortly and that he had something to take care of.

The Domme/AuntieAnna let her nephew/Master T in and started talking about when HE used to come and bring her lunch, AND while she ate HER lunch, HE WOULD HAVE TO EAT HER PUSSY and her ASS when she would put her long legs, NO panties, ON TOP OF HER DESK, then point for then a Younger teenage nephew/Anthony to "GET UNDER MY DESK."

The Domme/Goddess Aunt would then time him. When she finished her corned beef and Swiss on rye Deli sandwich, HE should have a mouthful of her PussyCum. The teenage nephew pussylicking lover would finish with a mouthful of HIS Aunt's Mango EVERY TIME before she finished her Deli sandwich. The Domme Aunt would get back to work while the Infatuated Nephew secret Lover would lick EVERY Stray drop off her long legs from UNDER HER DESK, then go home UNTIL THE

NEXT DAY after High School, when he brought his Goddess Auntie Anna WAITING for her lunch and HE would Eat his lunch (Auntie Anna).

So Today while he sat remembering as She was speaking, HIS FANTASY GODDESS Aunt took out a Corned beef and Swiss on Rye Deli-sandwich, THEN PUT HER LONG LEGS UP ON TOP OF HER DESK and pointed to the floor for her Slave/Master Loyal Nephew to "GET UNDER THE DESK" as his Goddess/Fantasy took a bite of her corned beef on rye.

Her Nephew Anthony, Master of all her needs, jumped to the challenge immediately as he ALWAYS did and started right away, SLURPING HIS GODDESS Up like Ice cream, poking his enormous, long, thick Lizard-like tongue in BOTH her holes back and forth.

The Master had been starving for His Domme Aunt's pussy now that Carol had been blowing or fucking him day and night lately. Mistress Auntie Anna KNEW this and had felt neglected. Needless to say AS SOON as half her Deli sandwich was eaten, THE NEGLECTED GODDESS AUNT WAS COMPLETELY DRAINED now, squeezing her Nephew and Master's head with her long, powerful toned legs YET AGAIN so he COULDN'T MOVE until she'd emptied every drop into his mouth.

"Thank You, Goddess Auntie, YOU STILL OWN ME, FOR SURE!" the Loyal Nephew said as his Fantasy Goddess Aunt from an infatuated teen finally let him up.

"NO, THANK YOU, SIR, I can't live without KNOWING you'll be here when I need you," the Goddess Aunt stressed with a kiss, then added, "Shhhh, Not a word!" the drained Goddess Auntie Anna whispered to HER FAVORITE PUSSY-LICKING SERVER EVER!

"I'LL ALWAYS be there, don't be silly," kissing her back softly before leaving. "Not a word!"

Master, Nephew and server agreed.

"THIS IS OUR THING, NOW AND FOREVER! Remember that, Gabeesh?" the Loyal Nephew assured his dream Goddess that had him trained.

Master T just had his mouth and oversized tongue buried deep In His Mistress/Goddess #1, taking a mouthful of sweet Mango from the Domme today, who had waited for the right moment to lure her favorite Oral-serving asslicker under her desk once again just like she had planned out for today while the girls would be out all day.

Master T had sent Joey to Alice's office, where Carmen and Alice would be in her new office to wait for him to get done SERVING his Domme Aunt.

He arrived to meet Joey after he was done pleasing Domme AuntieAnna and chatted about things. SO He knocked on the door and Alice was waiting for Anthony, SMILING and eager to start on ALL three like old times.

"Just Like the North End, only now I'm on salary, this time I get MY Pussy licked as a bonus by All three of you, AND by your Girlfriends too. What's hotter than this!" Alice joked.

"I hunted all three of you down all day to Suck your cocks on Saturdays, MY day off, NOW ALL three of you are right here where I work, My dream cum true! Now Get in a circle and stand in front so I can suck one and jerk the other two in my hands," Alice said, drooling for the three BIG HARD-ONS STAND-ING out in front of her face.

Alice took Carmen's cock out to say, "I KNOW the girls all know I was blowing you guys, one at a time at my Condo, but NEVER like this!" THEN Alice immediately took Master T's hard 10 right in her hot drooling mouth. Alice was now moving her head with a rhythm from the tip and AT LEAST 3/4 of the way down and back up to the tip again. Alice was drooling her saliva ALL OVER Herself and took her saliva-soaked blouse off and paused for a second to say,

"That's better!" THEN slurped down Joey's 11" cock, groan-ing and gagging over with the slightly bigger of the three cocks she enjoyed blowing weekly. Alice was going wild now, sucking one, then alternating jerking the other two. Alice Was making Loud Growling noises with her mouth FULL of cock for at least 45 minutes straight while the excited young men fondled and pinched her cherry-sized rock-hard nipples while She Visibly dripped pusscum on the floor From Sucking-Off her favorite three young studs.

Alice would HUNT down the trio on Saturdays at The Hay-market Fruit and Produce Market on Blackstone St., where the three stud friends worked on Friday and Saturday ALL day,

THEN Alice would blow them one at a time throughout the day, luring them to her condo nearby on Salem St., in the North End of Boston, But NEVER ALL three AT ONCE like this. She continued to remember dripping more pussycum on the floor, getting more horny, blowing three huge cocks.

Alice LOVED TO BLOW and today was a dream for her, getting all three of her favorite young men.

"WHAT ARE THE ODDS ON THIS HAPPENING??" Joey asked jokingly, lol.

"MMMMmmmm" was all Alice had to say, then she started to suck even faster and harder over the guys talking and toying with her like a $10 whore. Carmen got her up to sit her down backwards on the swivel leather office chair, taking off her cumsoaked Panties While STILL blowing the other two back and forth now.

Cock-hungry Alice was "growling" like a hungry Momma bear. Her sounds were now getting Demonic like while Alice was totally consumed with one ten-incher after another, getting fucked in both her holes, Spanked, fondled, hair pulled, while Master T was slapping her all over that Alice begged him to do to her, AND a total turn-on for the guys watching and FOR THE BIG COCK-SUCKING ALICE, still dripping to the floor, kneeling in her own Saliva and PussyCum.

Carmen was FIRST to Fuck his Supervisor Alice and GIVE HER A TREAT today that the Young Studs had really NEVER done before with ALICE. She JUST wanted to BLOW THEM

ALL DAY if she could without fucking anybody. Alice just LOVED to SUCK Cock. Period.

"NOT A WORD to Carol or the others," with a light face slap Master T said as he fucked her mouth while Carmen pounded her pussy from the back, MAKING ALICE CUM like she had never cum before she claimed, after she was drowned in three big loads from the three big dicks shooting cum on her face before SUCKING them clean.

"Alice, YOU are our personal gangbang Whore now," Master T added.

"Not a word to Anyone, Master T, I promise you! I want ALL THREE OF YOU to come back AGAIN, YOU guys ALSO Don't say anything to the other girls and we can meet here in my office weekly OR WHENEVER. Anthony/Master T says it's OK, DEAL?" Alice pleaded. "I'M here to USE anyway, just like the 'THE DOMME/Anna' wants anyway, AND that I agreed to also and well paid for, lol," Alice joked. "I LOVE LICKING ALL THEIR PUSSIES now too, they are ALL so beautiful AND Bi/Sexual. I don't want to mess this up. WE have come a long way and TODAY was just MEANT TO BE! That was the best Fucking I ever had, THANK YOU, CARMEN, for your assistance, lol," while kissing her new assistant on the cheek. "YOU'RE gonna LOVE being My assistant, Carmen," Alice giggled from her knees, kneeling in a puddle for at least two hours.

The Hardworking, HOT-looking, Fast-talking Carol and Patty are at their appointment with Phil LaBella, Executive Director

overseeing the Scanning Operations Department of the Massachusetts General Hospital in Boston, MA, just through the Sumner Tunnem In East Boston, home of the two gorgeous women Executives and home office of SIR, which they began to explain about to their "Target" and Potential business Client Phil LaBella.

Carol opened her New Journal with pictures and statistical information, Impressing the executive that really wasn't focused AT ALL! His eyes were wandering from the journal that Carol had placed on his mahogany desk in front of him TO Carol's Huge nipples as she was leaning in (NO BRA) and pointing out the MRI scanner machine to Phil.

Patty was smiling and nodded to Carol, then walked over to get Phil focused to GET THIS MGH ACCOUNT and began to talk to the dazzled CEO.

"Alice is our Radiology Technician with a Doctorate degree in Radiology and Bio-Chemistry," Patty pointed out to the CEO. "Alice does ALL our scanning, reads, develops, and we then deliver the disc the SAME DAY To you. WE have the best people for OUR NEW STATE-OF-THE-ART MRI SCANNER. Alice also said she KNOWS you, Phil," Patty said, getting Phil's attention quickly to Carol's approval, who was now smiling as the young CEO's eyes couldn't stop roaming back and forth. NOW Phil was looking at Patty's fitted Vest resembling a tailored Corset PACKING Solid Natural 38DDs and this Man COULDN'T stay focused for a second!

"So, how do you know our Alice?" Patty asked curiously.

"Alice who?" He drooled.

"Alice Capolla from the Lindeman Health Center in Cambridge. She works for us now and is very professional with a degree in Radiology and says she knows You, From College maybe?" Patty now said, searching for a professional conversation. "Carol and I also have degrees in Physical Therapy and work at Our New State-of-the-art facility in E. Boston. Carol and I BOTH do Physical Therapy sessions, sometimes we'll do four-handed therapeutic massages for special clients upon special request only. WE recently signed the Red SOX Organization account and are Now looking into the Medical field.

"Carol is Vice President and Co-Founder with her mom, Anna, and here is her picture," as Carol turned to a few modeling pages in her journal to show the sweating CEO as he looked at the pictures of VP Carol and her older carbon-copy mother.

"OMG! She's so beautiful," said the Jaw-dropping man. "I mean, YOU'RE ALL STUNNING! Not just pretty," he added. "Have either of you been models, just curious," Phil added.

"OH, NO," said Carol, "we were too busy getting business degrees," she Giggled. "But thank you very much for the compliment, and my Mom will be pleased what you said about her also, are you married, Phil?" Carol asked the CEO of MGH. "My MOM is single right now, you know," Carol said, smiling.

"You're kidding!" Phil shouted. "WHY? I'd love to meet someone like that, omg, SHE'S single? I'M single," he said. "Are YOU TWO taken? lol. Just curious," he giggled.

"IN BUSINESS! One usually will have to SEE or OPERATE a product before getting on board, I'M DEFINITELY INTERESTED, though. Can I see your Machine and the Facility you say is right through the tunnel in East Boston? On the waterfront?" the overheated CEO added.

"OH, YES!" Patty eagerly jumped in to say. "Carol and I will personally have a drink with you on the rooftop garden bar overlooking the skyline," as Patty showed pictures of the Grand Opening, skipping right by a topless picture of Carol showing her huge purple nipples, dropping his jaw.

"OMG," Phil shouted. "Go back!" he pleaded. "WAS THAT A NUDE PIC OF YOU, CAROL?"

"Yeah, Sorry, I thought I took that pic out when I prepared for our meeting!!" Carol grinned.

"NO, NO, that's fine, I NEVER SEEN ANYTHING LIKE THAT! THAT'S ALL, YOU'RE INCREDIBLE, CAROL, BOTH OF YOU! OMG, I'll be there tonight at 7 sharp. And Maybe I can get a four-handed massage like you offered? I'm SURE the account will be yours after tonight," Phil added.

"I'M POSITIVE the account will be ours," Patty concluded with a smile. "MGH's slogan is 'Ears, Nose, and Throat,' right?" Patty's Hot lips whispered in Phil's ear.

"Yes, it is," Phil replied.

"THEN, when you hold me by my EARS and my NOSE touches your belly, You'll know your cock is down my THROAT."

Patty nibbled his ear and said, "SEE YOU AT SEVEN SHARP! to sign your name."

Carol laughed and said, "OMG, GOOD ONE, PATTY!"

They all got in a good laugh as Phil adjusted himself and had to sit down.

Back at the Office, The Sly Mistress/Goddess of them all was waiting for Her first SIR Client from the Red Sox Organization. Today the team's Dr. Kehlman was arriving with a young pitcher who threw out an elbow and dislocated his shoulder. He needed an MRI scan on BOTH his elbow and shoulder.

Alice would greet the Dr. and baseball pitcher as well for the professional consultation and procedures, DommeAnna wanted to be sure EVERTHING went smoothly.

"Good morning, 'SIR,' MRI Physical Therapy, how may I help you today?" the Goddess herself answered the phone today, and she was waiting on Dr. Kehlman to call before his appointment with Alice for an MRI scan on the Red Sox star pitcher.

"Hello, It's Dr. Kehlman, we are on our way and will be there in twenty min. for the MRI," said Dr. Kehlman Goddess Anna.

"Very Good, Sir, we're waiting for you, and we'll valet your car for you. Just pull up in front. I personally will direct you to Alice, our Radiology Technician," said the eager Domme.

Looking out the front lobby window, the impeccably dressed Goddess could see the black Cadillac Escalade pull up and Carmen

walk over to open the doors for the VIP, giving the signal to Domme Anna to come greet them.

As Domme Anna walked out Dr. Kellman was startled from her beauty and told her so. "OMG, you're so beautiful, YOUR daughter looks EXACTLY like you," says Dr. Kellman, while the young 24-year-old pitcher was in Awe with his jaw dropped.

"Nice to meet you, Ma'am," the injured Pitcher stuttered. "Wow, you and your daughter could be twins," the young man agreed, complimenting The Domme.

"WE ARE! Lol," giggled the quick-witted Domme. "Let's get your shoulder looked at right away, FOLLOW ME," as she Planned to lead the way, giving the two men a view of the BEST HEART-SHAPED ASS they'd ever seen strutting like a Super-model on a runway.

"OMG!" whispered Dr. Kellman to the young man. "Close your eyes and take a picture Of that walk!! You're NOT going to see something that Gracious for a long, long time, IF EVER again!" said the Older 48-year-old Doctor to younger 24-year-old pitcher. With Both Men hypnotized by the Goddess in her new tailored Versace silk dress with 6" Stiletto Heels to match the belt Tied around her Tiny 24-inch waist.

"She's the best-dressed woman I've ever seen," said the young man.

Dr. Kehlman shot back, "She's the BEST OF ANYONE I HAVE EVER SEEN, and I got you by 25 years."

Smiling now from ear to ear, the Goddess could see the men Were indeed looking her over and whispering to each other,

walking from the glass on the front door's reflection as she opened the door for them, smiling and glancing down at the Doctor's bulging trousers.

There stood Alice, ready to take the star pitcher and his prepared information From Dr. Kehlman. "This IS a historic moment for 'SIR' and Your Organization," said the proud Domme. "OUR FIRST MRI scanning of many to come, Dr. Kehlman. It was Nice to see you again and hope you enjoyed our Grand opening recently," the smiling Domme replied.

The dazzled Dr. Kehlman was searching for words and could only say, "BELIEVE ME WHEN I SAY THE PLEASURE WAS ALL MINE, ANNA. I think I'll go home now and break MY elbow so I can back to see you again," getting a good loud laugh from ALICE, CARMEN and the PITCHER, AND THE IMPRESSED GODDESS HERSELF, as the Dr. Concluded.

Not to be outwitted, the Domme replied, "I LOVE MEN that can make me laugh and aren't intimidated. YOU, Dr. Kehlman SIR, can Come back ANYTIME to see me! We have a rooftop bar for our 'SPECIAL CLIENTS.' Just call first, here is my private card."

Waving Goodbye and walking away with confidence for ONE MORE LOOK, the Dr. closed his eyes to snap another picture of The Goddess Anna in his head.

MommeDomme got back to her desk in time to get her daughter's call telling her they were "on their way." Now to the BIDMC\ Beth Israel Deconas Medical Center, just down the road two

miles from Fenway Park and maybe six miles from the MGH, where they were leaving from. Also leaving was CEO of the MGH Phil LaBella, with the Hard-on of his life, AND a PROMISE by Deepthroater Patty And insatiable Carol to "SEAL the DEAL" Tonight! acquiring the MGH for all their MRI/CAT scans, not to mention follow-up Paid Physical Therapy sessions from their Insurance provider. Insurance Companies always preferring Physical Therapy sessions over an Operation, IT'S MUCH CHEAPER if the Physical Therapy sessions heal the injury first!

Carol And Patty joked to Mom about the meeting with the Dazed and confused 35-yearold engaged young man who was lying when he said he was single to meet the Momme Goddess, OR to get into the 21-year-old Carol AND the 22-year-old Patty's panties.

The Diabolical Hot Young Ladies went the extra mile today and WOULD GIVE the CEO Phil LaBella MORE than he bargained for! "JUST SIGN The contract!!" Carol and Patty Simply told the stunned and overwhelmed CEO.

Carol called MomDomme to say, "We should be back around six to get ready to meet CEO Phil LaBella from the MGH and have drinks on the rooftop bar and then show him the MRI machine, THEN we promised to give him a treat with our SPECIAL four-hand massage. So will YOU please make sure No one is in the massage room from 7-8, Mom, please, OK? Love you. See you at 8 with the signed MGH contract." Carol giggled.

"Maybe the BETH ISRAEL CONTRACT TOO, lol. Who knows," Alice said to the CEO.

"There is a hot Redheaded Woman, Patty is praying she's Bi/Sexual, See you soon, Momme," Carol concluded.

Patty pulled up in the Bentley as they were expected and greeted by the valet and shown where Monique Lasalle, Executive Director of The Radiology Department, would be.

Monique and Alice knew of each other from Boston College, where they both got their biotech degrees. They dated different guys, then Both married the guys soon after. The two promiscuous good-looking College-aged head-turners frequently went out dancing in the MANY nightclubs in the college-aged nightlife in The Back Bay Area of Boston, "Zelda's" and the "Other Side."

Dorm parties after hours were routine behavior and still are. This was HOW they knew OF each other. Alice and Monique still were in touch with old college friends frequently that knew both of them, THAT was how this meeting/Connection was planned for all the ladies today that were all now colleagues.

After the long walk down the corridor of this Massive Beth Israel Hospital, aka BIDMC, the two bombshells looking healthier than ANY doctor Stopping to watch them walk by in amazement, Carol and Patty were expected to present their presentation to Monique after a few brief words about their expensive tailor-made suits from Mom's Newbury St. Tailor and seamstress.

"OMG!" said the French/American Redhead, also size 4 and ALSO stunningly dressed. "Where in the world did you get those skirt suits?? I LOVE THEM! But I don't know if I'd be allowed to wear them here, lol, the Doctors wouldn't be able to work," they all laughed.

The girls were hitting it off right away. Monique was a little older by not by much; however, Monique was Alice's age of 32 and Patty 22, Carol 21 respectively, but they would share a lot more as they continued to talk clothes, shoes, Gucci handbags and just Girl talk.

Monique being a Natural Redhead was also met by two "All-Natural," NO plastic surgery, NO Hair dye, little makeup Or none at all, TO MONIQUE's surprise now staring at Carol's fitted silk blouse commented on her large protruding nipples.

"My mother would make ME wear Band-Aids over MY nipples when I was going out in summer tops to cover them up, But YOU need MORE than Band-Aids for those. OMG, they're the size of plums, lol," said the Redhead, still gazing at her while Patty was fixing her Vest to see if SHE got a look OR a compliment for Patty's DDs as well.

"I never heard of Band-Aids before, lol," Carol giggled.

"OH, yeah, MY MOM would tell me, 'Go get the Band-Aids,' lol, when she seen my inch-long nipples Sticking way out in my summer tops, OR 'Go put on a bra.'"

"'IT'S SUMMER!' I would scream back at her, Lol," Monique said while still staring at Carol up AND down, as Patty watched on wanting some attention too.

"YOU HAVE 1"-long nipples?" Patty jumped into the conversation, asking curiously.

"Oh, yes! Maybe longer, I wish they were wider or puffier like Carol's here instead of long like pencils sticking out of my blouses. Maybe I should have worn a vest like YOU, Patty," added the Curious Redhead Monique and turning to her attention to Patty, packing natural DDs in her vest. "Now THOSE are huge! And well covered at the same time. Very beautiful clothes, girls," Monique added. "Let's talk more another time about your tailor, but for NOW let's talk about Me and my Boss setting up a day to come see your facility, OR just by Myself maybe and do lunch there at Santarpio's Pizza in Eastie, 'MY FAVORITE,'" the hour glass-shaped French-model-turned-CEO said to Carol, STILL staring from her nipples up into Carol's amazing purple eyes with just enough purple eye shadow to make Monique so wet she was now speechless and just staring into Carol's eyes and then to her long straight thick black hair, AMAZED with her beauty.

"REALLY?" Carol and Patty BOTH jumped in to say and got Monique to focus. "OMG, Santarpio's is only two blocks away and it's OUR favorite Pizzeria too! WE CAN WALK THERE from OUR Facility. WE live on the Penthouse floor of our SIR Facility that leads up to our rooftop Garden and Bar. YOU HAVE TO COME NOW! PLEASE?" Carol pleaded, looking to Monique's crotch and then trying to peek into her blouse curiously to see the inch-long nipples now turned into stones.

Patty jumped in to say, "Come TOMORROW night! To-night the MGH CEO Phil is doing the tour of 'SIR' Rehabilita-tion Department to see how our MRI Operates.

"Tomorrow, then? Day OR Night! IS FOR YOU ONLY, Dinner is on us. We can EAT-OUT on the roof garden and walk to Santarpio's," Carol said softly, sexy, and very suggestively to a very wet Monique. "We have a Huge 24-jet jacuzzi, a sauna, ad-justable massage tables, and we just spent 1.f5 million to renovate our four-story brick building overlooking the Boston Harbor and skyline, and for the MRI scanner that will pay for itself soon with YOUR help and others in the Medical field," Carol concluded her PRESENTATION.

Carol and Patty kept talking/selling the wide green-eyed French beauty, Now glancing at Carol's heart-shaped Italian ass and long toned perfect legs as she Graciously walked and talked across the room, keeping Monique's Nipples at attention in her thin bra, NO Band-Aids. Carol was trying NOT to look at her SO the redhead WOULD keep looking at Carol.

Patty was watching them both and LOVING IT, smiling with approval, and Patty COULDN'T WAIT to lick BOTH of their PussyCumMango up while watching Carol work her Magic on Monique, who was mesmerized by Carol's beauty and Confident walk Carol learned from her mom, "The Domme" of them all.

"I can see NOW why your mom makes you wear Band-Aids! Lol," Patty joked, referring to the excited and now visible inch-long pink nipples showing through her light thin blouse, getting

a laugh from all. "Should I bring a bathing suit for the jacuzzi OR do you have a Robe for me?" the redhead curiously asked Carol.

"OH, of course, We'll have a robe for you! The jets only knock off our bathing suits anyway, ha-ha," Carol giggled to get this squirming redhead, even MORE wet, who was now adjusting her Italian knitted Blouse to her tight Pant suit that you could also now see her pussy crack that she was clearly soaking wet that Carol noticed and stared to let Monique know it was ok.

Carol was making this Redheaded Executive wetter than she had ever been for any woman before! This was what Alice was referring to when she said Monique MAY BE BI, but wasn't sure since she DIDN'T know Monique well enough but KNEW OF HER! And today Carol knew for sure she was going take this gorgeous ex/model by her Red hair and give her a taste.

TOMORROW night would explain a lot when they met and EXPLORED the facility, then relaxed in the huge eight-seat 24-jet jacuzzi after drinks and Pizza at Santarpio's.

"Will You be coming Alone OR bringing your boyfriend?" Carol asked curiously.

"WHY on earth would I bring him? Lol," Monique giggled. "I think just the three of us will have a LOT MORE to talk about. Let's just call it LADIES' NIGHT OUT, sound good?" Monique asked, looking directly at Carol's ass bending over to get her Journal off the chair.

"Sounds PERFECT!" Patty Added right away, needing to be included, and to Carol's approval nod.

"YOU WON'T WANT TO LEAVE!" Carol concluded.

Carol called MommeDomme right away with the great news about the BIDMC contract and to please make sure Nobody was using the Jacuzzi tomorrow night, Carol asked her Mentor and Mom, "This three-way will be a pizza Dinner on the rooftop lounge, followed by Mango Dessert in the jacuzzi to get the BIDMC account signed as well as the MGH account, so far! (one for Patty) (one for Carol).

The weekly agenda was starting off just as expected for ALL four Insatiable woman and three 21-year-old studs packing and ALWAYS ready for their Collared and Matched-up kinky female counterparts. A 21-year-old guy can cum two-three times EVERY DAY, at least Master T did, and also happy to meet ANY challenge for the Master/Nephew when demanded by Mistress/Auntie Anna.

Cousin Carol, However, was on a mission from her teen years and on up to "COLLAR AND OWN HIM" and cleverly succeeded.

Cousin Carol was about to further impress her Mom, the Original Goddess and diabolical clever BUSINESS Goddess, when Carol strategically mapped out her week to Promote and Escalate SIR, planned out and written into Carol's new journal, Not Mom's!!

Carol wanted Mom to retire permanently and just give AD-VICE, after all, WHO would be better Than THE DOMME/Auntie Anna to advise her new growing staff of skilled "Physical Therapists"?

Auntie Anna WAS NOT old or no longer able to DO the things SHE ALONE HAD DOMINATED for the past twenty years, Carol just DIDN'T want her DommeMomme to push herself anymore seeing the stress it WAS having on her, Period....

Carol wanted "SIR" Sports Injury Rehab/MRI-Services to be LEGITIMATE and LEGAL, WITH VERY FEW exceptions for Fetish Providing, of course! LIKE WITH CEO PHIL LA-BELLA at 7 P.M. tonight, and THEN with Monique tomorrow night, ALL NIGHT LONG!

Carol wanted Patty to believe that her Blowjob promise was the real reason why CEO Phil LaBella came tonight, Although IT WAS Patty's aggressiveness that sucked CEO Phil in. On the other hand, It May have been Carol's visible huge purple plum nipples when she was leaning over with No bra, showing Phil topless pictures of her (accidentally on purpose) in her journal.

Either way the CEO of the MGH had arrived at 7 P.M. as sched-uled. He was all cleaned up and with (two) bottles of wine, one for each of the (two) Beautiful Young Goddesses that were about to burn a memory into his brain HE WOULD NEVER FORGET.

Carol, of course, now had to show her position of Power from one CEO to another for the purpose of business first, THEN pleasure! Carol greeted him at the door in undoubtedly the best Fitted button-down blouse half-unbuttoned, NO bra needed.

"Beautiful Night, isn't it?" Carol said, smiling as she took Phil's hand and kissed his blushing cheek, then walked him into what seemed like HEAVEN.

"YES, it is!" Phil drooled.

"Patty is waiting for us at the bar on the roof to have a drink and a snack. Did you have dinner, Phil?" Carol asked.

"Yes, I did," Phil still gazing at Carol's natural beauty AND her fitted Donatello silk blouse. "OMG, I have to say you're so beautiful, you two beat out ALL these so-called Supermodels of today," Phil said confidently, shaking his head. "Just incredible!" Phil Stressed.

"Thank you for that, Phil, you're so kind," Carol giggled. "The elevator down the hall will take us upstairs quicker. It's four floors up to our rooftop garden and bar." As Carol started to describe the Facility floor by floor, the elevator door closed and started up to floor #1, where she explained all six rooms of SIR were located on, then continued on up.

Carol deviously hit the STOP button and leaned into Phil and KISSED HIM softly, grabbing his bulging cock in his expensive suit pants, then putting the bottles of wine down on the floor to unbutton her blouse ALL the way down. Carol stepped back a step to SHOW her AMAZING FIRM YOUNG BREASTS topped off with the largest PURPLE NIPPLES Phil or Anyone for that matter had EVER seen.

Carol then told PHIL to "SUCK ON THEM, PHIL. YOU will get a lot more later, I promise, but I want YOU to know THIS IS ONLY A TASTE of things to come tonight," Carol promised the CEO very convincingly. "Patty and I have a nice session planned out for you, IF there is a Special Request you

have, PLEASE! Just ask, Sir," Carol now dropping to her knees after Phil Was told to Suck On her hard purple plums, which HE DID for just a few minutes before she took them away to blow him.

Carol unzipped Phil's Neatly Tailored Expensive Linen pants to take out his VERY THICK but average-length seven-inch uncut girth cock.

"WOW!" Carol said. "Very Impressive, SIR!" Carol was excited to say as SHE sucked the 3.5-inch-in-diameter "Girth" cock Into her STRETCHED-OPEN drooling mouth, trying to take it in deep. Patty IS going to love to TRY and deepthroat this THICK DICK, But I'm confident she will. She's that good!" Carol added, But then Carol said to Phil's surprise, "I'D LOVE To try and get this Thick Dick in MY ASS and have you stretch Me wide open. Do you like anal, Phil? I'm really LOVING ANAL these days," Carol whispered to the overwhelmed and sweating CEO Phil La-Bella with Carol holding the Hard-on of his life.

"REALLY?" Phil Said with excitement. "I haven't had many women that could Deepthroat Me ALL THE WAY, Only one a long time ago could take my thickness in her throat." He added, "YOU, MY GORGEOUS ONE! WILL NEED A LOT OF VASELINE, BUT I will go easy and Your gorgeous Italian ass will open right up! I can't wait to open that ass up." Phil smiled, watching Carol gag, looking up at him with tears in her eyes from trying to deepthroat it.

Carol now stopped blowing Phil and got back up to say, "I Don't want to finish a perfect night in an elevator," Carol joked

as they both agreed and started up again to the rooftop to meet Patty, now talking on the phone to Alice,.

Patty was dressed in a similar blouse (easy access) for her DDs (NO bra), NO panties on this warm summer night, And about to get HOTTER!

Patty watched from the bar stool as Carol walked the Visibly excited CEO Over to Patty, dressed for the warm summer night, she had a thin silk top on halfway unbuttoned, NO bra with a matching Cotton dress with NO stockings OR Panties on. Her hair was slicked back in a Ponytail for THE OCCASION. Thick-Dick CEO Phil LaBella was drooling with anticipation to see if Patty indeed could swallow his 3+inch-wide cock All the way down just Like she said, holding her EARS, NOSE, touching his belly, into her THROAT.

Patty curiously asked, "DID YOU TWO START without poor little Me? lol," looking at his bulging thick cock in his thin linen suit pants (No suit jacket) on this warm HEATED night.

"Just a kiss or two in the elevator," Carol said, giggling. "JUST WAIT until you see!" Carol added.

"OH, REALLY?" Patty said with excitement, stroking his arm while smiling. "Let's take our drinks downstairs and show off Our Place to Phil first, Carol. Let's show HIM EVERTHING, Then I can See what HE can show me. I think WE have a New handsome Business Client, Carol," Patty concluded as the MFF threesome took the elevator down to the ground floor, where the Heated jacuzzi was put on for the occasion.

The large adjustable massage table was covered with fitted cotton sheets and pillows, along with three different Warmed oils and flavored lubricants for this New CEO Special Client soon to be in Carol's NEW SECRET JOURNAL!

Carol now needed to get focused on the impressive CEO SIGNING "SIR" as their Primary MRI/CAT scanner and provider for the MGH, the biggest-named Hospital IN THE WORLD.

Carol and Patty BOTH showed Phil around the MRI Scanning department, then the two Physical Therapy rooms, jacuzzi room, steam and sauna room, also used in treating patients as well as (Kinksters) in the STATE-OF-THE-ART EQUIPMENT.

Both Carol and Patty were VERY persuasive to the now HARD and HUNGRY CEO Phil LaBella, who would give his right arm right now as Carol took off her skirt with NO panties on.

Standing at the rim of the Jacuzzi PATTY "RIPPED OPEN" her thin blouse in Dominating fashion, Revealing her MASSIVE but firm and natural 38DDs with the Hardest Pink Nipples this Thick-Dick CEO had ever seen.

Patty started walking into the Jacuzzi, grabbing the CEO by the hand, telling him, "NOW SHOW ME YOURS, LOL," Patty demanded, Smiling.

BOTH Carol And Phil were in Awe from this Petite but beautiful Domme Patty from what THEY BOTH just witnessed, dominantly ripping off her blouse, exposing her flawless DDs bouncing right out, making Phil's thick cock get even harder and

thicker. Carol even became dripping wet now and BOTH were now wanting Patty's luscious body VERY badly.

Phil, answering Patty's request, dropped his trousers, NO underwear to reveal his 5.5"-GIRTH cock by an average 7" long, BUT about 7" around. Phil HELD his Un-Cut, THICK PACKAGE to Patty, still standing, while Patty was looking up from the Jacuzzi and said, "Oh, Yeah! NICE THICK COCK, SIR. This will be a challenge I shall enjoy, lol," Patty giggled.

Carol said, "PATTY, CAN YOU REALLY DEEPTHROAT THAT THICK DICK? I gave it a try in the elevator, Lol," Carol now admitted.

"I KNEW IT! YOU started without me, lol," Patty joked. "SIT DOWN HERE, PHIL, on the edge of the Jacuzzi," Patty ordered her new Submissive CEO, waiting for this moment ALL DAY long to see if Patty could "Ear/Nose and Throat" his girth.

PHIL was still in shock from the Dominant blouse-tearing-off display and hard as stone. The excited CEO Obeyed Patty's request without hesitating And sat with his feet IN the Jacuzzi while Now a very curious heated Carol sat beside him, taking Phil's hand up to play with Carol's huge nipples and to nibble on them while getting his THICK COCK SUCKED by the UNMATCHED, SKILLED, TALENTED, AND DEEPTHROATING QUEEN, "DOMME PATTY."

Patty moved in between his toned legs, running her hands all over his legs and teasing his hole. Patty was skillfully suckling on the Stunned CEO in foreplay fashion from his knees to his hips

Before taking the tip of Phil's HARD GIRTH COCK into her mouth and looked up him while Carol and the curious CEO watched in amazement as this Gorgeous Petite Bombshell slowly eased HIS WHOLE 3.5"-THICK GIRTH COCK ALL THE WAY DOWN!!

Patty's NOSE was touching this Moaning CEO's flat belly while Phil grabbed onto Patty's EARS AS PROMISED by Patty.

"OMG, look at that, Phil, EARS, NOSE And THROAT!" Carol excitingly said! "YOU definitely are the best, Patty. I can't believe that whole thick dick is down your throat," Carol said, giggling.

Carol replied, getting in the jacuzzi with her to suck Patty's awesome tits floating on the top of the bubbling water, driving Carol crazy for her while watching this ACHIEVEMENT from Patty, taking Phil's 7"-long-by-7-around-Girth Dick down her throat. Patty continued to Blow Phil until he was ready to explore IN her throat when Carol stepped in, Pulling the Pre-Cumming CEO into the jacuzzi To sit him down to try and fit Phil's THICK COCK INTO HER LUBED-UP Perfect heart-shaped Italian asshole.

Patty reached over for her flavored Lube and applied a handful to Carol's Asshole. Patty tongued Carol's asshole with her already hot tongue from SUCKING PHIL'S THICK DICK. Shocking the rock-hard CEO EVEN MORE was that Patty was really enjoying eating-out Carol's Asshole and Pussy for him to watch while the two beautiful women SUCKED ON HIM and THEN EACH OTHER in a 3way he would NEVER, EVER forget.

The Kinkster Sisters shared BLOWING the Impressive CEO's GIRTH COCK a little more, Butt now Carol WANTED IT PACKED IN HER ASS to make Phil Cum in her stretched-out winking Ass to finish him off.

Domme Patty took Charge and took them BOTH by one hand Each and led them to the table behind the door in One private Room of two. With the Massage table already prepared Patty told Phil to "Lay down" so that Carol and Patty could Massage him but first see IF Carol could take a seven-inch-around THICK COCK and STRETCH Carol open like Never before.

Carol told Patty and Phil, moaning and kissing them Both, to "VIOLATE BOTH MY HOLES," Carol demanded to them both.

Patty was now streaming for her beauty queen BDism sister and LOVED when she got Crazy like this and NEEDED TO MULTI/CUM to be pleased. The Stunned CEO Phil had Never seen anything like it.

Patty got up on the table to HOLD CAROL STEADY, watching as Carol EASED the hard THICK HEAD of the CEO Into her pulsating Lubed-up winking Asshole. CAROL WAS NOW breathing like a Woman Delivering a baby, screaming out, "YES! YES! OPEN MY FUCKIN' HOLES UP!!" First taking half, THEN to the amazed CEO AND to Patty's amazement, Carol rotated and circled on Phil's Girth Cock in a circular squatting position with a slow, steady rhythm until CAROL SQUEEZED IN THE ENTIRE THICK DICK ALL THE WAY IN HER ASSHOLE.

Phil just became Crazy as well and POUNDED Carol's Asshole VIOLENTLY, Just like Carol asked for it. Carol slurped and licked Patty's Pussycum as she stood up from HOLDING CAROL STEADY, NOW RIDING THE THICKEST COCK they had shared so far.

Master T was close In thickness but definitely LONGER To get at Carol's G-SPOT EVERY TIME! Carol was Riding this thick cock to Get at that G/Spot that made Carol Multi/Cum and Squirt heavily.

Patty knew Carol's G-Spot Secret that Master T had told Patty about and now Patty enjoyed as it well when Carol Multi-Came continually for minutes at time, soaking everything in sight, trying to drink Carol's Mango down.

Patty was now cumming on Carol's face and in her mouth, dripping down onto PHIL, who had his mouth opened, trying to catch the Mango dripping from Patty's MangoTree while Carol kept suckling and licking on Patty's oversized clit, not missing a drop.

Patty now wanted Carol's cum so she placed her next to Phil and began to SUCK AND LICK CAROL'S TWO STRETCHED OPEN HOLES, while Phil watched in amazement as Patty started using her whole hand, fisting Carol's Stretched-out Holes while Carol screamed into a pillow.

Patty was able to FIST CAROL'S STRETCHED-OPEN PUSSY and maneuver her fingers over her G-SPOT, causing Carol to Explode and squirt like a broken fire hydrant, soaking Patty and Phil while they BOTH were Eating, Fisting and Pound-

ing CAROL'S STRETCHED-OUT and USED-UP PUSSY, AND HER ASSHOLE, Passing Carol back and forth like a toy.

Patty and Carol now NEEDED TO FINISH off their business Client in Dramatic fashion, so Patty took charge while Carol followed the petite but sadistic blonde beauty.

Domme Patty told Carol to lube the CEO's ass while Patty started to blow Phil AGAIN to see IF he liked his ass played with.

"Ride my face, please?" Phil asked Carol while Carol fingered Phil's Asshole slowly while riding and humping his mouth in a 69 position. Patty was Deepthroating Phil once again while HE WAS ACCEPTING two fingers now from Carol and began to PreCum a bit.

Patty ordered Carol to GET ON TOP again, "RIDE THAT THICK COCK IN YOUR ASS AGAIN! MAKE HIM CUM IN YOUR ASSHOLE!!"

Patty's ordering made the stunned CEO EXPLODE DEEP into Carol's Asshole now that Carol had taken the WHOLE THICK COCK AGAIN ALL THE WAY IN just Like her kinkster sister Patty took the girth ALL THE WAY DOWN HER THROAT.

CEO and Director of the MRI/Radiology Scanning Department Phil LaBella was just as impressed with these Two Young Beautiful Insatiable Businesswomen AS THEY were with him. On the massage table he told The Dominating Patty HE DID likes his Prostate being massaged because he said It allowed more "bloodflow" to the penis, he had heard.

Patty replied that they mentioned that technique in Physical Therapy as well, Carol ALREADY has lubed up MR. GIRTH and had two fingers IN Phil's Asshole now, adding a third, massaging Phil right behind his large trimmed manicured balls Onto his prostate while Carol now Fed him more PussyMango while he was on his knees with Carol behind him, Massaging his Prostate gland DEEP now, twisting Her three fingers In the CEO's WIDE-OPENED ASSHOLE, massaging the CEO's Prostate Gland slowly.

Patty was violently facefucking this submissive Moaning Pre-Cummer. The three-fingered Prostate Massage was FORCING Phil's cum out while Carol stroked his THICK COCK to help him along, wiping his bursts of cum on her nipples, kneeling there for the CEO to lick off later LIKE MASTER T did for Cousin Carol.

Patty was giving this CEO Phil another Massive squirting Of PussycumMango all over his face he wouldn't forget anytime soon as well. The Sensual Bi-sexual excitement Carol was providing For Patty during this session made Patty Explode into a Multi/orgasm, choking the CEO.

Patty had become Obsessed with Carol's flawless body for five years now. Patty was SO TURNED ON BY HER BDISM SISTER CAROL than ANYONE ELSE, except Maybe MASTER T!

After an introduction to a delicious warm Golden Shower on THICK-DICK Phil by the two kinkster sisters, CEO Phil La-Bella SIGNED THE EXCLUSIVE MGH CONTRACT TO SIR, THEN BEGGED for ongoing Private sessions with Patty and Carol BILLED TO MGH, for MRI Scanning/PT.

Needless to say, the two Insatiable Young Goddesses WANTED THAT WIDE-GIRTH COCK AGAIN and welcomed Phil's "PRIVATE" Session request for Carol AND Patty @ $1,000 For a 2hr PT Session, Minimum!

The very next day, after a good night's sleep, Carol called Monique LaSalle to set up a time to meet for drinks on the rooftop lounge, THEN SANTARPIO'S for Pizza. Alice was speaking to The Domme/Mistress Anna About Monique Lasalle, now saying that she was married but Her marriage WAS NOT going well to NO SURPRISE of mutual friends from college.

Alice, Monique AND Mistress/Goddess Auntie Anna ALL took classes at UMass Amherst around the SAME TIME For their master's degrees. Their ages were only four years apart between ALL three Bi/Sexual Pussy Lovers (Alice recently): Anna 37, Monique 35, and Alice now 33.

Monique confided in an old friend that was ALSO a very good friend of Alice's named Kathy. Monique wanted some counseling or "Life coaching" by a professional to Let off some steam, she told Kathy, so Kathy suggested Alice.

Alice heard of the meeting and immediately Called Mistress Anna to "GET HER INVOLVED" to help seal the deal with BIDMC (Beth Israel Hospital).

The Diabolical Domme Anna, who did attend the same college as Future business Client Monique LaSalle and Collared and Owned Alice, asked Carol to stop by the office with Monique on

the way up to the rooftop to Chat about their college days AND talk to Alice Professionally, after the deal was signed OR MAYBE Alice could assist.

"I DON'T KNOW," Carol told MOM, "SHE MADE IT CLEAR, MONIQUE WANTS BOTH ME AND PATTY ONLY, MOM," Carol stressed.

"Yes! I understand, gorgeous, BUT IS THAT ALL? Did Monique say YES to the contract??! Or Does she JUST WANT BOTH YOUR PUSSIES?? Just drop by with her and then have a good time with her, OK, My lovely Clone?" MOMMEDOMME concluded.

"OK, MOM, I'LL DO AS YOU WISH, No problem," Carol replied as she waited on Monique and Patty to arrive.

Patty pulled up to Monique's Modest Ranch-style home in Winthrop, MA, next town over from East Boston, in the Bentley, where Monique was waiting outside.

"WOW, very impressive," said the impeccably dressed Redhead. "A Rolls? For Me?" Monique replied, smiling to a sexy dressed Patty. Patty was about to open the rear door for Monique but she said, "Oh, No, I want the front seat, lol, OMG! I LOVE ALL YOUR CLOTHES! We must go shopping on our days off REAL SOON," the well-toned voluptuous redhead insisted. "Is that blouse Silk or Satin? I can't tell," Monique asked, pinching Patty's shoulder strap holding up her DDs, protruding through the Giorgio Armani low-cut see-through Blouse with a matching

skirt in matching crotchless Panties. "Are ALL your outfits tailor made?" said the very curious and slightly Older 35-year-old drooling Monique To the 22-year-old knockout Domme Patty.

"It's a Georgio Armani," Patty quickly responded. "His Italian materials are mostly Silk and cotton, making it very light, durable, breathable, yet very comfortable and fashionable material to wear. Carol sends me to get fitted at her Mom's tailor for driving outfits for Special Clients that I have to pick up for meetings," Patty added, making Monique feel SPECIAL. "I'M GLAD YOU AP-PROVE, Monique! Feel the material on my skirt to get more of a feel than just the strap. We can pick one out for YOU when We all go shopping soon," Patty said as Monique jumped at the offer to FEEL Patty's miniskirt material.

Monique slid over a little closer to pat, then lift the material on Patty's smooth driving leg by her firm upper thigh, as Patty Cleverly suggested a minute ago.

Monique continued to comment on the blouse design while still sliding the skirt higher as Monique felt the Armani Italian material between her fingers up to Patty's panties.

"Omg, Patty, lol, Matching panties, I LOVE IT, are they are crotchless, lol?" Monique curiously giggled and was getting very wet.

"YES! They are, I'm So glad you like them, Monique. YOU look gorgeous today as well, I love your blouse too, where did you get it? Here in Boston? May I feel YOUR material as well?" Patty cleverly suggested, also smiling.

"OH, YES! YOU MAY." Monique took Patty's right hand from the wheel and placed it right on her firm left breast to feel Monique's nipple turning to stone and kissed Patty's hand. "Do you like My material as much as I LOVE yours, lol," Monique chuckled.

Patty took Monique's left hand now and put it right on her matching crotchless panties to feel Patty's Wet pussy with her very large clit and guided Monique's fingers over it.

Monique fingered Patty's tight Pussy and her jaws dropping for Patty's erect clit briefly before Monique licked her fingers to show her approval to Patty as they arrived at "SIR" on Sumner St. in East Boston, which was Only ten minutes away driving SLOWLY, as Patty got acquainted with their new Special Client Monique LaSalle, CEO of BIDMC in Boston, MA.

Both very HOT for each other, the two PussyEating knockouts DommePatty and Monique LaSalle couldn't forget they had an appointment this morning. They WOULD FINISH their clothing fabric fantasy LATER.

Carol walked out to greet Monique and Patty, while noticing Patty's strap was NOT on her shoulder, so Carol whispered to Patty, giggling, "DID YOU start without ME this time? lol."

"Someone wants to say hello first, then we can get started on the MRI and PT equipment tour before we ALL take a relaxing Jacuzzi on our Rehab floor," Carol said, greeting a very wet Monique LaSalle.

"OK," replied Monique to Carol, "I can't wait," turning to Patty, inconspicuously tasting her finger.

Alice and Mistress Anna were sitting as Monique was introduced to them by Carol. Patty was waiting and making sure the jacuzzi was on and getting the bath Oils warmed up.

"We ALL went to UMASS," stated the Domme Anna, "AND BOTH YOU AND ALICE went to BC and UMASS as well, What a small world," the Domme added.

"Yes, It is a small world," Alice replied.

"YES, it sure is," replied Monique, "And now we all have the opportunity to do BUSINESS together after today as well. This facility looks amazing, I'm so impressed," Monique added.

"Kathy Deveax, an old college friend, told me about you reaching out to Me, Monique, but things got too busy and nobody followed up on it," Alice apologized. "But WE WILL ALL talk later and catch up, But Today is for YOU to see our Facility and get BIDMC on board with SIR."

"YES! I REMEMBER NOW, YOU'RE ALICE!?" Monique surprisingly said. "OK, DEFINITELY ALICE, AND YOU, ANNA, and your daughter are definitely beautiful. You could pass for twins," Monique added, smiling. "Why don't you join us after this tour for a relaxing jacuzzi as well with your beautiful daughter and assistant Patty?" Monique curiously requested.

"Perfect!" said the Domme. "WE will when Carol says we can, After HER appointment, WE DO NEED a break soon so go ahead and look around and I believe SANTARPIO'S PIZZA was mentioned, so I won't miss it, enjoy your day!" the Domme Anna concluded.

MOMMEDOMME wanted Carol and Patty to Finish their planned-out day between the three Bi/Goddesses and NOT interfere in an already heated-up 3way to remember for life.

This was Carol's arranged meeting now escalating into a MangoSquirting feast, starting from Patty giving Monique a taste from the MangoTree earlier in the Bentley that would soon turn to a mouthful.

Carol walked in front to once again give her prey a glimpse of the best heart-shaped ass around, getting Monique even More wet for Carol's gifted young meaty pussy AND one-in-a-billion set of plum-sized purple nipples.

Monique had ALREADY seen Carol's gifts from God but wanted very badly to suck On the perfect firm set of young Italian titties, along with Patty's huge DDs to sweeten her day. Patty was walking close enough to Monique, guiding while touching her, showing Monique the way.

Monique was glancing AT BOTH OF THE BEAUTIES, back and forth, and getting all wet.

Monique's inch-long nipples were sticking straight out now, very excited for Patty AND Carol to notice. Patty DID notice first and jokingly offered Monique a "Band-Aid" as they ALL enjoyed a laugh about her mom's suggestions in high school to HIDE her long red nipples from poking through Monique's thin summer blouses.

"HERE IT IS, This is our State-of-the-art MRI scanner," Carol said proudly. "WE already did some scanning yesterday on a baseball pitcher's elbow AND shoulder, Alice read the results so

we know it works, lol," joked Carol. "Over here is two more rooms for Physical Therapy treatment sessions," Carol pointed out. "Beside those two rooms is the Jacuzzi room and sauna bath with a Walk-In shower, built-out seating ON the walls with mobile water heads to hold right in your hand and ALL our CLIENTS are treated like Royalty," Carol added. "Do you like Our new Facility, Monique?" Carol asked, staring at Monique's blouse.

"ABSOLUTELY! and Wow! That's a nice Custom-made Walk-In shower! Can we use it soon, lol," Monique curiously proposed, looking back at Carol's fitted blouse when Patty returned.

"ABSOLUTELY!" Patty Replied, Starting to TAKE OFF Monique's blouse with NO resistance from Monique as Carol quickly knelt down to undo Monique's belt. Patty held her arms up, kissing Monique's sweaty neck, pinching and twisting Monique's long hard nipples.

Carol Was trying to suck on them, undoing her skirt, then dropping her skirt to the floor.

Carol then took off Monique's soaking-wet panties, still kneeling down on the floor now while Patty was holding Monique's arms back for Carol to position Monique's long legs open wide for a licking of some sweet Redheaded Pussycum, which was already flowing steadily now, Stirred up from the two HOT young Bi/Pussyloving kinkster sisters Carol and Patty.

Monique was in HEAVEN now, breathing deep, forced back into the very Strong yet Petite Domme Patty feeding Monique to kinkster sister Carol, EATING her up like melting Gelato.

Standing very close to the Walk-In shower, the two Goddesses guided Monique to the shower and sat her down, opening Monique's smooth long toned legs while both Beauties licked and suckled Monique into her first series of PussyPeeCum that soaked Carol's face, Eating-Up the Red Ripe Monique Mango slurping down her Sweet Nectar of the Gods.

Monique was physically and emotionally in ecstasy, not moving an inch, surrendering to Patty's spankings as Patty turned Monique around on the shower seat, Passing her to Carol to spank Monique's firm pink ass. Carol reached around pinching, pulling and slapping on Monique's amazing inch-long red nipples on her lovely and still-firm 34DD-cup.

"YES, OMG! USE ME UP! I LOVE IT ALL," Monique Shouted, looking to Carol now, using her up like a toy while Patty held her for Carol to use now, seeing Monique loved being slapped.

"WOW," Carol said, "She's just like EVELYN, I think SHE may be a Masochist too," Carol said to Patty.

"YES, she is!" Patty agreed. "I'd like to get Monique up on the wheel of torture WITH Evelyn someday," Patty said, smiling.

"I'LL DO ANYTHING, JUST DON'T STOP," Monique said, visibly dripping More Pussycum to the shower floor while facing the shower wall, being sucked on, fisted, spanked, slapped, then fed Pussy from BOTH Carol, THEN Patty, TAKING TURNS ON MONIQUE, One Dominant kinkster sister passing Monique's red ponytail to the other for Pussycum drippings or swollen nipple nibbling off their NEW PUSSY SLAVE "MONIQUE."

"OMG! THIS IS WHAT I'VE BEEN NEEDING ALL
ALONG, I can't wait to work with you two and YOUR MOM,
OMG, Anna is also SO FUCKING GORGEOUS, I want her
too!" Monique cried like a teen on prom night. "Is Anna coming
down for the Jacuzzi with Alice too?" Monique was asking.

(Monique wanted even MORE), it sounded like, and Patty was
smiling ear to ear. Patty COULDN'T WAIT TO DELIVER
THE NEWS to the Domme of ALL DOMMES for her to witness the sexual cravings of Monique and Domme/Anna's collared
lover and masochist "EVELYN."

"OH, YES, Monique, My Momme said right after we showed
you around, she and Alice would be joining us for Jacuzzi time,
then Pizza at Santarpio's WHEN I send for her," Carol replied
to the eager Monique.

"I'll call up from the other phone," Patty pointed out to Carol,
who was now getting her ass licked and rimmed, tugging on Monique's ponytail. Carol was keeping her strong long legs wrapped
on Monique's Shoulders for an Oral treat given by this Pussy-
starved Redhead. MONIQUE HAD NOW FOUND HER-
SELF SEXUALLY, AND HER "DARKSIDE," along with the
MANY that would cross paths with these skilled Fetish Providers
at SIR, Especially with Domme/Anna, Domme/Patty, Carol OR
their loyal protector and partner Cousin/Master T.

"MOMMEDOMME will be right down With Alice," Patty
said to Carol, "to put the finishing touches on Monique," she
added, giggling.

"OMG! I can't wait!" replied The long red raw-nippled Redhead in a puddle of all their hot MangoJuice wasted on the shower floor.

"Let's shower quickly, then get on the massage table For Mom to work her over real good," Carol suggested.

"Take the long leather whip off the wall, your Mom's favorite!" Patty added.

MommeDomme Anna entered the massage room and greeted the eager Pussy-hungry Monique, caressing her long red raw swollen nipples from Patty nibbling on them, along with Carol slapping and pinching them to hear Monique moaning, BUT only asking for more, As a true Masochist would Do.

Carol was watching her Momme take Monique by her hair to the edge of the table, then lay her head OVER the side of the table while Monique started streaming down her leg.

The Domme opened Monique's mouth by squeezing her cheeks open, THEN PEEING on her face and into her mouth, covering her mouth tightly closed.

"SWALLOW!!!" THE Domme Anna ordered Monique!

Gagging just a bit but swallowing all the hot salty pee, Monique said, "OMG, YOU'RE SO FUCKING HOT! Should I call you Mistress? Madam? Are you a real Dominatrix?" Monique curiously asked, Now seeing Domme Anna dressed in a Dominatrix black leather Corset suit with thigh-high leather stilettos, taking her long leather whip from Domme Patty.

"YES! My PET. Call me Mistress or Goddess after I've Collared you in a few days and WE are working together with ALL

MY GIRLS after YOU give Us at SIR the BIDMC contract. You're going to LOVE it here with US, Monique, YOU'RE ONE OF US NOW, MONIQUE!"

As Domme Anna continued to whip Monique with Patty and Carol holding her still, then passing her back and forth that she seemed to really enjoy. BUT THIS TIME it was with TWO MORE insatiable kinksters, Bi/Sexual beauties from the same college.

Monique was eating up ALL their Pussycum, Pee, and Ass, one Goddess after the other for four hours, being passed around the room and LOVING being passed by her ponytail, squirting every time one took possession of her ponytail forcefully, like a TRUE MASOCHIST! Monique Signed the contract Immediately after Carol presented it to her, kissing her firmly on the lips, and then told Monique, "YOU belong to ME now, and I'll belong to you," Carol whispered with her hot wet lips to the Dazed Masochistic CEO Monique LaSalle of the BIDMC.

Monique was then asked Privately by The Domme, "WHO IN THIS ROOM DO YOU WANT AS YOUR OWNER to Collar you to be OUR NEW SLUT YOU CRAVE TO BE?" the DommeAnna asked.

The drained-out, cummed-on, pissed-on, fisted and rimmed-out Monique replied, "I WANT YOUR CAROL TO OWN ME. From the second I saw her standing before me, I Just knew I would LOVE to be used by this Goddess I was trembling over," Monique now admitted.

"DONE. I will have Carol perform your Collaring ceremony in two days, IS THAT good for you?" the DommeAnna asked Monique.

"ABSOLUTELY, Mistress Anna, the sooner the better," Monique answered.

Carol nodded in agreement to "Collar and Own" this beautiful Redheaded Ex/Model Monique as the bruised and used-up Monique nodded back to her New Owner, "Goddess Carol."

CHAPTER

20

MommeDomme/Mistress Auntie Anna watched closely as her carbon-copy kinkster daughter had scheduled MRI clients coming in daily now, Physical Therapy Clients from the follow-up MRI results as well as Carol's OWN (secret Journal) of "Special Clients" OFF THE CHARTS!

Carol and Patty were in Constant Demand from the BDism world for their fetish-providing skills, as well as being Beautiful Dommes to BOTH RICH MEN AND RICH WOMEN!

MONEY was NO problem for their services, however, getting a session with EITHER of the young Goddesses WAS the problem. The two persuasive knockouts only half of the eight Hospitals Carol had lined up for NEW BUSINESS to get SIR really rolling, and they got ALL eight.

Carol and Patty ALREADY had the two biggest Boston SPORTS teams on board, THEN to top that they landed the MGH AND the BIDMC Hospitals while landing the TWO CEOs of each Hospital into their own Special Clients Journal now and soon would Collar and Own Monique as Carol's own personal BDism Slave and share her with Carol's Co-Owned Domme/Patty, whom she SHARED EVERYONE WITH, Including Her Master T, "WITH PERMISSION ONLY!"

Patty had The Domme Anna and Evelyn for Herself, however, and sometimes played with the Clients when picking them up to drive them to "Special sessions" IN the Company's new Bentley.

TODAY Monique would be "Collared and Owned" by Carol to own. Monique was given a choice of anybody In the room by MommeDomme Anna and picked the young Unique Goddess Carol with a God-Gifted Anatomy and skills that amazed even Goddess MommeDomme.

Carol planned on persuading Monique, the BIDMC Director/CEO, to work side by side at SIR with Operations Director and Certified Radiology Technician Alice Capolla.

CEO Monique LaSalle of BIDMC AND CEO Phil Labella from MGH were acquired in just two days in Dominating fashion By Carol and BDism sister Domme Patty, THE TWO STAR-STRUCK CEOS DIDN'T HAVE A CHANCE!!

Phil was first, THEN Monique on the same day. BOTH submitted to their proposals and sexual advances almost instantly. Both CEOs belonged to Carol, Patty and Domme Anna, now

signing on with SIR, legally committed to refer ALL scanning patients to SIR for MRI scanning with follow-up Physical Therapy sessions billed directly to the patient's appropriate Insurance Company for Thousands of dollars at a time.

But these frequent visits to the Facility, which were also the Domme's home on the Penthouse floor, were Pissing the DommeAnna off and NOT in a good way, with ALL their cars double parked outside, troubling to the MOMMEDOMME! So Domme/Auntie Anna told her nephew Anthony/Master T to "DO SOMETHING ABOUT ALL THESE CARS."

CEO Phil From MGH was still Overwhelmed and hypnotized by Carol and Patty's talents and skills that took his GIRTH-WIDE COCK in Patty's throat, THEN Carol took every inch in her ASS as the insatiable Carol begged him for even more cock in her Italian Heart-shaped Ass.

Now CEO Phil was just showing up whenever he wanted, bringing friends to the rooftop lounge, where he had a good time with the Kinkster sisters, NOT a very good idea at all.

Phil was ON BOARD now with SIR and IN the Special Clients' Fetish list in Carol's New journal. CEO Phil had told at least five Golf buddies about the two 21- and 22-year-old gorgeous knockouts and THEY ALL wanted a piece and WOULD PAY ANYTHING.

@ $500 hr. was NO PROBLEM for the million-dollar membership club, all the golf buddies said, SO THEY ALL started to come around hunting down the two young beauties.

THEN WHEN MASTER T STEPPED IN, to say, "GET THE FUCK BACK IN YOUR MERCEDES AND GO HOME, NOW! NO appointment! NO Physical Therapy! YOU'RE ALL FUCKING ANIMALS, DON'T COME HERE THINKING YOU OWN THE PLACE, EVER AGAIN, GO HOME!" Shaking his finger at Phil, moving his car first.

Master T then angrily told Joey beside him all the way to "GO FIND THOSE TWO SLUTS OF OURS, I'LL FIX THIS!" Master T concluded.

Phil then approached Master T (ANOTHER BIG MISTAKE) to tell him "HE Made a deal" with Carol and that the rooftop garden/bar could be used by "Certain Clients," as he put it. "Also, I agreed to send you ALL our business from the MGH," Phil said in his own defense.

MASTER T, now steaming from his ears, nose and throat, said to CEO Phil, "WHAT? WHAT THE FUCK DID YOU SAY TO ME, ASSHOLE?" with a "SLAP" to his mouth, then wrapping Phil's silk tie around his neck, now screaming into his face! "YOUR MGH contract with SIR, DON'T STATE that You and your three friends here can DOUBLE PARK in front OF OUR PLACE OF BUSINESS, and THIS is where we live! DO YOU think you're going to spend an afternoon HERE away from Your wife and family PLAYING with young beautiful WOMEN?" asked a Violent Master T. "THEN YOU'LL BE DEAD WRONG," the Master concluded, letting Phil's tie go. "There are three owners here, NOT ONE, and five Stockholders, Now GO home!"

Joey and Domme Anna ran over to calm nephew/Anthony down now AFTER asking him to "DO SOMETHING," ANOTHER big mistake on her part.

"NO, NO hitting! Anthony," Joey stood in front of Phil and told his buddy as The Domme/Aunt Anna told Phil, "YOU, Sir, need to come back before the Police pull up and WE will straighten this out with Carol AND Patty ASAP. YOU CANNOT Bring FRIENDS here, What were You thinking, Phil? PLEASE GO now, This IS NOT a massage Parlor!" Domme/Anna added to the Shaken and Disappointed CEO. "You can't just pull up with three or four cars and park like that. We live here up in the Penthouse," persuading the Dazed and Confused Phil LaBella and friends to get ready to leave.

"OMG, I'm so sorry. Is THAT the same Anthony on the evening news they say threw Carol's fiancé off the Tobin Bridge???" the shocked CEO Phil asked Anna nervously.

"Allegedly," added The Domme/Anna, "and I wouldn't PUSH Carol's Cousin Anthony too far either. So Go home, please," she concluded with.

"NO WORRIES, I'm going and again, I apologize, I'll call YOU first, Anna, to make ANY kind of appointment at all," the worried CEO Phil said on his way, LEAVING AS QUICKLY AS THEY ALL ARRIVED!!

Master T's good friend Joey, As well as His Goddess Auntie Anna, had jumped in to calm Anthony down to NOT escalate this Confrontation in the middle of the street RIGHT IN FRONT of Their Residence AND Business. They BOTH knew his temper

and DID NOT want the Police getting ANY calls for trouble in-volving her nephew Anthony/Master T, especially right after HE was just suspended Of throwing Carol's Porn movie scout/Fiancé off a bridge and suspected of beating Patty's abusive Brother into Intensive care At MGH.

"Ironically," Phil was remembering the Names and faces now from the incidents on the news and Apologized to Domme/Anna and Immediately "GOT OUT OF THERE" like he was told.

All the cars were "Gone in 60 seconds!" Carmen, Joey or Master T Would now VALET park every car that arrived at the roped-off entrance, PROBLEM SOLVED!

Carol and Patty were BOTH in deep trouble with BOTH their Master T and The Domme/Anna now for "STRAYING & DIS-OBEYING." Carol was Collared and Owned by her Cousin/Master T, while Patty was Collared & Owned by BOTH Master T AND Mistress Anna!

The two head-turning, Insatiable, manipulative Goddess young Sluts had FUCKED And SUCKED CEO THICK-DICK PHIL LABELLA "WITHOUT PERMISSION."

"It's 'BREAKING THE RULES,'" said the angry MOMME-DOMME and to MASTER T as well. This WAS A PUNISH-ABLE Offense and WOULD be addressed by THE DOMME/Anna and Cousin/Anthony Master T, IF the offender Did NOT agree, they could be beaten, tortured, then SOLD OFF or AUC-TIONED Off By the Owner to Wealthy Kinkster Clients, OR ter-minated and replaced.

Carol and Patty arrived in the Bentley and Mistress Anna GROUNDED BOTH of them immediately, taking the keys from Patty. MASTER T and DOMMEMOM were now scolding Both the worried young Goddesses for STRAYING & DIS-OBEYING, punishable by a hundred whacks from Master T's Belt And various whips ready for use on the Large lowered Massage table just inside, where BOTH the Crying Young Sluts were about to get PUNISHED by a very PISSED-OFF Master T and MomDomme, who incidentally CO-OWNED BOTH OF THE SLUT SISTERS!

"WHAT DID I DO, THAT YOU DID NOT DO?" Carol pointed into Master's face.

"YOU FUCKED ALICE! Without permission from Me or Mom!! YOU FUCK and Use PATTY without ME!!!"

"GO AHEAD, BEAT ME!! THEN I'M going to beat YOU too for straying and getting blowjobs from BOTH of them," Carol yelled as she was bent over and tied, ready for the whip on her solid round ass. "YOU are Collared by ME too as well as Mom, those are her rules, RIGHT? AND YOU, MOMMEDOMME! you have a lot of nerve telling US what's Right from WRONG. YOU, SIR, Have NOT been exactly LOYAL To ME either," Carol Pled her defense.

MommeDomme SNAPPED back at her slut daughter, "What's WRONG what YOU did, was NOT telling Your target that THIS FACILITY IS NOT A FUCKING WHORE HOUSE! That DISILLUSIONED CEO Phil from the MGH pulled up here

with three friends ALL in different cars, ALL double parked, THEN They drank ALL of OUR liquor like horny teenagers, where WE live!" the Domme angrily screamed at her daughter, some in Italian. "WE JUST ESTABLISHED A NEW LEGITI-MATE, PROFESSIONAL, PROFITABLE BUSINESS. WE JUST SPENT A FORTUNE TO GET THIS PLACE GOING, AND YOU THINK That was OK?

I CHECKED IN ON YOU, JUST IN CASE PHIL WASN'T SOME KIND OF A SERIAL KILLER. I SAW YOU BOTH! SO I KNOW YOU BOTH FUCKED PHIL WITH-OUT PERMISSION, WHICH MASTER T WILL DEAL WITH YOUR PUNISHMENT NOW," Mistress concluded with the Charges.

Patty now said IN HER DEFENSE, "I WAS ONLY FOL-LOWING ORDERS FROM CAROL THAT I THOUGHT I HAD TO LISTEN TO SINCE SHE IS OWNED BY 'BOTH' CAROL and Domme Anna," Patty pleaded.

"VERY GOOD, MY little knockout manipulator," the Older Manipulator/Goddess and MOMMEDOMME suggested, "but NOT good enough! YOU COULD HAVE FOUND A WAY AND SHARED. 'YOU, MY CLEVER ONE,' could have slowed my daughter down a bit to THINK before you ACT. WHAT ARE THE CONSEQUENCES?? Or, IS IT WORTH IT?? MASTER T, TIE THEM UP TOGETHER, Back to back, NAKED, and open their legs wide, NO PANTIES," MISTRESS ANNA Ordered the punishment to the Kinkster Slut Sisters.

"Twenty whacks across their Nipples, then paddle those hard asses with butt plugs in them twenty more Times. DO YOU ACCEPT YOUR PUNISHMENT? IF YOU DO NOT ACCEPT YOU CAN BE SOLD, AUCTIONED OFF OR REPLACED!" the ANGRY DOMME ADDED!

"OH! NO! NO! NO!" Patty now Crying in tears. "PLEASE, MASTER T! Don't SELL ME OFF, PLEASE, MISTRESS! I WON'T STRAY EVER AGAIN!! PLEASE DON'T REPLACE ME, PLEASE! I DO ACCEPT MY PUNISHMENT! I WILL OBEY AND NEVER STRAY! I NEED TO STAY!!" Patty Crying out, begging NOT to be SOLD OFF to some kinkster Millionaire and be AWAY from HER MASTER T, OR HER MENTOR GODDESS, NOR HER DREAM OF SWEET MANGO DAUGHTER CAROL. "DO WHATEVER YOU WANT TO ME." The Goddess's very own surrendering words to Master T that drove him wild when he heard those words. PATTY PLED as she turned her head to HER MASTER, "READY" to be beaten, Used OR Violated by BOTH of them.

Master T had done the smartest thing He had ever done in the eyes of "ALL THREE" Of HIS Collared Beauties. HE had been caught straying as well and WOULD take his Medicine from BOTH HIS OWNERS He Had strayed from. Carol knew SOMEHOW Master T was getting BJs by Alice in her self-amusing circle of young men, along with Carmen and Joey.

Alice was totally out of control while the trio put her on her knees for her three favorite cocks she hunted down regularly

while living and working in the N. End. NOW Alice wanted them ANY TIME she wanted, but SHE COULD NOT, according to Mistress Anna's BDISM rules.

Alice WOULD FACE CHARGES soon with Punishment by Carol and Mistress Anna. Even Joey now belonged to Patty so Alice could ONLY have Carmen to play with, UNLESS Alice was given permission... not so complicated, right? Wrong! Lol.

It was not so easy when Alice started to get wet and her drooling lips wanted to suck the three ten-inch young hard cocks waving in her face while Master T slapped her, kneeling in a puddle of cum for two hours Straight!!!

Alice might just get off with a warning OR She might have to Eat-Out The two Goddesses, Carol and Domme Anna, For Blowing the two that were "Collared and Owned Personal Property." Mistress Anna had called Alice into the office!

"OMG, Mistress," Alice said, now defending herself. "I'm so sorry but I Didn't know who was owned OR who belongs to who."

"Master T and Joey are off limits to you, Alice, unless permission is given," DommeAnna told a worried Alice and shot back softly.

"YOU DID GIVE ME CARMEN, though, right? Can I use him, Mistress? Master T said He took the Punishment for the incident and that I should ask YOU for ME to Collar Carmen so I can then swap with the YOU and the girls? Can I PLEASE do that???" Alice curiously pled her case for justice to the DommeAnna.

"Well, I Guess So, Alice," Mistress Anna being easy on Alice because of nephew Anthony/Master T took most of the punishment. The Domme told Alice, "My nephew/your Master T TOOK A BEATING for you IN AND OUT of the Walk-in shower, where ALL three Goddesses soaked him. I DON'T even think it was punishment AT ALL." DommeAnna grinned.

The Domme now settled on a punishment. "ALICE, YOU WILL Collar and Own Carmen as Master T suggested, then You will be able to swap on couples night, YOU and MY TWO BEAUTIES and their Pets will schedule once a week or Bi/Weekly, that way YOU will still Co/OWN CARMEN With ME, AND YOU CAN STILL get to BLOW ALL THREE BIG hard cocks with their owners present while they whip you and use YOU as well. YOU will have to EAT YOUR DINNER at Rita's UNDER THE TABLE as your punishment. ME, MY Dinner guest Evelyn, daughter CAROL and on Probation PATTY will be your dinner and your punishment for 'Using Collared Property.' DO YOU ACCEPT YOUR PUNISHMENT? OR DO YOU WISH TO BE SOLD?" the DommeAnna gave Alice her choice.

"YES, DOMME/ANNA, I ACCEPT MY PUNISHMENT. I DON'T EVER WANT TO BE SOLD OFF, MY MISTRESS. I WILL Do ALL four Women, That's Fair, My Mistress. I have sucked four cocks in a circle before, I know I can handle four gorgeous pussies. MY PLEASURE, Mistress, and thank You SO MUCH for ME Collaring and owning Carmen as well," Alice said, kneeling to kiss The Domme Anna's stilettos. "I will look for-

ward to swap night now, AND I look forward to Rita's as well, My Mistress. Make the reservations and I'll be there," Alice smiled.

"VERY GOOD, Alice. You KNOW, I like you. You are a great asset to SIR and YOU will soon be working beside MONIQUE, another certified Radiology Technician From BIDMC as soon as we get her Onboard. She will be another Pussy licker for you under YOUR desk, lol," Mistress Anna giggled, "BUT YOU WILL SHARE HER," the Domme sternly concluded.

"I WILL SHARE MYSELF and EVERYTHING WITH YOU, GODDESS, YOU'RE THE BEST DOMME EVER. I'm So looking forward to Rita's more than you know," Alice concluded as The Domme helped Alice up from her knees to kiss her softly on her lips.

With All the confusion and the punishments handed down for straying, there was ONE MORE THING Carol needed to do and that was to GET MONIQUE COLLARED, as Monique now needed Carol in her sex life.

Monique desperately WANTED Carol's pussy VERY BADLY. Monique was willing to be collared and just MIGHT be willing to leave her position at BIDMC as CEO to come on board and work side by side with the young Goddess Carol. Monique had a daily Fantasy now to be USED and ABUSED by Carol OR Patty OR BOTH before going home to the boring Vanilla life Monique was stuck in with her boring vanilla husband, AND she would be PAID MORE for it too.

Monique had two kids and a mortgage like many other boring Vanilla Couples. Working next to THESE INSATIABLE BEAUTIES at SIR. This would be a DREAM COME TRUE for Monique, along with her new Mistress Carol, Domme Patty and Domme Anna, who would GET MONIQUE TO RITA'S in time for the Pussy-licking Feast as Alice's punishment.

ALICE might soon have five Pussycum dinners to Lap-up under the table at Rita's on her knees behind the low-hanging tablecloths in the circular Reserved Booth next to the warm fireplace.

The Domme's favorite Restaurant and Favorite Booth was Always well prepared for her Privacy with a fresh clean long tablecloth that reached the floor well before her arrival. The Goddesses always tipped $50 BEFORE the actual Meal tip. The waiter or waitress was NOT allowed back after the meals were served ON the table Until who would be serving UNDER the table was DONE, WHEN EVERYONE Invited by the Goddess Anna was PLEASED and It had taken two-three hrs. many times.

Patty was now very relieved that she would NOT be put up for auction to be sold off to a Wealthy Special Client for straying as Carol was also happy that her Cousin/Master T had kept his Word, Oath, and Loyalty to her and accepted Carol's punishment to KEEP Patty as well.

BOTH Master's Young Kinky Goddesses Needed to finish up with Monique; however, Monique had been Mesmerized by the two knockouts since their private meeting and Presentation of the MRI scanning Proposal To CEO Monique in her office at the Hospital.

Lately Monique's craving for pussy showed Monique now, after SEEING FOR HERSELF she needed to explore MORE with woman, But really wanted to be USED by Carol and Owned by her.

BOTH Patty and Carol now had Monique thinking ONLY ONE THING, and that was Monique rubbing Her inch-long pink nipples on Carol's purple plum 21-year-old nipples. Monique wanted nipple-to-nipple play, French kissing Carol While laying on her side, LOCKED Pussy to Pussy, humping their MangoJuices into a puddle.

Monique now walked around daydreaming of licking up Carol's young 21-year-old meaty pussy ALL DAY long, working for her younger Boss (V.P.) Goddess Carol AND her Mom, UNDER Alice in the MRI department. Monique dreamed while on lunch breaks Monique would be eating Pussy, not to mention three Young 10" studs that would pass her around on her 1-hr.-long lunch breaks.

IF Carol was ANYTHING like her Momme in the office, Monique would be spending A LOT of time UNDER all their desks OR Tied down to them.

TODAY as Monique Requested to be Collared and Owned, giving up her Vanilla life to Explore her cravings Into the BDISM world, Carol and Patty had promised to teach the borderline masochistic Monique Protocol into her hidden lifelong fantasy of exploring The Domination of OTHER Beautiful woman Using her forcefully and abusing her sexually.

Monique had chosen Carol over Patty and really WANTED CAROL BADLY. Being in the presence Of The Two younger Goddesses for the presentation left Monique sitting in a puddle of her own Pussycum on her office leather chair, not able to take her eyes off of Carol's Voluptuous body. BUT Monique would make That Presentation AND herself WORTHY, taking advantage of the STOCK OPTIONS and Position at SIR when "SIR" WENT PUBLIC.

Carol and SIR had to wait for a Certain amount of Revenue coming in with Assets to reach a Certain amount of money before STOCKS could be issued and sold OR offered to CORPORATE OFFICIALS or Investors.

Monique WAS also College EDUCATED With a Doctorate in Biotechnology right alongside of her colleague Alice. Mistress Anna had a double Master's to her credit.

ALL THREE were not only Gorgeous and Educated But IN-SATIABLE, Bi/Sexual, and ALL three could Eat Pussy ALL DAY LONG. ALL THREE WOULD apply their Education and Experience to take "SIR" TO ANOTHER LEVEL.

The Domme Had already SEEN the Numbers coming in. The revenue Coming IN was Only skyrocketing against the numbers going OUT, Confirming HER and CAROL "SIR" WAS ON ITS WAY To go public.

"GET MONIQUE ON BOARD," Mom and Alice told Carol. "DO whatever she wants! WE NEED her experience and her expertise in Radiology."

Alice stressed, "They ALL KNOW that Monique wants to be right next to Carol ALL DAY LONG if she can, NOW is the chance to 'Collar and Own' this gorgeous Ex-Model French beauty WITH Brains to match."

Patty Might NOT be as well educated Intellectually, but Patty WAS More Street Smart with Unmatched Oral skills, Socially outgoing with abilities to Manipulate EVEN the Mistress and her Master T MANY TIMES to get her way.

NOT always, though. Patty would watch from a distance, however, for her BDism sister and FAVORITE FLAVOR Carol and would have NO objection to the Domme and Spoiled Clone Daughter Carol Dominating the masochistic Monique in Private sessions.

MANY TIMES one Purple-eyed Goddess after the other had used Monique up secretly.

Patty would NOT interfere as long As she was INCLUDED sometimes in three-ways! Patty had a lot on her plate already with Special Clients, BUT would NEVER want to lose Carol, NOR her Master T. Patty would rather DIE than to lose either one. So, Monique was NOT an issue with her.

Monique was ready to be Collared and Owned as She looked at Carol in Awe, holding her custom-sewn burgundy leather Collar with Black ornament stones and light green jade stones to match her green eyes lined with a cluster of diamonds spelling out her OWNER'S name, "PROPERTY OF GODDESS!" On top and in Green Jade stones reading "CAROL," under that,

which ABSOLUTELY melted Monique's heart and wet her panties at the same moment, when she was told to kneel and recite her oath To Carol.

"I PROMISE TO OBEY, I WILL NEVER STRAY, I PROMISE TO DO WHATEVER YOU SAY, I PROMISE TO SERVE, AND WITH MY MISTRESS CAROL I WILL STAY. YOU WON'T BE DISAPPOINTED, YOU WILL SEE! I WILL BE THE BEST SLAVE AND PUSSYSLUT I CRAVE TO BE," Monique repeated proudly.

"DO YOU ACCEPT MY COLLAR?" Mistress Carol asked Monique firmly.

"YES! OH, YES!" Monique again eagerly answered, smiling and ready to be inducted while Cousin Master T, Patty, Alice, and the Mistress all looked on at Carol's Control and Dominance over her submissive slave Monique entering the BDism Darkside forever.

Carol WAS BECOMING Just like her MOMMEDOMME Before their eyes. Master T's jaw dropped with an Immediate hard-on for HIS Property Carol. Cousin Anthony/Master T now would witness And participate in the induction of this NEW inch-long-nippled Redhead with an always moist, puffy pussy, size 4, READY to be Used, abused, clamped, nibbled, slapped, whipped and cropped Until visibly sore and raw.

Monique was still looking up at her New Owner, "Property of Mistress Carol," who Was now placing the very expensive Handmade Leather burgundy Collar around Monique's very sexy

neck. Monique was so visibly excited also. Monique's Long thick nipples were sticking straight out above her matching burgundy corset's edge that Carol made her wear to the ceremony for All to see her amazing long erect nipples.

Her amazing long, thick pink nipples were complementing Mistress Carol's plum-sized purple nipples, also visibly on display in her tailored midnight blue Corset for her New PussySlave to see what she would be SERVING and nursing from in appreciation for her Submission to the Younger flawless Goddess.

Monique's long wavy red hair was in a ponytail for the Collaring, now held Tightly by Mistress Carol pulling her surrendered prey in close to pinch and twist the masochist's Long tingling Nipples while kissing her hot wet lips, welcoming her to serve on the Darkside and be shared whenever Carol gave Permission to the kinksters present, witnessing her Collaring ceremony.

Carol was now buckling the Custom-made collar on Monique's neck, who was holding the back of Carol's thighs as she knelt inches from her Fantasy and was drooling for a taste of what was to cum. With NO panties on Monique's Mistress Carol lifted up her leather skirt that matched Monique's new collar with one hand, Then Carol took her new Collared PussySlave's ponytail with the other hand to wet the Redhead's mouth to BEGIN SERVING HER Voluptuous 21-yr.-old Goddess Carol.

Mistress Carol whispered down to Monique, "IT'S TIME FOR YOUR INDUCTION INTO OUR BDISM LIFE-STYLE, YOU BELONG TO ME NOW. YOU are My prop-

erty to share with the people in this dungeon if I tell you to, ONLY with MY PERMISSION. They all may Use you OR YOU serve them, Do you understand, MY Slave?" Monique's Mistress/Goddess Carol was now explaining the rules to her.

"YES, My Mistress, This is what I have chosen and I DO UNDERSTAND, I WILL OBEY THE RULES 100%," the eager Collared Slave Monique agreed now, saying, "I AM READY, MISTRESS CAROL. I need you to Use Me up like YOUR Pussy Slut/whore I crave to be. Do to me what YOU and Patty did To Me in the shower that I crave every day now. I loved every minute of it, Mistress Carol. I NEED to serve You EVERY DAY as your Collared slave" (Referring to the day the two Goddesses Held and Ravished her Into BDISM Forever).

"OK, My Slut/Slave, Patty, will take you now over to the WHEEL OF TORTURE Behind the door to see If you're as Masochistic as My MommeDomme's Masochistic Evelyn?" now looking towards her Momme, who was smiling.

"Evelyn will be here shortly for dinner," MommeDomme replied quickly.

Patty was now walking over, Remembering just a few days ago, slapping this masochistic 32-year-old Redheaded Beauty into a squirting multi/orgasm that soaked all three of them on that day.

But TODAY Mistress Carol passed the eager Collared Redheaded Ex/Model Pussylicker To Patty to TIE-UP the dripping Monique onto the tall wheel by her Mom. MOMMEDOMME held the thick soft silk rope to tie the excited Masochistic Monique

onto the Wheel of Torture to be turned while whipped, paddled, sucked, fucked, slapped, then fed Pussy by The four extremely wet kinky women present for Carol's first Collaring Ceremony and Monique's induction into BDism.

There would be only one big dick from the Master in the Dungeon today Monique would have to serve for the amusement of Momme and Carol when he fucked Monique in her ass deep and hard with ten inches of hard meat.

Master T and Carol had straightened out ALL their differences of straying and had AGREED on sharing concerns with who and who NOT to play with, Period.... Carol won THAT war, of course.

Patty and Her Mentor MommeDomme had finished tying up this hourglass hard body and started to spin her slowly to see if she was tied firmly with her legs apart, wide enough to whip or fist-fuck her pussy into one orgasm after another for the eager masochist.

Patty told her DommeAnna, "YOU go first, MY MISTRESS," looking at Monique, anxious for the first strike from the long leather whip held by The Domme Anna.

"WHACK! WHACK!" TWO hard strikes to each waiting and tingling long hard pink nipple. Monique Only let out a deep breath of air while the Slightly older Goddess inserted two fingers into her pussy, then sucked on her marked swelling nipples from the whipping, Now stepping back a bit to order Domme Patty, "YOU now, my Pet! Just Like I taught you," the Mentor Goddess added.

"WHACK! WHACK! WHACK!" Three consecutive strikes to Monique's inner thighs and one on Monique's visibly wet puffy pussy, this time letting out a low moaning sound to her satisfaction. Whack! Whack, right after Patty by the MommeDomme on the same spots as before, right across those gorgeous long erect nipples.

MommeDomme was pinching her raw marked nipples while suckling and biting them to see her limits of pain. Monique was feeling more pleasure than any pain, moaning even louder and saying, "YES! Give me MORE. Just Like that," the Collared Monique said to the older Goddess Anna, "DO IT!" Monique adding in a demanding tone. "Bite them!" Looking down now at her new owner Mistress Carol also biting her long, bruised erect nipples while pulling her ponytail over to the older goddess, who had four fingers in Monique's streaming pussy, ready to be fisted any minute now by the two Sadistic Dommes whipping her into continuous long Orgasms.

"Monique is Definitely a true Masochist just like Evelyn," MommeDomme said, agreeing with Patty.

"OK, OK! You two Sadistic Dommes, This is MY Party!" Mistress Carol joked to All three Wet Women while Alice sat fingering herself but would rather be blowing Master T, who was there close by now, but Alice OR the Master didn't have permission, lol.

Monique kept saying, "DON'T STOP! Please Don't stop! Mistress Carol, WHIP ME MORE! Turn the wheel around so I can reach your pussy and EAT YOU some more, My Goddess," Monique begged.

"YES!" the New proud owner Mistress Carol agreed with excitement. "Put MY Collared Slave/Slut upside down So I can feed her All three pussies while eating Her 'RED SNAPPER' as well," Mistress Carol ordered, slapping the insatiable Redhead on her puffy thick pussylips.

Monique's sweet Pussy was squirting Mango everywhere and on everyone as the three Pussylicking co-workers took turns to the wheel to make this masochistic beauty SCREAM out, squirting her juices for each abusive FemDomme, using her up like a toy with a whip, crop OR Strap-on Dildos just as Domme Anna and Patty did to Evelyn, not so long ago.

Patty now told Carol, who wasn't there that unforgettable day when Mistress Anna PUSHED Evelyn's limits to the sky! Evelyn Only asking FOR MORE ABUSE on that day.

Mistress Carol's final request of HER new Collared Slave Monique was to spend the rest of the night with Mistress Carol and Cousin Master T alone to share and use Monique together.

Carol had planned to lay down the hard Master so Carol could put his 10" cock in Monique's Ass while laying on top of his hard 10 into her winking nasty hole WHILE MONIGUE ATE Goddess Carol into Her Multiple Orgasms, standing over both their heads, dripping Carol's sweet Mango onto both their faces and into her cousin's mouth.

Mistress Carol still had access from this position to abuse Slave Monique's abused red, raw, swollen nipples AND Belting Monique's squirting pussy with her Cousin Anthony's wide

leather Belt right on Monique's erect clit, sticking up Red and raw as well just above her swollen puffy pussy lips.

Carol was using the custom-made long leather whips lined up on Master T and Carol's bedroom walls to beat their Beautiful Masochist Monique as she just begged Carol to Use-up her hard sculptured body even more. Monique HAD DISCOVERED what made her squirt now, What she had been missing sexually, and did NOT ever want to leave Carol's side now.

Monique just kept saying to her new Owner/Goddess Carol in front of Master T, "I BEG YOU, GIVE ME MORE, MY GODDESS CAROL, KEEP USING ME UP, BEAT ME HARD, MAKE ME THE SLUT SLAVE WHORE I CRAVE TO BE."

MGH CEO Phil LaBella called to once again apologize to Domme Anna and to say He had referred two New patients to "SIR" today. The two patients needed MRI scans and possible follow-up Rehabilitation Physical Therapy. Phil went on to say He had a Free Membership to give to Master T to the Colonial Country Golf Club In Lynnfield, Mass., and to show there was NO disrespect, only a misunderstanding of the use of the Facility's Rooftop garden lounge.

The Elite Country Club was only ten miles north of East Boston from the "SIR" Facility.

The Domme AuntieAnna told her nephew/Master T of the membership suggestion, THEN SUGGESTED He take the

Membership AND explained WHY it was a good idea, thinking in her Diabolical way, of course.

Phil could STAY on the Special Clients Fetish/Massage list and allow ONE friend Only at the $500-hr. Rate. THIS would allow Master T and his Longtime Fantasy Mistress/Auntie Anna to CONTINUE their Fetishes And Fantasies with Permission from Carol.

Carol in turn had Permission to Use the Thick-Girth Cock of the CEO Phil LaBella, along with Patty, in their four-handed Special Prostate massages he COULD NOT forget AND wanted to schedule ANOTHER two-hr. session soon but Only with Carol and Patty @ $750.00/hr., for ANAL and DEEP-THROATING, Carol insisted!

WITH PERMISSION NOW, Mistress and Goddess Auntie Anna would be able to have her favorite skilled tongue-lashing nephew again and hadn't had her Corned Beef w/Swiss on Rye in a while with her nephew Master T under her desk EATING-OUT the Domme/AuntieAnna until she let him up WHEN she was done feeding her nephew long, hot Multiple-Orgasms, "Soaking him."

The Domme's nephew Anthony, now her Master T, ALSO missed the Unequivocal Taste of the older Goddess's PussyPee-Cum mix she provided to him, Nor the smell of Shalimar perfume Master T went WILD for and she knew it.

The manipulative Goddess Aunt applied Shalimar to her inner thighs AND a splash to the dimples on her flawless lower

back and ass, KNOWING Master T would Eat her out for hours, asshole included! IF SHE SAID, OR NOT!

Master T TOTALLY agreed, then told Carol to go ahead and schedule the CEO Phil for his Prostate-massage Fetish. "Tell Patty to get her fist up there in Phil's ass, lol, YOU have MY PERMISSION," Her Cousin Anthony and Master added, laughing. "By the way, Phil Gave me a Golf membership to the Country Club in Lynnfield. Your Mom thinks it will be good for Business and for me to make Vanilla connections for An ACTUAL Physical Therapy SIR Clientele, which is already OFF THE CHARTS with revenue and our cash flow. WE are about to go public on the (NYSE) STOCK MARKET, Carol. Your Monique, along with Alice, was offered STOCK OPTIONS already by your Momme so be careful!" Master T told Cousin Carol during dinner in their Penthouse suite.

Carol agreed, saying, "I KNOW! We NEED to be sure WE ALWAYS HAVE CONTROL of the Company, MORE THAN 51% of the stocks WILL belong to US, our lawyer Evan told me. He will show US on paper as well, so NO worries," Carol added to Her Master while taking him by the hand into the Shower before bedtime.

MommeDomme gave a call to her twin/Goddess daughter Carol to tell her she'd been thinking about the Fantasy Carol approved of, The MOTHER/DAUGHTER Live sex show for 100k. MommeDomme wanted permission to use Carol's Cousin Anthony/Master

T in ANOTHER three-way. "ALTHOUGH I DO own him too! I GROOMED MY NEPHEW ANTHONY LONG AGO TO COLLAR HIM, but I still want to OBEY the rules so I'm asking your permission To MAKE HIM use that tongue on BOTH OF US TOGETHER, then give him the Golden Shower of a Lifetime for ALL THREE of US TO REMEMBER," Carol's MOMMEDOMME pleaded.

"OMG, I'm getting wet just thinking of that three-way now with Grace and Paul! NOW THAT was Fun," Carol remembered, "AND the money went into the business, just so you know, Mom," Carol added.

"I KNOW, my pet!" said MommeDomme. "I'LL SHOW YOU How Master T can EAT A PUSSY from under your desk, MAKING YOU SQUIRT before you can finish a 'Corned beef on Rye with Swiss' sandwich from Pressman's Deli! lol," Mom joked. "We've been doing that challenge for years. IT'S YOUR CHALLENGE NOW, lol," the older Goddess said, surrendering to her younger Goddess Daughter, who undoubtedly HAD THE SAME HOLD on Master T now.

MommeDomme continued to talk to her Up-and-Coming Dominating Daughter with a submissive DARKSIDE ONLY TO A CHOSEN FEW (Master T and Patty), Just Like her Mom had Already surrendered now to her groomed and collared nephew/Master T.

Goddess/Domme Anna had submitted to Evelyn's endless tongue lashings more often now as well. "Evelyn can lick Pussy

and Tongue an ass like a hungry dog on a bone," she added jokingly. "Evelyn wants to retire from the Phone co. with her stock options and their retirement package they offered her, worth well over a Million dollars, And wants ME to Semi-retire with her as well," MommeDomme told Carol. "I WON'T tell you what I have stashed away, BUT I'M PRETTY CLOSE to Evelyn, lol, besides, I'M getting tired and going on forty soon," the MommeDomme was looking for a response OR her daughter's opinion.

"MOM, FORTIES IS NOT OLD! YOU'RE STILL GORGEOUS, NOT EVEN A WRINKLE OR A GRAY HAIR." Carol added, "WHAT'S WRONG? Take a nice three-wk. vacation With Evelyn. You're working way too much," Carol said, searching for answers.

"Nothing's wrong, my Love! I SHOULD BE spending MORE TIME Traveling and be with Evelyn exploring more places and things. I'm Putting YOU And your cousin/Anthony, OUR Master and Protector, in charge to run things. I'LL BE YOUR SENIOR ADVISOR, very close by at Beaver Lake with a Snowbird condo in Florida or San Diego In the winter," MommeDomme suggested to Carol, looking for an OK. "I'll STILL BE just a phone call away! But for right now I DO ADVISE that YOU use Alice and Monique's brains MORE than their pussies," the Domme advised. "THEY ARE BOTH brilliant in their fields and WE ARE GOING PUBLIC NOW. Offer them LIMITED stock options like I already told you, AND DON'T forget to offer Patty some as well. PATTY would die for you And Anthony.

It really showed when I had to discipline you and Patty for straying. OMG! I NEVER seen her worried like that before," the MommeDomme was remembering. "Well, maybe once before...

"SO, DO I have permission to arrange for two corned beef sandwiches for tomorrow's lunch-and-munch? One sandwich for Me and One for YOU? Then we BOTH can get pounded side by side With his hard 10? IT will be fun making some more memories with You," MommeDomme curiously asked Carol again.

"OMG, YES! You have an incredible imagination, Mom, I LOVE IT. YOU'RE the reason I'm so Kinky, lol," the Younger cloned Goddess Carol joked to Her Kinky Mom.

"YES, I KNOW! I see it every day more and more, and ALSO our Master T told me when I was blindfolded that Paul and Grace's Mother/Daughter Live Sex show that HE MADE YOU EAT MY PUSSY? Did YOU know that also?" Mom asked Curiously.

"YES, I KNEW, MOMME, lol, but I wanted to do it anyway and give the couple their money's worth. IT WAS $100K, you know, that's a lot of money to ANYONE!" Carol answered truthfully. "We will meet tomorrow At 1:30 for some corned beef/Swiss on Rye, YOUR OFFICE DESK, OK?" Carol suggested.

"YES, MY DESK is Your desk! Then after 'LUNCH' I want YOU to arrange for Your Masochistic Monique to meet MY Evelyn for a short session to see the similarities up close, OK? Do YOU have the time to arrange that with Monique?" Mom surprisingly added.

"I'll MAKE TIME FOR THAT, that'll be SO HOT!" the eager Carol Replied to her kinky DommeMomme, getting wetter by the minute.

"WE need to make sure WE keep Monique happy and on board at 'SIR,'" the Domme concluded to her hot daughter Carol.

Master T was on his way to the Exclusive Colonial Country Club In Lynnfield, Massachusetts, with HIS PERK, a one-yr. membership given to him From CEO of the MGH Phil (Mr. Girth) La-Bella. Phil plainly (fucked up) Bringing buddies to the Sir facility and was trying to make peace with Master T, MISTRESS ANNA, CAROL and PATTY if he Ever wanted his wide-girth Cock throated by Patty or buried deep in Carol's Asshole Ever AGAIN.

Carol and Patty BOTH had strayed over Phil's thick dick, then were Punished severely for doing so, scaring Patty into a panic that she might be sold off to the highest Kinkster bidder.

Master T got settled in with registration and proceeds to get a drink at the complimentary bar and saw a very Familiar face. IT WAS WEALTHY KINKSTER PAUL TRAVELLO. He was From the High-Priced real Estate Town of Lynnfield. Paul had a membership at the club as well. So did Eddy "Showers" Dugan, ALSO here today on this particular Sunday for a round of golf (When he was NOT getting pissed on by The Domme's private GS sessions).

OMG, I'M going to like it here, Master thought to himself, lol, while waiting to run into Phil to give his Permission personally

to have private sessions with Patty and Carol again @ $750.00 an hour.

"Look who's here! When did you start playing golf? Lol," Paul joked to Master T. "How's Carol and her Mom, THAT WAS THE BEST, ANTHONY, thanks so much for arranging that, MY wife loves you now!" Paul added.

"I was given a membership to see if I like it," Anthony said to Paul. "I like handball OR Racquetball with four walls preferably Inside OR outside Against a tall wall," Master T added. "But I'll play here inside for the summer and see to get to meet some nice people here on the North Shore, I need to get away from the City," the Master added. "Carol and her Momme are great, OUR company 'SIR' is going Public tomorrow! Monday is going to be VERY SPECIAL For the three of us," Master added, smiling to Paul.

Carol called Monique Sunday night to report to her Monday Morning and to BE READY to come on board with US at "SIR."

"Do you need to give a two-wk. notice at BIDMC?" Carol asked of her newly Collared and Owned Submissive Slut/Slave, in true BDism terms.

"YES, My Goddess Carol! I can't wait, I'll be on board in the morning, AND to serve YOU as well. I want to be a part of YOUR Vanilla world AND Working for YOU at SIR as well. We can go over everything as we go along, My Goddess. I'M ALL YOURS," Monique said seriously. "Alice and I will take SIR to the Moon with the four major organizations YOU ALREADY ACQUIRED. I'M

impressed with your Marketing skills, Mistress Carol, I'm ready to serve My Mistress, IN EVERY WAY, EVERY DAY," the hot Monique eagerly told her new Owner.

"AWESOME, Monique, That's what I like to hear," said the pleased new Owner and Mistress Carol. "PLAN ON celebrating with ME, Your Master T, MOM and Evelyn will join us in a session after dinner for some REAL FUN you're gonna love, lol," Mistress Carol giggled to her New Sub/Slave.

"OMG, YES!" Monique excitingly giggled back. "YOU WERE JUST WHAT I NEEDED ALL ALONG, MY MISTRESS CAROL. You won't be disappointed, I promise," the masochist drooled over the phone. "I'LL BE THERE EARLY TO DO THE NECESSARY PAPERWORK, THEN I want to meet this EVELYN You ALL are talking about that is also Masochistic like I crave to be," the eager-to-serve Monique concluded to her New Goddess Carol.

CHAPTER

21

It didn't take long at all after the paperwork was signed and Carol's new Pussy Slave/Monique was on board and her reward was given to Monique when Evelyn was walked into the room by a leash held by her owner, The Domme/Anna.

Carol took Monique's hand and walked her over to the two massage tables joined together and just let nature take its course.

Almost immediately Monique and Evelyn were "Locked," grinding onto each other sideways. The two gorgeous Redheaded Masochistic streaming lesbians were passionately French kissing while being circled and whipped gently at first ALL OVER their well-built hourglass bodies, with Mentor Momme leading the way for BDism Domme apprentice daughter Carol.

WHACK! WHACK! Twice with Authority! Momme told her daughter, "That's what YOUR Submissives are NEEDING from

you! DOMINANCE IS what they Expect and need as Pussy Sex Slaves," Momme explained.

The more the masochists took the Beating on their firm, hard breasts, Ass and dripping-wet pussies, the more Monique and Evelyn would Hump harder, taking in More of their portion of the double-dong dildo given to them by DommeAnna and demanded to "TAKE IT ALL" (until It was buried deep in BOTH their pussies). Mistress Carol and Mom Wanted to see BOTH clits touching, THEN they would know the 18" DoubleDong was ALL THE WAY IN.

Whack, Whack, Whack!! three times on Monique, making her groan Louder and move while Evelyn took the Top position now, fucking Monique like the Submissive Slut/Slave she craved to Be.

Whack! Whack! Two More hard strikes from Mistress Carol across Evelyn's swinging Voluptuous big, firm breasts as she fucked Monique deep and harder with the dildo BURIED inside Both of the Masochists!

"HARDER!" Monique was yelling to Evelyn on top, fucking her with the dildo buried in both of their stretched-out RED swollen Pussies. Evelyn was whipped continuously Now until SHE was on the bottom and Monique started to RIDE the Older pussycum eater into several orgasms one after the other, leaving both of them in a puddle of their Own Hot, sweet MangoJuice!

Holding on to each other tight While Still kissing Passionately, the marked-up Masochists KEPT the 18" double-dong sil-

icone toy BURIED "Out of Sight" up into each other's Cum-Squirting pussies as they kept the Double-Dong held in, OR-DERED by Mom Domme for HER amusement.

Monique and Evelyn were putting on a Live-Bi/Sexual Display that even the Domme Anna HADN'T SEEN Before In her many years as THE DOMME. These Two gorgeous voluptuous women that were both married to men had craved another woman's pussy for years. Both women were Redheads AND the best part to these BDism lifers that now had collared them was that they were both Insatiable Masochists! They had now met their match and now WOULD BE satisfied forever by their Sadistic Dommes that had Collared and Own them, a Masochist's Dream.

The 32-yr.-old sculptured body of Monique and a solid 45-yr.-old Evelyn looked like twin sisters as they started to FEEL each Crack of the whips and Master's Belt applied to the other while LOCKED pussy to pussy, moaning in harmony while passionately French kissing each other, rubbing breast to breast, hiding their marked and bruised nipples from the stinging whips as their FemDomme Owners targeted the swollen RED Raw, long nipples repeatedly as they circled the Slaves, "growling" like animals in heat.

After each STRIKE The moaning Redheads tended to each other by licking the mark of the latest CRACK of the whip, OR open-hand SLAP to their nipples. Monique showed to be an Equally compassionate Masochistic Protecting Evelyn after every Strike, Pushing Evelyn's Limits By her Sadistic Goddess/Domme Anna.

Monique was reaching for Carol's Pussy while Teasing Monique's open mouth as the younger Goddess Carol followed her Mentor Mom As they circled around to Inflict yet MORE PAIN with MORE WHIPPING across her visibly oozing swollen, raw, long thick Nipples.

Evelyn's firm DDs were lined with long red whip marks Inflicted by the Hard Snaps of her DommeAnna while Monique tended to them with suckling licks to cool them down, leaving BOTH of the Bruised Masochistic Redheads in a puddle of their own mixed PussyJuice.

Each Owner now had to Pry EACH Consoling Masochistic apart by their ponytails to use them up for some Forcefully Face-Fucking and ass licking to finish things off.

It was time to squirt on their collared masochists that were just waiting to please their Mistress/Owners in that way, making sure they were completely pleased.

"JUST WHAT THE DOCTOR ORDERED, and just what these two Slaves have been NEEDING all along," Momme told her daughter Carol.

"I think YOUR new Sub/Slave Monique you have Collared will work for YOU for free now if you made her. I CAN TELL Monique has been NEEDING to be treated AS A MASOCHISTIC PUSSY SLUT/SLAVE she craved to be all her life, THEN Monique finally saw YOU as her Goddess to serve Carol."

Monique was looking for just the RIGHT woman to submit to.

"NOW YOU GIVE HER WHAT SHE NEEDS and Monique will serve YOU forever, JUST LIKE EVELYN WILL Serve Me now!" MommeDomme concluded to her daughter, mentoring Carol in EVERY way!

What Monique really needed NOW was her Goddess Carol's Wet Pussy to taste and to please her new Young Goddess she had surrendered and submitted to. Monique was Immediately put on her knees by Mistress/Domme Carol right in front of the lowered massage table in the Dungeon while Carol sat before her Pussy Slave.

Monique, happily kneeling, was removing Goddess Carol's wet panties to get at her puffy, meaty, and very Juicy pussy, and Without hesitation Monique spread her Goddess' wet pussylips apart to suck on her clit hard, cleaning ANY stray drops of Carol's MangoJuice from her inner thighs and into her asshole.

Monique licked and sucked on her Goddess Carol, sent from Heaven, EVERYWHERE, even her toes. Monique was sucking on each toe and back up for MORE PUSSY and ASS from HER NEW young Goddess Carol that Monique had been WAITING FOR most of her 32 YRS.

Monique moaned while being used up BY CAROL and Now PATTY was ordered over to join in to abuse Monique JUST as the day they met and just what Monique had asked Carol for today as well. Mistress/Carol would keep these sessions going to KEEP MONIQUE from Ever straying AND to give the Masochistic PussyLover what she craved, AND had been missing.

MommeDomme has already seen this display of LOYALTY, AFFECTION and DEDICATION from Evelyn, she told her apprentice daughter, "BUT NOT to lose sight of Patty, KEEP PATTY just as close to you!!" she warned Carol. "This lifestyle IS NOT EASY and will drain more than Your Pussy," Momme-Domme again stressed to Curious Carol. "Your cousin, My Nephew Anthony and BOTH our Master, is OURS forever, lol. HE'S NEVER LEAVING!!" MommeDomme giggled.

Master T, however, had Bad news. He had just been told One of his Mentors and father figures, "Sonny Sarro," Freddy's brother from the N. End Fruit Market that Anthony worked for, had just passed away from complications with diabetes and was VERY Upset.

Sonny and Freddy practically brought Anthony up from the Pushcart Days at Haymarket in Boston's North End since he was twelve yrs. old and considered BOTH brothers like a father to him.

Anthony was just turning twelve when the Sarro brothers hired him to sell fruit and vegetables on the pushcarts at Haymarket Square in Boston's North End. BOTH brothers looked after the troubled East Boston skinny, hungry kid, ALONG WITH young Anthony's Mom and Auntie Anna, of course.

Both Sonny and Freddy were close to Anthony when there was trouble in his life and Sonny OR his Auntie Anna could calm him down, and feared he was losing both of his father figures so close together, EVERTHING was happening too fast for the Master.

Nephew/Anthony was very worried about losing His Goddess Auntie Anna. She wanted to retire with Evelyn and was feeling it out with Carol. HIS MISTRESS AUNT ANNA HAD ALREADY TOLD HIM, BUT the news was hurting her nephew MORE than it was hurting the Domme Aunt's less-affectionate daughter Carol.

Master T/Anthony started drinking and doing More Cocaine now than he should after losing MORE CLOSE FRIENDS AND FAMILY from drugs, Mainly Jack (Michael Giacalone), from E. Boston and then Bobby Paglia from the N. End/Boston, along with his wife Patty, both killed in a home invasion In Lynnfield.

THEN two family members died. The first was Anthony's biological Father, also named Anthony, died at 52 yrs. old without ever resolving some issues with his young son Anthony. Soon after ALL that, Anthony's well-connected Mafioso Uncle Angelo in California was hung on a meat hook in SanDiego, which would finally send the Master/Nephew OVER THE EDGE! and out of control!

Anthony in a few short months was a TOTAL WRECK and Out of control, Violent, neglecting his responsibilities to The Domme/AuntieAnna, his Cousin and soulmate lover/Carol, AND watching the business, Without thinking the Master would get stopped, and the State Police found two packages of Cocaine and he was charged with Distribution of Cocaine (NOT just simple possession). The State Police were TARGETING Master T anyway and wanted him in jail to begin with.

He was being watched along with Nicky for the Tobin Bridge Incident, when Carol's Fiancé (Louie Lipstick) was thrown off the bridge, and then Patty's brother was beaten into a coma for abusing her sexually and tried to stop sister Patty from moving out.

At the court hearing Anthony's (good-luck lawyer, Evan Gellant of Chelsea, as He called him) made a deal with the Court that (Anthony) sign himself into the Betty Ford Clinic in Palm Desert, California, and complete a drug Rehab program INSTEAD of Jail time.

The Betty Ford Clinic is located in a wing off the Eisenhower Hospital in Palm Desert, CA. Founded by Betty Ford, President Ford's wife Betty, back in 1982.

Anthony's Uncle Tom was the Radiology technician at the Eisenhower Hospital who helped get him enrolled (NO special help), just guidance. Anthony ALREADY KNEW what He HAD TO DO, and wanted to do this for Himself AND for the people standing by him, waiting for the Master to get his head on straight again.

COUSIN CAROL in particular, who told her love and soulmate for life Cousin Anthony, "I'LL BE RIGHT HERE WAITING FOR YOU! RIGHT HERE WHERE YOU LEFT ME!" Carol said to her Broken Master in a river of tears!

ONCE signed into the Betty Ford Program for the 60-day program, Anthony MUST REPORT WEEKLY by phone AND send counselling reports SIGNED by the certified Counselor holding the meeting he had attended, three nights A week, and sent back to E. Boston Probation Dept.

"THESE Counselors at the Betty Ford were the BEST PEOPLE I've Ever had the experience to meet and I'VE MET ALL KINDS OF PEOPLE in this cruel world," the Broken young man Anthony/Master T confirmed and remembered the WISE WORDS of one counselor in particular who changed his ways of thinking, FOREVER!

"'YOU, It's All up to YOU. YOU came here to help YOU, Not me. I will help YOU be YOU again, after all YOU were the one who took the wrong turn at the fork in the road, NOT ME. I will give 'YOU' directions to get back to the fork in the Road, But I'm NOT driving your fucking car. 'YOU' Drive your own car, I'M NOT your fucking chauffeur or your butler or whatever you want to call me. BUT if 'YOU' pick the wrong road AGAIN, THEN FUCK YOU," He said.

It was SO SIMPLE. In one minute with that guy, In that one session! It came down to one word, 'YOU.' You are the only one that can help YOU!

These Counselors at the Betty Ford ALSO volunteer time to the State of California's court system (or at least they did) in the late 80s to the (State's Diversion Program), in which a person with a felony Drug offense Gets a SECOND CHANCE. But the felon facing jail time MUST complete a three-month program with them three times a week, and THEY are very strict!

ONCE "YOU" complete the program, the State of California drops ALL charges (like it never happened), BUT there is one important factor: YOU better not come to one of these Counselor

meetings HIGH, Or smelling of booze or pot. They WILL simply send YOU straight to jail (NO BAIL) with your charges still pending and waiting for trial, for Failing the Diversion program.

Anthony made a few adjustments mainly with his attitude and knew he needed to get OUT of the North End and East Boston A while, Out from the DRUG CIRCLE he hated anyway and met a lot of NEW friends that started calling him TONY, which most Italians will call you anyway when you're older and in your twenties people tend to call you Tony or T. So I kept it Tony.

I was Tony now, SO I Even changed my name coming home to my FemDomme Devil's Angels. I missed My Cousin Carol the most, I realized, being away.

Cousin Carol needed her Strong Man to lean on again but My Goddess/AuntieAnna was getting sick and I had to pretend it wasn't killing me inside, but I needed to let her go slowly.

We all feared The Goddess's Leukemia was returning, Evelyn put in for full retirement to care for her Mistress/Lover Anna. We were ALL waiting for test results to come back with OPTIONS or treatments if they found anything. In the meantime, Everyone that knew the Goddess visited her daily while she still tried to be her independent strong self with Evelyn watching over her, EVERY step of the way.

The murder of My Uncle Angelo DiFronzo in San Diego, California, was an INSULT to his brother, my Uncle Johnny DiFronzo, in Chicago, and sad news for My Grandmother (My Father's Mother "Millie" DiFronzo, who was Uncle Angelo's

sister). It was well known within the family I was IN California getting my act together when I got a phone call at my Uncle Tom's, where I was staying at the time In Palm Desert, CA, home of the Betty Ford Center.

The call was from My GREAT UNCLE "JOHNNY BOY," BOSS OF CHICAGO during the 60s. Johnny DiFronzo, "I want YOU to go and see Your Aunt Julie in San Diego and Get the Names She has for you. Bring them to the North End when you get home and they'll get them to me!" My ANGRY Great Uncle "Johnny Boy" yelled over the phone.

"I HEAR you're very well liked and respected already, and you're only 22!" THE DON of Chicago proudly said to his great nephew. "Good Man, but YOU STAY OUT of this one! Gabeesh?" Uncle Johnny added. "Now that THEY all know YOU are my nephew, you'll be Untouchable Just like Me," Uncle Johnny laughed (John DiFronzo), DON of Chicago for something like fifty years, was NEVER convicted (On multiple Trials) and NEVER met his maker like all his Rivals OR counterparts had. Uncle Johnny DiFronzo died of natural causes in Chicago at the age of 89.

There was ANOTHER MAFIA WAR going on, this time in San Diego. WHILE IN CALIFORNIA I did go see my Aunt Julie, Uncle Angelo's wife, and met MY Cousins, Angelo Jr. And Julie, they were awesome people and I kept in touch with them when I eventually left California after completing THE BETTY FORD PROGRAM. I still visit Palm Springs, CA, AND San

Diego, CA, On my vacations. I have BOTH sides of my family's relatives Established there Since the 1940s. It's VERY hard to come back to Boston once you live in Southern California.

I did, however, return to the North End in Boston with the names and addresses of a few rivals, I guess you would call them. All the Men in the room had to say was "WOW, T, DO YOU REALLY KNOW WHO YOUR UNCLE IS? WE WILL TAKE IT FROM HERE. Your Uncle Jonny Boy said that I make sure YOU STAY OUT of it! So please, for MY sake, just go home now and I'll see You around, Anthony."

"HEY, KID!" Before I could walk away the "Wise Guy" said to me, "STAY CLEAN, KID! MANY PEOPLE LOVE YOU, and Say hello to your Auntie Anna for me," HE concluded and assured me My Aunt Anna was only ONE Of MANY people that needed me healthy, as the other rough-looking men looked on nodding their heads.

I Always thought it was a 1ˢᵗ cousins thing in only MY family to be involved with another 1ˢᵗ cousin sexually or sexually promiscuous. In my family on BOTH SIDES I have First Cousins Joanne (Auntie Louise's Daughter), who immediately HOOKED My other First Cousin Joey (Auntie Judy's son, Both My Father's sisters), THEY are still married to this day.

THEN there was an incident with another promiscuous female cousin on my mother's side who was in an open BDISM Relationship that turned bad.

So, IF YOU CAN'T TAKE seeing your spouse or lover with another man or woman, THEN THE BDSM LIFESTYLE IS NOT FOR YOU!!

2nd Cousin Kathy Was married and had a live-in Guy tenant that she and her husband had a three-way open relationship With. When Kathy was feeling the urge to get her pussy fucked OR licked she would Just DO IT With or without her husband's permission (which went against The Domme's rules, for starters).

So, one day her husband came home to see her in bed with the Young stud tenant, shot and killed Cousin Kathy AND her boy toy tenant, THEN KILLED HIMSELF! It was a three-way of a Whole different kind!

A LOVER'S TRIANGLE, they called it in the newspapers. IT Was something my cousin Kathy's husband just couldn't live with anymore, some friends had said of their Open BDism relationship. INSTEAD of joining in like he usually did, He ended the Open kinky relationship for good.

There are SO MANY examples I could write about! BUT This kind of Taboo sexual behavior Is EVERYWHERE. EVERY FAMILY has a story to tell about a "Secret Closet" OR a "Secret Journal," A promiscuous Curious Cousin, sister, brother, OR Even a gorgeous Aunt that you fall over in love with that keeps a Personal Journal that WILL be found one day.

Auntie Kathy was Close in age to Auntie Anna and My mom by five or six years, AND was also a HOT Italian Insatiable brunette. I would hear her refer to Kathy as the SLUT in family when

She was on the phone while I was UNDER Auntie's desk eating MY lunch (Auntie's Pussy) while she ate her lunch (Corned Beef /Swiss), but Kathy was the Slut In the family? Go figure! Lol.

Kathy LOVED multiple men at once, Domme AuntieAnna would say on the phone, and it drove her husband to go crazy one final day. I listened to her say things about Kathy to family members calling in the day Kathy was killed, So I took my time Eating-Out Auntie Anna that day.

While meeting Alice One day with two other kids from Haymarket, I REMEMBERED that conversation Of Auntie Anna's while she filled my mouth, about woman craving multiple men.

I had NEVER seen a real situation with a woman craving and needing multiple cocks to suck OR fuck at the same time, THEN I also learned the meaning of "Nymphomaniac" and meeting Alice, watching her go wild when there were MORE than two guys to Suck-Off over her condo on Saturdays.

Alice taught me about the G-Spot and where to apply my two tickling fingers just up inside her pussy behind her clit. Alice would show me while blowing two or three of my work friends at lunchtime in the North End.

I would always Eat-Out Alice's pussy when the others wouldn't. SHE LOVED MY TONGUE and I've Always loved to Eat Pussy. Alice would cream for minutes at a time before squirting, making these loud Demonic growling noises that drove us younger guys Wild. We couldn't wait to see her again on Saturdays to line up three or four of us in a circle, and just suck-off

one dick after the other, making Noises while swallowing ALL of our cum, continuously.

Speaking of Alice! Today Alice got her promised prize from her new Owner and Goddess Carol. Master T was given Permission for today to be One of the four guys Alice had been waiting to blow all morning and Master T was to supervise the session as well as getting his dick wet, so nobody got out of control.

Lenny and Allie were in town for a session and had made an appointment with Carmen. Lenny had "Come Out" thanks to Carmen and Mistress/Domme Anna, as you remember, but now Carmen was Alice's assistant to use whenever she wanted.

Lenny and Allie hadn't forgotten the incredible session of the two men fucking each other while being whipped by mean wife Allie and Domme Patty that day and were BACK FOR MORE.

Lenny had to agree to be the 4th cock for Alice to blow today as a reward by ALICE'S NEW BOSS, Collared and owned now by Domme Carol.

Allie and Patty would discipline their two men today. Allie LOVED to Dominate as did Patty. Alice wanted to show everyone today SHE WAS the most submissive cocksucking slut ANYBODY had ever seen lining up her PREY in a semi-circle in front of her as she knelt in her own saliva mixed with the young men's cum.

Lenny and Carmen got to rub cocks discreetly without anybody seeing, waiting for Alice to blow them next. Carmen didn't want his work friends Anthony or Joey to watch him suck cock OR Especially take Lenny's thick cock in his Ass, Lubed up by

Patty OR Allie spreading Lenny's Ass open for Carmen. Allie and Patty would whip them into the next room when Alice was finished Blowing The four Young Hard cocks for today's special session, treating Alice to her Fantasy/Fetish, A GIFT from her Goddess/Mistress Carol.

Master T would have some fun this morning serving Alice "with permission, of course," but is told BY HIS Goddess, and insatiable lover Cousin Carol to SAVE SOME for her later.

Domme Patty would be there dominating the session with Allie. Patty would report back to Carol Later, So Master T/Anthony WOULD OBEY and just get his dick sucked a bit with the three others that Alice drooled over daily at work, and SAVE SOME for Cousin/Carol tonight.

Master T walked over to Alice sitting at her desk and pointed to the floor, where she immediately Jumped Up to kneel before her Co/Owner while he placed her collar around her neck to show Alice she also belonged to Master T, and would lead her around the room on all fours.

Patty opened the door to let the young men in, all jerking their Cocks slowly walking toward a Visibly drooling Alice, still kneeling being held back by her leash/collar by Master T.

WHACK! Patty snapped the whip right on her Collared Property Slave/Joey's ass, ordering him and Carmen to GET IN THE HALF-CIRCLE with Lenny and Master T so Alice could begin blowing one hard cock while jerking two others in her hands. This drove Alice WILD and she began to growl like

a "Lioness," the young men have said while getting their cocks sucked.

THIS was just what Carol and Master's Collared Slut Alice wanted today for her Bonus. It was also the PERK she was granted for signing on with SIR. One man today, "Lenny," would be whipped to fuck Alice's Pussy by BOTH ladies (Master T DID NOT have permission to fuck Alice today).

WHACK! On Lenny's hand, jerking his thick dick, and he was told by HIS BOSS/DOMME WIFE to stand beside Carmen so they could touch or jerk each other while waiting when the other two guys were not looking (as Carmen wanted it FOR NOW), until he was very comfortable with "coming Out" around his lifelong work buddies Anthony and Joey.

Master T let go of Alice's Collar to stuff her mouth first with a short SLAP to her face as she growled submitting to her Master T, taking his 10"-hard cock deep with a slow rhythm that turned faster by the second with a few more short slaps and hair pulling that Alice LOVED by Anthony/Master T getting him harder and harder, ready to explode.

Grabbing Alice's Ponytail and pulling her head back, Master T cummed hard, opening her mouth, and dick slapped some cum on her face, then passed Alice off Joey, waiting next in line.

WHACK! Cracked the whip on Joey's ass as his Domme/ Patty told Slave Joey, "YOU'RE NEXT" and "YOU SAVE SOME TOO!" Patty ordered her collared Slave/Stud to feed the drooling cock-slut Alice. Slave Joey would have to serve Domme/

Patty later also in a full swap with Carol while glancing over to a smiling Master T, Both enjoying this session immensely.

Alice was making her Demonic Growling noises AGAIN as always, a "BIG TURN-ON" for a young guy getting blown that had never heard of this before! Alice growled so loud with her mouth completely stuffed that each young Man came in a matter of ten minutes Or less!

ALICE SUCKED COCK THAT GOOD! She Didn't Deep-throat All the way down, but Alice's tongue and rhythm "TECH-NIQUE" was even better.

Alice would take the time to suck BOTH of your Balls at once and rolled them around in her mouth with her tongue humming on them as your balls vibrated in her hot mouth. Alice would even tongue your Asshole periodically, especially if She was Blowing multiple men like Alice LOVED to do so she could catch her breath, then continue to suck even harder and faster, making you explode!

The NOISES Alice made while blowing you were such a turn-on to a guy to know she was ENJOYING what she was doing, and YOU were giving this cocksucking nymph what SHE needed.

Alice would be masturbating herself violently all while sucking you hard, humming with a rhythm until you Cum in her mouth. Alice would ONLY slow down when you were ejaculating and would hold your ass with both hands pushing you towards her, making sure she COMPLETELY drained your balls and swallowed every drop, "Unbelievable!"

Alice, Patty, Carol and Auntie Anna were the best blowjobs EVER! I COULD NOT say one was any BETTER than the other, really. They were ALL THAT GOOD in their own way!!

Tonight, Patty would be rewarded personally by HER Mentor, Domme of ALL Dommes, OUR Mistress Anna. Tonight Patty would be presented with 5,000 Stocks opening at $10.00 a share on the NYSE. Patty would own 5,000 shares x 10 dollars = 50,000. In value as "A GIFT"!

500,000 Stocks were available and up for sale. IF ALL THE STOCKS OLD the potential revenue for SIR Inc. would be approximately five million, BUT Carol and Cousin Anthony/ Master T WOULD HOLD BACK Or buy 251,000 Stocks to CONTROL the company.

My Mistress/Auntie Anna and Carol's Mentor Momme-Domme GAVE US THAT CONTROL, THAT 251k in stock was our present and her blessing before Silently retiring into the background ONLY to advise SIR Inc.

Collared and Owned Bi/Evelyn would stand by her Mistress/Domme Anna's side and care for her IF things took a turn for the worse.

THE FLAWLESS GODDESS would have to Finally SLOW DOWN Her lifestyle she had been accustomed to and Mentored for 18 Yrs. straight at full speed, right after putting her leukemia in remission, but now WE ALL feared for its return that would take this true GODDESS/AUNTIE ANNA/The Domme from us for good.

Evelyn, The Domme's lover and partner till death do they part, assured US ALL, "I WILL be there for her Anna every day and every night, now and forever," Evelyn promised in tears.

"THAT KIND OF LOYALTY and UNCONDITIONAL LOVE IS REAL LOVE,"

Auntie Anna would call to say to Carol and I, Master T. "YOU TWO MAKE SURE TO HAVE THE SAME LOYALTY FOR EACH OTHER THAT YOU HAVE ALWAYS HAD! I'M ONLY A PHONE CALL AWAY! OR AN HOUR'S DRIVE," the Goddess concluded from her Lakefront property in Derry, NH.

When the NYSE introduced SIR On opening day, the stock was priced at $6.00 a share and almost doubled at the closing bell to $10.00. The clever Mistress Anna had Already Bought and held back the controlling 51% Of the stock to KEEP CONTROL of the company.

Mistress Auntie Anna now wanted her cloned daughter Heiress Carol and her groomed collared nephew Anthony/Master T to Have the controlling stock of SIR. Patty would get a BIG BONUS stock option as well for her Loyalty, Promoting, Marketing and advising Domme Anna while bathing the Goddess most mornings before pleasing the Pussy-loving Goddess/Anna with her Oral skills to start her busy day, ALWAYS to satisfaction by the blonde bombshell.

Patty's Loyalty and Priorities were ALWAYS to Mistress Anna First, then Patty had the backs of Mistress Carol, Alice AND Master T in IN EVERY WAY, EVERY DAY.

Patty had Bi/Sexual unmatched Oral Pleasing Skills with STREET SMARTS, and HOT as they came! Finally, she had also now been GROOMED by the most sought-after Dominatrix in ALL of New England. But the blonde knockout refused to GO ON HER OWN. Patty had found herself, and it was right here at SIR, with her new family spoiling Patty DAILY.

The Private meeting was Between Mom And her cloned Heiress Carol, Anthony Her Groomed nephew, their Master, Protector, Lover, and workaholic for the company. The meeting was a presentation for Patty's BONUS and appreciation award.

Tonight, Patty would get what was cumming to her finally for the all torture they put her through In the beginning before "THE DOMME" really got to know Patty PERSONALLY!

Patty sat with Carol and Cousin/Anthony in front of Domme Anna, sitting at her custom designed desk big enough for her perfect Long legs In her Italian-made six-inch heels, OR to HIDE an entire body Under her desk with her legs spread Far apart, just like her nephew OR Patty had served the Goddess many times before.

Patty and Master T BOTH had seen OR been ordered "UNDER THE DESK" many times as they now stared at their Goddess sitting at the same desk, and were reminiscing.

The BossDommeMomme asked her CEO daughter Carol to present Patty's Bonus and Appreciation GIFT to Patty as Carol took the folder to read off the Amazing Amount of Stocks she would have for herself to do WHATEVER she wanted with them.

5,000 Stocks of SIR with a face value of $10.00 each in only one week from $6.00 each, Mistress/Anna said to her Loyal Collared Property/Servant AND Employee of the month!

"MANY TIMES, THANK YOU, PATTY! So Much," Mistress came around to congratulate Patty and kissed her cheek softly, whispering in her hot ear, "Thank you for EVERYTHING, especially under that desk many times you have DONE Me as well."

WITH THAT BEING SAID! Patty broke into tears and knelt down before her Mistress, throwing her arms around the Goddess' long legs, and cried. "NO, Thank You SO MUCH, Mistress, for bringing ME into your life and treating me like Family. I will be worthy, I Promise. How about having your nephew walk ME under your desk right now and WE ALL make an Orgy out of this amazing gift presentation you have given Me?" Patty suggested.

"MAY I, CAROL? Do I have permission to participate in this Orgy Patty has just suggested?" the Curious bulging Cousin Anthony asked a very wet Carol watching Patty press her face into MommeDomme Anna's crotch and crying on her knees over this overwhelming stock option just given to Patty as a GIFT in a Ceremony fashion.

"YES, YOU MAY!" Carol answered. "But you must share, those are OUR rules!" Carol now kissed the eager Master, unzipping his suit pants to take out his throbbing cock and START the Stock Option Orgy Patty had just begged her Goddess Anna for.

MommeDomme was already down on her knees to take her Nephew/Master's massive Cock from her daughter Carol, putting it right into her MommeDomme's mouth, telling her to "SUCK OUR MASTER so we can ALL watch," Carol commanded.

"Patty wants to Eat-You-Out to THANK your sweet Pussy while YOU suck a big dick and I can watch MY lover/Cousin FaceFuck you, Momme," the kinkster daughter added to her Momme, getting everyone "READY FOR AN ORGY."

"Let's go over to the sofa! WE WILL make a memorable Orgy out of this Celebration today! BUT three on one isn't fair, lol," Master joked to his three Sub/Bi Sluts.

Carol was sucking on both her cousin's balls, sharing his cock with her Momme for a few minutes at a time, then going back down, licking Patty's dripping Pussycum. Carol alternated sucking Patty's big firm, smooth, milky-white DDs and biting on her thick, hard Red nipples.

Patty was cumming in buckets in minutes between being face-fucked by her Goddess and Mentor/Mistress Anna while EATEN-OUT by best-friend Carol, then slapped while Master T fucked BOTH her holes that made the Mother/Daughter get a taste of each other. While I knelt before ALL THREE Of their SQUIRTING pussies as they RUBBED ONE OFF on me, CAROL INSISTED SHE WAS GOING FIRST To squirt her Mango in my mouth. "HE BELONGS TO ME," Carol giggled.

"YES! But I always taught you to share, lol!" Quick-witted Mom replied jokingly.

"BUT Wait, This was supposed to be MY DAY. Do all I get is Stocks?? LOL, PLEASE share OUR Master with ME too," Patty QUICKLY joined in on the joke!

"OF COURSE," Carol replied to her very pleased Momme and BDism sister Domme Patty as they ALL were excited and eager as always to hold my head, waiting for their turn to hold me still with my mouth open to fill it full of their PussyPeeCum to swallow.

I LOVED WATCHING The looks on their faces and the noises they made when squirting on my face OR filling my mouth. I STILL CAN CUM JUST THINKING ABOUT EATING OUT MY THREE BEAUTIES TOGETHER FOR THE PRE-PLANNED STOCK PRESENTATION FOR PATTY that turned into an ORGY that day. With Carol's permission, of course!

Patty WAS very smart and realistic to the fact that THIS session might be her last with the slowing Domme Anna causing Patty to break down in tears when the sometimes COLD-HEARTED Domme whispered in Patty's ear, "You WERE the best I ever had!" Patty took it as PAST tense and Patty could NOT handle losing her Goddess and Mentor, not now that things were going so great at SIR.

The stocks meant Nothing to Patty without the three people in that room. They meant everything to Patty, NOT the money! The way Patty licked and slurped-up her Mistress that night and didn't move an inch while Her Mentor/Goddess finally Squirted Squeezing her Collared Patty's mouth open said it all.

Patty wasn't stopping and wanted More. WE had to tear Patty away from The Goddess' streaming pussy to get some of her sweet and juicy ripe MangoCum, right from the Mango tree, Goddess/Domme Anna tasted like NO OTHER.

Mistress Anna was looking as gorgeous as ever, only worried a bit as always, whatever it was ailing the long-legged Goddess it surely didn't show it while presenting Patty's 5,000-share stock option In appreciation for "ALL HER SERVICE."

Patty had dropped to her knees for ONE MORE Service in tears before Eating-Out her dripping-wet mentor and savior before Her Domme/Anna could leave for N.H. for a while. Patty pleaded to make the Stock presentation an Orgy to remember, which WAS a memory for life.

"PLEASE, Master T, HOLD HER DOWN FOR ME!" Patty begged, getting back down.

I can still hear those words in my head that gave me an instant Hard-On I'll NEVER forget, and when Auntie Anna voluntarily leaned back into me to HOLD HER DOWN so Patty could lap-up the Goddess' visibly throbbing clit Patty was sucking on, I thought I was going to cum in my pants when all of a sudden Mistress/Domme Anna squirted Long and Hard right in Patty's mouth, pulling her hair while I HELD HER DOWN, and I jerked-off on My Aunt's face, "SO HOT."

Cousin Carol and I would make weekly trips up to N.H. and take Domme Patty, of course, when requested OR special Family members, like Mom Joan OR longtime friends approved by The

Domme OR her Partner, the very hot 45-year-old Evelyn, now retired, to care for Her Mistress/Anna if things took a turn for the
worse and the Leukemia made a return. WE ALL WAITED FOR
THE PERIODIC TEST RESULTS, But The Domme Anna just
kept saying, "Fuck it, Whatever happens, happens! I'M OK WITH
IT! I'm Semi-Retiring and passing things on to My brilliant Goddess Daughter, My Loyal Master/Nephew Anthony, and a VERY
talented YOUNG CAPABLE CREW, I FEEL BETTER AL-
READY," said the satisfied Goddess, leaning back against her desk
after being RAVISHED by Patty and her hung Nephew/Master.

Everyone smiled along with The Domme, while she joked in
conclusion. Patty still shed a few more tears while Carol and their
Master Both hugged a worried Domme Patty, fearing the worst.

Back at SIR business Couldn't be better, OR COULD IT? Carol
was suggesting something a few of the wealthy women clients had
been talking about ALL ALONG how the Men had ALL the fun
spending Company money on Sex Retreats.

EVERY MASSAGE PARLOR or GOLFING COUNTRY
CLUB out there WAS for successful, cheating rich MEN, sneaking around with YOUNG PRETTY WOMEN that Sold their
bodies to them for SEX.

"WHAT ABOUT WEALTHY WOMEN? Where do THEY
get to go to be pampered and served sexually to satisfy OUR insatiable sex drive when we get the URGE? Especially women
approaching their 40s, which is a woman's sexual Prime AND

usually WELL OFF by then. WOMEN HAVE MONEY TOO, you know, AND WILL PAY for a good Pounding with a big dick OR two, lol," Carol laughed, knowing she frequently had two cocks in her Pussy OR Ass.

"Women need a Retreat or Woman's Spa of some sort 'SERVICING ALL OUR NEEDS,' Just Like the Exclusive ALL-MEN'S Country Clubs and Massage Parlors do with their Happy-Ending Hand Jobs OR Blowjobs. WE like our Pussy-Blowjobs too! Right, ladies?" Carol was curiously looking for Ideas from her ladies.

Evelyn said it best to her Mistress Anna five years earlier, when they met for Private Massage sessions, that there WAS NO-WHERE for her to go and be pleased sexually like rich Men did. Evelyn confided that her husband just DIDN'T DO IT for her anymore and asked the Domme if SHE knew of anywhere to go to.

Evelyn would be teased sexually one day during a Massage session by the clever Goddess Anna when Evelyn got a wet face full of the Domme's sweet PussyMangoJuice. Evelyn couldn't resist Eating Out the Domme Anna's nectar while being spanked lightly at first while being FED the Domme's streaming Mango-PussyCum, THEN Evelyn was whipped into One orgasm after another when Domme Anna KNEW exactly what Evelyn really needed, and the rest is history.

"You're right, EVERTHING IS FOR THEM," the Domme told Evelyn that day their relationship would last a lifetime, all while Evelyn was looking for a CLUB just for VIP Women.

Then there was Monique! Carol and Patty had lured the Hypnotized Monique to SIR to show off the MRI machine one day, but mostly to GET MONIQUE in the Jacuzzi OR into the walk-in shower, Vibrating oversized Massage tables and a rooftop garden bar.

Monique had ALSO said, "YES! THIS IS WHAT ALL WOMEN NEED TOO! A women's PRIVATE CLUB, Like ALL the rich prick men have."

THAT NIGHT would not only get Monique as an MRI client but Carol would have Monique "COLLARED and OWNED" in just days as her Pussy slave AND employee to USE her and her long stiff pink nipples, DAILY.

Carol Remembered that day and called in Monique to discuss a few things and give IDEAS as well on a SPECIAL CLUB or Ladies' Retreat.

Monique was there at Mistress Carol's Desk in a matter of minutes, HOPING to serve Carol today since Carol had Been so busy With Momme getting SIR to go public. BUT TODAY MONIQUE WOULD get to kneel on the padded floor UNDER BossDomme Carol's custom-made desk While Mistress Carol ATE her Deli Sandwich and Monique ATE-OUT Boss/Goddess Carol until dismissed.

"NO challenge here!" Carol joked. "I'll expect YOU to STILL be eating YOUR LUNCH when I'm done with My corned beef on Rye," Carol joked.

Carol WAS done eating her Deli Sandwich while Monique was STILL eating her lunch as she was told, THEN all of a sud-

den, the long-nippled Monique was choking trying to swallow the GUSHING Mistress Carol that could Squirt MangoJuice like NO other.

Carol reached under her desk to pinch and slap Monique's 38s with long erect nipples before pulling her up by her red ponytail, sitting Monique up with her long legs apart right ON CAROL'S DESK, for Carol to have dessert, "Strawberry shortcake," as the PussyCraving Cousin Carol called her sometimes when sharing Monique's CreamyCum with their Master Pussy-licker Cousin Anthony.

In the Walk-In Shower they discussed an idea of forming a "Private Women's Club," kissing and washing each other gently, then changing clothes before Carol Called a "Special Meeting" to discuss a Private VIP Women's Club.

The Newly appointed CEO Goddess Daughter Carol was calling her first very important meeting without MommeDomme present but was advised beforehand and WOULD BE briefed after to hear ALL the ladies' opinions.

Carol sat at the head of the long oval Custom-made Mahogany table in their brand-new Conference room. Patty Would ALWAYS be sitting on her right, then Alice On Carol's immediate left with BossDomme Carol's newly Collared Slave Monique on the end.

Allie was invited for opinions and availability if the idea of a "Private women's Club" went forward and would be a "Perfect Domme," as Patty suggested.

Patty mentioned Allie had Magic fingers and was Dominating with a whip, especially on Submissive husband Lenny. They discussed a NAME for the club, what OPTIONS for massage, waxing, Bathing, and of course FETISHES these Privileged Women might be needing.

"EVERYONE AT THIS TABLE LOVES PUSSY, So that's NOT a problem!" Carol joked as they ALL laughed at the Boss' joke. "WE ALREADY HAVE a few Exclusive women In MY new Journal, I'd like to keep servicing them at a slightly Higher rate for the NEW Facility and NEW OPTIONS we will offer them that Momme could not in her smaller Chelsea place," Carol said.

"AND THEY WILL PAY IT!" Domme Patty said confidently, nodding.

"OR their Company's Expense Accounts will, lol," Alice giggled as they ALL enjoyed the laugh at WHO would be paying EXPENSIVE MEMBERSHIP FEES, And "TIPPING" thereafter.

"THAT IS THE TRUTH!" Carol agreed instantly. "ALL of The Domme's Special Clients were billed that way for years!" Carol added. "WE WILL TARGET ONLY successful VIP women with expense accounts OR WEALTHY, preferably married OR LOOKING for DISCREET Bi/fun with our ladies, OR OUR THREE HUNG YOUNG MEN that WE also own," Carol joked again.

Monique raised her hand and was called on by her New Owner and Goddess.

"Yes, Beautiful, what would you like to add, Monique?" Carol was complimenting her new Pet.

Monique suggested a few places WHERE to find and TAR-GET "Successful VIP Women" in Powerful Positions of their Companies OR OWN their own Business Colleagues, if you will. "WE will show them how the billing will be done, LIKE YOU TARGETED ME! Lol," Monique giggled, and NOT ONLY in the Medical field, But in the Private sector as well. *Fortune 500* magazine and OTHER publications like that, We can search THESE VIP WOMEN Out and I WILL HELP You there if you need ME, MY Mistress/Carol," Monique added.

"YOU KNOW I WILL, MY MONIQUE! YOU ARE AL-READY a great asset To ALL of us here, that's why I MADE SURE WE got you on board here," Carol said, standing, staring and smiling at Monique, exciting the long hard-nippled Slave Monique (NO BRA on today).

"Anyone have a few Band-Aids for Monique, lol," Carol giggled as they All applauded Monique for her suggestions. PROUD Mistress Carol now asked Monique to "Stand, Please, my Pet. Show your co-workers how awesome you look today," Carol added with a giggle. Carol then asked ALL the ladies to "Open your folders and find copies of ALL Suggested Names. I like 'Club Paradisa.' What names would attract YOU ladies In?" Carol suggested.

"Then SERVICES women masseuses only? OR Both? I want Both for the women that DO LIKE BOTH Men and Women

sexually as well as sensually on the Massage table. WE can even have special COUPLES that will come, So WE will have to get OUR HUNG MEN To massage and serve, NO SINGLE MEN!" Carol stressed. "I DON'T WANT to bring in strangers. THIS WILL BE A PRIVATE CLUB!! THIS IS FOR VIP WOMEN ONLY!" BossDomme, Mistress Carol, Demanded while visibly Exciting Patty to rub Carol's right inner thigh quickly UNDER the Long Oval Table for NOBODY to see.

MommeDomme had her Secret Journal filled by word of mouth, NO ADVERTISING! "And WE will do the same, WE DON'T NEED to jeopardize 'SIR' OR ourselves for Rich Kinky Neglected Women OR Couples we don't know. WE want OUR VIP WOMEN to HAVE OPTIONS, that's ALL, Just like the Rich prick Men Do!" Carol said to HER loyal crew. "WE will have THIS conference room available for WOMEN executives ONLY and OUR GUYS and OUR ladies can serve the WORTHY ones right Under the table After the meeting has ended! Like at Rita's, Momme's favorite place," Carol continued.

So without further delay, BossDomme Carol pressed the security button under the conference desk to automatically OPEN the Custom-built heavy Mahogany Doors.

Master T, Joey and Carmen were waiting eagerly to walk into the Conference room to "SERVE" lunch to their favorite three FemDommes.

The three Hung Young men, led by Master T, with corned beef and Swiss on rye sandwiches from Pressman's Deli for their

Excited and surprised Ladies, the three Hung Men were fashion-ably dressed in tailormade Smoking jackets with matching bibs for the Occasion.

Master T would be servicing his soulmate Cousin Carol while Joey would kneel and serve HIS Domme Patty. Carmen would assist and service HIS TWO FemBosses Alice AND Monique from MRI Under the table on all fours side by side with Joey and the Master as well. The Boss Goddess/Carol had instructed the session and would be done.

"Alice can take the rest of the day off after WE are pleased with our three young men to show OUR appreciation. ALICE WILL ENJOY 'OUR' THREE Hung Guys as much as they will enjoy her Oral skills with MY Permission," the BossDomme Carol concluded, smiling to Master T On His way DOWN To Please and serve kissing HIS Goddess/Carol on her smooth, toned inner thigh to begin her extensive foreplay.

As the five Kinkster Sisters were halfway through their Corned beef and Swiss Deli sandwiches, they ALL started to LEAN BACK in their expensive swivel office chairs, each "SIR" VIP fondling on a close-by Nipple or two, getting ready to squirt in a mouth under the table.

The Hung Young men were being EXTRA SPECIAL today because they were recently TRAINED by Master T on EATING PUSSY to completion, drinking ALL the MangoJuice Down and how NOT to move until the Lady let you up while they were squirting.

Carol and Patty would be "GRADING" Joey and Carmen on their performance today. Alice loved the news and couldn't wait to Blow her three favorite Young men From the Haymarket push-cart days, exploring her Taboo Fantasy even further, taking Alice deeper into her Darkside by taking multiple cocks lined up in a semi-circle, sucking off three big ten-inch cocks one after another, AND getting paid for it as her Bonus.

Alice giggled to Carol and Patty "NOW I GET TO HAVE THEM ALL AT ONCE while working with them!! OMG! With your Permission, of course, MY MISTRESS," Alice repeated what Carol had already said!

"YES! Of course," Carol smiled. "THEY ALL LOVE your Growling Blow jobs, I'm told, lol. I'M blessed to have YOU And Monique on board our MRI Department, I'll do EVERY-THING I CAN for BOTH of you to keep you working here at SIR," Carol said to Alice, smiling as they BOTH slowly closed their Eyes and gave EACH young man still serving under the table a MOUTHFUL of FRUITI D'MANGO JUICE.

That very night the tired, Hardworking young Domme Carol checked in on MommeDomme to give her the details of the meeting in the VIP LADIES ONLY Conference room, even up to the kind of sandwiches Master T bought, AND WHO he brought with him To SERVE all the Ladies under the table.

Carol continued to ask MommeDomme If she liked the name "Club Paradise" OR "Club Paradisa." "The OPTIONAL services

would be offered ONLY AFTER careful screening of a new Women VIP Special client to avoid Illegal activities, ONLY A FEW more than what YOU have already have established OR with YOUR PERMISSION, I'll keep them so they can have what they are used to and are always pleased. THEY WILL LOVE THE NEW OPTIONS just like they have ALL loved YOU, Momme," Carol strained to say to her Semi-Retired MommeDomme.

"I LOVE IT, ALL OF IT, my genius Daughter! By ALL means, YOU can keep My Special Clients. THEY absolutely NEED a place to go for their unique FETISH, each of them having something special," MommeDomme continued. "ASSIGN specifically WHO is comfortable with each fetish and KEEP YOUR SAME people with each Special Client ongoing. Great Job, I LOVE YOU," Momme assured Carol. "I'll be back on the weekend for shopping and lunch with you. I feel great not working 12 hrs. a day, lol," Mom concluded. "Evelyn says hello too and see you soon, and again, GREAT JOB," the Domme concluded.

CEO/Chairwoman Goddess Carol of "SIR Inc.," also beneficiary to DiNunzio Enterprise Trust Co., would now be adding, "Club Paradisa," A discreet private membership Club/RETREAT for VIP Women in Power of Major Corporate Businesses in Boston, or wealthy and on their own.

When Domme/Auntie Anna was starting off at the Parisian Massage and Sauna Baths in Danvers, MA, "The Parisian" was An Exclusive Men's Club, only serviced by young gorgeous

women, all over eighteen, but no older than thirty, with the same selection of services, and the same basic exercise equipment, a Steam and Sauna room, Large walk-in Jacuzzi, a lounge with Sofas and a full bar, a large-screen TV for watching Sports, especially on Saturdays and Sundays with Frankie Fingers taking all bets at the bar.

Wealthy, successful men came from ALL OVER N.E. Domme AuntieAnna had said BIG MONEY was all over the place, from ALL Ages and walks of life! From younger Drug Dealers with big money to your older Mafia Gangster types, or just Filthy-Rich Businessmen, THEY ALL shared ONE THING in common: "SEX."

Leo was the name of the owner and the Domme Anna's boss that hired ONLY Beautiful, skilled and talented "Fetish-Friendly Women." The select few young beauties were WELL PAID for their services. The Parisian Sauna was where DommeAnna, "The Domme," got her name AND her reputation would follow her well after the Parisian was closed down in a SEX sting operation.

Domme/Anna had already collected a whole Private Journal of names she took on "Privately," Especially for Golden Shower and Strapon/Pegging Kinksters. DommeAnna WAS THE BEST! The MEMBERSHIP to join The Parisian was also VERY EXPENSIVE, with 90% of the Wealthy Men belonging to corporations with expense accounts and billed to their companies. The rest were wise guys and dealers that the very connected owner Leo kept in line, OR thrown out!

THE DAY the Parisian Sauna was raided for Prostitution in a sex sting operation, Domme/Auntie Anna said, "There were car license plates from EVERY STATE in New England in the parking lot on that Sunday when ALL the men were watching football, making bets with Franky Fingers and just relaxing in the Jacuzzi AND getting their dicks sucked, fucked and whipped, maybe even a fetish performed, OR getting a tasty Golden Shower from 'The Domme' or some other gorgeous 22-year-old."

There were maybe six Fetish-Friendly young Goddesses that worked EVERY SHIFT for ten to fifteen Wealthy Men present at ANY given time with CASH in their Roman Robes.

"THE PARISIAN WAS JUST TOO BUSY, AND TOO OBVIOUS," the Domme told Carol and Master T. "I was one of the lucky ones of three of us that snuck out the back and wasn't noticed as working there and walked right to my car down the road," the Domme explained. "I ALWAYS parked AWAY from the place so Family and Friends WOULD NOT KNOW I worked there as a masseuse and think bad of me. I wanted to be known as a real estate agent and NOT A DOMINATRIX, whipping and pissing on these rich Kinky pricks For $500/hr. Which in 1969, THAT WAS BIG MONEY. DON'T EVER become that busy! Just keep your 'Special Clients,' THAT'S ALL! You have 'SIR' now, a legitimate business, AND now your 'Club Paradisa' for VIP women? YOU have more than enough!!" MommeDomme STRESSED adamantly to her cloned daughter! "YOU ARE one of those wealthy women too, SO PLEASE

BE CAREFUL!" the Clever MommeDomme pleaded to her daughter.

Monique and Carol would target JUST TWO VIP women for now that they had read about in *Boston Magazine* and *The Phoenix* newspaper, "Trisha Sullivan," an Irish Blonde knockout, and Donna Puopalis, a Greek Goddess with Jet-black hair, Two Boston CEOs in Power of Major Companies, One of which Monique said she went to Boston College with around the same time for her Business Degree as well as her Doctorate in Microbiology AND Radiology.

Monique said Trisha was BRILLIANT as well as beautiful and probably had fucked her way to the top at Schrafts Chocolate Co. In Charlestown, MA, right next to the N. End of Boston, seven miles from The East Boston Facility for "Club Paradisa."

Monique and Trisha Both went to Zelda's nightclub nearby in Brookline, MA, when Zelda's had LADIES NIGHT with ½-price drinks for the ladies, Which brought in a lot of ladies that, of course, brought in a lot of MEN.

Monique told Carol that Trisha was a WILD ONE when drinking. Carol, Momme, Patty and now Monique ONLY wanted gorgeous women in Power, so it seemed, just like them.

"NOTHING WRONG with mixing business with pleasure, IF WE CAN, lol. It just so happens these women happen to be beautiful and USUALLY ARE the ones that GET TO THE TOP. UNFORTUNATELY! unattractive WOMEN OR MEN just don't cut it in the business world."

All the girls nodded in agreement, as The DommeAnna concluded.

According to the background check on Trisha Sullivan, she was still divorced, So Carol set a little trap for her, one like Phil LaBella fell for with Carol's nipples Photo (accidentally on purpose). Carol had a nice Photo of ALL THREE of HER young men at work in Wet Speedo Bathing suits, ALL Showing perfect outlines of their ten-inch cocks in a Photo shoot for Club Paradisa Clients to PICK ONE, OR TWO for Double the fun, the DP Special!

Shraffts Chocolate Candies was a popular local Chocolate Factory in Charlestown, Mass., in a Massive Building Owned by the Shrafft family for decades. According to the girls searching Trisha's profile, Trisha Sullivan had expanded and doubled their business with her charm and good looks (sound familiar). Good looks, Perks, and sex sells and that IS A FACT!

Trisha was given a chance right out of college, Alice found out, AND that Trisha was fucking the OLD MAN Jerold Shrafft on the side on business trips, eventually presenting her own ideas to "THE BOARD" and Old Man Shrafft that eventually put her in charge as CEO of Shraff's Chocolate Inc. "Trisha was that good!"

The fashionably dressed jet-black-haired beauty in 6" heels greeted Carol and Monique, smiling and eager to hear about their "Club Paradisa" that Trisha had been briefed about earlier that week.

"Please! Tell Me more, I am SO interested in this 'Women's-Only Club and Spa.' Everything IS about the Men, WE need a place too," Trisha said in total agreement with Carol's new venture.

Carol opened her presentation folder with all the OPTIONS, on-site equipment, then the rooftop garden lounge with a view of Boston skyline with a FULL BAR, which caught Trisha's eye, Trisha loved a good Martini!

"I REALLY love this OPTION," she pointed out to Carol, pointing to the table shower in the photo with grooming and moisturizing, followed by a four-handed Hot-Oil massage by two Men For a strong, relaxing massage. "THIS looks really relaxing," Trisha giggled to Carol.

Carol laughed back, adding, "THEY will relax you, alright. All our young men are very skilled and certified, THEY CAN DO ANYTHING YOU WANT! They All are Fetish-friendly too, once they get to know you, of course."

Monique added, "You will love it here relaxing with ALL our VIP ladies," Monique said confidently with her long nipples visibly excited, listening and looking at Carol talk to Trisha the knockout VIP, getting Monique soaking wet.

BOTH Carol and Monique could see Trisha glancing at their protruding gifted nipples on BOTH Monique and Carol, But NOT saying a word.

As Monique stood straight up and got even closer for Trisha to glance ever so obviously at Monique's long hard nipples, Monique looked into Trisha's wide-open eyes to say softly, "Would

YOU like to come for a drink tonight and SEE our place, Trisha?" Monique suggested to SEIZE THE MOMENT and reel Trisha in to "Club Paradisa" and a WILD grinding.

"YES! I'd like that very much," Trisha shot back immediately, looking ever closer now at both sets of very unique nipples. "I'd love the Limited membership You're offering and if I like 'THE EQUIPMENT,' I will definitely take the VIP Membership," Trisha stressed, looking again at the three young men in their speedos, then handing back the journal to Carol, looking directly into the Side opening Of Carol's buttoned-down silk Versace top (NO bra).

"OK then, TONIGHT," Carol said, "we will order Pizza at Santarpio's and then a few drinks out on our Rooftop Lounge over-looking the Boston Skyline before WE show you our State-of-the-art Sauna, Jacuzzi, and custom-built walk-in seated shower, AND Remote-Controlled adjustable Massage tables. I'm so glad we got to meet you today, Trisha. I know how busy you must be and we will see you later for DRINKS and Pizza, then a nice, relaxing ja-cuzzi if you have time. You can bring whatever you want to wear, But we have plenty of Towels and Robes, though," Carol concluded.

"I'll be there by seven, is that ok?" Trisha was walking the ladies to the door with her hand on Monique's shoulder, glancing AGAIN at her long pointy nipples. THIS TIME Monique looked down at Trisha's shiny legs, smiling and nodding.

"YOU'RE going to love our place!" Monique assured Trisha.

"I have a great feeling I will." Trisha was now In awe, shaking Carol's hand and watching Carol's Huge Plum-sized nipples

shake as well UP CLOSE as Carol's silk buttoned blouse Partially unbuttoned.

Carol smiled widely at the jaw-dropping Trisha, adding, "See you at seven? Carmen will valet your car when you arrive." Carol walked out gracefully saying goodbye and Monique was just as wet as Trisha watching Carol's presentation and watching how Carol gracefully moved (JUST LIKE MOMME did At 22).

Trisha loved Men but was so overwhelmed today with these two ladies in their Tailor-made Italian Threads and 6" heels. They made Trisha soaking wet, "Curious" for some pussy as well.

TRISHA HAD NOT TRIED WOMEN. She had come close, she told Carol and Monique in the Jacuzzi, BUT JUST COULD NOT. Trisha also said SHE HAD NEVER seen in all of her life two different ladies standing right in front of her with SUCH UNBELIEVABLE NIPPLES that actually made her spot a bit in her panties, IN ENVY.

Trisha was drooling and craving to suckle on each set of different, yet unique sets of firm protruding nipples, one a 22-year-old Goddess and the other the 32-year-old Monique, Trisha's age exactly.

Trisha arrived to find Carmen waiting at exactly 7 P.M. and opened the door for the impressive and Curious Trisha dressed to kill OR excite WHOEVER tonight.

Carol came walking right out to take Trisha's hand and into the elevator up to the rooftop lounge, where Monique was having a drink and a piece of Santarpio's Pizza with Joey, who was waiting for Master T to meet him.

"This is Joey," Monique introduced Joey as ONE of the guys in the photo that was certified in Massage therapy "for your pleasure and relaxation," Monique added.

"Very handsome young man, I must say! I bet you have strong skilled hands, WHICH I NEED for my stiff shoulders," Trisha giggled.

"YES, I DO, when you're ready, I'LL be ready too," Joey added, walking away to meet Master T. Now Trisha had seen Joey in person, not just in a photo. Trisha really LIKED HIM In his tight jeans with his protruding 11" outline of his big package for her to see (accidentally on purpose).

It wasn't long after a few strong drinks with some pizza and stories about college days with boys, Boston nightclubs, and dorm party stories before ALL THREE ladies relaxed in the Jacuzzi when Trisha would witness Monique taking off the top of Carol's bikini set and massaging her while Carol talked about "Club Paradisa," dropping Trisha's jaw seeing Carol's plum nipples.

THIS sort of pampering was for the successful VIP women at Club Paradisa as Monique started to suckle Carol's HUGE throbbing nipples very passionately, back and forth, One then the other, like the Collared slave Monique craved to be for her Mistress Carol.

This sent Trisha streaming into her FIRST orgasm of MANY of that night. Trisha (No longer just Curious) would become another pussy lover in a matter of minutes once she stepped into that jacuzzi and saw these two sets of firm amazing Breasts with UNIQUE rock-hard nipples on such beautiful women.

Carol would be FIRST to open Trisha's legs to reveal an enormous shaven clit on a meaty set of pussylips a lot like Carol's thick Labia sometimes covering such a beautiful Clit and preventing stimulation.

BUT NOT TONIGHT, however, the two ladies promoting "Club Paradisa" tonight BOTH LOVED PUSSY and knew how to eat it out until the last drop.

Trisha would have multiple orgasms, then held by both women to GIVE A FEW orgasms to Both Pussycum sluts Carol and Monique tonight. Suckling on both their nipples was on Trisha's mind the entire time she drove to meet the two teasing, luring beauties in her office earlier that day, AND TRISHA MADE SURE SHE DID, ALL NIGHT LONG for Trisha's first time ever with another woman, AND TRISHA.

Trisha had a nice smaller set of firm 32C cup Breasts, however, with nice cherry-sized nipples like stone, great for biting and nibbling on. Carol and Monique were doing exactly that to the screaming Trisha while squirting over and over on the massage table as they ravished Trisha, holding her still, taking turns Flicking and Licking on her Amazing long, thick Clit.

Trisha LOVED being held down as did Carol by her Cousin Master T.

Trisha HAD a greater asset than nipples. Trisha had at least an Inch-sized-thick long clit, the size of a tiny little dick, and looked like one too. The girls were having a party SUCKING and SLAPPING Trisha on her long erect clit, watching her squirt like

a teen, then trying to drink her MangoJuice down like Master T tried to do with Carol's gushing orgasms.

"Before you leave, would you like Carmen and Joey to fuck you now while we hold you down, our newest VIP Member? lol," Carol giggled to Trisha.

"OMG, YES! Ten times YES, I DO love men more than women, you know!" Trisha laughed. "I am a member for life, girls, WHERE DO I SIGN, CAROL? This is fuck'n unbelievable! I'll be here every weekend and YOU CAN COUNT ON IT. I can't believe I ate pussy tonight and I LOVED YOU BOTH using me up, I KNEW I WOULD, BUT I do love FUCKING more for a good pussy pounding," Trisha said confidently. "THANK YOU BOTH, CAROL and MONIQUE," Trisha concluded to Carol, Just before Joey and Carmen fucked Trisha together into PARADISE, making Trisha cum like a broken water balloon three more times easily while the girls held Trisha down, Just like Trisha asked them to do!

CHAPTER

22

Carol called Master T five times but the line was busy for half an hour now, annoying his spoiled Goddess Cousin Carol. Finally her Master/Cousin Anthony walked into Carol's office, ranting and raving about a call he got from SDPD Organized Crime Unit, asking Questions about some retaliation murder for the death of their Uncle Angelo that left two rivals violently assassinated in San Diego, CA.

"The bodies of two Reputed rival gangsters were dumped on the Exclusive LaJolla Beach, a suburb of San Diego, CA," the SDPD told Anthony.

"CAN YOU IMAGINE DYING THAT WAY? FCK'N ANIMALS! Meathooks up the ass and hog tied," the Master vented out on his soulmate Cousin. "LET'S GO SEE YOUR MOMME!" the confused and angry Master Mumbled to Carol.

"I called My Mom already and we'll go tomorrow to see her after work. Mom wants Patty to come too with a few toys from the dungeon wall Evelyn asked for, AND FOR YOU TO BRING DELI SANDWICHES. So I guess Momme's not feeling THAT bad, lol."

Carol giggled, "BESIDES, A very attractive Woman VIP from the G.E. Co. in Lynn, MA, Is stopping by at 6 P.M. Her name is Donna Puopalous. Monique scouted her out last week and she will be signing on with 'CLUB PARADISA.' She Picked YOU from The Brochure we sent to her, and wants to meet you IF you're not busy. SO YES! YOU DO have my permission to-night at 6 to PERSUADE her totally over drinks and Pizza up on the lounge. I told her, 'Wear the tight-worn Sicily Jeans you have with (NO briefs).' Those jeans make your cock look like King Kong's, lol," Carol joked. "I think this HOT-ASS Donna is just a cock slut, BUT WE WILL SEE," Carol added, Smiling.

"Wear YOUR Thin white Italian knit sweater," Master T added, "YOUR PURPLE PLUMS SHOW right through, there's NO BAND-AID EVER MADE that would cover those nipples, lol," the Master joked. "Let's see WHO she's glancing at the most!"

The two Inseparable kinkster cousins joked as they kissed.

Carol's nipples were STILL tingling from Donna's chilling voice, so she placed her Cousin's hand and magic fingers on her throbbing plum toppings to soothe them as they kissed, that Only her Master knew how.

It was 6 P.M. and CFO of General Electric in Lynn, Mass., and the Stylish European Donna Puopalous were right on time. Carmen was waiting Dressed in a light tight Pair of slacks SHOWING a perfect outline of HIS 10" package to park her Car. Carmen stood tall as Donna, took his hand to get out of the car, Donna's face was Literally six inches from Carmen's bulging cock outlined in the skin-tight jeans as he lifted her Up from her seat with authority.

"Omg, and YOU must be Superman," Donna joked.

Carmen had on a muscle tank top as well, showing his toned-out weightlifting biceps and 44-inch chest. Donna's tongue was already hanging out, as Carmen joked, "I CAN BE WHOEVER YOU WANT ME TO BE," Carmen said, smiling. But Donna hadn't seen ANYTHING yet of what Carmen could do.

Carmen AND Lenny would be doing (Mano e'Mano), which was on the Club Paradisa Optional "Fetish/Fantasy Menu" For Women VIP Memberships ONLY.

Mano e'Mano was A Two-man GuyOnGuy live Sex show. As she watched with the OPTION of getting her pussy and Asshole licked clean OR Pounded for the ninety-minute live show, Carol and Master T BOTH watched as Donna was lifted up by Carmen, getting a fantastic side view of Donna's PERFECT heart-shaped European Ass, looking A LOT like Carol's ass.

"OMG, Look, Carol! HER ASS is just like YOURS! AMAZING!" Master T added. "I'll bet 1000 to one, she loves dick in that ass just like you do, lol," Cousin Anthony teased again.

"MINE IS BETTER!" Carol joked and grinned at her Cousin and Master. "NOW SAY IT!" Carol ordered to her Cousin Anthony to SAY IT as she would tell him in their teen days.

"YES! of course, YOURS IS BETTER, LOL," Anthony Cleverly Answered. "BUT that ASS is as perfect as you can get, just like your Momme too, AND the Graceful walk IS the same as well," her drooling Master/Cousin said to his Goddess Carol, still watching Donna walk with Carmen from the front door window.

"With ALL that Solid packed Meat behind you, YOU BETTER know how to carry it, OR FALL DOWN! Lol!" Carol joked to get a laugh from HER Cousin Anthony/Master T, the love of her life.

Carol introduced herself and Partner/Cousin Anthony to Donna Puopolous as Co-Owners of the "Club Paradisa," a Division of "SIR," as they All shared a drink and Santarpio's Pizza at the rooftop Bar overlooking the Boston skyline.

"WOW, This View is Spectacular!" Donna surprisingly said. "Where did you find this place? I've been looking at Waterfront real estate In the Lynn, Nahant, and Marblehead area and NEVER thought of East Boston, and with the water and skyline view right in front of you!"

"WE HAVE AN OFFICE in Chelsea, MA, My Mom started years ago," Carol replied back. "We'll Have our agents look around here for you Also. WE gutted this whole building out and made it BRAND NEW again. WITH ALL OF OUR HELP,

WE made it a Medical Commercial Facility WITH FOUR Penthouse Condos just below us, AND THIS is our Rooftop Lounge," Carol added, looking over Donna's amazing curves with her toned legs crossing over back and forth as Carol drooled. "Relax and have another drink, Donna, then We can show you downstairs after WE explain ALL WE HAVE TO OFFER YOU as a Business Woman VIP Member at our 'Club Paradisa.' CLUB PARADISA IS FOR VIP WOMEN ONLY. We want WOMEN to have their own outlet too, just like VIP Men do with ALL their Country Clubs and so-called Retreats, ANYTHING YOU WANT OR NEED, and 'I MEAN ANYTHING,'" Carol giggled.

Carol put Master T/cousin Anthony in front of Donna and pulled his arms back, revealing the bulge in his jeans that Dropped Donna's jaw. The outline of Master T's 10" semi-hard-on in his tight Sicily jeans was enough to make her wet her panties as she squirmed in the swivel, stool crossing her legs over once again, opening them a bit wider each time for the Master to see in.

"Hmmmm!" Donna said, staring at the Master's big bulge in his worn-out Sicily jeans. "I understand, Carol, and was that Superman Carmen downstairs in your Brochure as well? BOTH of these young men in particular look MUCH BETTER in person, I must say, Carol, AND YOU are absolutely gorgeous, YOU must have to be fitted by a seamstress also with that ass like I have to also, lol," Donna joked.

"I have to Say, there are NOT MANY ASSES like you two," Master T Joked. "I'm just curious, BUTT DO YOU LIKE

447

ANAL as much as MY Cousin here does?" Master T Joked, look-ing to Carol for approval.

"ASSOLUTELY, Lol," Donna jokingly replied to get a big laugh by all three.

"WHY? DO YOU COUSINS PLAY AROUND WITH EACH OTHER?" Donna now curiously asked after the surpris-ing ANAL question arousing the Greek Goddess Donna.

"OH, YAH! Lol, since we could crawl," Carol said, giggling. "WE LIVE TOGETHER right beneath your beautiful legs in the Penthouse Condos down below from the lounge. We DO have a Vanilla business life, however, So WE don't just tell ANY-BODY. WE are very open with it as it IS a part of OUR CHOSEN BDISM sexual lifestyle, BUT WE DO REQUIRE EACH OTHER'S APPROVAL AND PERMISSION to swing with others, just those two loyal rules, mostly." Carol Continued to glance at Donna's fantastic curves on the well-toned 32-year-old, which were Monique and Alice's age. "HOW do you keep your legs so beautifully toned?" Carol asked, taking a CLOSER look at her inner thighs. "Your thighs are SO defined and solid," Carol asked, getting Donna to SHOW Carol a little MORE of what Carol Really wanted, "Donna's MangoJuice."

"I DO some squeezing exercises with light weights for my inner thighs and running for the calves just about ½-hour work-out with my coffee to wake up, AND from the advice of my per-sonal trainer," Donna admitted. "I'd like to see YOUR equipment you have here! IN BETWEEN MY JACUZZI TIME WITH

YOU AND YOUR FETISH-FRIENDLY THERAPIST COUSIN. How do YOU stay TRIM at the waist like that, you're like a 22-inch waist, FLAT and solid belly," Donna was now changing the subject.

"I DO a lot of squatting!" Carol joked, looking to HER Master T. "OVER HIS Face, Mostly," Carol getting Donna's attention back and very curious now IF her pussy was going to be treated sooner than Donna expected, and becoming soaking wet. "Donna, YOU can choose Whoever you want once you're a member, BUT HE HAS BY FAR the biggest and fattest tongue for Oral. MY Cousin IS the reason why I love Oral and Anal the way I do, AND He is the MOST Dominant of the three guys, TO BE HONEST, But HE needs MY PERMISSION first," Carol Stressed.

"REALLY! OMG, I LOVE THAT! I could NEVER get a guy to eat MY ASS for more than thirty seconds OR spank Me harder than a four-year-old, lol," Donna Joked. "I DO NEED DOMINATING, I need to be very specific with you, Carol and Anthony. I DO LOVE ANAL, but mostly I love the Anal FORE-PLAY of RIMMING IT, tonguing and SPANKING My Huge ASS, VERY HARD! I THINK I can be honest with you two, LOL. I LUV being spanked with a Paddle or wooden spoon or something like that. CAN YOUR EXCLUSIVE WOMEN'S CLUB PROVIDE ME with that? Then I'M ALL yours! I'M 32 yrs. old and NEED to have this done to me 'REGULARLY,' I DON'T have time to find a guy and waste time knowing he's

NOT going to please me. I'd rather seek MY FETISH out right here with 'Club Paradisa' and KNOW I'm going to get what I need," Donna desperately admitted, confiding to Carol after her 3rd Martini.

"Cousin Anthony! SHOW Donna How your tongue can touch your nose." Carol was now looking to get the Giggling and Buzzed Anal slut Donna Downstairs in the Jacuzzi and onto the Massage table for the spanking and RIM JOB of Donna's life.

Donna was now looking very closely At the Master's pointy oversized tongue while he showed Donna how he could stick his tongue right up into his nostril, THEN reaching down touching his chin with his long, thick tongue, getting Donna all excited.

"OMG! It's like a long Pink lizard!" Donna said, squirming back and forth on the swivel chair. "Carol, You do your squatting on THAT? Let me know what time YOU do your workout? Lol, CAN I JOIN YOU? With your PERMISSION, of course," Donna joked, giggling.

Carol replied, "I WAS JUST GOING TO DO A WORK-OUT WITH HIM, ISN'T THAT RIGHT, COUSIN?" Carol said, pointing to the floor.

"YES, MY GODDESS," Now kneeling and lifting Carol's skirt to SHOW Donna how things work at "Club Paradisa," "Just COMMAND your selected STUD to perform and It's DONE!"

The Kissing Cousin kissed Carol's toes first through her open-toe heels, then up to her Perfectly toned calves, causing Donna to become wetter by the second. She reached under her blouse to play

with her own aroused nipples first, Just watching in Amazement, Carol getting ALL her toes sucked one by one and her Cousin Kissing up to Carol's Asshole was driving Donna Crazy.

Anthony, Carol's Master, caressed Donna's knee first, looking for Carol's approval, GOT the nod to KEEP GOING! Carol was now stroking Donna's ears and well-groomed fine jet-black hair for Donna's approval AS WELL.

Carol wanted VERY badly to get this new Hot-Ass VIP Member for a Special Client as well as for "Club Paradisa." The Kinkster Cousins now walked a very ready and eager Donna downstairs to the Jacuzzi, THEN planned to hold Donna on the adjustable massage table for a Tongue/Rimming by Cousin Anthony and Pussylover Carol to FEAST ON Donna's dripping Pussy AND winking Asshole TOGETHER! and IT WOULD NOT TAKE LONG!!

Once in the Jacuzzi, ALL three kissed and splashed around, fondling and fingering each other, creating A puddle of their Pussy-PeeCum. Now the two voluptuous VIP Asses were taking Cousin Anthony's ten-inch Cock Deep in their ASS while Beating them Both on their PERFECT MEATY ASSES with the Special Handmade long Wide Mahogany Paddles from Master's workshop,

Donna LOVED her Ass Eaten-Out/Rimmed and said THAT WAS THE FIRST time ANYONE had ever satisfied her Spanking Cravings, EVER! OR had her ASSHOLE tongue fucked before for that long.

"AMAZING! THIS WAS THE ONLY TIME EVER, also I'd allow a woman to use me like that. THANK YOU BOTH

Sooo fucking much!" Donna said, trying to HUG both cousins. "LIKE I SAID, I'M ALL YOURS NOW! LOL, I'M a VIP Member for life. I'll be here constantly to work out with you, AND your guys. I'm feeling so good, I can Cum again on your Cousin's tongue, if that's ok with you, Carol?" Donna seeking permission, touching them both gently to continue.

Donna kissed Carol's pulsating nipples and stroked Master T's still semi-hard Cock with juice continuing to stream down Donna's inner thigh as the kinky Cousins surrounded her like PREY and held Donna down on the desk slowly while Carol slapped her tits on Donna's face.

Master T saw a great opportunity here to LICK EVERY DROP from these two solid voluptuous Asses. Donna was STILL Visibly streaming down her leg while nursing on Carol's throbbing nipples and jerking Master T's hard 10, causing Donna to keep creaming while being paddled with a partially CRACKED Mahogany paddle right down the middle from beating Donna's ass so hard that she was needing so desperately done to her.

Donna had neglected her ASS Fetish/Craving to be SERIOUSLY Spanked, whipped, PADDLED, wanting to have her Asshole Stretched-Out and used, Until now.

Carol's Master/Soulmate Cousin ordered Carol and Donna to Lay down ON THEIR BACKS, touching "ASS TO ASS," with their heads at opposite ends and to hold their legs UP on the Long Massage table to be throat fucked as well as grinding pussy to pussy, and Ass to Ass.

With Each Eager Anal Slut holding their LEGS UP Ass to Ass, Master T was still paddling their NEW ANAL WHORE, CFO Donna Puopalous, "Mercilessly HARD" with NO limits on her smooth yet firm rounded Greek Ass, exploring deep into Donna's hidden "Darkside."

Cousin/Master took turns lubing, THEN FUCKING each ANAL WHORE while they still lay on their backs, WAITING their turn for their Ass to be Violated, Alternately.

"HARDER, SIR! HARDER, FUCK MY ASS HARD!" Donna begged, and Carol would echo the same words.

Master T was in heaven as He BURIED HIS HEAD Right in the MIDDLE of BOTH ASS TO ASS, PUSSY TO PUSSY, as they continued to Grind, then SQUIRT Violently on his long, hard tongue, and soaked his entire head of thick black hair in a FOUNTAIN of PussyCum.

Sucking, slurping, licking and lapping up Donna's Mango-Juice, then Carol was STILL Multi/Cumming as Cousin/Master took it ALL down. This WAS VERY NEW to Donna and she was Amazed at the Cousin's RAVISHING her and WAS already "HOOKED" on them.

THIS alternate BDism lifestyle of being paddled, whipped and forced to Rim Master T and Carol's Ass while Being PAD-DLED on Donna's Ass HARD WAS EXACTLY WHAT DONNA WAS LOOKING for at "Club Paradisa" AND Donna WOULD have her dream fantasy come true.

Both Carol and Cousin/Master T KNEW and had seen this Submissive behavior in Monique recently and Definitely In Evelyn even more as well. Donna now realized She required the same Intense ANAL Play of Dominant Spanking, Flogging, Whipping, Paddling OR sometimes called "Canning" to stimulate blood flow to her Clit, releasing Multiple/Orgasms, JUST LIKE CAROL, MONIQUE AND EVELYN needed this foreplay.

"YOU TWO CAN BE SISTERS, OMG," Master T seeing a great resemblance in ANAL Craving and the "LOVE FOR ANAL PLAY" needing their Asses probed and stretched.

JUST AS the Ass-Eating Cousin was telling these two gorgeous Anal Sluts of their similarities, THEY BOTH squirted up in his face almost simultaneously. PussyPeeCum! a Fountain of BOTH flavors squirted out from the sides of their Meaty Mediterranean Pussies and into the Master's mouth while the ANAL SLUTS were humping LOCKED onto each other's pussy side by side.

GRINDING violently Clit on Clit, He tried desperately to Catch and DRINK DOWN as much of their Mango/Mix as he could while they pulled his wet head of hair, giving the Cousin More.

"I'M CALLING UP CARMEN Downstairs to come up and Help Me fuck your Asses some more! WOW! You're NOT done Cumming yet, are you?" the Soaking-wet Master/Cousin asked Carol from behind, Fucking her Ass as the Anal Sluts GRINDED and continued to Cum.

"YOU TWO ARE TRUE ANAL SLUTS! You Both can cum from a cock IN YOUR ASS," Master T said to them. BUTT THAT ONLY MADE THEM HOTTER and WETTER!!!

Like when Mistress ANNA called her Nephew/Master "YOU FUCKING ANIMAL" OR "Do whatever you want to me!" Only made him harder, Calling to Carol, "YOU FUCKING ANAL WHORE" Only turned Carol on more!!

Master T had "DP" in the ASS in mind For BOTH of them, While EACH ANAL SLUT lay down on one 10" Cock IN THE ASS, The OTHER 10" COCK Fucked "THE SAME HOLE" From on top while standing facing the Already penetrated Ass-hole, Cock on Cock, allowing TWO cocks to fuck the SAME ASSHOLE or PUSSY "Double Penetration."

Master T Knew Carmen was Bi/Sexual and MIGHT cause Carmen to get excited as well for some cock too. So Master T might have Carmen blow him later and have the girls watch FOR the end of a perfect evening AND a VIP Club Paradisa Membership welcoming For the Greek VIP ANAL SLUT, Donna Puopalous.

Carmen opened the door to find Master T fucking Donna's Asshole and beating her with the Rounded ping-pong paddle. Her Ass was Visibly Black and Blue, squirming on the lowered Cum-soaked leather massage table, and Donna moaned loudly taking ALL ten inches in her Ass.

Carol was laying UNDERNEATH Donna AND Her Master while he was standing pounding away IN Donna's asshole. Carol was Eating-Out Donna's Pussycum drippings and sucking her

Master's Swinging balls, BUTT When Carol saw Carmen's hard 10" READY to "DP" DONNA'S GREEK ASSHOLE, Carol Immediately bent over in the SAME POSITION right next to Donna and OPENED HER ASS CHEEKS With BOTH HANDS, signaling Carmen to violate her ASSHOLE as well.

After The two Studs were done Fucking Donna's Ass DP STYLE, which they gladly did, they Fucked Carol's big round Italian ass as well.

BOTH ANAL SLUTS eventually took two cocks DP style butt the Master and Carmen went one step further and MADE Donna and CAROL suck and lick the two cocks Clean (ASS TO MOUTH). Donna was moaning like a dog sucking two CUM-COVERED COCKS right from her own Greek asshole BUTT would NOT stop until Master T pulled her up by her hair, KISSING the Anal whore and telling Donna, "YOU BE-LONG TO US NOW! HERE IS WHERE YOU BELONG NOW, TO CAROL AND ME!" Cousin's Anthony/Master T AND Carol TOLD a drained-out, black-and-blue-ass Donna Puopalous.

The Cousins then added Donna to a NEW membership into Club Paradisa AND into Carol's NEW Special Client Journal as well to be passed back and forth by the kinky Cousins.

"YES, SIR! I DO!" Donna cried out with tears while still cumming uncontrollably as Carol continued slapping and tapping, then lapping on Donna's swollen erect inch-long Clit, making her squirt continuously. Carol looked up into Donna's eyes

while she was screaming and streaming and told Donna she tasted just like Hazelnut-Gelato, "Carol's favorite Ice-Cream."

Patty parked the Bentley and watched HER Master T walk into Pressman's Deli to order Corned beef and Swiss sandwiches for his lifetime Fantasy Goddess/Auntie Anna as Carol told Patty of the Awesome "ASS Worship" session with Donna last night and wished Patty was there!

Patty was getting all excited just talking about it with her Idol kinkster sister Carol and just listened getting wetter by the second, "TELL ME EVERYTHING," Patty pleaded.

"My Cousin Anthony and I are going to Collar Donna when we get back! DONNA WANTS US TO COLLAR HER. She fucks like an ANIMAL when it comes to taking it from behind in her Ass. DONNA LOVES ASS PLAY, her Ass, My Ass, Master's Ass." Donna was obsessed with "ASS Worship" and Giving OR Receiving Anal in ANY way, Donna admitted to Carol while Tonging and Rimming Master's Asshole last night.

"No guy has ever made her come more than once In a Whole day, Donna told me, and NEVER from Anal!" the Greek Anal Slut/VIP Donna Puopalous had confided to Carol and her Cousin Master T. "WE MADE HER SQUIRT LIKE TEN times ALL OVER THE ROOM, and all over everyone just like Evelyn does, lol," Carol laughed to Patty, who was getting soaking wet from the story.

Patty was listening BUTT daydreaming and needed some licking also from HER Master's thick talented tongue, facefucking him

frequently on drives to N.H., hiding the Bentley off the road, but not lately. Patty was missing out on HER Private time with Master T but couldn't say a word.

But not tonight, SHE THOUGHT TO HERSELF, WATCHING HIM WALK OUT with the bag Full of corned beef and Swiss on Rye sandwiches and Smiling directly at Patty squirming in her sticky panties.

Cousin Anthony's Mom Joan might be up at the cottage in N.H. to see her sister Anna and LUVED Patty's outgoing personality and SHE WAS his Vanilla girlfriend, don't forget. So When Patty had to PLAY Anthony's Vanilla girlfriend "SHE WENT ALL OUT, VERY CONVINCINGLY," especially to Joan, who she liked as well.

Patty had been Pre-Approved ALREADY for tonight to Ravish HER Master, So no penalties for straying tonight with Patty's Co-Owner and Master. Carol's Cousin/Anthony loved these occasional situations and HAD FUN with his Vanilla girlfriend Patty as well, watching Carol get all STEAMED-up as Her Kissing Cousin had Patty sit on his lap, then hugged, kissed and fondled the 23-year-old's solid DDs on this petite sandy-blonde Goddess with an hourglass figure dressed to Slay ANY prey!

Carol WOULD ride shotgun and keep Patty driving with Master T IN THE BACK SEAT on the ride up to see The Domme/Goddess Anna and Lover/Partner Evelyn today, Cousin Anthony's Mom Carol's Auntie Joanie WOULD be there as well.

It was a quick 45-minute drive to Derry, N.H., from Pressman's Deli Right up Rte. 1 to Rte. 95N in the Bentley OR thirty minutes in the Corvette. MommeDomme Anna was starving for her Deli Sandwich when the Bentley pulled up with her three Favorite Kinksters to be greeted by the Auntie Anna/MommeDomme, Evelyn and Anthony's concerned Mom Joan, who was there to visit her sister Anna.

"OH, LOOK! YOU brought your girlfriend Patty!" Joanie was so happy to see PATTY as always, hugging and kissing Joan whenever Vanilla Patty saw Joan and went ALL OUT as Carol ROLLED HER EYES to the sky, watching Patty work her Vanilla magic.

MommeDomme/Auntie Anna turned her head for a laugh with Evelyn when she heard her sister say right in front of her son Anthony's Cousin/Lover Carol, directly TO Patty, "I didn't know YOU two were coming or I would have made plans to stay longer," Joanie said, Still hugging the cheerful smiling Patty, Joan's favorite OF ALL her son's past Girlfriends. "IS THAT SHALIMAR you're wearing, Patty? That's My Anthony's favorite perfume," Joanie added as she sniffed Patty's neck, squeezing Patty and giggling.

"OH, YES, I know it is. HE bought it for me for Christmas!" Patty proudly said, smiling to Joanie, hugging her right back and fixing Joan's coat collar and hat.

"He bought EVERYONE a bottle for Christmas," Carol shot back, laughing for All to share a laugh.

"Well, I can't stay too long, I have to be home by 2:30 today but MAKE SURE YOU COME TO VISIT ME, PATTY, with or without my son. I enjoy seeing you as ALWAYS," Joan said, hugging Patty again.

Carol rolled her eyes AGAIN while Patty smiled over to Carol, sarcastically enjoying EVERY SECOND of this Vanilla Girlfriend game they played FOR BUSINESS MEETINGS and MOM JOAN only.

Anthony walked HIS mom Joan out to her ride and also to greet her 3rd husband George, who drove Joan Everywhere because Mom Joan JUST WOULDN'T get her license!

Master T said his goodbyes, then ran for HIS Corned beef and Swiss Deli Sandwich before HIS Domme/Aunt Anna ate them all.

Mistress/Goddess Domma Auntie Anna had been known to eat two whole Deli sandwiches while getting her Pussy drained "UNDER HER DESK" at her office in Chelsea, MA, after school by Her sixteen-year-old PussyCum-loving Groomed Nephew Anthony. He brought HIS GODDESS he was IN LOVE with Deli Sandwiches to their TABOO Secret Oral Pleasing sessions for his Dominant Aunt ALMOST DAILY by bus after School.

Nephew Anthony, NOW her Master, grabbed his half-eaten sandwich, looking over to HIS still Goddess Aunt Anna, now smiling ear to ear at him, KNOWING what was on his mind.

"I KNOW YOU CAN EAT TWO OF THESE!" the Nephew laughed to his Goddess/Aunt, remembering very well

their earlier years together when her sixteen-year-old hung nephew with amazing ORAL skills fell hopelessly in love with her.

The seventeen-year-older Aunt Anna realized SHE couldn't live without her nephew's skills, either FALLING hopelessly IN LOVE with him and continued to Groom her nephew into a Master of BDism, Satisfying the Domme Aunt Anna's needs and Desires in the kinky lifestyle.

"Patty and Carol was just telling Me THEY soaked you with a Golden Shower right here down by the stream with Alice, my Nephew? Is that so?" the jealous Domme Aunt asked. "I didn't even know that lovely trail and beautiful Brook belonged to US. Evelyn wants to try giving/receiving GS with You and Patty right now while I speak to my Carol for a few minutes Alone. Is that OK with you, Our Master?" the Goddess Aunt asked her nephew. "THEN Carol and I will walk down and give you a lot more while Patty holds you down for ME, lol, I'll start to drink some Iced coffee right now, SO BE READY! How does that sound, Our Master?" the Mistress/Aunt teased the GS lover softly in his ear.

"YOU KNOW I LOVE YOUR ICED COFFEE," Nephew/Master T whispered back into her ear.

Patty heard this and QUICKLY asked Carol for permission for PeePlay time with their Master T since Momme brought it up.

Patty was happier than an Anal slut with two cocks up her ass KNOWING Master T would finally fuck and suck her brains out before Patty had her turn, facefucking her Master, giving him a mouthful OR two. Patty had to be quick before Cousin Carol

came walking down with Momme, "Queen of the Golden Showers," to PeePlay in the secluded Brook ON her Nephew.

Patty got her permission and QUICKLY took her BAG OF TOYS, wasting NO time. "HAVE A NICE LONG CHAT with your Mom," Patty said, smiling, closing the door behind.

Evelyn the Masochist was anxious and READY FOR WHA-TEVER Domme Patty had in mind for Evelyn's torture today. EVELYN HAD BEEN WAITING ALL DAY for Domme Patty's Sadistic Dominating techniques since Domme/Anna told Evelyn, "Patty IS coming Today!"

Evelyn got WET just hearing Mistress Anna saying Patty's name! Evelyn had been Infatuated with Patty since the day Patty picked her up that day in her new skimpy driving suit and fondled Patty's huge DDs while Patty drove Evelyn to meet The Domme Anna in a session, eventually joining in on that session that night, making Evelyn Squirt Uncontrollably in a 3 Way.

Evelyn then requested to her Mistress/Goddess that Patty BE PART OF EVERY SESSION from then on before The Domme Anna would finally "Collar and Own" Evelyn. Patty made Evelyn Squirt like crazy with her ORAL skills, "which Domme Anna AL-READY Knew." Master T would provide his 10" cock and long, thick tongue following Domme Patty's instructions, Also using Evelyn up like the Masochistic Slut/Slave she craved to be.

The shack by the stream was fixed up somewhat once Domme Anna learned it belonged to her and was now used for storage while sitting IN the Brook on the large stones.

Patty noticed a nice heavy curtain rod above her head in the shack and tied Evelyn's hands high above her head onto the curtain rod to Evelyn's satisfaction, eagerly waiting for the first CRACK of the long leather whip placed next to her, along with TWO other whips and a long Riding crop, teasing Evelyn as she begged, "Use Me, Beat Me, Domme Patty, I've been so BAD."

Domme Patty pointed to the floor while kissing HER MASTER T, waiting for him to kneel down, lifting her skirt with NO panties on, WAITING for his prize.

Patty Squeezed his mouth open for a taste of Patty's ALREADY dripping-wet pussy that had been MISSING HIS TONGUE and oral-pleasing skills very badly.

CRACK! CRACK! CRACK! Now whipping Evelyn across her thick pink nipples three quick, HARD strikes placed directly on Evelyn's swelling nipples, marking the light-skinned Masochistic Pussycum squirter, and Pussy Lover.

Domme/Patty took the riding crop now, Tapping Evelyn's inner thighs to open Evelyn's legs wide for Master T to start slurping the constant dripping. Evelyn's Pussycum was now running down her leg, calling out to the Sadistic Domme Patty, "HARDER! I WANT MORE! You make me Cum so fucking much, Patty, I CAN'T STOP!" Evelyn cried out, still squirting.

Master T LOVED watching this and was trying to keep up with Evelyn's multi/orgasms, lapping-up as much as he could while she took a beating from Domme Patty without Domme Anna present.

Patty was now biting on the 42-year-old Evelyn's swollen thick pink nipples, hearing her scream as Patty pinched them after biting them, nursing from Evelyn's big tits like a hungry baby lion, this "NIPPLE TORTURE" was making Evelyn Squirt in "BUCKETS." It was a favorite of Evelyn's and she loved how Patty could be so SADISTIC with her big tits and stone-hard nipples.

Patty's Dominant behavior drove the Master T crazy for her, and he now took Patty by the hair from Evelyn, DRILLING the petite Young Domme Patty's tight Wet pussy HARD and DEEP, until Patty would drop the crop, surrendering to be USED along WITH Evelyn by the Master. Domme Patty had been waiting ALL DAY to submit and be USED BY HER MASTER T anyway today. Patty needed HIS Dominance and Power over her for now before Carol and Momme came to take THEIR PROPERTY from her.

Patty was bent over, being POUNDED doggy style in BOTH holes by her Master and making Patty Eat-Out Evelyn's dripping-wet pussy as Evelyn begged to be Fucked also.

Patty screamed out to her Master/Vanilla Boyfriend when she squirted HER HOT MANGO repeatedly while suckling on Evelyn's constant stream of PussyPeeCum.

Master T pulled Patty's hair, guiding her like a RAG DOLL across Evelyn's pussy and onto the Masochist Evelyn's asshole while He fucked Both Pussy lovers back and forth.

Master T was now totally in charge, taking the Crop from the floor, whipping Patty to her knees to throat fuck his favorite Blonde Pet/Sub of all time.

While facefucking Domme Patty, Master T was slapping and whipping Evelyn repeatedly until Evelyn GUSHED AGAIN like a broken water balloon, SCREAMING even louder now.

Evelyn was now being tortured by the Master AND Patty was being beat as well, LOVING EVERY SECOND, not letting an inch of HER MASTER'S hard 10" cock out of her mouth while he slapped Patty's DDs and pulled her hair.

Patty sucked Her Master DOWN DEEP as she could, taking the hot exploding Juice, gasping while she swallowed ALL OF IT. The Master continued SHOOTING his huge built-up load right down her throat, holding her head as Patty kept his hard 10 all the way down.

Patty took a quick breath of air, then took his Cum-Covered 10" right back down, MAKING SURE she completed the job on HER FAVORITE cock in the world, and always waited for Master T To pull his cock out first, and that was when She'd done!

Patty LOVED IT when her Master/Vanilla BF Anthony kissed her as he always did when he was done cumming, showing his appreciation, tasting his own cum to Patty's satisfaction as well.

Patty was definitely peeing, she said, when she was having Multiple Squirting Orgasms from being pounded so hard. Patty hoped she had more Pee for the Golden Shower session today for her Master's Favorite Kinky Fetish. So she quickly went for the fridge to get two sweetened Iced coffees to drink right down for the occasion.

Evelyn drank down two large Ice waters as well AFTER a few more slaps and cracks from the Master's strap across her thick,

swollen, raw nipples, making Evelyn scream some more louder and louder, which made her squirt "Uncontrollably."

Evelyn had waited ALL DAY for this moment to laugh AND CRY all in the same breath while being whipped, slapped and nipple tortured by the Petite Domme Patty, who NOW KNEW Evelyn's NEEDS. This was who The Masochistic PussyPeeCum-loving slut Evelyn craved to be.

Patty only had a little time for herself and Evelyn to give her Master some Hot Pee/Play and teach Evelyn how he liked it, Holding Master's mouth open and how to squat for his amusing Fetish, showing Evelyn just HOW to "Give her warm salty pee."

The Master loved when Patty Dominated this session for this Particular Fetish, JUST LIKE HER MENTOR DOMME/ AUNTIE ANNA, "Queen of the Golden shower," taught her.

Patty was working FAST to get by the stream before Carol came down with Domme Anna and spoiled Patty's PRIVATE Time with her Master, who WAS NOW begging Patty to blindfold him AGAIN for fun and playing the guessing game to please his Fantasy Goddess Aunt that missed out the last time. He wanted to make her smile for As long as He possibly could SO Patty ripped Evelyn's Wet panties Off and used them as a blindfold.

PATTY BEGAN TO PEE FIRST, not being able to hold in four iced coffees anymore. Wasting No time while tying the panties over her Master's eyes, Patty Busted like a Firehose right over Master's entire head, face and chest and over the wet panties as well.

PATTY, STILL WASTING NO TIME, pulled Evelyn by her arm over to Master T, laying back blindfolded on a large flat stone right IN THE FLOWING BROOK, and told Evelyn to listen to the running water splashing over the rocks and THAT WOULD MAKE HER PEE quickly and longer.

"YES, IT REALLY DOES MAKE YOU PEE," quickly the beaten but satisfied Evelyn Admitted, aiming into Master's squeezed opened mouth, held by the FAST-WORKING anxious Domme Patty before BOTH of Master/Anthony's "OWNERS" came for him to TAKE her Master from her and END Patty's Private time today with Domme/Anna's Evelyn AND Slave Nephew/Cousin Anthony. He was ALSO Vanilla Boyfriend Anthony belonging to Patty, however, but had limited time and CONTROL over him, "Only with Permission."

"SIT DOWN AND LAY BACK! NEXT TO MY MASTER," Patty commanded to Evelyn, lowering Evelyn next to Master T to "RECEIVE" Patty's yellow salty rain as well before the Domme came with daughter Carol. Patty slapped open Evelyn's mouth for some of her warm salty pee to taste, NOT letting Master T see just yet but could HEAR Evelyn's mouth being filled by the ruthless Domme Patty.

"DO YOU LIKE IT?" Patty again slapping her face, asking the gagging Masochist Evelyn receiving her first Golden Shower from a Very Dominant Patty "GIVING" the Golden Shower.

"YES! Very Much, Domme Patty, ANYTHING YOU DO TO ME I LOVE, PATTY!" Evelyn told the petite Goddess as she licked a few stray drops of pee off Patty's curvy legs.

"I was asked to see if you liked the PeePlay, SO YOU WILL get more later today, but right now we will play the guessing game for Mistress Anna and DO some more Pee/Play on our Master T, BEFORE they come for him!" Patty whispered to Evelyn.

"HERE THEY COME!" Evelyn warned Patty. "SLAP ME HARD JUST ONE MORE TIME, PLEASE!" Evelyn begged Patty.

Patty SMACKED Evelyn's face hard TWICE, then BIT BOTH her nipples, almost making Evelyn bleed, making Evelyn Scream, causing her to ooze out and Cream immediately.

"YES! OMG, YES! I'M COMING AGAIN!" Evelyn cried out into Patty's Pussy to muffle the screams so The Domme/Anna and Carol couldn't hear Evelyn being tortured.

CEO Trisha Sullivan, a 32-year-old VIP bombshell, just left Carol and Monique after being taken to the shower from the massage table, sitting her down, hand showering her sculptured body, Carol held Trisha's arms up from behind to play with her long erect nipples.

Monique was teasing Trisha's inch-long-thick Clit with the handheld showerhead while suckling and lapping up Trisha's still streaming used-up, beet-red, puffy pussy.

To really finish things off, Goddess/Carol Ordered her Collared Masochist Monique to sit down beside Trisha, pulling Monique by her hair close to Carol's pussy to "Rub One Off" on the masochist's face and into her mouth to SHOW Trisha that Mo-

nique was a true Masochist and COULD USE HER as well once Trisha had a Permanent VIP membership pass, with Permission, of course!

Monique COULD BE AVAILABLE as Trisha's Fetish-Friendly provider, a/k/a Trisha's "PRIVATE Physical Therapist," To which Trisha said, "OH, YES! I want Monique AND those two Young Men EVERY TIME I'm here, AND YOU TOO, Carol, IF you're available, of course.

"THAT WAS SO FUCKING HOT, CAROL. Thank you sooo much for tonight, I'M IN 100%, and for the BDISM sessions you mentioned also, AND YES, I'll accept YOUR COLLAR Any day! Omg, I'm still cumming being a permanent VIP member," Trisha concluded, giggling with another spurt of Nectar D'Mango, wetting herself on the way out!

Carol and Monique were Just as pleased as Trisha while Monique was reminded of the similarities of being seduced sexually by Patty and her New Goddess/Owner Carol.

Monique was eventually Collared And Owned by Carol just two days later, opening Up her Darkside and welcoming her Masochistic cravings by DommePatty, her Sadistic BDism pleaser.

Domme/Patty, Mistress/Domme Anna, AND the very capable beautiful BossDomme Carol Monique's Mistress, together with Master T, would ALL SHARE the voluptuous Redhead.

Speaking of Patty! Carol turned to Monique and was now worried about the office, so Carol began to give orders to Monique.

"Check in on Alice and Carmen and make sure Patty is OK, then check your messages and get back to me in an hour. YOU may need to go help Patty and Allie in today's session," Carol demanded.

Carmen was supposed to be available for Lenny today's session, instructed by Patty. "YOU go see if she's ok and if Carmen is there yet, THEN YOU come see me later for my bath," Carol concluded in a rush, needing to see her cousin Master T as well.

Carol was Still worried sick about Her Momme. Carol WAS NOT used to be in TOTAL CHARGE like the MommeDomme was Consistently, the cloned Goddess Carol was getting a taste of just how hard her Momme worked for EVERYTHING she was leaving to her and her Groomed loyal Master Nephew/ Cousin Anthony.

Carol still needed to check phone messages for Real Estate business, AND what Momme wanted Master T and Carol to do with the business Momme had used as a front for years as well.

Master T had been checking in on the real estate office with an agent the Domme had hired for the time being, Master T assured Carol, "You just need to SHOW property when a prospective buyer calls to see a new listing they like. It's a good 'FRONT,'" he convinced Carol.

"An hour at a time here and there, you MAY even sell a few houses a month. It Has been A GREAT FRONT for your Momme and IT'S HOW SHE FILES HER TAXES, so don't go changing things too much with the IRS, be VERY careful," Master T advised Cousin Carol.

So just like that, Carol called back her second appointment, Donna Puopalous, the Greek goddess with the gorgeous ass just like hers with long curvy legs also, smaller Firm Breasts BUTT EVERYTHING ELSE!!

Carol told Donna to come see HER at the facility when she had time and would explain up on the rooftop bar at her convenience.

Carol was realizing SHE may have bitten off more than she could chew, OR lick, But was doing a hell of a job TRYING, and had already established a Retreat/Club for successful VIP Women to congregate and relax. "Just like the 'rich prick Men' do," as The Domme/Anna quoted.

It had been an exciting day For Monique and about to become HOTTER when she walked into Patty's session while whipping Monique and Alice's assistant Carmen across his muscular Italian ass. Allie was whipping her hubby Lenny while in a GuyOnGuy session (Manoe'Mano) live show that Allie had requested ongoing Bi/weekly, and billed to her NBC expense account.

Allie had a disappointing miscarriage a few months back, BUT was still producing Breastmilk, Allie was squeezing and squirting her Breastmilk ALL OVER the guys; faces while they Fucked each other's ass in this Live Sex Show, "Extra Cash," as a VIP member of "Club Paradisa."

"OMG!" Monique said in shock, watching this live Mano'eMano show while being beat by their Woman/Owners. A very wet Monique grabbing her own nipples in excitement knelt in front of Patty, lifting her blouse, begging for a WHACK OR

TWO across her already swollen nipples as well, and a taste of some tittie milk.

"Please, Domme Patty! Can I join in just for a few minutes?" Monique begged.

"SURE, MY MASOCHISTIC SLUT!" Patty, Lifting her skirt up to Monique's face, said.

"EAT SOME PUSSY FIRST," Patty insisted, to which Monique eagerly did for a beating by The TWO sadists Allie and Patty, THEN taking mouthful of Patty's MangoJuice, along with a BONUS mouthful of HOT BABY MILK from Allie's big lactating Breasts while WHIPPING Monique into a Another puddle of her own Pussycum.

Monique was watching her assistant Carmen take Lenny's thick cock deep in his asshole, moaning heavily right beside her, still being whipped as well by the vicious Domme Patty, who ENJOYED beating the Redhead Monique, who SQUIRTED so intensely From a whipping, with All the extras In THIS VERY HOT SESSION, requested by Sadistic wife Allie to watch her CUCKOLD husband Lenny TAKE on a big dick, OR have him WATCH HER take a big dick while she beat him and HUMILIATED him, calling him Nasty names.

Monique rushed back to tell Carol, "ALL IS WELL WITH PATTY! Carmen is there doing his part, Mistress/Carol, and I HELPED JUST LIKE YOU ASKED," Monique giggled with sore bruised nipples, easing Her Mistress Carol's mind of a Very busy SIR Agenda ahead today.

Carol's message machine was FULL and Alice had some MRI visits written down. When Monique checked IN on Alice she was reading MRI results of The Domme/Anna.

It was NOT A return of Leukemia, but rather "Symptoms of Parkinson's disease," and Alice insisted Her Domme/Mistress Anna NEEDED REST, mild meds and a Parkinson's Specialist.

Evelyn would tell Carol Exactly what Domme/Anna's Doctor wanted her to do and Carol would see to it that Momme AND Evelyn got whatever they needed from that day on.

Carol and her lover/cousin Master T were relieved A LIT-TLE bit for now! At least Mom was not going to die anytime soon. So they had more time to spend with the Goddess at their Lakefront Cottage in N.H. Just forty minutes away in the Bentley OR thirty minutes in Master's yellow Corvette when His Goddess needed a Deli Corned beef and Swiss on Rye FOR LUNCH.

The Domme/Anna was not showing any shaking symptoms just yet, but this WAS a progressive disease, Dr. Anastopoulis told Everyone on a scheduled consultation visit to the Beth Israel Hospital in Boston "BIDMC," where Monique Once worked, then TAKEN by Carol.

"Just comfort her and make sure she takes her Meds daily," the silver-haired Greek Dr. Harry Anastopoulis told The Domme's Auntie Anna's family, EAGER to care for their Goddess every day in every way.

The next Very Important message on Carol's machine was from The East Boston Police Chief Detective Bobby Faucette,

looking for Cousin/Anthony to ask him a FEW questions on his whereabouts on July 5th, 1975.

When The Dick finally got to ask his questions, the Brawny 6'8" Detective Looked down on 5'9" Anthony/Master T tapping his head with the Infamous flashlight he carried constantly.

"I HOPE FOR YOUR SAKE you were here in Boston that day because the SDPD Homicide Dept. in San Diego, CA, WANTS TO SEE YOU if not," Detective Bobby Faucett arrogantly said. "WHY WERE YOU asking questions on the street about your Uncle Angelo that was murdered? AND THAT'S NOT ALL!! Two gangland rivals of YOUR UNCLE ANGELO were then killed, 'Meathook style,' Just how your Uncle Angelo was killed," Bobby added. "YOU wouldn't know ANYTHING about that, though, Anthony, would you?" the Det. Said.

"OF COURSE NOT!" A calm, innocent Anthony/Master T was looking up, saying to the very pissed-off Chief Detective Bob Faucette of the EBPD on Organized Crime. "I WAS RIGHT HERE! I've been back here in Boston for a while working ten hrs. a day, taking care of My Cousin and MY sick Aunt." Anthony was getting mad now himself for the allegations against him. "YOU TELL SAN DIEGO to call me personally then, FUCK THEM, They weren't doing anything for my Uncle's family," an Angry Master T said to the Detective staring in his face. Great Nephew Anthony of his Grandfather's brother Angelo and "Anna's Uncle" was still curious over the new developments and asked the Detective Faucette, "WTF happened, anyway?"

"WELL, it turns out SOMEONE retaliated on YOUR Uncle Angelo's murder and killed two rivals IRONICALLY with meat hooks just how your Uncle Angelo was HUNG on one. SDPD found them in LaJolla, CA, on the beach, EACH with a meathook up the ass and one in the Mouth with the two meat hooks 'Hog-Tied' together, VERY MESSY and very violent, 'Cosa Nostra Style,' as the San Diego Homicide described it," Detective Faucett added. "I DON'T SEE THAT IN YOU, KID, But Close!! You're NO Nicky Flemia and stay away from guys like him, HE'S TROUBLE, KID! Your Aunt THINKS he's a nice guy And HE WAS when we were all kids fifty years ago, But NOT NOW…," the Detective concluded with a tap on my head from his heavy flashlight to make his point. "I'll have San Diego Homicide call you Just like you said, AND WE WILL check out your alibi, SO with that being said, WHAT'S WRONG WITH YOUR AUNT ANNA? I WISH HER THE BEST, KID, WE GO WAY BACK, AND YOUR MOM JOANIE TOO. Tell Anna hello from me, please," THEN concluded with, "Palm Springs Police, ALSO IN California DID say you completed a program at the Betty Ford Center in Palm Desert, BUT you were in touch with Family members there as well. Phone calls and Surveillance show YOU asking about your Uncle Angelo's death, making YOU a person of interest, Anthony. Just answer them NICELY when they call you, kid," Chief Det. Faucett added as he left.

The next message was a very tantalizing, sexy broken English voice on the Answering machine. She spoke eloquently, slow, sexy

and as deep as you could get from a woman's voice. This message had Carol squirming in her office chair and needing to calm the tingling in her blouse with a slow pass of her hand and a pinch onto her hardening nipples.

IT WAS THE GREEK CFO, Donna Puopalis, from General Electric (GE) in Lynn, Mass. Donna was VERY INTERESTED in the limited membership offer for the Exclusive VIP Women's retreat "Club Paradisa" in East Boston inside the four-story brick building, along with "SIR MRI" scanning, Only fifteen minutes South from G.E. Corp. through Revere, right into East Boston.

Carol Immediately returned Donna's call, getting her on the phone just before 5 P.M. when she was leaving. Donna talked to a very excited Carol, still grazing her fingers across her tingling nipples from this tantalizing sexy woman's voice, making the pussy lover Carol wetter by the second as they spoke on the phone.

"Today was a crazy day, BUT what about a weekend night to show you our Club Paradisa, what's YOUR availability, Donna?" Carol curiously Asked Donna.

Donna replied, "I'd love to see that rooftop bar overlooking the Boston Harbor and skyline in the brochure you sent me. Tomorrow after work for a drink at least is good for ME, Then MORE if or your 'Male Assistants' in that brochure prove to be real. The club's Male Physical Therapists/Masseuses are very impressive and a nice feature, I may add!"

"OH, YES, Donna, They're Very Real and I WANT TO show you personally with MY Cousin and Co-Owner Anthony.

He is pictured in the Club Paradisa Brochure I sent to you. He's the middle one on the very first page," Carol proudly added.

"OH, YES, I love ALL three, lol, YOU'RE a very lucky lady, Carol, I'd love to meet with both of you tomorrow after work. Is tomorrow good for you and your Cousin?" Donna replied curiously in her very sexy European dialect, once again sending tingles to the young insatiable Goddess Carol once again.

"I'M SURE TOMORROW WILL BE FINE! Make it around six and your car will be valeted for You. I'll greet you at the door Personally," Carol Assured Donna about No worries about parking. "JUST SHOW UP," Carol jokingly replied.

"I CAN'T WAIT! I love the brochure and the three Handsome GIFTED young men standing with the three gorgeous women. Are they MODELS for the brochure, OR are they actually your workers? I was in advertising a while and I know a little about what they will do to Market something new," Donna joked. "IF ALL these male and female club assistants are for real, AND this Club Paradisa is as nice as these pictures in the brochure, I'M IN, l can tell you THAT much," Donna replied, sending goosebumps down Carol's Arm. "I'M NO LESBIAN, BUT I sure ENVY these three young gorgeous ladies in this Brochure for sure," Donna joked.

"WELL, THANK YOU very much for the compliment, Donna. I'M THE BRUNETTE ON THE LEFT, first page," Carol NOW in wet panties waited for Donna's reply.

"REALLY? Wow! You're so young and gorgeous and YOU'RE the OWNER? along with your cousin, THE GUY IN THE

MIDDLE? Can I come NOW, lol," Donna giggled. "NO, I'M kidding, BUT EXPECT ME at six Sharp so I can look over your VIP Membership paperwork AND your Cousin Anthony. I'll be applying under General Electric's Executive VIP. Was that how you explained you would do your billing?" Donna curiously asked.

"ABSOLUTELY! These Women VIPs usually have Company expense accounts, OR Well-Off and have a business of their own," Carol assured Donna.

"I saw YOUR photo as well in an article about successful Younger women in the *Boston Phoenix Magazine*, YOU are gorgeous as well, I must say, and have great ASSETS yourself, lol," Carol joked about Donna's gifted European Greek ass.

"SEE YOU AT SIX then, OK? We'll have pizza from Santarpio's and drinks FIRST before we show You EVERYTHING 'Club Paradisa' has to offer our Women VIPs," Carol concluded.

The horny Goddess Carol now rushed looking for an outfit for tonight's meeting with a Greek Goddess named Donna while calling her Kissing Cousin to GET this VIP Membership.

Patty meanwhile, still by the stream in N.H., was waiting to present BOTH anxious submissives to her Mistress/Mentor, DommeAnna AND Daughter Carol.

Evelyn and Master T had been tied together and blindfolded by Domme Patty and were sitting back on a large flat rock IN the stream of flowing water, very APPROPRIATE For the Out-

door Golden Shower Session "Domme Patty" had set up for her two Mistresses to enjoy.

Evelyn was so excited how Sadistic Domme Patty was Using her up and Slapping her silly that Evelyn was STILL streaming visibly between her legs. Her Master's ten-inch cock was as hard as the rock he was tied on from Domme/Patty USING him up in ways HE LOVED from the blonde bombshell before the two Goddesses USE their Nephew/Cousin PussyPeeCum lover NEXT.

Patty HAD accomplished what she was sent out to do, Patty now HAD TO turn over Domme/Anna and Mistress/Carol's PROPERTY that had been TOLD TO USE, with PERMIS-SION, of course!

Mistress Carol Took the long leather whip from the Smiling and pleased Domme Patty, then looked to the MommeDomme attending to her two "COLLARED AND OWNED" Favor-ites, propping them up for THEIR NEXT TASTE from The Domme/AuntieAnna, Goddess and Queen of the Golden Shower.

"Are they still alive? lol," Carol Joked as they ALL enjoyed a long laugh KNOWING Domme Patty's Sadistic practices.

"YES, they are both fine, sweetie," replied Mom!

THEY WERE SMILING and wanted to play that guessing game now. Master T was asking Carol for Permission to play the guessing game of WHO was doing the peeing on him while blindfolded again, for whoever didn't enjoy it last time, mainly (AuntieAnna).

"Evelyn wants to play too," Mistress Carol was giggling As Evelyn turned to look around BLINDFOLDED, asking for permission to play, and wanted to pee with the others on the Golden Shower Fetish-Lover Master T as he tried to guess who was squatting and squeezing his mouth open to listen as the girls filled his mouth with their warm salty pee, OR their HOT Mango/ Juice as they Dominantly "RUBBED ONE OFF" on him when they had finally EMPTIED ALL THE ICED COFFEE, and multiple bottles of water.

The Domme Auntie Anna lowered her manicured PuffyPussy onto her Nephew's face softly, allowing only the taste of her Streaming PussyCum first, TEASING HIM, making him wait for the warm yellow rain.

The Domme Aunt was playing with her Nephew/Master, humping his mouth, then moving away, humping slowly some more juice on his long thick tongue, flicking and probing her holes, then she moved away again, THEN A FEW HARD SQUIRTS FILLED HIS MOUTH Unexpectedly.

The Goddess/Aunt demanded, "SWALLOW!" then again MORE LONG SQUIRTS OF HER HOT SALTY PEE, along with dominant short slaps to his wet face, pulling his hair back as She Demanded again, "SWALLOW IT, ALL OF IT!" The Goddess Dominated her submissive recipient of the Golden Shower, allowing ALL the Ladies present to WATCH her technique.

The Domme Anna was now Grooming and Training the potential Golden Shower, Domme's present, and AMAZED watch-

ing and learning for THEIR New Special Clients entering the BDISM Lifestyle seeking a FemDomme to guide HIMor HER into the Darkside. This very kinky and Taboo Fetish known as the "Golden Shower"/PeePlay/Water Sports was NOT for just any kinkster!

Carol and her MommeDomme switched positions now. MommeDomme would hold him down while Carol GAVE the "GS" to HER Property and Cousin/Soulmate for life, making sure Patty was paying close attention how Master T Submitted to HIS Goddess Cousin Carol.

PATTY KNEW IT, But Patty wanted and Needed him too... Period. Domme Patty DID get to him eventually, even though she might have to wait a bit, making it all worth the wait. Patty Cleverly and carefully had figured it out now, she just waited HER TURN or waited to be INVITED by the insatiable Pussy-CumCraver Carol in their three-ways with the Master.

Carol had finished off THREE ICED COFFEES with lots of sugar for the SWEETNESS her Cousin had requested she do, Carol now was DOING EVERYTHING she just had seen her MommeDomme do, AND watched just how much HER Master/soulmate SUBMITTED and ENJOYED being used by HIS TWO Goddesses.

The Master/Cousin/Nephew's ten-inch cock was sticking straight up, swaying like a FLAGPOLE in the wind as Carol emptied her bladder, squatting over her Cousin's face, holding him by the piss-wet hair.

Momme Goddess sucked on his Big Dick first, watching her Daughter proudly fill her Nephew's mouth in a long, hot stream of her "YellowRain," then passed it to Evelyn to suck that, passed it to Carol when she was done squirting, who then passed the Master's Flagpole to Patty LAST, so Patty could learn her place.

The Master's 10" FLAGPOLE EXPLODED, squirting a beautiful stream of HOT Cum right back into Patty's mouth and throat. Patty's Unmatched deepthroating Oral skills made the Master Cum intensely every time and HE WAITED for Patty to Cum in Appreciation as they ALL got a great laugh when she choked on a huge, thick load.

Carol laughed along with Kink sister Patty, then "Sucked and Cleaned" off what was left of her Cousin's Hot Cum still oozing from the tip as MommeDomme cleaned off his Cum-Covered balls, BUT PATTY GOT THE PRIZE, FIRST.

Patty and Evelyn would Pee next and the guessing game would last for another thirty minutes. Master would have HIS TURN as the "GIVER" before All enjoyed a swim to WASH OFF in their newly discovered Nature's landscaped stream, now used for the Kinkster's "Water Sports."

The reason behind MommeDomme, sending Patty down to the shack by the stream for a while with Her nephew and to Whip Evelyn into ecstasy, was to discuss business with daughter Goddess Carol.

"DON'T bite off more than you can chew. Keep it LOW KEY, and always have a 'Front' business doing as well as your

Special Kinkster Clientele. You WON'T last if everyone knows your business," the MommeDomme stressed. "Between Crooked Cops looking to make money for themselves, Then the WannaBe Gangsters that think they deserve A PIECE of your hard work, OR the young punks that think they can rob you without having their hands cut off later, JUST ASK YOUR COUSIN AN-THONY. He Knows ALL of them and PROTECTS You and I from Assholes like them. Don't EVER take him for granted and I am trusting MY Nephew to you now, so take good care of him," Momme pointing to her daughter. "HE BELONGS TO YOU NOW! BUT as long as I am alive, I TOO WILL STILL BE NEEDING THE YOUNG MAN I GROOMED TO BE OUR MASTER, Gabeesh? Do I have your pre-Approved permission?" MommeDomme FIRMLY asked while lecturing her younger 22-year-old Goddess Daughter Carol.

"ABSOLUTELY and ANYTIME, Momme. YOU don't ever have to ask for MY Permission again, I promise! Without YOU Cousin Anthony wouldn't even be in MY life," Carol sincerely answered The MommeDomme.

"I'll never question him If he's coming Up to see you, EVER!" Carol added with a tear in her eye, knowing it might be Anthony's last visit with (Momme), his Fantasy Goddess AuntieAnna.

"Now TELL ME about this menu of OPTIONS and WHO is doing this Mano e' Mano? I LOVE IT," MommeDomme giggled. "Now THAT would keep MY interest for sure watching two guys getting it on in front of my face in a LIVE sex show

for VIP Women Only, Brilliant!" MomDomme praising Carol once again.

"Carmen and Lenny OR Joey and Carmen," Carol answered. "THEY WERE AWESOME together under Allie's Control. Lenny's wife, Patty, could stand in if Allie wasn't able to and is very dominant with Patty's Slave/Joey."

These live men's shows were by APPOINTMENT ONLY and Extra "Cash Only." The VIP must plan way ahead, Carol also added to her VERY Curious MommeDomme.

"CAN I see this LIVE Men's show FIRST? My Birthday is in a few days, you know! YOU TWO DIDN'T FORGET, DID YOU?" MommeDomme giggled to Carol, smacking her tight Italian ass walking past her.

"OF COURSE NOT, MOMME, lol, and I'M ALMOST SURE Carmen is meeting with Lenny in MRI TODAY and using the dungeon for Something. ALICE HAS THE KEYS and MY JOURNAL with appointments for today. She's letting them in with Allie. I'LL HAVE CARMEN AND LENNY COME HERE FOR YOU TONIGHT, MOMME!! HAPPY BIRTHDAY, MOMME! Lol," Carol picking up the phone To CHANGE LO-CATIONS with Carmen and Lenny's Mano e'Mano session.

Carol told a busy Alice and Monique working on MRIs, "Alice, Tell Carmen, Allie and Lenny to up DRIVE UP TO the cottage in N.H. on BEAVER LAKE. My MOM wants to see the Mano e'Mano live show for approval, 'AND IT'S HER BIRTH-DAY,'" Carol giggled.

This would be a Great debut for a Mano e' Mano performance In front of four Excited women, All present, watching as both Men each take a BIG Cock in their fruit-flavored lubed-up ass. Allie Will do the Dominating on her hubby whipping Lenny, Momme and Evelyn would like to see Sadistic Domme/Patty Dominating Carmen! "Patty was born for this!" MommeDomme joked to Carol!

"OK THEN, Momme, it's settled! You will have your birthday wish!! Today at 5:30 they All WILL be here," Allie assured Carol.

EVERYONE was doing their part to comfort the LONG-REIGNING Domme/Anna in ALL New England, everything WAS running smoothly at SIR and with her "Special Clients" under Carol and her Cousin Anthony's control.

Monique and Alice BEGGED Carol to watch THE LIVE MEN'S SHOW and promise ALL their work was done for today. "WE want to bring a Birthday Card and be there for our Mistress too. WE DIDN'T KNOW it was your Momme's birthday!" Alice and Monique Pleaded to Carol.

"PLEEEEEZ? We will leave right after the show, WE WILL BOTH EVEN LICK YOUR ASS if you let us come, lol," Monique jokingly pled to Carol's weakness with curiosity.

Carol wittingly replied, "Ha-ha, YOU DO THAT ALREADY! YOU KNOW that's a LOT of licking to do, BUT OK, MAKE SURE ALL your work is done and get right back there after the Cake and the Mano e'Mano Show. Carmen and Lenny are great together, I watched them already once!" Carol concluded.

Allie and Lenny were minutes away from Meeting Carmen, so all they had to do now was to head North up Rte. 95 for thirty more minutes just over the Massachusetts, NH, border into Derry, N.H., onto Beaver Lake, then find Onessimo Village.

Onessimo Village was where seven brothers and sisters OWNED seven lots of the eight. The Domme Goddess/Anna real estate agent FOUND the last Forgotten Lakefront Lot with the broken-down cottage UP FOR GRABS, and grabbed it, Renovated it and NOW IT'S BRAND NEW! The Onessimo MEN DID NOT COMPLAIN, however, after losing out on purchasing the lot.

All the Brothers get to see A Goddess/DommeAnna, her clone Gorgeous young daughter and DommePatty every summer in custom-made bikinis lounging around on the private 200-ft.-long sandy lakefront beach, sometimes TOPLESS!

The STAGE was set, and ALL the participants were present For The "Mano e'Mano" performance inside the cottage's renovated extended patio addition leading RIGHT OUT through the sliding Glass Doors, just steps to their Lake designed by Evelyn.

Evelyn, Carol, Patty, Master T, Alice and Monique wanted to be sure Everyone sung "HAPPY BIRTHDAY" from The CLOSEST people to Anna besides her sister Joan.

"NO WAY Mom Joan was seeing Mano E' Mano tonight," ALL the kinksters agreed.

"Light the Candles before 'The Show' starts. Not everyone can stay after the show, SO let's sing Happy Birthday, relax and enjoy the show," Carol Excitedly said to everyone.

"AND let's remember this date, MAY 10th, YOU'RE ALL INVITED NEXT YEAR ALSO here to the Lake for a HAPPY BIRTHDAY WEEKEND PARTY. Put it in your journals when you get home," Mistress Carol said softly.

Carol Pulled Patty aside in Private to say, "Momme wants YOU out there with the Riding Crop on Carmen. She requested Domme Patty," Carol whispered while biting on Patty's earlobe, sending goosebumps and tingles through Patty's body as always.

"I'D LOVE THAT, Then I want to crop YOU while I lick you clean, lol," Patty giggled.

"THAT CAN BE ARRANGED! We'll talk later, but for now GET YOUR WHIPPING CROP and we'll meet you out there in a few minutes," Carol concluded to Patty.

Domme Patty wasted NO time sliding the partitioned doors open that separated the sitting guests WAITING to see the Mano e'Mano show. The live show Option was listed for the VIP Women's membership at a staggering $1,000.00 an hour.

The Well-Hung Bi/Men would be dominated and whipped by A Gorgeous female, either Allie OR Domme Patty Preferably, and would be Domming these Pre-Booked Live-Show performances.

The Mano/Mano On-Stage live SEX Show was an Anal, Oral, TWO-Man SEX SHOW performed directly right IN FRONT of the VIP WOMAN MEMBER that reserved the Private show for

a Pre-paid $1k an hour, Non-Refundable! THE VIP WOMAN MEMBER Reserving the show had another OPTION, TO JOIN IN WITH A STRAP-ON to fuck the men (OR) BE FUCKED BY THE TWO BI/STUDS FOR "ANOTHER $1,000." "CA$H".... Period!

"What's 1,000 An hour to a Multi-Millionaire, OR PAID for by her Company's PERK expense account for the time of your life?" as Carol laughed when saying this promoting "Club Paradisa" to these CURIOUS Wealthy Women VIPs.

Crack! Crack! Patty Whack! Allie simultaneously whipped their Submissive Slave Men on their calves, dropping them to their knees. BOTH men were wearing their Mistresses' Collars with leashes today and were told to face The "BIRTHDAY GIRL," who was smiling ear to ear, clapping, accompanied by her Very excited lover and partner Evelyn.

Crack! Crack! Again across Carmen's bubble ass as Patty pointed to the padded barstool and had told Carmen, "HE will be bending over to receive 'BOTTOM' for Lenny's Thick Dick in his Crop marked ass."

Allie holding back HER hard thick seven-inch husband Lenny by his leash, who was ready and eager to "TOP" Carmen while Patty applied a generous Handful of fruit-flavored edible lubricant using three of her petite fingers directly in front of Patty's Mistress and Mentor, The Domme Anna, TO SEE up close.

The Domme was nodding and smiling with approval, watching HER FAVORITE ruthless Domme Patty work her fingers, opening

Carmen's Hole. Domme Patty was prepping her Male/Slave Anal slut Carmen to take ALL of Lenny's Uncut Girth Cock with ease. Carmen and Lenny had "Topped AND Bottomed" Each other ALREADY under wife Allie's Dominating crack of the whip, Scolding HER very Obedient and loyal husband For Her pleasure, as well as HIS.

Lenny had finally "COME OUT" of the closet when Carol and Allie tricked him into sucking Master T's cock while couple swapping one evening. Goddess Carol WAS AN ANAL SLUT, everyone knew, Anal Slut Carol had taken ALL of Thick-Dick Lenny's cock deep in her perfect meaty heart-shaped Italian Ass that same night Lenny sucked a cock for his first time, taking them into Lenny and Allie's Darkside, Forever!

Lenny then was tricked AGAIN to "Take/Bottom" Eddy Showers' cock in his ass for BI/CURIOUS reasons as was Carmen, but Carmen didn't want his friend Joey knowing YET for fear of his Bi/Sexuality and WELL-PAID Mano e'Mano Shows, getting back to his old-fashioned Italian neighborhood in the North End of Boston.

Master T already knew about Carmen and Joey but couldn't care less what others thought of anyone else's Sexual preference. "YOU DON'T EVER ridicule a GOOD FRIEND of mine OR FAMILY of Master T. OR he will make you wish you didn't," Nephew Anthony had said.

Carmen WAS Anthony's true friend and now MUST tell Joey to respect what Carmen had chosen as part of his lifestyle and on the "SIR" payroll as well so "DEAL WITH IT."

"Respect OUR friends NO MATTER WHAT!" Master T told Joey Adamantly, pointing while seriously speaking, demanding his attention.

"OF COURSE, ANTHONY! I respect HIS decision, I would jump in front of a train for EITHER ONE of you," Joey said seriously in return.

"I PERSONALLY LOVE ONLY PUSSY but That's just ME. I've noticed Carmen looking at our cocks before at Alice's house when we were getting sucked off by her and always wondered about that. Carmen can like both women AND men if he chooses and I would NEVER judge him, THAT is his decision," Anthony/Master T now told Joey.

"YOU BEGGED PATTY to Collar and Own you, right?" Master now asked Joey. "NOW, IF Domme Patty Orders YOU to let Carmen Suck you someday for her amusement, YOU MUST OBEY HER Or lose her! Did YOU know that? Did you realize WHAT you were doing asking a mean Domme like Patty to Collar you? Did you think THIS LIFESTYLE was all fun and games, my Pal Joey?" Anthony asked Joey Curiously once again, but still very seriously.

"WELL, I guess I could close my eyes and have Carmen DO me, I just think of Patty and playing with those Big tits. I DON'T EVER want to lose that little Deepthroating Goddess. I'LL DO WHATEVER SHE SAYS, ANTHONY," Joey confirmed.

"GOOD! Because YOUR MISTRESS and deepthroating Domme Patty WANTS YOU BLINDFOLDED and on stage today. IT'S OUR MISTRESS/DOMME ANNA's birthday party.

Patty wants two guys to Suck on your eleven inches while you're blindfolded because Carmen don't want YOU to see him blowing you. CARMEN IS ONE OF THE GUYS AND OUR CLOSE FRIEND doing the live sex show with Lenny, Mano e'Mano. This NEW Mano/Mano Live show for IS for Women VIPs ONLY at $1,000 a pop. Patty will dump you So fast, Joey, SHE ALREADY TOLD ME. So do the right thing IF you're still up for this and want to keep playing with her. SHE surely is playing with YOU, lol," the Master joked to his buddy Joey. "She is mean, Joey, don't go getting serious with Patty OR she will hurt you bad. I already told you that, Patty is Stone COLD. Just obey her or lose her, It's that simple," Anthony/Master T warned his pal Joey AGAIN.

"OK! OK! I'm kind of UP for it now, lol," Joey joked. "IF YOU CAN DO IT, I CAN TOO." Joey looked to his friend and Mentor Anthony/Master T. "LET'S DO THIS!" Joey concluded.

No sooner than Joey finished his sentence To Master T that Domme Patty opened the door to ask Master T, "Who is letting Joey Into the cottage to GET ONSTAGE today?"

"Have you seen MY JOEY, Master?" Patty asked.

Joey standing behind the door said to HIS Mistress Domme Patty, "HERE I AM, MY GODDESS/PATTY, READY TO SERVE MY MISTRESS in ANY way!"

"AWESOME, So glad you made it and even happier to hear that," Patty told Slave Joey.

"Master, Would you please Blindfold YOUR PAL JOEY and walk him out there for ME and THE OTHERS?" Domme Patty

smiled to her Master AND to her Collared Slave Joey. "MY SLAVE JOEY, I hope you're ready for this today. Prove your loyalty and Obey. You will be rewarded when GOOD but punished when BAD," Mean Domme Patty told "Slave Joey."

"ANYTHING YOU WANT!" Master T agreed to Patty and proceeded to walk out a Blindfolded Joey now JUST IN BREIFS with eleven inches of Hard Meat sticking out from seeing HIS Blonde Bombshell Goddess and hearing her Dominating voice guiding him to be "Used."

OR Was It Joey's Mentor Master T that Curious Joey envied beyond words that sexually aroused this confused young 23-year-old Stud/Slave packing BIG MEAT!

CRACK! CRACK! CRACK! Patty whipped HER collared Slave/Joey twice across his nipples and one down to his HARD standing long cock, ordering her Slave to "Sing Happy Birthday to THE DOMME."

After Joey was done singing, he was ordered to sit and jerk his cock for ALL the ladies' Amusement just before BOTH men would be sucking on the 11-incher In a SHARING Scenario UP CLOSE in front of Domme Ann and Evelyn while they kissed and fondled each other.

Carmen didn't know yet that Joey knew that it was him sharing Joey's Cock with Lenny.

"What a nice surprise, Domme Patty!" the Birthday Girl giggled. "YOU'RE SHARING your own collared property with Us? We should ADD HIM as an Option as well to do Mano Mano

shows, THAT IS a big dick for the VIP Women to see OR USE," the Domme suggested.

"IF that pleases YOU, THEN I THINK I WILL, Mistress Anna, THANK YOU!" Domme Patty smiled to the Goddess of ALL Goddesses.

From The Domme/Anna's suggestions to her apprentice Domme/Patty, in an instant just like that Slave/Joey was about to be turned into a Man/Ho and a Mano/Mano Slut for Club Paradisa's Exclusive Women VIP Members' Cash as well.

IF SLAVE/JOEY WANTED TO CONTINUE WITH PATTY'S DEEPTHROATING SKILLS, Or Full Swapping with the brunette Goddess Carol and his best friend Anthony/Master T, Joey would have to choose FAST!!

Then, in an instant, CRACK! CRACK! CRACK! Domme/Patty ORDERED Joey to turn around in his seat and open his HOLE wide for a waiting hard 10" cock from Carmen (NO Blowjob today) and JOEY OBEYED!!

Master T enjoyed a good laugh with Carol, MommeDomme and Evelyn as Joey Moaned like a Virgin on Prom night while Carmen rode Slave Joey's lubed Asshole to a very surprised Domme Patty, BUTT Ruthless Patty LOVED the look on her Slave Joey's face as CARMEN POUNDED HIS BEST FRIEND'S VIRGIN ASS, While Allie joined in to paddle Carmen, telling him to "FINISH UP SO MY LENNY CAN HAVE HIS TURN TOPPING JOEY!!!"

"Good thing MY Slave Joey is blindfolded so HE DON'T

SEE Lenny's Thick-Dick ready to RIP HIM A NEW ASS-HOLE, FOREVER," Domme/Patty joked to Carol.

"GOOD CHOICE, Pal Joey," Master T laughed to the slow-walking, sore-ass Joey, Who has just Totally surrendered his man-hood to the two Mano e'Mano Stars while Blindfolded AND Blindsided, led by a Ruthless FemDomme Patty Dominating her Sub/Slave Joey all the way.

Joey NEVER stood a chance against Patty's Diabolical per-sonality to ALWAYS GET HER WAY. Master T KNEW enough to keep his distance from Patty, who was IN LOVE with him, and now Slave/Joey knew it too, a little too late, however.

Joey got to STAY AND OBEY, Butt JOEY WAS DONE when he asked to be Collared by the Hot blonde deepthroating Goddess Patty. Joey WOULD now be rewarded tonight by his Owner Patty in a Full-Swap THAT SHE ALREADY PROMISED her Slave Joey, tricking him to drive to the Birthday Party to USE HIM in the Mano e'Mano Show to please HER Domme Anna.

Patty WOULD WIN once again tonight, getting Master T, Slave Joey AND Carol to LapUp and POUND her juicy FruitiD'Mango while the Pussy-Loving Patty would be draining EVERY DROP from her Insatiable 22-yr.-old Mistress/Goddess Carol AND her Cousin Anthony with approval that Patty had Pursued and now HAD for the last six years.

Anal Slut Carol would keep ALL of eleven-inch Slave Joey's cock in her ass for the night while Carol kept her mouth busy Feasting-Out on Patty's always flowing MangoJuice Carol AND

Master T enjoyed sharing with the Diabolical Blonde so much, WIN, WIN, all around.

THE DOMME stood applauding and "Thanking Patty" while laughing her ass off while Joey LIMPED off from the stage. "GREAT JOB, MY GORGEOUS LITTLE ONE! THAT was the best Birthday present EVER, YOU WERE BORN FOR THIS! Thank You ALL for being here tonight, and Evelyn and I will say goodnight until we all have breakfast in the morning," Goddess/Auntie Anna cheerfully said while kissing her daughter's cheek with a THANK-YOU for putting it all together like a Professional, Then a wet kiss goodnight to her Nephew/Master.

Boss and Goddess Carol had a brief discussion with her Cousin/Master before they started to Swap with Patty and Joey that "Joey and Carmen" should Do the Mano/Mano shows From NOW ON and NOT Lenny, OR only for specials," Carol asking Cousin Anthony to arrange it.

"I will tell Joey and Carmen, THEY are Mano e'Mano now," Carol's Master laughed in agreement, NEVER letting his Soulmate down, keeping his promise, Spoiling HIS Insatiable Goddess since birth, "Till Death do WE part." The Kissing Cousin sometimes kidded to Carol,

"And I will tell Patty SHE will Domme the Show." Carol Nodding with certainty while the clever Goddess took Her Master by the hand into the shower to get ready for tonight's Full- Swap, IF JOEY WAS STILL UP FOR IT, lol. The Cousins joking about the limping off the stage.

Master T and his soulmate Cousin Carol kissed and fore-
played a little on their King-sized bed, Waiting for Patty and Joey,
"Butt MY Slave Joey WAS NOT UP for it tonight," SAID THE
EAGER DIABOLICAL DOMME PATTY as she let HERSELF
in for the evening to be Ravished and Used-Up by the Kinkster
Cousins, With Permission, of course!

CHAPTER

23

After the Pleasingly SURPRISE Birthday Party from the Kinksters last night, breakfast was on the table to reminisce of last night's Live Show event "Mano e'Mano." Suggestions were made by the Domme and ALL the others seated at breakfast before hitting the road and back to work.

There WAS a very busy Agenda today they were forgetting about, but not Boss/Goddess Carol.

"LET'S GO, EVERYONE, take your coffee with you and LET'S GO NOW!" Carol said, walking over to kiss her Mom-meDomme and Evelyn goodbye. "WE HAVE AT LEAST EIGHT MRI reports to read and deliver to Longwood Ave., and AT LEAST FOUR 'Special Client sessions' THAT I KNOW OF, including two NEW ones, Trisha and Donna," a very excited Carol told her crew.

"Ha-Ha, Relax, my Clone. It's NOT going to be easy But YOU have the help now, AND REMEMBER WHAT I SAID! YOU have enough right now so Don't take anything else on right now and just keep up," the Senior advisor MommeDomme To DiNunzio Enterprises And Trust told her successor and CEO daughter while rubbing her Nephew/Master's back.

Sensually and slowly with her fingertips, Domme Auntie Anna made him squirm, giving him a hard-on while Nephew Anthony kissed his Goddess/Aunt's wet lips goodbye, for now....

"I'LL BE BACK UP SOON With Deli-sandwiches next week for lunch while you do your paperwork, Mistress, like old times (Permission granted)," he whispered to his Auntie Anna.

"PURRFECT," replied the Master's Goddess with goosebumps on her arms from her Master's hot breath and deep voice, along with the wet kiss to her long hot neck and ear on his way out, that NOBODY saw.

"LET'S GO!" Carol opened the door, trying to smile for Momme at the same time!

Cousin and Master to all her needs reiterated, "LET'S GO! Back to work!"

They rushed one by one, walking out, saying goodbye, smiling and kissing the Domme's cheeks, Alice, Monique, and Carmen of MRI, Patty and Joey, Lenny and Ali (Optional) Mano/Mano).

1st Cousins Carol and Anthony Executive Directors of Operations (Special Clients & (SIR) Operations), with Evelyn, Now a

Board member Trustee, Caretaker, and Senior Advisor To The Domme. The only other adviser NOT present for the Party/ Show was Evan Gellant, the Family Lawyer and Legal advisor to DiNunzio Enterprises & Trust.

Carol had now organized A Business Conglomeration with Multi-talented Physical Therapists for Sports Injury Rehabilitation, a/k/a "SIR," for MRI/CAT scanning at the newly renovated million-dollar Facility On Sumner St. in E. Boston right across the street from the waterfront known as the Boston Harbor to everyone in Eastie.

Special Clients OR SIR Clients could drink and dine overlooking the Boston Harbor from the rooftop lounge for Men OR Women VIPS from Club Paradisa, along with Top-Ranking Boston Sports Figures waiting for an MRI.

The chosen FEW that became an Exclusive Member of CLUB PARADISA were treated like A QUEEN, OR whatever she craved to be had "After-Hours" access to the rooftop lounge.

The Domme's handpicked selected skilled Staff would see to it personally THE CURIOUS WOMEN VIPS would end up begging to Stay and Obey.

Master T had now trained HIS crew of HUNG men to be servants to the Women VIP Membership Goddesses that came to relax and reap the rewards for all their Hard work.

Each Woman VIP got to pick from Options from the Assorted MENU of Fetish/Fantasies for their pleasure on a Pre-Arranged Day. They were billed through HER Company's expense

account under Complimentary Spa/Gym perks, JUST LIKE THE PIG MEN DO," Carol joked.

A daily staff of up to six skilled certified Physical Therapists, Men, Women OR Both, You pick, AND in bold print to reassure they WOULD BE taken care of sexually, it read.

"ANY FANTASY/FETISH WILL BE PROVIDED TO ANY CLUB PARADISA VIP MEMBER THAT'S NOT ON THE OPTIONAL MENU FOR AN EXTRA HOURLY RATE."

Meanwhile, Best friends Carmen and Joey Must get the Mano e' Mano Experience OUT INTO THE OPEN, said Anthony/ Master T to Joey, "YOU, Joey, Need to tell Carmen you knew it was Carmen all along when Patty ordered you to turn around on that stool and OPEN UP your hole to be used for the Show. It will make Carmen feel better that YOU too have been Bi/Curious ALL ALONG, Haven't You?" asked the curious Master.

"Well, to tell YOU the truth, I HAVE," said the very confused Bi/Curious Joey. "Patty now told me she wants to watch ME sharing YOUR cock with her, imagine her saying that to me? OR Patty threatened to sell me off or dump my ass. That's why I faked being sore and Didn't show up for the full swap after the Mano/ Mano show she tricked ME into. I Really WAS sore, though, lol," Joey joked, "Butt I will tell Carmen OK, Anthony, AND I will tell Patty She CAN have her wish of sharing IF THAT'S OK WITH YOU, MASTER T?" Joey asked curiously to his buddy Anthony but calling him Master this time.

Joey was being turned into a "CUCKOLD" by the ruthless DommePatty having Joey ask for permission to Share HER Master's cock with the controlling blonde bombshell Joey was OBSESSED with and Didn't want to lose her. Joey was being BITCHED-OUT and humiliated and didn't seem to mind at all.

"ONLY IF that's YOUR choice, Joey, YOU DON'T HAVE TO, you could walk away anytime, I told you before. I don't care one way or the other," the Master and friend Sympathetically told his Pal Joey. "There's Plenty of other women out there," Master T added.

"NO! NO! I'm sure, I want to now, I need to explore ALL of this lifestyle with Patty and please her, the more I see, the more I need to learn of the lifestyle now. I know it sounds crazy but I love it now," Joey said with excitement. "Patty is just Pushing MY LIMITS, as she put it in BDISM terms," Joey concluded.

"OH, YAH! Patty WILL do that to you for sure, lol," Master T agreed.

"OK then, NEXT TIME!" Master T suggested. "Let YOUR DommePatty take the lead and hold back till she whips you, that's what ALL FemDommes love doing."

"Yes! I will take your advice, Master," said Bi/curious Pal Joey, as he limped away.

"HEY, JOEY! Make sure you keep that limp for the Mano/ Mano ending when you're done taking Carmen's big ten, The Domme Loved it, SHE LAUGHED FOR AN HOUR watching you limp away after taking two dicks for an hour, lol," Master T

laughed to conclude the interesting conversation between the Master and his pal Joey, now Patty's Slave/Cuckold.

Master T was trying real hard to make Joey walk away BE-FORE Joey would become a REAL-LIFE SLAVE FOREVER to the RUTHLESS BLONDE DOMME/GODDESS PATTY, A lot like Joey's friend Nephew/Anthony HAD eventually become when HE was groomed, controlled, then Collared and Owned VOLUNTARILY to be a Slave to BOTH his Fantasy Women growing up with, first being Cousin Carol, then stolen and groomed to be Master of ALL her needs by the Ruthless Dominatrix, "His Domme, Auntie Anna."

BUT that was from a younger Nephew/Cousin Anthony's Fantasy dreams from a young teenager when He got his first Real Hard-On peeking at his gorgeous Auntie Anna taking a shower, then would watched her get dressed. His WELL-AWARE teasing Goddess always left the doors OPEN a crack for the Fascinated teenage Leg-and-Ass-Worshipping Nephew.

Cousin Carol, NOT to be outdone, then led the horny young Cousin Anthony by the hand On the same day into her Secret Closet to "Feel-Up" Cousin Carol when she was starting to develop HUGE puffy nipples that would become unmatched by any other woman. Nephew and Cousin Anthony fell in Love HARD with Both of the Gifted Goddesses, FOREVER.

Master T had come to Realize that HE stayed as long as he did because he could NOT deny the Love he had for the Mother AND Daughter AND the Love they had for his Loyal Service

and Respect that the Domme Aunt would SOON teach him as she groomed him to be their Master.

Maybe a bit more for Cousin Carol, EVER SINCE THEY COULD CRAWL TO EACH OTHER AT TEN months old, The 1st Cousins would ROLL AROUND ON THE FLOOR TO SEE WHO WOULD END UP "ON TOP."

Joey had been given a CHOICE By his Friend in their world that Joey WAS NOT really familiar with YET and warning Joey to walk away. Joey's buddy Anthony/Master T had NO CHOICE ANYMORE So he needed to be sure his friend Joey wouldn't get hurt by the Ruthless gorgeous Domme Patty, Who had already Collared him and was Using the confused Hung and Hypnotized 24-year-old Slave/Joey.

Domme Patty was now turning her Bi/curious Slave Joey into a Cuckold to be put on DISPLAY for her own amusement, also pleasing HER Domme/Anna at the same time, AND to show her Delicious Idol Carol just how Dominant DommePatty could be to get a taste of her.

Joey reminisced when Master T, along with his Pushcart working buddies Joey and Carmen, had a great time on weekends working LONG days together, having a few beers together, lunch together, OR bringing lunch to Alice's Condo on Cross St. next door to (Joe Candy's) Candy Store, when Alice hunted the Hung Trio down on Fridays and Saturdays to satisfy her Fetish of blowing the three Hung Young Men at once in a semi-circle being lightly slapped.

Alice would become DEMONIC-like, making growling noises, and loved her submissive Fetish that made her PussyCum Flow uncontrollably while she was passed around the room OR had her head passed by her hair to the next-to ten-inch cock, waiting to be sucked off standing over Alice In a half-circle while she made her loud growling noises with her mouth STUFFED with Hard young cock until she made us explode in her mouth.

ALL three of us would go back to work, leaving Alice in a PUDDLE of OUR CUM, HER OWN PUSSYCUM and her drooled saliva, literally from head to toe.

"SEE YOU THREE NEXT WEEK?" Alice would ask to plan out while putting on a dry blouse from her bedroom closet, where she just Sucked-Off three Huge ten-inchers on a Cum-soaked blanket.

"THIS IS DIFFERENT!" Pal Anthony tried to explain to Joey that Patty was Not Alice. NOT even close! and that Joey was under Patty's spell, although Joey LOVED the petite body on Patty and getting what he wanted, But Slave/Joey at the same time was being manipulated to GIVE WAY MORE of what Patty wanted than Joey got in return.

"Just give it some more thought, Joey," the Master/Mentor advised his BDism apprentice Joey. "DON'T fall in love with her, IF you haven't already! THAT'S The best way I can say it, my friend, this is NOT for everyone, I told you, and YOU can get hurt very badly. I DON'T want to see MY friends hurt If I can prevent it, and that's all, my friend. That's it, Joey," the Master concluded.

BUT IT IS TOO LATE! Joey thought to himself and didn't answer as Master T walked away to his day's agenda AND the only lifestyle ANTHONY had accepted with open arms for The past ten years Already. Master T DIDN'T know any other life NOR did he want to. His two Goddesses Auntie Anna and Cousin Carol WERE HIS LIFE NOW.

Deep down inside Master T Knew Patty wanted to be Intimately involved with her Co/Owners Master T and his Cousin Carol equally. Patty MAY even be more likely to want Carol's pussy EVEN MORE than cock from what the Master had seen from Patty already. SHE LOVED TO BE EATEN, AND LOVED TO EAT PUSSY EQUALLY, But Could Suck Dick better than most women could with her unmatched No-Gag Oral skills, and she Craved a Pussy Pounding that made her squirt intensely, So Patty was definitely Bi/Sexual.

Patty was Especially addicted to her Master's Oral skills and oversized long pointy Tongue since high school, when he teased her sticking his tongue up his nostrils, grossing the girls out in the cafeteria. Sometimes After school Patty would make out with Carol, then eat Carol out ALL afternoon while Cousin Anthony Licked Patty's Pussy clean-out, THEN His Cousin Carol's Pussy too while they sucked each other's nipples.

Cousin Anthony would get a "Double-header Blowjob" from BOTH the Bi/Curious Nympho teenagers SHARING his ten-incher to finish a perfect afternoon before all their parents got home from work.

There WAS a time when the fifteen-year-old Cousin/Anthony would Fuck BOTH of them side by side while they kissed, bending the Bi/Curious Sluts right over Carol's bed before Auntie Anna got home.

But NOW Patty needed permission and it was killing her to have to ASK Carol to share her Master/Cousin Anthony when Patty had him ALONE twice a week or even more WITH Carol included.

Patty would NEVER forget Master T rescuing her from her older abusive brother, who wouldn't let her go until he went to the house in person and threatened to throw her Brother out the 3rd-floor window, THEN the stubborn brother was Mysteriously beaten into a Coma AFTER MOVING HER OUT to Cousin Carol's and Mistress Auntie Anna Condo Unit.

THERE HAD BEEN ONLY ONE MAN FOR PATTY AFTER THAT, AND EVERYONE KNEW IT WAS NOT JOEY. Besides being a NATURAL Blonde Bombshell, Patty was intelligent, very Diabolical, and just WAITED HER TURN, Not rocking Goddess Carol's boat On such SMOOTH waters.

Today Was about to become another bad day concerning friends of the Domme's and nephew/Anthony when ONCE AGAIN Chief Detective Bobby Faucette would come knocking On the Sumner St. Facility in East Boston without a phone call first.

The Detective had seen the Corvette and knew Anthony OR his Aunt was available to answer "ONE QUESTION," as Bobby put it.

"Have You seen YOUR GOOD FRIEND, NICE GUY, NICKY FLEMIA, LATELY? Seems like NOBODY has seen Nicky since the 'BLACKFRIERS RESTAURANT MAS-SACRE,' Which NICKY FLEMIA is a Prime suspect in the Bloody Massacre of five men in the restaurant's basement, tying the infamous record Of 'The Boston Massacre,' the most men killed on one day in Boston's history, NOT a good Day!

"I already warned BOTH of you once, HE WAS a nice guy once, But stay away from him NOW. The word is NICKY is rip-ping off EVERY Cocaine dealer for his Expensive bad Coke habit! TELL your aunt to call me, please, I KNOW YOU WON'T!" said The pissed-off Head detective, concluding his warning, pointing his 18" infamous Flashlight/Billy club.

"WELL, HE won't come around HERE then, ALL WE DO IS MRI Scanning, NO DRUGS, SIR. But I'LL tell MY Aunt Anna you were asking for her. Have a nice day!" Master T Added to the disturbed Head Detective of East Boston's BUSY Drug unit.

It DID NOT take too long in a City like East Boston For Nicky to MEET HIS MATCH.

It seemed the word was out about Nicky ripping off Cocaine dealers and soon found Nicky DEAD soon after the BLACK-FRIERS Incident, putting a lot of people at ease. His bullet-rid-den body was found on Condor St. in East Boston by the Chelsea Creek's Filthy dirty water, it said in the Newspaper."

"People who live by the gun, Die by the gun," Auntie Anna and My Mom would tell me when they learned about their

OLD-SCHOOL FRIEND who "Once was a nice kid," they cried. "Some people just take a WRONG TURN at the fork in the road," as my Counselor once told me.

Being brought up in East Boston OR the North End of Boston, you could count the amount of people you could trust ON ONE HAND, the amount of people you could CALL, THAT WOULD SHOW UP AT 4 A.M. with bail money in their Pajamas for you, NOT counting the ONE at home waiting for you. She must never know about the trouble you're in, "For her own protection.

"ON THE OTHER HAND, if you lead a clean Vanilla life WITH SOME of your Darkside friends to explore with AND actually Enjoy exploring with, you have NO worries. JUST MAKE SURE YOU INCLUDE the one at home waiting in her panties for you to come home or Don't even keep her around, period.... She shouldn't have to wait around for you if She DON'T KNOW WHO YOU ARE, or who you crave to be!"

The Domme/Auntie Anna was the only one of those handful of people that were ALL of those people on one hand... (one) The ONE I would call FIRST, (two) the one to keep it quiet, (three) the ONE that was waiting in the wet panties, (four) The ONE I needed to keep exploring with, and (five) Auntie Anna KNEW exactly what I craved.

"Don't just do something to do it!" MY Fantasy Goddess Auntie would Always tell me, "Take it to the moon, my Nephew,

and Master it! Make it as good as it can be, Like YOU have Mastered Me," the Domme/My Auntie Anna would tell ME one more time!

The Worried Master was starting to face the reality now that His Fantasy Goddess Come true and His Vanilla real-life Auntie Anna that helped raise, guide, and groom him was retiring and getting sick At only 39 years old.

Carol could ALWAYS see the fascination, dedication AND Loyalty her young cousin Anthony had for her Gorgeous Mom. Carol KNEW that devotion could be easily transferred to her over time, WHICH Carol made sure of, BUT slowly, and carefully to ease the pain from her Soulmate Lover/Cousin IF her MommeDomme would finally say goodbye one day.

But only IF things changed and The Flawless Goddess made a turn for the worse and the Leukemia returned OR the Parkinson's Disease worsened, but everything was Fine, the Dr. said.

TO LOSE Auntie Anna would be another close-to-the-heart loss to a very young man of only 22 years old. So like a good Soulmate Carol NEEDED to reassure her Cousin Anthony, HER MASTER, Her Lover, HER business partner, that she would NEVER be going anywhere WITHOUT HIM. Too many close friends had left him TOO SOON already to a life of crime OR drug and alcohol Abuse, including his own Father that had Deserted his wife Joan, six-year-old Anthony and His three-year-old brother Steven that devastated them for life.

Carol was paying CLOSE ATTENTION to Patty's every move, however, being EXTRA cautious Domme Patty was NOT going to play the sympathy card, NOT ON CAROL'S WATCH!

Carol was standing behind HER Man, watching closely as he stirred his coffee in a daze, staring into the cup and thinking His Soulmate Cousin Carol knew exactly what was on his mind and picked up the phone to call her Mom.

"HI, MOM," Carol said loud enough for Cousin Anthony to turn quickly to glance at his young Goddess Carol. "SOMEONE wants to drive up today to check on you," Carol pleasantly told HER MommeDomme.

"LET ME SPEAK TO OUR WORRIED YOUNG MAN," Mistress Auntie Anna speaking loud enough to Carol for her groomed Nephew and Master to hear.

Goddess Carol handed the phone over to a nervous and worried Nephew, who began saying how many things were hitting him at once, and NOT being able to tell his Mistress about them, who was usually there to put his mind at ease every time.

Cousin Carol listened closely, stroking his thick black hair, also concerned about HER MOM, of course. But Momme and her soulmate Cousin were closer than ANY relationship could get that Carol had accepted for a while now.

But SLOWLY Goddess Cousin Carol WAS taking the groomed Nephew/Anthony's Leash and Collar From her Momme into HER Own hands Now.

"I'm going to take a nice ride in the Corvette to see you and get back here for dinner, MY STRICT GODDESS AND BOSS CAROL told me she's making my favorite meal tonight so she knows I'm coming back. Carol is making Scungilli Diavolo for dinner. Apparently She can cook too! Lol," Master/Nephew, now laughing, told his Goddess/Auntie Anna, but missing her badly.

"OK then, Do what she tells you now, you know better, YOU BELONG TO CAROL NOW!"

As Carol heard Momme's Dominating and Reassuring voice, Carol proudly smiled from ear to ear, finally letting Master's hair out from her fingers, and rushed to get Cousin Anthony's jacket and keys for the Yellow 1972, 4-speed, 454 ci, T-Top, Chevy Corvette.

Carol handed Over the keys and kissed her Gleaming Master/Cousin and Lover Anthony like she had never kissed him so early in the morning, long, wet and hard! Raising the Master's eyebrows as he replied, "WOW, I AM COMING BACK, YOU KNOW! lol," Anthony joked.

"I'll COME LOOKING for you IF YOU DON'T, lol," Witty Carol joked back. "Give a kiss to my Momme For me, please, and don't worry, SHE WILL BE FINE For a long time, Dr. Anastopalous said," Carol added, reassuring the worried Master of his Fantasy/Goddess Auntie Anna.

"I know, I know, I'm NOT used to seeing this yet, I guess, SHE Just seems so alive when we are there with her, and yet we know she HAS TO slow down," the Master told Carol in a confusing tone.

"Yes, I know, and WE will learn to live with it as we go along," Carol explained softly, hugging her Cousin, Lover, and Master before he left for the thirty-minute ride up to the Lake.

NO SOONER than her cousin pulled away in the Corvette, Patty came knocking on the way to work, saying, "I just passed the Master in the Corvette FLYING up Rte. 1, What's Up!" Curious Patty asked a Heated-Up Goddess Carol.

Carol, still smiling ear to ear, told Patty, "JUST RUN ME A BATH, I GOT SOMETHING FOR YOU TO DO WHILE YOU BLOW BUBBLES in the water," Carol said, pinching Patty's protruding nipples in her thin summer blouse.

"MMmmmm, REALLY, so early in the morning, My Mistress Carol?" Patty added, smiling.

"OH, YAH! I'M SOAKING WET THIS MORNING!! I'll need My short whip this morning for those hard pink nipples while your mouth is busy blowing bubbles, lol," Carol giggled. "IT'S A BEAUTIFUL MORNING!!" Carol shouted out to a very confused Domme Patty, who was about to be Dommed and Whipped herself in a big way by her Idol Mistress/Goddess Carol. Patty would be slurping plenty of Carol's Multi/Mango this morning to wake Patty up and keep her quiet while the Brunette Goddess guided Patty's head by her Blonde Ponytail.

Derry, N.H., from East Boston IS about thirty miles, @ 60 MPH is thirty minutes, BUT in a Corvette @ 90 MPH you can do it in twenty, especially if you're "Eager to Please" your Goddess.

The Domme and Evelyn were sitting Outside by the Stream, watching as a bobcat looked on at them from across the Stream from Henry Onessimo's Property, when the bobcat was scared off from the roaring 454 Yellow Corvette that pulled up to the Sexiest Semi-Retired couple ever.

The 38-year-old Italian Silky Black-haired Goddess DIDN'T even have a grey hair yet. The Domme's complexion was still flawless, It was Domme Anna's INSIDES that were the concern.

Fully Retirement Partner For life, 44-year-old Evelyn Had a few Greys that blended beautifully into her Strawberry-Blonde Professionally Styled Hair-Do from Newbury St.

Evelyn was a Naturally light-skinned beauty, NO freckles, NO wrinkles, NO Extra makeup, just enough for her green eyes and full set of lips, Just STUNNING for 44, STILL with an hourglass figure, firm DDs and marble-sized Nipples for The Domme's Sadistic Fetish of "BITING" that the Masochistic red-headed Evelyn went wild for.

Evelyn dressed In Taylor-made Corset Skirt suits, ALWAYS showing off her Hour-Glass body for The Domme to take notice, just like Mistress Anna ALSO dressed to "Slay her Prey."

TODAY, THE MASTER WAS IN FOR A TREAT WITH MASOCHISTIC EVELYN.

"YOU SCARED THE CAT!" Shouted the excited Domme AuntieAnna, laughing.

Evelyn was in a revealing skin-tight one-piece bathing suit, looking BETTER than a 22-year-old (half her age). His awaiting

39-year-old Mistress Auntie Anna was in the latest Tailor-made Body summer suit looking just as old as her 22-year old daughter.

"We were having coffee and cake and the Cat wanted some, lol," the Domme joked to her nephew, SO happy to see her.

IT WAS OBVIOUS that They were SO excited to see Master T as well, who was now their ROCK more than ever before. Evelyn was so visibly excited that her hard pink marble-sized nipples were protruding right through her one-piece spandex swimsuit as she took Master T by one hand.

Master's Fantasy Goddess Auntie Anna took her Nephew/Master's other hand and strutted her walk close by his Loyal side! The two Goddesses had been waiting patiently for him to arrive and loyal Nephew wouldn't let them down Just as he promised already, WITH PERMISSION from now on.

EVERYONE KNEW, especially The Domme/Auntie Anna, that her nephew Anthony's WORD WAS written with his blood, WHEN HE SAID HE WOULD DO SOMETHING, IT WAS 99.99, IT WOULD GET DONE, Especially NOW in Auntie Anna's uncertain health. HE had come to realize together through the eyes of his lifelong Soulmate and 1st Cousin Carol that her Momme needed rest and medication to keep her alive for as long as they could.

Each of eager Cock-Starving, Bi-sexuals now sexually PEAKING Cougars held their much younger 22-year-old Stud/Master tight between them as they sat him down together to passionately kiss him. They wasted no time fondling him, unzipping

his bulging Sicily jeans and caressing the Hard Nephew's bare muscular chest, unbuttoning his shirt, Together.

The first soft kiss was from His Goddess, now only a Submissive Auntie Anna, THEN a second wet kiss of passion to her Nephew that would show him just how much HIS Goddess had missed his touch, having him only occasionally, But now was with Carol's permission.

Waiting For Evelyn's turn to be kissed, Evelyn slowly rubbed her Mistress Anna's Master's toned masculine biceps and chest with permission, waiting for her Lover/Goddess Anna to pass her HARD ten-inch Nephew over to Evelyn to kiss.

"Mmmm," replied the Very wet Evelyn, taking Domme Anna's Stud Nephew as he was passed to Evelyn's waiting arms. "Have you been working out, Master T?" Evelyn said, caressing his toned-out chest, then kissed his hot wet lips, lowering her hand to his six-pack abs.

"I always work out a little in the morning, But I have a feeling I'M IN FOR A REAL WORKOUT THIS MORNING, lol," Master T joked.

French kissing Evelyn right back in a kissing frenzy, His Sub/Slut Goddess Aunt caressed HER Nephew on his lower back, grazing across his firm young bubble ass with her skilled fingers and softly onto his hole. Evelyn ran her fingers through Master's long, thick black wavy hair but had HIS HARD COCK in the other hand while STILL French Kissing him a bit harder and deeper again and again. Seemed Nephew Anthony AND Evelyn LOVED to kiss a lot!

Master T Already knew this was going to be A DAY TO RE-
MEMBER when his dripping-wet Mistress Auntie Anna began
to remove Evelyn's one-piece suit slowly, lowering Evelyn down
to her knees in the streaming brook while Evelyn was licking the
Master's NIPPLES, down to his hard flat belly, STILL holding
his hard 10" Cock in Evelyn's hand, now tapping his long Hard
Dick onto her DDs as Evelyn was being forced down to her knees
to "BLOW HIM," the Goddess told her Masochist Evelyn.

The Hard Nephew's Goddess Auntie Anna was now French
kissing him, Sucking on his oversized tongue (ONE OF her favorites) while Evelyn was Sucking her Nephew/Master's Hard
Cock deeper than he could EVER remember from Evelyn,
"Throating" ten inches ALL the way.

Evelyn was now Deepthroating ALL 10" inches while kneeling in the Brook and partially sitting on a flat rock, getting her
Red hair pulled and slapped lightly by BOTH the Master and his
now Sub/Slave Aunt Anna.

They were ALL READY TO GO INSIDE to tie Evelyn up
for some Sadistic torture play that Evelyn enjoyed from the
Master and her Bi/Lover Domme Anna, Who also loved to watch
Evelyn being "USED" by Domme Patty as well, but Not today.

"THE DOMME" ANNA LOVED HER LOVER EVELYN
TO ENJOY herself when she was squirting like a water hose all
over everyone and Everything. The two middle-aged Bi/Sexual
Nymphomaniacs were sexual PEAKING.

THEY DID LOVE TO FUCK, although they preferred the tongue mostly for a more INTENSE Multiple/Orgasm as Mistress Auntie Anna said before at her Office while fucking my face into a river of her hot Pussycum, SHOWING ME the difference!!

Master T had made an arrangement with his Goddess Aunt and Evelyn that "ON OCCASION," He would drive up to "Serve" his BDISM /Goddess AND her Masochist lover Evelyn and for them to Share the Master/Nephew to one another. Co/Owner Carol WOULD NOT question the visits To Momme/Domme as long as HE WAS BACK IN TIME FOR DINNER!...period.

Cousin Carol's Collared and Owned Master WOULD BE SURE to make it home in time for dinner to his soulmate with a gift from MommeDomme FOR BEING SO UNDERSTANDING.

Although A normal vanilla person may NOT think anything special or kinky about Carol's Cousin/Master leaving to go visit his Aunt OR, Mother-In-law OR Boss that he worked for, Nor a visit from Carol's best friend and employee Patty just stopping by to say "What's Up" right after morning's coffee, then winding up being whipped and sexually used, These Fetish-providing Kinksters were NOT EVEN CLOSE to a Normal Vanilla life.

Goddess/Domme Auntie Anna and her gorgeous Red-head partner Evelyn were FEEDING the 22-year-old stud Nephew continuous Multiple FruitiD'Mango Orgasms, going wild watching him swallow, making gulping and gagging noises to please the Goddess even More.

Evelyn was going WILD for Master's Big Cock now that since she DIDN'T have her husband AT ALL anymore and STILL enjoyed a nice Pussy Pounding, OR in her Ass as well.

Evelyn was also impressed with the Master's Oral skills and lasting stamina. Evelyn was MORE OPEN when the Nephew was ALONE with Evelyn, and He was not visiting with Carol OR the staff.

Evelyn also now showed she was a proud Deepthroater like Patty to Master's surprise (NOT MANY woman can deepthroat ten inches without gagging), Evelyn had given Master T a SAMPLE BlowJob performance to show him what to expect from now on, WHENEVER HE VISITED ALONE to be Shared.

Evelyn could see the Passion, Love and LOYALTY that the hung Nephew had for his Domme Aunt Anna, So Evelyn was thinking ahead and wanted SOME of that same Devotion as well. If things took a turn for the worse for their Goddess Anna, Daughter Goddess/Carol had already agreed to take Evelyn in IF Evelyn was to be alone.

Boss/Goddess Carol had Domme Patty BATHE her as soon as their Master drove away to see his Domme Aunt Anna and Carol was Dominating a Submissive Patty in a very Juicy session, whipping Patty's ass as Patty Lapped-Up Carol's Nectar from her flowing Mango Tree.

The spoiled and somewhat Jealous Goddess Cousin Carol was squeezing Patty's head with her toned powerhouse thighs. Patty knew NOT to move until her Idol Goddess Carol was pleased, releasing ALL her hot sweet Mango, then licking her clean.

Goddess Carol NEEDED to show Domme Patty that Carol was BossDomme now and that "Master T BELONGS TO CAROL, HE IS COLLARED" and Owned by Carol now. The ONLY exception to use his services without permission WAS MOMME!...Period.

Patty had ALREADY accepted the fact She would have to wait for her turn, SHARING the Master in three-ways, OR in FULL SWAPS with Joey and the occasional invites from Carol, but NOW today.

Today while in the bath Patty was "Feeling it" as a Dominant Carol showed through giving her best friend a Dominant "Multiple/Squirting Orgasm" that Patty had been addicted to since high school and still craved to be Used-Up by the Goddess Brunette with Unique Huge nipples.

Protective Cousin Carol showed Strict DOMINANCE to Patty to protect "HER PROPERTY."

The blonde bombshell Patty had been Bi/Carol's GO-TO Female as well, only now with Monique a VERY CLOSE second, and invited over on weekends now, SO PATTY BETTER BE MORE CAREFUL what she did OR said around the STRICT, Protective, Boss/Goddess Carol, gradually becoming more and more like her mentor MommeDomme.

Cousin/Anthony Stopped for gas for the gas-guzzling 454 Corvette and made a phone call to Carol at the pay phone to say he was on his way and asked if Carol needed anything, and also to say her Momme was fine and sent her love.

"I LOVE YOU! Very much, You do know that, right?" the guilty Used-Up Cousin Anthony curiously asked his soulmate for life, which melted Carol's heart, and the witty but ALSO guilty Drained-Out DOMINANT Goddess Carol responded right back, "I LOVE YOU MORE."

Master T could smell the Ossobucco "Veal shanks" roasting In the oven, along with the homemade burgundy wine brown gravy Carol had Mastered FOR Her Master T. He immediately went to the oven and opened it, then PRAISED his awaiting FemDomme soulmate Cousin for life.

"THE BEST SO FAR!" Master yelled out to Carol, looking over her Journal, "and YOU smell great too. Is that YOUR new Special Bubble Bath Oil you bought?" the Master curiously asked.

"Yes, it is, I took a VERY SPECIAL, very relaxing Bath today while YOU were out," Carol said, smiling as she deviously sniffed Momme's Shalimar Perfume from her Master/Cousin's chest.

Goddess Carol had become an Excellent Italian cook by any vanilla life Standards acquired from Old Italian/Sicilian family recipes handed down from both Cousins' Grandmothers.

During their PRIVATE dinner for a change Carol mentioned that Monique was on the payroll ninety days now, according to "HER NEW JOURNAL," and needed to call Monique in for EVALUATION as Carol promised Monique when "SIR" acquired the talented MRI scanning specialist when Monique was persuaded AND Hypnotized by Carol's beauty to leave BIDMC.

Although Monique was more impressed with Carol's beauty and see-through blouse, along with the PERKS Monique was introduced to on that special presentation day by the Dominating Duo, Goddess/Carol and Domme/Patty.

Monique WAS ALL IN and Comfortable with "SIR Inc." since Carol and Patty gave her exactly WHAT MONIQUE HAD BEEN MISSING for years.

Monique was GIVEN "Multiple/Orgasms" Via Domination during an unforgettable two-on-one Bondage session at their New Facility.

THAT would be the Day Monique would discover her "Masochistic Darkside" promised to be explored even MORE once she was "Collared and Owned" as promised by the younger Goddess Carol, which DID happen very soon after.

Only one day after meeting the two young beauties, Carol in particular would become a sexually addictive craving for Monique TO BE THE SUBMISSIVE MASOCHISTIC SLUT/SLAVE SHE CRAVED TO BE! Monique NEEDED to be under Carol's Complete Control.

"WE need to spend MORE time with Monique Privately. Is that OK with you, My love, My Master?" Carol asking for permission. "Monique IS OUR dedicated Masochistic beauty that needs a LOT of attention, SHE IS one of the best in her field and I persuaded Monique to come on board. So now I need to keep MY promise to make her stay," Carol pleaded to her Master for permission to SHARE the Masochist Monique on some

weekends. "WE have been so busy to appreciate Monique and Alice, and this week WE need to TREAT Them right, You OK with that, Master?" Carol concluded with a wet kiss.

"YOU'RE THE BOSS," Master T quickly agreed. "I'M there for you, just have a plan in place and I'll make sure it's done this week," Master assured his Goddess, and Boss/Carol.

"Awesome, Thank You, MY love, I'll call Monique tonight to make plans and put her mind at ease, AND FANTASIZING, lol," Carol Joked. "Also, my love, Set SOMETHING up for Alice as well with Phil LaBella and his Golf buddies from your Lynn-field Golf Club at a nearby motel on Rte. 1 'OUTCALL' so they DON'T come here and hang out all night in OUR Lounge," Carol suggested to her lover/Cousin. "Give Alice half Of Phil's billing in cash when she's done, But Alice won't want the money, JUST MORE DICKS TO SUCK! Lol. Keep a GOOD EYE on Phil and his buddies with her, please!" Goddess Carol joked.

"OF COURSE! I'll hold PHIL RESPONSIBLE if they act up, they're his buddies, and I WILL KEEP MY EYE ON ALICE as always," her Master told Goddess /Boss Carol, Who was now SHOWING A far more Dominating presence than ever.

"Especially today in the bath," Carol began to tell Her Love and Master. "I feel like I'M BECOMING my DommeMomme in EVERY WAY," Carol began to tell her Cousin Anthony/ Master T, wrapping her arms around him, giving him a spank on his bubble butt, and explained just how much.

Carol whispered in her kissing Cousin's ear, "She enjoyed whipping Patty today in the bath when she showed up unexpectedly and asked ME why Master Flew past her in the Corvette.

I didn't answer Patty for prying, I only wanted her to run ME a hot bath, like she did for my Momme, and then the words just came out," Carol admitted to her Master.

"WASH ME and EAT ME," while I slapped and whipped her ass and big tits, then I pulled her hair while Patty drank ALL My Juice.

"The ONLY person I want Dominating ME, IS YOU, SIR, MY MASTER!" Carol whispered into his ear. "DO YOU THINK I WAS TOO CRUEL TO HER TODAY? OR WAS I TOO PROTECTIVE TOWARDS YOU when Patty asked about MY Man, MY Master?" Carol added.

"YOU ARE YOUR MOMME! Lol," Carol's Master said jokingly. "You have ALWAYS been protecting ME from Patty, which you don't have to anymore, EVER! I'm just Happy when YOU'RE NOT mad at Me! But you DID smell great after that bath, lol," He joked. "I SEE You are Enjoying yourself being the Dominant one watching your Subs ENJOY being under your control. That makes YOU enjoy Dominating your willing Submissives, I KNOW I LOVE IT," Master T added. "YOUR MOM HAS THAT GIFTED DOMME PERSONALITY, and YOU DO TOO, YOU'RE JUST SEEING IT NOW," the Master added to his Domme/Soulmate Carol.

"YES, I AM just seeing it now, I seen it in ME big time today in the bath overtaking Domme Patty, Submitting so EASILY to my commands. I can't wait to get Monique over here with us, Master, WE WILL HAVE OUR MASOCHIST MONIQUE SCREAMING," the Delicious, Devious, Domme/Carol added with a wet kiss in conclusion.

"Just call Monique now if it makes you feel better. Tell her to come for DESSERT after this Delicious Ossobuco you cooked up, and Thank you very much for that," Master T said. "I'll follow your lead with Monique, YOU TAKE CONTROL TONIGHT, ALL THE WAY, EVEN WITH ME, OK?" Carol's Master insisted, wetting Cousin Carol's panties. "I'll have MY turn with you as always, BUT I WANT YOU BAD RIGHT NOW! I'LL BE IN THE SHOWER WAITING, OK?" Master Begged.

"OH, YES!" Carol all visibly excited was Ready to Give her Cousin/Master "A GOLDEN SHOWER" that the Kinky Cousin was hinting for, and quickly undressed after drinking down three glasses of water for his kinky request and Favorite Fetish.

Carol made the call to the overwhelmed Masochist, and within the hour Monique was at their door with an overnight bag as requested by the Collared Slave Monique's Mistress/Owner Mistress/Domme Carol TOLD Monique, "She would be spending the night with BOTH Cousins, Maybe the whole weekend," causing her Red-hairs to stand up on the back of her neck and soaked her panties.

Carol took Monique's Gucci overnight bag from her and kissed her slow and deeply at the door, apologizing for neglecting her for a while, making Monique even wetter since the phone-call an hour earlier, when she was creaming from Carol's overnight invite, and Monique would be SHARED with Cousin/Master T in a three-way sex-marathon, pushing her Masochistic limits.

Monique actually had Creamed right in her panties while on the phone from her first Command from BDism Goddess Carol to SPEND THE NIGHT with her AND Master T.

The Plan WAS for Master T to be IN the walk-in shower as Monique was taken downstairs by Goddess Cousin Carol, where the S&M supplies and equipment were kept neatly hung on the walls.

Whips, Crops, Paddles, Nipple clamps, Rope and Restraints were chosen TO BOUND AND TIE MONIQUE to the Massage table, the WHEEL of torture, and In the Harness SWING.

But first Carol wanted Monique in a sexy fitted corset to show off those Inch-long nipples that WOULD BE clamped, Sucked on, pinched, nibbled, bitten and slapped ALL night Until morning by BOTH Kinkster Cousins Master T, and Goddess Domme/Carol, "A Masochist's Dream Session"... OUCH!

Master T wanted his Golden Shower in the Dominating Style Domme/Auntie Anna had provided for his Favorite Fetish For years and that Patty AND daughter had been taught by the MommeDomme.

COUSIN CAROL WOULD MASTER THE TABOO PISS FETISH NOW FOR "HER MAN, LOVER AND MASTER."

"NOBODY ELSE! EVER! GABEESH?" CAROL OR-DERED WHILE CAROL STOOD OVER COUSIN AN-THONY, YELLING THOSE WORDS AS SHE PEED, HOLDING HER MASTER'S MOUTH OPEN WHILE MO-NIQUE WAS WATCHING IN AMAZEMENT.

MONIQUE WAS THEN ORDERED TO "COME HERE, MY SLUT/SLAVE" BY THE DOMINATING GOD-DESS CAROL.

"ONLY WITH MY PERMISSION!" CAROL WAS POINTING TO A STARTLED MONQUE AS MONIQUE LISTENED TO THE HEAVY STREAM OF SALTY YEL-LOW RAIN AS GODDESS CAROL'S HOT PISS FILLED MASTER'S OPENED MOUTH.

DOMME CAROL POINTED AND ORDERED MO-NIQUE TO SQUAT OVER HER COUSIN'S FACE AND PEE, TEACHING MONIQUE TO FOLLOW ORDERS, AND HOW TO "GIVE" A GOLDEN SHOWER, AS WELL AS "RECEIVING."

DOMME CAROL NOW DEMANDED TO HER SUB/MASTER, "SWALLOW IT," HOLDING HIS MOUTH SHUT AND HIS ARMS BEHIND HIM TIGHTLY AS HER SUBMISSIVE MASTER SWALLOWED TWO WHOLE MOUTHFULS OF GODDESS CAROL'S AND COLLARED SLAVE MONIQUE'S HOT SALTY PEE.

"YOU MAY GET UP NOW," JUST LIKE THE MOM-MEDOMME/ANNA HAD TAUGHT PATTY WHILE

CAROL WATCHED HER DO TO "EDDY SHOWERS" DUGAN ONE DAY.

Monique was in total shock, Cumming uncontrollably as she was forced down on her knees while her Owner/Goddess Carol and her Cousin/Master T began to pee on her beautiful hard inch-long nipples and a tease taste to her lips. The Demanding Domme Carol told her Master/Cousin immediately to lick the hot salty pee Off her big tits while nibbling the long thick nipples on a Firm 36C cup, slapping the hot pee onto her face.

MONIQUE WAS LOVING IT! And this was just the beginning of the night that was to come for the Masochist Monique in her glory tonight, SERVING her Owner Goddess Carol.

The Kinkster Kissing Cousins brought Monique upstairs to bed after Using her in more PeePlay AND more Foreplay. The Cousins BATHED Monique, poured her a glass of wine that Monique sipped as they BOTH kissed her Softly, but slapped her Hard!

"OMG, YES! I can't stop cumming, Mistress Carol! I JUST WANT MORE!" Monique cried out loud, grabbing onto Carol's Long legs as Goddess Carol approached Monique on her knees, who was BLOWING Master T and just waiting to be USED by her Goddess Carol next.

Goddess/Mistress Carol had done it AGAIN for Monique! Taking a SHOCKED Monique deep into Monique's Masochistic Darkside, NEVER to return to Vanilla sex ever again!

Master T AND Carol Fucked Monique into multiple orgasms ALL NIGHT while they Slapped, Clamped, Nipple tortured,

Fisted BOTH her holes, then forced Monique to eat Carol's Constant Squirting of her Mango, OR Master's Cum with her hair being pulled while he jerked off on her face for Cousin Carol to lick off, only to CUMSWAP French-kissing Monique SPIT-TING Master's load in Monique's mouth.

CHAPTER

24

Master T woke up to the smell of Monique cooking breakfast for her BDism owners Mistress Carol and Monique's Master as well, with Carol's permission, of course!

Goddess Carol's smiling face said it all, looking into her Cousin's opening eyes to see her face, the ONLY face he wanted to wake up to, until He didn't wake up again.

"I LOVE YOU, you know that, right?" the convincing purple-eyed Goddess Cousin Carol whispered inches from his ear.

"I LOVE YOU MORE" the Curious Master whispered back, "YOU were Fantastic last night as YOU ALWAYS ARE, but yesterday was like WOW! All day long. Starting from the morning YOU were the Strict Domme you crave to be," Cousin/lover Anthony told his Rising Domme Carol with a long morning kiss.

Monique knocked On the opened door to say, "Goodbye and Thank You for a wonderful evening, and breakfast was on the table," Monique said. "I be here exactly as I was told, Mistress Carol, EVERY Saturday Night for dinner following the 1st of every month for an overnight session with just the three of us, I WILL BE LOOKING FORWARD TO IT MORE THAN YOU KNOW!" As The visibly excited Masochist Monique concluded with a kiss to both of her S&M Kinksters and was off to work at SIR Inc.

Monique's inch-long nipples were visibly bruised, swollen to twice the size from the clamping, slapping, whipping and biting them to Monique's approval, submitting to be Used and Bruised for the night at the request of her Owner/Domme Carol in Full control.

Carol's Cousin Anthony/Master T followed Carol's Orders, dominating the session with HER NEW SLAVE Monique, and DID exactly whatever his Goddess 1st Cousin made him do.

Domme Carol got the approval she needed from Master T to USE Anyone SHE wanted for sexual satisfaction (Male OR Female) as long as Spoiled Cousin Carol "SHARED."

The Domme/Auntie Anna was still OK for now with NO advancement of the Parkinson's WE would have to watch for, NO leukemia rebounding, which was our worst fear.

Evelyn was breaking loose and VERY COMFORTABLE around her Mistress' Nephew Anthony/Master T as HE was also COMFORTABLE around Evelyn and were BONDING to-

gether with PERMISSION, of course, while caring for the Domme of all Dommes, "Goddess/Anna."

MASTER-T WAS NOW GIVING EVELYN EVERY-THING SHE NEEDED, TO BE THE NATURAL-BORN MASOCHIST SHE CRAVED TO BE!

Retired Partner and Masochistic lover Evelyn to the Sadistic Domme/Anna were the PERFECT couple!

Goddess/Auntie Anna's Nephew ENJOYED SERVING BOTH Cock-Starved Bi-Sexual Lovers joining in weekly sessions, taking full control of their Special three-way sessions when the Master was Called-on to SERVE, inducing the two Pussy Lovers INTENSE SQUIRTING when Domme/Auntie Anna SUBMITTED into becoming "A SECOND MASOCHIST" Locked-On to Evelyn's Pussy, taunting her Hung Nephew and Master every week now, telling him, "DO WHATEVER YOU WANT TO ME! FUCK ME LIKE AN ANIMAL!"

"YOU'RE A FUCKING ANIMAL!" driving the Domme's 22-year-old Groomed Nephew WILD Fucking and whipping "TWO" eager, Submissive, Masochistic Sluts into multiple-orgasms for hours, screaming and SQUIRTING their MANGO-JUICE All over Everyone and everything!

Meanwhile, Patty was STILL patient to get her turn with her Master and USED a very confused Joey to get at him. But Patty had a lot on her plate at work, NOW IN CHARGE of Massage Therapy, along with discreet CASH MONEY Fetish Providing for ALL kinkster clients, "Old and New."

Boss/Goddess Carol had Patty supervising ongoing MRI Physical Therapy referrals with Monique, Alice, and Carmen ALL WEEK LONG, taking up ALL her personal time as well.

CAROL HAD PATTY SO BUSY WITH HER WORK SCHEDULE, Patty worked singing, "EIGHT DAYS A WEEK!" LIKE THE NEW BEATLES HIT! The only shot Patty had using Master's lizard tongue and big dick would have to be at the weekly Business Board Meetings for the Infatuated Domme Patty, and We all knew THAT WAS NOT HAPPENING on Carol's watch.

Allie and Lenny CALLED TRYING DESPERATELY to get a session from Carol's busy agenda set schedule, but WANTED ALLIE as an employee now and making Allie wait.

"MAYBE," Allie kindly responded to a desperate and busy BossDomme Carol, So ONLY "limited one-hr. sessions" are set instead of three-hr. marathons for the Bi/weekly Fetish kinkster Couple UNTIL Carol got Allie "On Board" to Take-On some Special Kink Clients!

Allie was HOT, Dominant, Young, and fit right in with the other girls. Allie even had her Own Collared Hubby Bi/Lenny to work with in SOME Special sessions as well. The kinkster Couple were PERFECT Fetish Providers, especially with Millionaire Paul Travello and his Kinky wife Grace, OR Eddy "Showers" Dugan that Allie liked her Slave/Husband "Topping."

Eddy Dugan a/k/a "EddyShowers" was scheduled with Lenny soon in a Coming-Out tribute for Allie and Domme Patty to Instruct in a one-hour session very soon.

Phil LaBella of MGH and three eager buddies were ALL SET with Alice with Master T to supervise this weekend IN THE COUNTRY CLUB'S CONFERENCE ROOM to be sucked off by cock-lover Alice.

Special requests were handled by Collared Monique and her younger Owner/Goddess Carol at a MUCH HIGHER rate!... With permission, of course!

Trisha Sullivan, the Hot CEO From Shrafts Chocolate Co. with the incredible big cock/clit who Monique shared some MangoCumJuice with, was also down for a scheduled FULL TREATMENT. Trisha wanted two Hung Studs from the Club to rub her down slow and easy, But Fuck her HARD in a Dou-blePenetration (DP) style, THEN to have her oversized Cock/Clit Sucked real good until she squirted, giggling to Carol over the phone.

"IF Monique is available HAVE HER THERE, PLEASE, VIP," Trisha Added, giggling.

Donna Sullivan, the Greek Goddess with the European Ass like Carol's, and a sexy voice that made Carol wet, was ALSO making plans for the weekend to visit Club Paradisa for a FULL 2hr TREATMENT.... CAROL WAS STRAIGHT OUT BUSY AND CALLED MOMME!

MommeDomme advised her Stressed-Out Boss/Goddess daughter, AND her groomed Nephew to GET ONE MORE HOT YOUNG BEAUTY on board at this NEW "Club Paradisa."

"LET THEM do all the sessions and YOU TWO just do

the scheduling and Billing. You're creating a Mountain of Legal Paperwork, AND quarterly TAX reports to prepare for now.

ENJOY EACH OTHER AND KEEP UP!" the older and wiser Goddess explained over the phone to her Younger Domme Daughter, who was Loving it all while Her Cousin and Master kept a close eye on his Insatiable Soulmate Goddess. Always!

Carol LOVED being involved with a whip in her hand, and her Master LOVED watching Carol fulfilling a Fetish for Her Special clients to its FULLEST, NO LESS WOULD DO!

"Carol, YOU have become your Mom 'ALL THE WAY,'" Master Joked. "The ONLY difference I see is YOUR NIPPLES are MUCH bigger, like plums are to strawberries, and THAT'S ABOUT IT, Lol," Cousin/Anthony added while turning her around in amazement, "Yup! Same Ass." As They enjoyed a laugh together. "But your Momme is absolutely right, you know, You CAN'T be in two places at the same time. YOU Make the arrangements, YOU do the billing and to what Company OR person, YOU make sure the clients are happy with Our services. IF YOU DECIDE WE SHOULD PARTICIPATE WITH A SPECIAL CLIENT, WE WILL, With YOUR permission, of course, AND I WILL WATCH OUT FOR OUR CREW."

Master T convincingly talked softly in her ear in his deep voice that drove his Gorgeous soulmate wild. Carol was listening closely,

leaning into her Hard Lover as He massaged her shoulders, teasing her huge nipples while talking into her HOT ear from taking calls ALL DAY.

"YES! I KNOW, You and Momme are right, BUT 'IF' I WANT TO HAVE FUN WITH CERTAIN CLIENTS, YOU WILL ACCOMMODATE ME?" the curious Goddess Carol added to her Rock/Cousin Anthony.

"IN A HEARTBEAT! YOU MAKE MY HEART BEAT," Cousin/Anthony Sincerely said, Then kissed her hot neck softly, sliding his fingers slowly down into Carol's partially unbuttoned silk blouse to softly twist her hardening puffy nipple.

"They DO expect ME to be there now when they come In to Club Paradisa seeking their Fetish OR Fantasy that I have Promised them I would provide to them. YOU STAY CLOSE BY, IF OR WHEN I NEED YOU, OK, MY LOVE, MY MASTER?" As his Goddess/Cousin Carol thanked him for Permission to Participate in SOME Sessions.

"ANYTHING YOU WANT, just slow down like your Momme said, AND I also suggest you do so from your stressful agenda, TOO MUCH IS NOT GOOD for YOU, as it IS GOOD for business," Carol's Master advised to protect his busy Goddess Carol from a breakdown.

"Thank You For the massage, My Love, lol," Carol joked. "I won't take-on too much anymore, I promise You and Momme," Carol concluded, all visibly excited while she rebuttoned her tailor-made Versace' silk blouse.

The Non-stop BossDomme Carol had convinced Cousin An-thony/Master that she would only be involved "Hands On" with CERTAIN Club Paradisa Members at Carol's Private Club brainstorm for Woman VIPs In Powerful Corporate positions... OR wealthy business Women.

Powerful Women Like to talk with OTHER powerful women (JUST LIKE PIG MEN DO) as MommeDomme once told Carol that she once told Evelyn, now semi-retired Lovers.

Today TWO Of those Powerful VIP women had scheduled their weekend "Spa-Massage" Pampering-Perks that would be billed to their Company expense account.

Trisha Sullivan, CEO at Shrafts Chocolate Co., had already been introduced into Goddess Carol's BDism world the day Carol brought Monique with her for the Club Paradisa presentation, teasing Trisha, flaunting two very unique sets of nipples on the two Goddesses Trisha had NEVER seen before, soaking Trisha immediately, CRAVING TO SUCK BOTH of the impeccably dressed stunning ladies.

Trisha Sullivan was straight sexually and had NEVER craved another woman's Pussy Or Breasts before that day, BUT TRISHA HAD NURSED FROM BOTH OF THESE BEAUTIES THAT DAY, and couldn't stop suckling on BOTH of their unique nipples like a crying HUNGRY baby needing to satisfy their "HUNGER," as did Trisha while Goddess Carol held her head in close.

Trisha DESPERATELY wanted to be collared now by the in-credible Goddess Carol and enter the lifestyle Carol was intro-

ducing to the Craving Trisha, just as her Momme had introduced the lifestyle to her AND her Cousin Anthony, who had Mastered BOTH Mother AND Daughter now.

Trisha was hypnotized by Carol's beauty and Insatiable sex drive to Dominate and Discipline women AND Men, something Trisha had NEVER seen before, With permission, of course!

Donna Puopolis, VP at General Electric in Lynn, Mass., had Insatiable Carol hypnotized with her sexy Greek broken English voice over the phone when Carol left a message for Donna to call her back about the VIP Cub Paradisa.

Goddess Carol met with Donna soon after for an Ass comparison by her Master to witness. It seemed as though these two gifted Ass enthusiasts shared a similar interest, "ANAL SEX," And BOTH of them had awesome meaty heart-shaped Asses to take a Big Dick with ease.

Donna was practically Limitless to Pain from ASS spankings/Flogging/whipping/paddles, etc. DONNA LOVED IT ALL when it came to ANAL SEX (and So did ANAL SLUT CAROL!).

Donna and Carol already took an ANAL pounding By Master T and Joey, and now DONNA HAD RETURNED FOR MORE, requesting weekly scheduled sessions, the voluptuous Greek Goddess with a perfect European Ass had requested two of the well-hung young men in the brochure for today's session at "Club Paradisa."

Today Master T AND Carmen would "DP" Donna's Ass While Carol fed Donna her plum-sized nipples Donna had adamantly requested as well, Carol WANTED DONNA'S MAN-GOJUICE real bad. While Donna was being DP'd in her ass just inches away From Carol's mouth, kinky Cousin Carol wanted to be Eating-Out Donna's dripping pussy, making sure BOTH COCKS were being held deep in Donna's lubed-up ASSHOLE for an "ANAL DP" FantasyFuck.

Donna told Carol about her old "Massage Palace" in Lynn, MA, that had been closed down. The massage parlor was caught giving handjob happy endings and NOT paying off the Lynn police. Four Asian women worked all day in three shifts in a nice quaint building with two huge Redwood saunas and an Inground jacuzzi seating eight people, Donna explained.

"POOR GIRLS, now they have nothing and I still need my weekly massage relaxing in their private spotless place. I'M so glad YOU came along, IN MORE WAYS THAN ONE!" Donna giggled.

Carol, listening very closely, was SO INTERESTED in hearing of these Masseuses not working, AND wondering about the Equipment in the closed-down massage parlor. So Goddess Carol asked Donna for their number to talk about hiring a few of the out-of-work licensed Masseuses and Maybe even BUY-OUT the business for all the equipment, especially the two Redwood Saunas with Lava stones for steam that caught Carol's interest.

The Genius/Goddess Carol wanted to get the equipment to East Boston at the facility to fully equip the second floor with the two Redwood Saunas, a full bar/lounge, Big TV screens, a Jacuzzi with PRIVATE dim-lit rooms, making THE ENTIRE SECOND FLOOR "Club Paradisa" AND THAT WAS JUST WHAT GENIUS/GODDESS CAROL DID!!

Carol had called the number on a business card Donna gave her, and within a week Carol HIRED two of the four HOT younger Brazilian Masseuses, and bought the two Redwood sauna stalls and installed them in her building In East Boston.

The two NEW Brunette Beauties were WARNED, BRIEFED, SCARED and INFATUATED all at the same time, by The Domme Anna, THEN by Domme Patty, and finally by Boss Goddess Carol, who told the two stunned gorgeous Brazilians with knockout bodies, "DO AS I SAY, NEVER STRAY OR DISOBEY, and you can STAY! Forget ALL your other customers, YOU WORK FOR ME NOW!" Their NEW BossDomme Carol had given them their first orders. "I'm assigning both of you 'Special Clients' only, AND I'm doubling the salary you made before. So YOU be nice to me, and I'll be nice to YOU," Boss Carol drooled in conclusion, watching the two Brunette knockouts comfort each other.

Carol had to schedule Greek Goddess Donna and Sexy Talking Trisha in separate two-hr. sessions because all three Hung-Studs NOR Insatiable Bi/Goddess Carol could be in two places at once, SO Trisha would be scheduled first and Carol wanted to share Donna's Greek Ass last.

Dick-Clit Trisha was first to finish squirting when Joey hammered her Special Pussy missionary style while Carol held her legs high by her neck, squatting and RIDING Trisha's face from above, feeding Trisha a gagging mouthful of Goddess Carol's Hot MangoCum.

Joey stood up and exploded right on Carol's huge Nipples while Goddess Carol took Joey's 11-incher in her mouth to clean him off, And so did Joey CLEAN HIS OWN CUM off Carol's Breasts AS SHE ORDERED JOEY to do so, Just as Cousin Carol made her Cousin Anthony do.

Now well-satisfied and well-drained, Trisha asked in her sexy voice to wait for Carol and Donna at the rooftop bar until Donna's Fantasy was completed as well so the three VIPS could have dinner together and just talk about girly things.

Carol agreed as Trisha washed the Goddess' throbbing nipples and perfect Ass In the shower, STILL amazed by Carol's plum-size Nipples while Carol pinched and pulled on Trisha's Erect-Clit, NOW TOLD TRISHA SULLIVAN, "This Special Pussy belongs to Me now, I'm going to Collar You," Goddess Carol told Trisha.

"I'd LOVE to wear your Collar, Mistress Carol, whenever and wherever you say, I will obey!" Trisha said with a wet French kiss, giving Goddess Carol a taste of HER own MangoCum!

Carol was now waiting for Anal-Slut Donna to arrive for her two-hr. FULL session, Master had given Permission for the insatiable Bi/Goddess Carol to join in with HER VIP LADIES

on some weekends, because that was all busy Goddess had time for lately.

Just like these VIP business women, Carol had become a workaholic as well, but now MAYBE her concerned Cousin/ Master T could have Carol relax more and visit her Momme more.

IF the busy Goddess Carol was AT her Club Paradisa WITH the VIPs relaxing AND getting a TASTE, then Cousin Carol could do her CEO workload and not be so stressed-out.

Master T saw Cousin Carol LOVED to Domme Other beautiful women infatuated with her, taking full advantage of those SUBMITTING to Goddess Carol.

Bi/Goddess Cousin Carol LUVED PussyMango more than they knew! But Carol loved her Cousin/Master T even MORE so he was NOT worried at all with Carol joining OTHER WOMEN at her Private VIP Club Paradisa. The young insatiable PussyLoving Goddess did get to relax.

Domme Patty was right behind Carol every step of the way but would NEVER interfere in their life. Patty understood Carol's Protection towards her hung Cousin Anthony/Master T.

Patty would have her turn with the Master's Lizard tongue and hard 10", Just NOT as often as Patty would LIKE it. Patty HAD her Master often enough. However, Domme Patty's stock option that Domme/Anna handed Patty kept her smile lately.

Business at the totally renovated "SIR" facility was off the ground and running Smoothly. The stock had TRIPLED, MGH referrals,

BIMDC referrals, other Medical clinic referrals, Boston Sports contracts for the MRI Scanning Department WAS BOOMING.

MRI Dept. HEAD Alice, and Mgr. Monique were keeping Slave/Carmen CRAZY BUSY running MRI Discs and reports to Boston ALL DAY, EVERY DAY.

Physical Therapy sessions were BOOKED weeks and months in advance for "Sports Injury Rehab" THAT WAS JUST FROM MOMMEDOMME'S NEW VENTURE CAROL HAD IN-HERITED AND HELPED TO SET UP, DESIGN, BANK-ROLL, AND ORGANIZE FROM LOUIE LIPSTICK'S 2M POLICY.

CAROL'S NEW JOURNAL AND MOMME'S OLD SE-CRET JOURNAL OF "SPECIAL CLIENTS," ALONG WITH CAROL'S NEW "CLUB PARADISA FOR VIP WOMEN ONLY" TOOK CAROL AND HER MASTER/ COUSIN ANTHONY OVER THE TOP!

The two NEW Certified Physical Massage Therapists from Venezuela were LEGAL immigrants now. Carol was very impressed with Madeline, one of the gorgeous brunettes she hired after buying their place out. Maddy was a Miss Venezuela beauty pageant winner At 22 years old. The other 24-year-old Martha WAS also a stunning caramel knockout with great curves, and legs to die for.

Carol ONLY hired two of the four girls and bought out the Massage business in Lynn from the older two ladies ("NOT A GOOD FIT FOR 'SIR' LIKE YOU TWO ARE," CAROL EX-

lllllllllll

PLAINED TO THE NEW GIRLS). Besides, They were always TARGETED by the Lynn Police for CASH payoffs, free blow-jobs and free massages, Carol was informed.

"YOU TWO WON'T have that problem here with ME! OR problems with our 'Special Clients,'" Carol added. Monique had come to the briefing to show them around Before giving the two young South American stunners MORE WORK TO DO In the Physical Therapy Dept. with two scheduled Red Sox players with shoulder injuries.

Monique And Alice would be their supervisors with assistant Carmen for delivering MRI reports To medical Facilities and Fenway Park.

Monique told Carol, "Thank You So much! What a BIG difference the two new girls will make taking some of the Therapy sessions coming up. I owe you one, Mistress, lol," Monique joked.

"You're welcome, Now YOU have more time FOR ME, lol," Carol joked back.

"ANYTHING YOU WANT!" Monique shot back, licking her lips as she closed the door behind her, letting her Boss/Domme Carol get back to work as well.

Carol needed more than two massage therapists. Carol now needed a Certified ACCOUNTANT or two. The PAPER TRAIL of Checks and Business Credit Cards for "Services Rendered" were overwhelming the Goddess.

MommeDomme told her workaholic Clone daughter, "DON'T EVEN TRY! The IRS will eat you up for breakfast, AND NOT

"OK, I'm going now," Nephew/Master told His Mistress/ Goddess Auntie Anna.

As the Nephew's Domme/Aunt handed him a load of Bank Statements in a large folder, the Flawless Goddess showed a slight shake that worried Her Groomed young Lover/Nephew for a minute and glanced towards Evelyn, VERY concerned, looking for an answer of some kind.

"I'm going to Call the Deli FIRST and order sandwiches. I'll send Evelyn in to pick them up to save time," now pointing to Evelyn to take the ride, "OK, EVELYN?" Master T pointed to Evelyn.

"Please come with me for the ride so YOU can run in And I don't have to find a parking Spot?" Master/Nephew suggested while both The Domme/AuntAnna and his Mistress/Carol agreed was a good idea, AND their Master wouldn't have find a parking spot at the Lawyer's office EITHER. The Nephew/ Cousin convincingly said to BOTH his Love/Goddesses.

BUT the Worried and very Protective Nephew NEEDED to ask Evelyn about Auntie Anna's health PRIVATELY, and IF ANY advancement with The Parkinson's Disease to His Goddess/Auntie Anna that he still worried about daily.

Evelyn was so wet in her panties over the idea and QUICKLY Stood up and agreed to the thought of being ALONE in the car with the 22-year-old Stud Nephew.

Evelyn had been daydreaming lately about waiting for her screaming, squirting three-way WEEKLY sessions when her

Goddess Anna's Nephew/Master visited them up at the Lake, pleasing them both in 2hr. S/M sessions now that HIS Auntie Anna SUBMITTED as a Masochist.

Master T had been Pleasing BOTH Evelyn and his Mistress/Auntie Anna in Sado/Masochism sessions LATELY on his visits that Domme/Auntie Anna had already taught her groomed Nephew/Lover Anthony when BECOMING the BDism Master he WAS today.

As their Master/Nephew Lay the two Eager Masochists Evelyn AND his Goddess/Auntie Anna side by side to LOCK PUSSIES, grinding onto each other, He TIED the two French-Kissing Lesbians, groaning like two animals in heat.

The Domme/Goddess Auntie Anna AND her Bi/sexual Lover Evelyn were now just two Eager SUBMISSIVE Masochists tied together and helpless, BOTH WAITING to be whipped, paddled and Slapped into a puddle of their own MangoJuice by the Master. They WATCHED as the Pussy-Loving Nephew Sipped, Slurped, and Licked-Up their Surprise Squirting of Hot salty Pee/Cum, along with their Multi/Creaming Orgasms of MangoJuice that made them Cum even MORE INTENSELY and CONTINUOUSLY for the whole 2hrs he was visiting.

Master T and Evelyn left by the back door, where Evelyn BEGGED to take HER CAR. "Please? I keep a blanket in the back seat for the summertime, lol, I DON'T want to ruin the Rolls or your Corvette, from the way YOU make me squirt, Master, lol," Evelyn giggled.

"OK, Evelyn, but FIRST! HOW IS MY AUNT ANNA DOING?" Master T asked. "I just seen some shaking going on when she handed me this Manila Folder. How long has THIS been going on, Evelyn?" a very concerned Nephew Anthony asked while he started to unzip Evelyn's designer Zipper blouse, revealing Evelyn's Surprisingly firm DDs for 42 years old. "Amazing!" Master T complimented them with a hard nibble to her excited thick Pink Nipples between his teeth as she grabbed his hair, pulling him in closer to nurse on her. Evelyn began panting like a Cougar In heat.

Finally, Evelyn answered, "About a month now. Your Aunt Anna is on mild medication and what YOU Saw only happens with HEAVY objects like that Large Awkward envelope. Doctor Anastopolous said it may take YEARS before We see anything life threatening, and just keep her physically moving around and active like the Goddess has been doing, NO sitting around," Evelyn told him, lifting Anthony's head OFF her stone-hard wet nipples.

Evelyn pushed him back in the seat, leaning on him, telling the Master/Nephew, "I WANT TO SUCK YOUR COCK," Evelyn said after just getting her nipples bitten, pinched and slapped. "FUCK MY THROAT! just like you do to my pussy!" a very excited Evelyn begged to be abused yet again by HER Master T as Evelyn called him now WHEN the Master was called upon by Mistress Anna for their weekly S/M visits.

Cousin/Anthony already HAD PERMISSION from his Mistress/Carol to please Momme, But NEVER asked about Evelyn.

"WILL CAROL APPROVE?" Evelyn asked Master T curiously.

Master T pulled Evelyn's hair hard to lean her over the back seat and began to pump her wet Pussy with a rhythm, LONG, DEEP AND HARD, slapping her face from behind her and backhanding Evelyn's solid Ass on both solid cheeks HARD while holding Evelyn down tightly Bent-Over the car seat, NOT moving an inch, Crying and Begging, "SLAP ME HARDER, SIR!"

The Open-Handed Slaps to Evelyn's red face came Harder and Faster as Evelyn just EXPLODED, Squirting and Screaming so loud Master covered Evelyn's mouth fearing someone may hear her in the car. Evelyn was Cumming so heavily into the thick blanket that in a matter of minutes her Cum/Juices were SOAKING right through the quilted blanket she put right up to her Pussy, knowing "Draining" every drop of her Sweet Nectar from the Cock-Starved Redhead.

Master T got to Lap-Up a good amount of Evelyn's Mango/Juice from her STILL-Streaming Red and bruised Pussy, considering most of it dripped onto the blanket, BUT Evelyn got to Swallow, choking down ALL of Master's thick creamy Nectar of the Gods into her throat while having her hair pulled, asking for her face Slapped-Hard, like the Masochistic Bi/Sexual Evelyn was, AND loving all the NEW Weekly abuse with her lover's young stud Nephew Anthony.

"Let's get out of here and get to the lawyer's office right now!" the Master shouted out to Evelyn. "I'll order the sandwiches from

there AND! NOT A WORD ABOUT THIS, NOT EVEN TO MISTRESS ANNA, OK? I WILL TAKE CARE OF YOU for the long term also, JUST DO WHAT I TELL YOU!" Evelyn's Master demanded to her with Evelyn's approval.

Master T had promised HE would be Evelyn's everything in the Domme/Anna's absence!

"The Masochistic/Slave Evelyn now WANTED to be Collared and Owned, Used and abused to show Master T, She HAD BECOME the S&M Slut she had craved to be, FOR only One Master In The Domme Anna's absence, BUT WOULD it be approved by Cousin Carol?

Meanwhile at Attorney Evan Gellant's office in Chelsea, MA, The Domme's private attorney "Evan" took the large Manila envelope from Nephew/Anthony with another white standard-sized envelope inside the Larger one. The Second envelope was sealed with "EVAN ONLY" written on it By the Domme/Anna.

Evan slid the sealed white envelope into his Brooks Brothers suit jacket and said, "Tell your Aunt Anna Thank You," then handed Nephew/Anthony a business card of the BEST CPAs he knew of.

"THESE PEOPLE ARE GREAT, I already called for an appointment and that YOU will be coming in tomorrow!" the family AND Business lawyer Evan told Nephew/Anthony with confidence. "GET EVERYTHING IN ORDER FOR TO-MORROW AND GO THERE, I'll meet both of you there at

11:00 sharp!" Evan demanded Of the Cousins Anthony AND Carol be present for signing legal Tax documents as Controlling Officers of the DiNunzio Enterprise and Trust Co.

"I'LL BE THERE! With my Cousin/Carol," Nephew/Anthony assured HIS personal attorney and consultant in recent past legal matters. Evan was NO stranger to Nephew/Anthony.

On the way back Evelyn ran Into Pressman's Deli and picked up the waiting Corned-Beef and Swiss on Rye Sandwiches VERY QUICKLY to get back without suspicion, and DID get back NO QUESTIONS asked!

"Thank God," the Master whispered in Evelyn's bruised ear with a slight redness from SLAPPING her face from behind, FUCKING Evelyn Doggy-Style in both her holes just ninety minutes earlier, pulling her Red-Ponytail and making his new PRIVATE Masochistic S/M Slut Squirt like a broken garden hose.

As the main Corporate Officers of SIR and DiNunzio Enterprise and Trust were going over LEGAL paperwork, Eating Deli-Sandwiches, THE BIG QUESTION was brought up by the always cautious Domme/Anna: "WHAT IF! OR WHEN? Domme Anna keeps hinting on about her being Disabled OR inevitable death, YOU TWO BETTER TAKE CARE OF OUR EVELYN! and NOT just leave MY Evelyn in the Fucking gutter like some Families DO with Blood Relatives, nevermind Non-Biological blood relatives. She retired to be with ME and YOU better take care of HER! Evelyn retired to Care for ME,"

Domme/Anna spoke in a broken voice. "BUT I'M NOT DEAD YET, I feel fine, in fact, but tomorrow we can all die in a plane crash, YOU JUST DON'T KNOW when it's your time," the Domme pleaded for Evelyn's future.

"OH, STOP IT!" Carol interrupted her MommeDomme. "DO YOU THINK THAT BAD OF US? We All LOVE Evelyn! She IS Family now! My Cousin and I would take her in a second! She stays with Us, FOREVER! Momme! What Do you think we are, anyway?? WE say it now and We'll said it later! We will sign ANYTHING you want," Carol added with confidence, hugging the startled Evelyn, then looked right to her Soulmate/ Lover to say, "ISN'T THAT RIGHT, COUSIN?" Carol waited on Cousin/Anthony for an answ.er

"OF COURSE, IN A SECOND, you have MY word, Mistress/Auntie Anna, EVELYN IS OURS FOREVER!" Cousin/ Anthony answered daughter Carol and his curious AuntieAnna, looking over to their Loyal Masochist Evelyn that begged to be Used by Either one.

THAT STATEMENT "Evelyn is OURS FOREVER" was all Evelyn had to hear as she smiled ear to ear in relief, looking to her Gratifying Master for reassurance of what he said about THE LONG TERM as he smiled back nodding, knowing HE would have to back up his word soon.

THERE WOULD BE A COLLAR COMING for Evelyn sooner than Master T thought,

Goddess Carol just gave her approval as far as EVERYONE was concerned to COLLAR Evelyn that dreamed of being daughter Carol's and Nephew Anthony's Submissive Masochist to Use and Abuse as their Human Fuck-Toy in The Domme Anna's absence.

IT was Evelyn's turn to say, "THANK YOU, BOTH," and added that SHE considered Nephew/Anthony and the younger Goddess/Daughter Carol HER FAMILY AS WELL, Accepting and Welcoming the Taboo Couple in her Vanilla life AND BDism Family life as well.

"YOU ALL have opened up my world AND I finally ENJOY MY LIFE now since meeting Domme/Anna AND her family almost ten years ago now. I have TWO MORE young adults now besides MY own kids, '1st Cousins Anthony and Carol,'" Evelyn said, smiling. "However, I have had the pleasure of ENJOYING the young Adult Cousins in OUR S/M Lifestyle WE have chosen. I want to continue our relationship of exploring OUR Darkside with them in this BDism lifestyle, WITH PERMISSION by MY Owner and Lover/Goddess Anna. SO, I will now ASK MY MISTRESS ANNA TO PASS MY COLLAR From DOMME ANNA to her DAUGHTER/DOMME CAROL and NEPHEW ANTHONY/MASTER T in the event of The Domme/Anna's passing," Evelyn curiously asked, directly to her Goddess Anna.

"DONE! It's ALREADY Legally written separately, ready for my daughter Carol and Nephew Anthony/Master T to sign.

SOME documents will be kept separate, But Our Evelyn WILL NEVER have to work again, I can tell you that, and besides all that, Evelyn retired with a GREAT severance package, SO Money is NOT the problem, lol," Domme Anna joked. "I'm just concerned about Evelyn needing simple things, like a ride to the hospital, OR that She HAS SOMEONE to call to come pick her up at the airport, OR if her car breaks down, The Little things Evelyn can rely on," the Domme Anna pleaded.

Anna DIDN'T EVEN FLINCH about PASSING Evelyn's Collar to "The Cousins" to OWN Evelyn in Every way. Evelyn was visibly Excited and Wet from asking the question of BEING PASSED from one Domme to Another. She was thinking of being Slapped HARD.

THEN, FROM THE REASSURING ANSWER FROM HER PRESENT OWNER MISTRESS/ANNA OF PASSING HER COLLAR DOWN TO HER FANTASY COUPLE THAT WILL USE HER UP DAILY in the future, was so Overwhelming for Evelyn she began dripping right through her panties, she was SO WET.

Used and Abused Evelyn couldn't have written it ANY BETTER, it was exactly what she wanted to hear. She WOULD NOT WANT for Anything OR ANYBODY. Evelyn would be a 1/3 owner of the family cottage in Derry, N.H., on Beaver Lake, OR Stay over in The Domme's Office Suite when visiting "Club Paradisa" up on the penthouse floor right NEXT DOOR to Domme Patty, Domme/Goddess Carol and her Big-Cock Master

T, THREE SADISTIC ANIMALS to Use and Abuse her "PRE-FERRABLY ALL AT ONCE!"

At the attorney's office Evan presented Exactly what they ALL were talking about requiring Cousin Carol and Anthony to sign. BOTH Cousins agreed to the terms and conditions that were already discussed over Deli sandwiches.

SPECIFICALLY, Evelyn be shared Immediately with full permission from Evelyn's Mistress Anna, the same as Nephew Anthony was shared, then GIFTED to her Daughter Carol for her Spoiled Daughter's happiness.

At breakfast Cousins Carol and Anthony walked over to Momme-Domme and Evelyn having coffee and reading over some of the paperwork that WAS SIGNED as requested by Momme-Domme/AuntieAnna.

"I LOVE THIS ONE!" Evelyn holding up and waving a signed Document that read: "IF MASTER T and DOMME CAROL prefer to arrange their own Collaring Ceremony to PRESENT their own designer Collar on Evelyn, PERMISSION IS GRANTED by Goddess Domme Anna," the BDism document read.

"OH, YAH! I LOVE doing My own ceremonies like My Momme taught me, MUCH MORE PERSONAL, and I love MY leather Collar designer Walter Dyer, from Lynn, MA. I'll order you a SPECIAL COLLAR next week, Evelyn, since you're so excited about this Co/Ownership. So It will be OUR

PLEASURE, Evelyn, for everything YOU DO for MY Momme. Thank you so much!" Goddess Carol said very sincerely. "AND WHY SO FAST, MOMME? Is everything OK?" Carol asked her Momme, sipping her coffee and looking at Evelyn so excited she would NOT be alone, EVER! "ARE YOU SURE YOU'RE OK?" Carol very curiously asked Momme of her health.

"YES, She's fine, Carol," Evelyn snapped back to put Cousins Carol and Anthony at ease now, Overthinking the whole collaring ceremony. "SHE STILL CAN MAKE ME SCREAM, Lol," Evelyn joked.

"AND WHERE THE FUCK IS DOMME PATTY?" MommeDomme asked to Carol! Changing the subject to what was really bothering the Domme.

"Patty is ALWAYS here to see me! Did YOU tell her I WAS HERE?" Momme knowingly asked her spoiled Jealous Daughter Carol again. "Well, Did you?" Asking twice!

"I thought I did!" Carol rolled her eyes and picked up the phone to call Patty In to see Momme.

"I'LL BE RIGHT THERE!" Nervous Domme Patty and all excited told her Boss Goddess Carol.

MommeDomme and Evelyn both enjoyed a laugh together when Evelyn asked the Nephew, "Does Domme Patty still drive Special Clients in her sexy tailored driving suits YOU make her wear, Master T?" Evelyn's sudden sarcasm was so hilarious that her Mistress Anna laughed in her coffee at Carol's "Rolling-Eyes" expression she was known for.

"NO! Patty is much more valuable downstairs with Clients AND works her ass off ALL DAY LONG!" Carol said in all honesty. "Patty still enjoys the Bentley, though," Carol added.

"OH, YAH! We should get A Vanity license Plate that's says PATTY on it and not 'SIR,' lol," Master T jumped in for a Group laugh.

Patty rushed in and ran right over with tears in her eyes and hugged her Mentor and Goddess/Anna tightly. Patty didn't let go until she stopped sobbing so her BossGoddess Carol, OR her Master wouldn't see she had missed The Domme/Anna very badly and WASN'T told Mistress/Domme Anna was here!

The ONLY thing that mattered To Domme Patty WAS THAT MOMME missed Patty too, and NOT being there to greet The Domme Anna was bothering Domme Patty's Mentor.

"...I DIDN'T KNOW, MISTRESS, or I didn't get the message, I'M so swamped with work now, WE ARE DOING SO WELL NOW, YOU KNOW!" Patty went on and on to the smiling yet concerned Domme/Anna for HER neglected favorite Pet Patty.

"Yes, I know, my Pet, WE are doing VERY well and WE have hired an accountant today so I hope YOU can work a Little LESS now!" the Domme/Anna said, so disappointed right in Carol's direction. "You're OFF for the rest of the day!" Patty's Goddess/Anna said, stroking Patty's blonde hair and taking her by the hand and signaling to Evelyn that it was time to go. "IN FACT, PATTY! WE are going to catch-up on things and get our hair

done while Evelyn and I are in Boston today." THEN the pissed-off Momme/Goddess arrogantly Said to her selfish Goddess Daughter, "CAROL! PATTY IS TAKING EVELYN AND I TO NEWBURY ST. TO GET OUR HAIR DONE! 'IN HER ROLLS'!" MommeDomme firmly said as Momme walked Patty out with Evelyn to catch up on things and get their hair done at "Jacques" on the elite Newbury St.

"OK, Momme, fine, have fun, and sorry, Patty, I REALLY THOUGHT I told you she was coming," Carol apologetically said to Patty on the way out, BUT too little too late.

Before a neglected Patty could respond to the apology, MommeDomme Quickly took Patty's hand, rushing out, sparing Patty any more embarrassment in front of The Domme/Mentor.

NOTHING MORE was said, but Master T standing there said and assured Carol, "THIS ISN'T OVER! YOU KNOW THAT, RIGHT? I want YOU to fix this! Patty didn't do ANYTHING to you, SHE LOVES YOU, for God's sake. And if you're thinking about Why PATTY Is being SO close to me because of what I done for her by TAKING HER IN with us,

I DID THAT FOR YOU! Because YOU told me she was being beaten, raped, used and abused by her own scumbag brother. 'I WOULD HAVE DONE THAT FOR ANYBODY IF YOU OR YOUR MOM ASKED ME TO,'" Cousin Anthony, Soulmate and Rock, continued to plead with his stubborn young jealous Goddess, Cousin Carol. "YOU KNOW I NEED YOU AND I LOVE YOU, RIGHT?" Master T added.

"YES, of course, I know That," Carol answered with her head resting on Master T's chest, hugging him, realizing he was right and looking for forgiveness.

"STOP TRYING TO PROTECT ME, THEN. I'M NOT GOING ANYWHERE WITH PATTY, I'M HERE FOR YOU! ONLY YOU! NOW FIX THIS WHEN YOUR MOMME GETS BACK! OK? WE GOOD?" the Master/ Cousin and Lover concluded to his stubborn Goddess that HE had spoiled, and WAS responsible for now in the eyes of The Domme/Anna.

"I'm ON IT, right now!" Carol began to scroll her Rolodex and found contractors and her decorator to begin a renovation of Patty's office, ordering the biggest picture window to install.

Patty's Penthouse office/condo would now have a view overlooking the Boston Harbor Like MommeDomme's corner office. A Brick wall needed to be knocked out, the contractor told Carol.

"JUST DO IT, PLEASE, Make Patty's office the best office you ever renovated," Carol told her contractor. "I CAN'T LOSE MY BEST FRIEND," Carol added to the contractor.

Hours had passed, many calls were made and arrangements were made to renovate Patty's office as a makeup gesture for overwhelming Domme/Patty's schedule.

MommeDomme, Evelyn and Patty Walked in to interrupt Carol in a pile of paperwork, All with NEW KILLER OUTFITS and NEW HAIRSTYLES, Giggling after dinner and a few drinks on Newbury St. in Boston.

Carol rushed over to hug Patty and told her, "YOU LOOK SO GORGEOUS, PATTY. YOUR OFFICE IS GETTING A COMPLETE MAKEOVER MONDAY. I'VE BEEN SO BUSY AND NEGLECTING YOU, I'M SO SORRY, MY BEST FRIEND, Please forgive me?" Carol Asked Patty for forgiveness, wiping tears from her face as they hugged to THE DOMME'S approval, looking on closely with a nod over to her Nephew Anthony and Master for taking care of the problem.

HE WAS GROOMED TO KNOW HIS GODDESS/ AUNTIE ANNA'S EVERY THOUGHT and WHAT IT TOOK TO PLEASE HER. THIS APOLOGY FROM CAROL WAS EXACTLY WHAT SHE EXPECTED WHEN SHE GOT BACK FROM GETTING HER HAIR DONE!

The younger Goddess/Daughter, however, NEEDED to learn these important values FOR HERSELF, and MommeDomme was worried SHE hadn't much time to Mentor Vanilla values along with the BDISM lifestyle She had Dominated for years. Carol's Cousin/Anthony WOULD HAVE TO TEACH BOTH SETS OF VALUES TO A SPOILED COUSIN CAROL NOW.

Patty hugged her idol and Mistress/Carol back, then took her Mentor's hand, standing very close by for approval and to reassure there were NO bad feelings.

"We're good," Patty said, smiling. "I can't wait to see MY new office, Mistress/Carol. Thank you so much, Your Momme, Evelyn and I loved our time together today. I'll remember Newbury St. for the rest of my life after today, I LOVE YOU ALL, YOU'RE

MY FAMILY. I need to get to bed now," still wiping tears of joy, saying goodnight to her Master T, with a "THANK YOU," Patty whispered.

"No worries, Patty, Get some sleep. I'LL CALL JOEY TO-MORROW AND WE'LL ALL DO LUNCH NEXT WEEK IN YOUR NEW OFFICE SUITE, lol," Master joked softly.

"OR MAYBE DINNER?" Carol suggesting mildly that they CONTINUE "Swap Night" Carol had put on hold.

"OH, YES! I'd like THAT even better," smiling ear to ear, Patty pointed to Carol with appreciation AND approval!

Evelyn and her Goddess Anna were also tired, but Evelyn HAD to remind Carol about next week as well. "PLEASE, DON'T FORGET ABOUT MY NEW COLLAR," Evelyn whispered with a soft kiss to both a happy Master T and the compromising Stubborn Domme Carol.

BUT BEFORE MOMMEDOMME RETIRED FOR THE NIGHT, She would preach to her spoiled daughter one last time for the day, "YOU KNOW, MY LOVELY CLONE GOD-DESS! WE DON'T HAVE MUCH TIME HERE ON EARTH TO GET ALL THINGS RIGHT, AND WHAT YOU DID TO MAKE THINGS RIGHT WITH PATTY TO-NIGHT WAS RIGHT, ESPECIALLY FOR SOMEONE WHO WOULD DO THE SAME FOR YOU, OR MORE! IT'S CALLED LOYALTY!

"WHEN PEOPLE DON'T MAKE THINGS RIGHT, LIFE HAS ITS OWN WAY OF MAKING THINGS RIGHT.

YOU DON'T WANT THAT! SET YOUR OWN DESTINY AND HAVE NO REGRETS. STAY LOYAL TO THOSE LOYAL TO YOU, AND WHO ALWAYS HAVE YOUR BACK! AND BE THE BEST AT WHAT YOU CRAVE TO BE."

With that being said, MommeDomme gave the Stubborn/ Spoiled Goddess Carol something to think about for the night, then kissed her Daunting Daughter on the forehead and walked gracefully out the door with her LOYAL Evelyn right by her side.

Domme/Patty, Slave/Joey, Boss/Goddess Carol and Loyal Master/ Cousin Anthony CONTINUED their Date-Night out as best friends, then back to Master's Dungeon for Swap-Night. Patty ALWAYS looked forward to Family OR Business Events, being her Master's Vanilla GF as HE introduced Patty as HIS FIANCE while Carol pretended to be a happy girlfriend to Slave/Joey. Only Carol SMILED more now, and didn't roll her eyes anymore.

Monique would STILL stay over the first Saturday night of Every new month to be used and pleasingly abused while passed around the room by the kinky cousins while tied in bondage being whipped, spanked, and nipple tortured for the night until Sunday morning. Monique would have to SERVE breakfast in bed to the Dominant Sadistic Cousins waiting to be dismissed, Sometimes NOT UNTIL Monday morning IF Domme/Patty and her Slave/Joey were invited.

Alice was being rewarded by Boss/Goddess Carol with a nice Monthly Perk, giving her the three hung young men she had

hunted down in the North End, where they worked selling fruit. Alice would Suck-Off ALL of the three hung cocks, seducing them to her Condo on Saturdays. That was HER day off from work at her old job, But now All three (Joey, Carmen & the Master) worked at "SIR" with Alice.

Carol had arranged for the Same three young men to accommodate her Craving for Sucking-Cock. Some weeks Alice was in Heaven, when Phil LaBella, CEO of MGH, and three of his buddies showed up for Blowjobs at the Country Club, arranged by Master T and Cousin Carol. Alice was in her glory for those Special Client Sessions, Making BIG TIP$ while Sucking-Off Multiple Men. That was what Alice LOVED to do, and looked forward to it.

Evelyn had been collared in a private ceremony, NOT to take Anything away from her Original owner Goddess/Domme Anna in any way, just for Security reasons.

Master T and Domme/Goddess Carol had Evelyn stay-over in Momme's Office suite when she got the urge to be used with NO LIMITS, screaming into Uncontrollable Orgasms while paddled with wide Mahogany wooden paddles, handmade by Master T in his dungeon just for Evelyn and Monique's Masochistic "Ass-Beatings."

Allie continued with scheduled sessions where Allie could participate while supervising her husband's Cuckold Fetish sessions now that Lenny HAD COME OUT.

"NO WAY," Said Domme Patty to Boss/Goddess Carol. "Let's get Allie to come on board with us and take-on a few Special Clients."

Carol quickly agreed, "YES! OR WE CHARGE ALLIE/ NBC MORE MONEY, Allie can't be taking OUR Carmen For two hrs. AND Eddy Showers IS OUR (GS) Special Client. He's NOT for her to use for Cuckold Hubby Lenny," Boss/Domme Carol insisted! "Patty! You take charge of this one since you're aware of what Allie is doing when she comes in," Carol gave Patty the credit, then added, "Tell her it's $100.00 more per session, OR She gives you a 'Yes' answer before she leaves today to work for us, AS A DOMME."

Domme Patty and her Mistress/Boss Carol were back in sync now. They had each other's backs, socializing with their Collared hung men, Cousin Anthony and Slave/Joey, AND a few Lucky women.

Patty and Monique were now regulars for Dining out to eat, the movies, museums, weekend getaways. The world was spinning slowly again for Goddess Carol and Cousin Anthony, AND very Lucrative at the same time.

Domme Patty NEVER strayed in spite of being slighted in respect to her Master T AND especially to her Caring Goddess and Mentor, Mistress/Anna, THAT NOTICED Patty's absence and DEMANDED her attendance immediately to spoiled Daughter Carol.

Patty's patience, respect and loyalty eventually paid off. She knew it would eventually when Carol finally realized her Loyal Lover/Cousin Anthony would NEVER leave his Soulmate Cousin Carol's side for ANY other woman.

Master T's fantasy Goddess Domme/Auntie Anna, Carol's Own Momme, was the ONLY other Goddess Carol realized that could Seduce Cousin/Anthony, THEIR MASTER, to stray.

HOWEVER! Loving and Pleasing them BOTH, the Master knew enough to STAY and PRAY for his #1 Goddess Auntie Anna to live another day.

The Domme had given her Blessing, AND WITH PERMIS-SION, of course, for her clone Goddess Daughter Carol to take the Leash and Collar of her Groomed Young Nephew that HAD MASTERED BOTH OF THEIR NEEDS.

Goddess Auntie Anna knew of the inevitable and was accepting Her fate. ALL SHE WANTED in the end was her Nephew and Daughter Carol to be able to have what SHE and the Loyal Handsome Hung Nephew that protected her once had, Including FORBIDDEN times the Aunt, Nephew, and Daughter love triangle they SHARED together that The Domme would take to her grave, "WITH NO REGRETS."

Nephew/Anthony's fantasy Goddess Aunt Anna had always been his Fantasy since he was a wise-ass hung fifteen-yr.-old that teased each other, flaunting what they had often openly. She felt fine and still looked gorgeous, but the Domme/Goddess showed signs of the Parkinson's getting worse and would fight it off like A LIONESS she craved to be.

Auntie Anna would HAPPILY take him weekends while her nephew's Mom Joan worked sometimes when he acted up and stayed out late. The Goddess enjoyed How Daughter Carol and Herself Could calm the teenage Devil In a matter of MINUTES!

His Aunt Anna was flattered by the way her young Demon/Nephew Anthony's eyes would POP open and his jaw drop at

such a young age, NOT EVEN KNOWING or caring he was visibly Excited to be in their Presence, DOING WHATEVER DEVELOPING COUSIN/CAROL OR HIS FLAUNTING AUNT ANNA TOLD HIM TO DO.

Cousin Carol LOVED to lure her young Demon Cousin's attention away from her Momme's flaunting presence, SATIS-FYING her Sexual-Craving Cousin's needs in her Secret Closet.

Cousin Carol was JUST AS Diabolical AND sexually developing into a Goddess at a very early age of fourteen and infatuated with her handsome/Hung teenage Cousin/Anthony. Carol communicated her thoughts with him while drawing or painting together through their art, OR in her "Secret Closet," showing Cousin/Anthony her HUGE nipples getting bigger every day.

His Dominant Auntie Anna would always have Control over HER Cocky wise-ass Italian teen adolescent Nephew/Anthony right up until the Professional/Dominatrix Aunt Anna would eventually "Collar" her sixteen-yr.-old Nephew, then GROOM him into the BDism lifestyle to SERVE her personally at her office (Sixteen was the controversial consenting age at that time).

His Fantasy Goddess/Auntie Anna would smile ear to ear, Knowing she was ONLY CALMING the Demon Nephew's sexual desires AND advances towards her, But NOT eliminating his kinky thoughts of pleasing her completely.

The Devious Domme needed the aggressive attention of the young/Devil Nephew's twisted sexual suggestions that drove her crazy, and WERE NOT for everyone. But the Dominant Aunt

was NO MATCH for the inexperienced teenage Nephew/Sex-Demon that would whisper in her ear how he wanted to EAT her Pussy until his lips bled, while leaning his Big Hard-Dick right against her perfect ass.

The Goddess/Domme AuntieAnna MELTED the Cocky-Kid with a big dick and long oversized tongue TO HIS KNEES, then trained the Wise-Ass-talking Nephew to "SERVE" both his Fantasy Aunt, and his Cousin Carol "FOR LIFE"…. The cocky-kid never knew what hit him!!

The Domme/Auntie Anna stressed all the time, "Be Loyal to those that are Loyal to you." The young Diavolo/Nephew Anthony would be greatly rewarded for his Loyalty, pleasing her almost DAILY when his Dream Fantasy Domme Aunt would shortly in life whisper into his ears,

"DO WHATEVER YOU WANT TO ME." These words alone would turn his cock to stone.

MommeDomme made sure her Daughter Carol was present most of the time to teach her the BDism lifestyle values as the INSEPARABLE Soulmate Cousins grew older together.

Cousin Carol would always be second, but she would come to realize the Loyalty and Devotion her soulmate Cousin/Anthony had for his fantasy dream come true in the Lifestyle that her Momme led with her Nephew/Anthony, but NEVER worried too much.

Goddess Carol knew that kind of LOYALTY could easily be passed down to her. Make NO mistake, Cousin/Anthony came RUNNING when Carol Called as well, but today and every day

until Momme's last day, Carol WANTED her Momme/Domme to be First.

Today would be no exception when the Loyal Nephew took his second ride in a week up to the lake to be by her side for lunch and listen to her speak to him with her favorite Deli/Sandwich, Corned beef with Swiss on Rye, pre-approved by Carol, who now had her Master's Collar, AND his heart after Momme KNEW to step aside for her Nephew's happiness, AND the happiness of her Daughter Carol, Then telling her daughter earlier on the phone, "Take care of MY Nephew, OR I'LL BE BACK FOR HIM!" Scaring her curious Daughter.

While The Domme sat and reminisced with her Loyal Nephew/ Anthony, the alert Goddess Aunt snuggled in close to her Master for his protection and his warmth, her loyal lover Nephew/Anthony squeezed his Goddess Auntie Anna tighter as she put her arms around him.

His Goddess Auntie Anna's unique purple eyes looked straight up into his tears to tell him with a soft kiss, grasping his thick black wavy hair, "BEFORE I DIE, YOUR FACE IS THE LAST ONE I WANT TO SEE, THEN I'LL GO! I LOVE YOU, ANTHONY, I ALWAYS HAVE AND I ALWAYS WILL. I'LL WAIT FOR YOU AND CAROL ON THE OTHER SIDE...."

Printed in the USA
CPSIA information can be obtained
at www.ICGtesting.com
LVHW061257081223
765655LV00059B/743